AMERICA'S
FIRST ADVENTURE
IN CHINA

AMERICA'S
FIRST ADVENTURE
IN CHINA

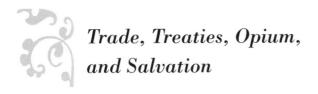

*Trade, Treaties, Opium,
and Salvation*

JOHN R. HADDAD

TEMPLE UNIVERSITY PRESS
PHILADELPHIA

TEMPLE UNIVERSITY PRESS
Philadelphia, Pennsylvania 19122
www.temple.edu/tempress

Library of Congress Cataloging-in-Publication Data

Haddad, John Rogers.
  America's first adventure in China : trade, treaties, opium, and
salvation / John R. Haddad.
    pages cm
  Includes bibliographical references and index.
  ISBN 978-1-4399-0689-7 (cloth : alk. paper) —
ISBN 978-1-4399-0691-0 (e-book) 1. United States—Relations—
China. 2. China—Relations—United States. 3. United
States—Commerce—China—History—18th century. 4. China—
Commerce—United States—History—18th century. 5. United
States—Commerce—China—History—19th century. 6. China—
Commerce—United States—History—19th century. 7. Opium
trade—China—History—19th century. 8. Missions, American—
China—History—19th century. 9. China—History—Opium
War, 1840-1842. 10. China—History—Taiping Rebellion, 1850-
1864. I. Title.
  E183.8.C5H174 2013
  327.73051—dc23
                                                    2012040901

∞ The paper used in this publication meets the requirements of the
American National Standard for Information Sciences—Permanence
of Paper for Printed Library Materials, ANSI Z39.48-1992

Printed in the United States of America

2 4 6 8 9 7 5 3 1

Contents

Acknowledgments

This book would not have been possible without the generosity, support, and insights of several people and institutions. I thank the leadership at Penn State Harrisburg for granting me the sabbatical that made the early stages of this project possible. I am also grateful to the Fulbright Program for placing me in a research-teaching position at Hong Kong University. There I joined the American Studies Program, whose director, Kendall Johnson, was a wonderful host, a helpful colleague, and a terrific friend. I would also like to thank Glenn Shive of the Hong Kong–America Center who coordinated much of my Fulbright experience, enriching it immeasurably.

I owe a debt of gratitude to those who read my work at various stages: Paul Van Dyke of Sun Yat-sen University in Guangzhou, Peter Buck of Harvard University (retired), and Steven Conn of Ohio State University. Along with saving me from mistakes, these readers generously provided me with access to their knowledge and expertise. My editor, Janet Francendese, who guided me every step of the way and was a true joy to work with, deserves my maximal gratitude.

I also acknowledge the friends, colleagues, and mentors who offered continuous encouragement. At Penn State Harrisburg, I benefited from the unwavering support of Simon Bronner, Charlie Kupfer, Anne Verplanck, Erin Battat, Anthony Buccitelli, Michael Barton, Catherine Rios, David Witwer, Greg Crawford, and Oranee Tawatnuntachai. Two others merit special mention. A longtime friend, Daniel Medwed, was with me in Japan when I first developed an interest in Americans in Asia; later, in graduate school, the late William H. Goetzmann taught me how to convert this interest into narrative history.

Finally, I thank family members. My parents, Richard and Betsey, provided vital support and good cheer every step of the way, as did my brother,

Rich, his wife, Sandy, and their three boys, Tim, Alex, and Sam. Similarly, I am grateful to my wife's family in China—in particular, my parents-in-law, Wang Qingyi and Yang Xiurong—who epitomize the Chinese tradition of respecting scholarship. To my wife, Catherine, and my children, William and Elizabeth, I have this to say: you helped me in profound ways you may never understand. Though perhaps it did not always seem like it, this effort was for you all along.

A Note on the Spelling
of Chinese Words

The Romanization of Chinese poses problems for historians because, for any given word or proper name, several different spellings can exist. In the 1950s the Chinese adopted Pinyin as the state's official system on the grounds that its spellings most closely approximate the true sound of Mandarin Chinese. For this reason, this book uses Pinyin system as its default system. That said, there are two exceptions to this rule. First, some Chinese personal and place names, when converted into Pinyin, appear unrecognizable to many of today's readers, they being more familiar with an older spelling. In these cases, the author has opted to leave certain names in their older and more familiar form. Second, when certain names appear repeatedly one specific way in primary source materials, the author has elected to retain these spellings. For example, since nineteenth-century American sources, without exception, referred to the city of Guangzhou (a Pinyin spelling) as Canton, the latter spelling is used here. Likewise, Beijing appears in this text as Peking.

Introduction: America's Early Adventure in China

A Story of Tea, Treaties, Opium, and Salvation

We begin with two scenes from two different times. The first takes us back to 1784. Samuel Shaw has recently arrived in Canton aboard the *Empress of China*, the first U.S. vessel to reach China. As supercargo, Shaw handles the business side of the venture—the buying and selling of goods and the payment of duties and port fees. Every day, a local Chinese merchant drops in on Shaw, points to the same article of merchandise, and offers to pay an amount Shaw considers low. "I treated him politely every time," Shaw later writes, but "adhered to my first demand." After cycling through this routine for several days, the man finally accepts the higher price, and Shaw happily sells him the article.

Though the transaction is complete, the man is not finished. Throughout the process, he has shown a strange interest not just in Shaw's merchandise but in Shaw himself. Something about Shaw's behavior mystifies him, and he is determined to get to the bottom of it. "You are not Englishman?" he finally asks. After Shaw confirms that he is not, the man's face brightens. The British always treat him like an inferior, he says, whenever he approaches them to bargain. "Go to hell, you damned rascal," they sometimes scold. The anomaly of a polite English speaker now explained, the man becomes chatty. He has never heard of the United States but nevertheless pays it a compliment: "China-man very much love your country." Though these words flatter Shaw, the ones that follow carry an ominous tone. "All men come first time China very good gentlemen," he observes. "I think two three times more Canton, you make all same Englishman too."[1] Shaw has made a favorable first impression, but will he and the Americans who follow him to China come to act more and more like the British?

For our second scene, we vault forward eight decades to the year 1867, descending on a farewell banquet being held in Peking for a departing American. Anson Burlingame plans to head home after serving six years as the American minister to China. Overflowing with charisma and bonhomie, Burlingame has endeared himself to European and Chinese colleagues alike. In particular, he has won over both Prince Gong, the leader of China's ruling faction, and the members of China's Foreign Affairs Office, the hosts of this gathering. As Burlingame says his good-byes, the Chinese blindside him with an astounding offer. "Events of such importance have transpired within a few days," his flabbergasted wife informs their son, "that I take advantage of the Russian mail . . . to write you something about them." Her "astonished" husband has just been appointed "Ambassador from China to all the Treaty Powers!" The Chinese government rapidly confers on Burlingame an official title and rank and empowers him to represent China in Washington, Moscow, European capitals, and—most important of all—London. Days later, he and his delegation embark for San Francisco.[2]

What do these two scenes tell us? In the most practical sense, they set the temporal boundaries for this book, which begins with the *Empress of China* (1784) and ends with the Burlingame mission (1867–1870). More substantively, the scenes describe Sino-American relationships, which lie at the heart of this book. In writing it, I wanted to tell the story of early Americans in China, explaining how the two peoples first met in the eighteenth century and how that relationship matured in the nineteenth. In the first scene, Shaw and his Chinese counterpart both appear cautious, circumspect, and perhaps a little suspicious as each tries to ascertain the other's motives. Their guarded behavior is typical of the early stage of the Sino-American relationship, in which each side operated within a fog of ignorance with respect to the other's language, customs, and values. By the second scene, that fog has dispersed. Impressed by Burlingame's character and his knowledge of Chinese values and needs, these officials make a supreme gesture of trust: they place in his hands their hopes for an effective Western diplomacy.

The two scenes also illustrate the method I use to tell this story: this is a work of narrative history with a biographical focus. Though I address the larger historical, economic, and religious forces driving American activity in China, I refract these through the lens of individual lives. The chapter on the missionary movement, for example, not only discusses the theological currents carrying Protestantism into China; it also examines the dreams and anxieties of the volunteers themselves. What compelled these individuals to bid farewell to family, give up comfort and security, and accept a hard life in an alien culture? What strategies did they employ to win over the Chinese, and how did they maintain morale amid setbacks and failures?

Finally, the two scenes illuminate the chief findings of this book. Henry Luce, the son of American missionaries in China and the founder of *Time* and *Life* magazines, famously called the twentieth century the "American century." Today, consensus appears to be building to stamp the twenty-first the Chinese century. Neither, however, could claim superpower status in the nineteenth century, which indisputably belonged to the British. China and the United States, in other words, forged their relationship during Britain's period of global dominance. Given this context, the connection between the two scenes becomes clear: the first implicitly poses a question that the second answers. Would Americans in China carve out a distinctive identity for themselves, the Shaw encounter asks, while operating in the shadow of the British goliath? The answer embedded in the Burlingame episode is an emphatic yes.

This conclusion was far from obvious. In fact, while reviewing existing books on Americans in China, I tentatively formed the contrary view. I should state here that these sources do not cover the American experience in China in its totality. Each one, rather, explores a single category of that experience—the commodity trade, opium smuggling, missionary activity, official diplomacy, or intellectual achievement. When I viewed the American experience in China in this way, broken down into separate components, I received the impression that Americans largely imitated the British, though always on a smaller scale and with a shoestring budget. Like Britain, the United States conducted trade with China, but Americans handled a lower volume of goods. Americans copied Britain's smuggling networks but imported far less opium into China. In matters of diplomacy, Americans merely piggybacked off the British, who handled all the heavy lifting by sending formidable fleets to China. Though American missionaries proselytized in China, they simply adopted the British evangelical model. Intellectually, Americans took a back seat to the British, who produced the authoritative works in the field later named "Sinology." The American presence in China, in sum, amounted to a lesser version of the British presence, or so my early thinking went.[3]

However, to write this book, I needed to consider the American experience in China *holistically* rather than in *itemized* fashion. When I stepped back to widen my field of vision, a different picture emerged, one in which the American and British experiences contrasted sharply. Most British subjects shipped out under the auspices of some larger entity—the East India Company, perhaps, or the Royal Navy. In China vast institutional and governmental structures dominated their lives. Small cogs within large machines, these men tended to behave according to clearly delineated protocols that left little room for improvisation. Americans faced the opposite set of circumstances in China. For much of the 1800s, the official U.S. presence was so small, poorly funded, and militarily weak as to verge on insignificant. The British sometimes scoffed at it. This absence of bureaucratic structure affected American behavior in two profound ways.

First, *it intensified the already-pronounced individualistic tendencies of Americans.* For white male citizens of the United States, the decades before the Civil War provided the high-water mark for individualism. In this period, Americans celebrated the Western pioneer and the Yankee trader, aspired to become Jacksonian self-made men, or heeded Ralph Waldo Emerson's stirring call for self-reliance. When transplanted in China, this individualism became further amplified, unchecked as it was by much familial, institutional, or governmental oversight. The result: *hyperindividualism*. Americans imagined China as a field of potential, a vast canvas on which they could project gaudy visions of self-actualization. To open China to the West, to get rich, to save millions of souls, to acquire total knowledge of China, to assemble vast Chinese collections, to introduce modern technology to China, to introduce Chinese culture to Americans, to reinvent Sino-Western relations, to command a Chinese army—these were some of the fantastic dreams spun by Americans in China.

If the American Dream found expression in China, so too did its dark side. Driven by class aspirations, many traders turned to opium smuggling as a means to hasten their rise. Like the protagonists in novels by F. Scott Fitzgerald or Theodore Dreiser, these men willingly traded morality for quick wealth. Other Americans were led astray by a different sort of dream. Harboring the grand ambition to change China in a profound way, some individuals believed so much in their own importance as to ultimately succumb to megalomania. When their elaborate plans collapsed around them (as they almost invariably did), they typically descended into states of depression. Fortunately, the failure of a China dream did not always lead to personal ruin. Some recovered, set realistic expectations for themselves, and enjoyed meaningful careers in China.

Second, *the lack of official structure forced Americans to adopt pragmatism in their dealings with the Chinese.* Unlike the British, American expatriates could not depend on protection from their government. Therefore, to achieve a favorable result in China, an American needed to adjust his behavior in a way that a British expatriate did not. The latter, though encumbered by bureaucratic structure, benefited from the respect and fear his nationality commanded; he could prosecute his business with the reassuring knowledge that the greatest power in Asia backed his activities. If he could make demands of the Chinese, an American, in contrast, had to strike compromises with them, form partnerships with them, and approach problems with flexibility rather than dogma. However, while befriending the Chinese, Americans had to remain conscious of the British. Since all Western activity in China—missionary work, the commodity trade, or opium smuggling—took place under Britain's protective shield, Americans could not afford to provoke the British. This was difficult terrain to negotiate.

While acting as individuals, Americans *when taken collectively* constituted a new force in China, one that placed stress on British and Chinese systems. American traders stunned the British East India Company by transporting cargoes faster and more efficiently than the mercantile colossus could. Americans also competed effectively in opium trafficking; indeed, when the Chinese cracked down on smuggling in 1839, they were reacting to both British and American contraband. As for American missionaries, they largely adopted the English model; however, they injected so much evangelical fervor into that model as to make it their own. It is also safe to assume that the Taiping Rebellion (1850–1864), a massive civil war that cost roughly twenty million Chinese their lives, either would not have happened or would not have assumed its quasi-Christian form without the involvement of American missionaries. Finally, in the area of diplomacy, two American officials, Caleb Cushing (who arrived in 1844) and Anson Burlingame (who arrived in 1861), brought substantial change to Sino-Western relations. Crucially, they did so not by following their government's instructions but by acting on their individual initiative.

This book proceeds mostly chronologically, beginning with three chapters on American merchants. Chapter 1 offers an account of the *Empress of China* (1784), the first American vessel to reach China. Though the voyage advanced the nation's interests, it was nevertheless a private enterprise organized by men who dreamed of tapping the unrealized potential of a trade with China. A modest commercial success, the voyage sparked a debate within the merchant community: should the United States follow Europe's model by founding an East India Company to control its Asian trade? When the United States opted to forgo that model, China was left open as a field of competition. A magnet for ambitious men, the China trade grew robust over the ensuing four decades, despite strict Chinese regulations that included confining foreigners to a small area in Canton. Chapter 2 approaches the China trade from a microeconomic perspective, examining the company built by Thomas Perkins, a Boston merchant who achieved dominance in this laissez-faire trading environment by imposing a system over his commercial activity. Shifting to a macroeconomic lens, Chapter 3 describes the collective resourcefulness of American traders as they tried to offset the trade imbalance caused by America's passion for tea and China's apathy for American goods.

Chapter 4 considers the missionaries who began arriving in Canton in 1830. Of all Americans, missionaries perhaps brought the most ambitious dream: they believed that their efforts to convert the Chinese would help bring about the Second Coming. However, being limited to Canton, missionaries struggled to reconcile the vastness of their holy objective with the smallness of their space. Unable to engage in direct evangelism, they instead launched projects in writing, translating, science, medicine, and education, discovering in the process talents they did not previously know they had. Since their home institutions wanted to see conversions, missionaries often pursued these interests against their sponsors' express wishes. However, as this chapter shows, it was in these projects, not in proselytizing, that missionaries achieved lasting influence.

Chapter 5 discusses the potent role that opium played in the dreams of Americans, both those who smuggled it and those who opposed its importation. The former had entered the China trade aspiring to become self-made men; they saw easy profits from opium sales as accelerating their progress toward this goal. Though the latter had also come to China for the purpose of self-making, they envisioned for themselves not just an *economic rise* but a *moral ascendancy*. By taking a vocal stand against the opium trade, they hoped to establish their moral superiority to their peers. This chapter also examines Americans' involvement in China's dramatic attempt to crush the opium trade in 1839, the event that prompted a determined military response from Britain.

Britain's victory in the First Opium War roused Washington into action. As Chapter 6 explains, the United States sent Caleb Cushing to China to secure the same rights and privileges as contained in Britain's Treaty of Nanjing, such as access to four new ports. Though Cushing had planned only to execute his government's instructions and no more, a series of setbacks forced him to improvise in China. Indeed, he returned home with a treaty that exceeded his government's expectations, securing from China concessions of far-ranging significance. Chapter 7 considers the great changes wrought by the ending of the Canton confinement. Specifically, this chapter shows how the opening of the treaty ports triggered the rapid dispersal of people, goods, capital, and ideas previously concentrated in Canton.

On one occasion, the transmission of Christian theology contributed to massive upheaval in China. As Chapter 8 explains, individual Americans played a large role in sparking, nurturing, and finally suppressing the Taiping Rebellion and did so by acting contrary to the wishes of their government and home institutions. Chapter 9 discusses the amazing diplomatic career of Anson Burlingame, Abraham Lincoln's minister to China. Not backed by any American military presence, Burlingame's predecessors had all complained of the powerlessness of their post. Undeterred, Burlingame dreamed of big things: he aspired to reinvent Sino-Western relations by replacing gunboat diplomacy with his own model based on cooperation. In 1867 the Chinese government, believing that Burlingame both understood and cared deeply about China, took a remarkable leap of faith by entrusting its Western diplomacy to his capable hands.

Our story begins in 1784 with a gamble of a different sort. The American Revolution having just come to an end, the officers and crew of the *Empress of China* are readying their vessel for departure. For them, China looms as terra incognita. For introduction, Congress has just drafted an official letter that the captain is to carry to Canton. Upon arrival, he is to present the letter to Chinese authorities, who are unaware that a country named "United States of America" even exists.

1

First Contact

The Voyage of the Empress of China

n January 1784 Captain John Green received a letter bearing the seal of the Congress of the Confederation, the governing body of the United States. He was instructed to present the letter to Chinese authorities after the ship under his command, the *Empress of China*, reached China, the first American vessel to do so. Strictly speaking, the purpose of the voyage was to conduct trade, but the *Empress* also carried a quasi-diplomatic mission: the officers were to initiate relations with the Chinese. However, since the Revolution had only recently ended (Congress ratified the Treaty of Paris days before composing the letter), the newest nation on earth feared that China, the oldest, might not respect its representatives. Should the Chinese question the nation's legitimacy, Green would produce this letter and erase any doubts about his country.

That, at least, was the hope. Unfortunately, the letter began with the following sentence:

Most Serene, Serene, most puissant, puissant, high, illustrious, noble, honorable, venerable, wise and prudent Emperors, Kings, Republicks, Princes, Dukes, Earls, Barons, Lords, Burgomasters, Councillors, as also Judges, Officers, Justiciaries & Regents of all the good Cities and places whether ecclesiastical or secular who shall see these patents or hear them read, We the United States of America in Congress Assembled make known that John Green Captain of the Ship call'd the Empress of China is a Citizen of the United States of America and that the Ship which he commands belongs to Citizens of the said United States and as we wish to see the said John Green prosper in his lawful affairs, our prayer is to all the beforementioned, and to each of them separately, where the said John Green shall arrive with his Vessel & Cargo, that they may please to receive him with goodness and to treat him in a becoming manner, permitting him upon the usual tolls & expences in passing & repassing, to pass, navigate and frequent the ports, passes and territories to the end to transact his business where and in what manner he shall judge proper: whereof we shall be willingly indebted.[1]

The more worldly Europeans knew better than to carry letters such as this one to foreign ports. Its absurd formality, intended to show that the United States belonged in the diplomatic arena, would almost certainly lend the opposite impression to the Chinese.

However, it is in the letter's awkwardness that we find its true meaning. For one thing, the letter makes clear (albeit accidentally) that Americans lacked an appropriate language for international relations, an unsurprising shortcoming given the severe restrictions England had imposed on American shipping with the Navigation Acts of the 1650s and 1660s. By granting the British East India Company (BEIC) a "commercial monopoly in Far Eastern trade," the Crown prevented American colonists from undertaking commercial voyages to Asia. With no American experience in China to serve as a guide, the voyage to Canton became, according to Kendall Johnson, one launched into "uncharted territory."[2] Understood in this way, the *Empress of China* appears in our imaginations not only on a crinkly mariner's map of the world, where we see it cruising in an easterly direction toward Asia, but also on a sheet of graph paper, where we track its vertical progression on a steep learning curve. This was an experimental voyage, one replete with blunders and embarrassments, all of which had to be patiently endured.

Mishaps aside, the voyage did yield a profit. Financially, it brought back a return for its investors substantial enough to convince others to enter the China trade. However, the voyage's most valuable gains cannot be measured in silver dollars. Diplomatically, it allowed the United States to initiate contact with China. Metaphorically, this American-made ship carrying an American crew and cargo provided the United States with a triumphant symbol of its independence from Britain. Commercially, the voyage educated those on board as to the specific rules of the Canton System, the complex bureaucratic machinery China used to control Western traders. This chapter describes this system, which structured the activities of all Americans trading in China before the First Opium War (1839–1842).

The voyage was also significant from a historical perspective because it marked the first appearance of three themes that would shape the American experience in China. First, the voyage exhibited the hands-off approach of the American government. Instead of dispatching an envoy, the United States requested that a merchant vessel carry a letter. Though this expediency made sense in the Revolution's wake, the United States continued to practice low-budget diplomacy throughout the 1800s. Second, three men associated with the *Empress* epitomized Americans' tendency to project their dreams onto China. The idea for the journey sprang from the imagination of John Ledyard, who dreamed of becoming fabulously wealthy selling furs in China. After the voyage, Samuel Shaw and Thomas Randall, both of whom sailed with the *Empress*, tried to dominate the American China trade while it remained in its infancy. Third, the voyage raised the issue of national character. After a major Sino-British conflict forced all Westerners in Canton to take sides, Americans took a decisive stand that separated them from the Europeans.

Horn or Hope?

In January 1784 dockhands stowed one crate after another into the lower compartments of the *Empress of China*. As soon as weather conditions permitted, the vessel would sail east across the North Atlantic, taking advantage of the Gulf Stream. Upon nearing Africa, it would then proceed south, cross the equator into the southern Atlantic, and round the Cape of Good Hope. It would then sail in an easterly direction toward the Malay Archipelago and pass between Sumatra and Java (the Sunda Strait) before reaching Canton. By taking this eastern route, the ship would reach the fabled Chinese port in about six months. Of course, there were other routes. The choice of route had less to do with making time and more to do with obtaining a cargo. The western routes involved initially sailing south, rounding Cape Horn, and then stopping in the Pacific Northwest to barter for furs before proceeding to Canton. In fact, in the earliest configuration of the *Empress*'s mission, furs from the Pacific Northwest constituted the major thrust of the entire venture. As late as the autumn of 1783, the venture's itinerary included Cape Horn, not the Cape of Good Hope.

The ambitious fur scheme was the brainchild of one man—John Ledyard. An adventurer from Connecticut, Ledyard had joined Captain Cook's ill-fated third voyage in 1776. In 1778 Cook's ships, the *Resolution* and *Discovery*, explored Nootka Sound on Vancouver Island, where crew members encountered Yuquot Indians, who presented them with an array of furs. For Ledyard, the showcase was remarkable for both the "variety of its animals" (he listed fourteen species) and the "richness of their furs." Needing warm coats for the freezing temperatures, Cook's men purchased furs, buying more than they needed since the price, sixpence sterling for each, seemed an unbelievable bargain. In 1779 (after Cook's death in Hawaii) the ships harbored in Macau, where the Chinese stunned Ledyard with their willingness to pay one hundred Spanish silver dollars (the world's de facto currency) for a single fur. There was an "opportunity," Ledyard wrote, to turn an "astonishing profit."[3]

This epiphany activated in Ledyard an entrepreneurial spirit that, heretofore, had lain dormant. A vast fortune was just sitting there, unidentified and waiting to be claimed. To seize it, all the enterprising individual had to do was connect the dots: Ledyard could sail a ship to Nootka Sound to obtain a cargo of furs, transport these to Canton where they would fetch a high price, and then use the profit to purchase tea for the return trip to the United States. The triangular trading scheme consumed Ledyard, and he waited anxiously onboard the *Resolution* for the conclusion of the expedition so that he could begin to execute his plan. He was probably the first American to concoct a China dream.[4]

After returning to Connecticut in the early 1780s, Ledyard began writing his account of Cook's final voyage for publication. In doing so, he hoped to capitalize on Americans' hunger for information about a heroic expedition that had ended in bloody tragedy. However, as Ledyard rushed his manuscript to completion, he remained preoccupied by his fur scheme, which he realized would not be simple to execute: it would require a substantial outlay of capital to purchase, provision, and rig a ship; hire a captain and crew; and obtain a suitable outgoing cargo. How could he obtain the requisite capital?

Opting not to waste precious time with small investors, Ledyard started his search at the apex of the commercial world. He audaciously sought, and surprisingly obtained, an interview with Robert Morris in June 1783. A signer of the Declaration of Independence and responsible for financing a large part of the Revolution, Morris had emerged in the 1780s as one of the new nation's richest men. As Morris listened to the animated Ledyard, he found himself captivated by the charismatic storyteller and his predictions of profits of 1,000 percent, an astonishing figure Ledyard could support with sound intelligence gathered during Cook's voyage.[5] In Morris's judgment, the plan was nothing short of inspired. For Ledyard, the meeting went so well as to trigger euphoria: "What a noble hold he instantly took of the enterprise!"[6]

Morris did not want to back a far-flung trading mission alone. Hoping to locate partners willing to share the cost and risk, he approached Daniel Parker, a well-connected Bostonian and former officer in the Continental army, who quickly brought in his business partner, William Duer, a New York speculator. Parker and Ledyard promptly traveled to Boston with two main objectives: to line up additional investors and order a vessel from John Peck, America's best shipbuilder. In New England the shrewd Parker and the glib Ledyard effectively pitched their proposal to a consortium of merchants who, greatly intrigued, expressed an interest in backing one-third of the venture. Their third, when combined with one-third from Parker and Duer and a final third from Morris, would complete the funding for the venture. In the summer of 1783, Ledyard watched with satisfaction as the pieces of his China scheme came together faster than he had expected.[7]

Then the enterprise began to unravel. The Boston consortium, which had withheld a firm commitment, abruptly pulled out for reasons that remain murky. The merchants might have harbored doubts as to the moral and financial integrity of one of the investors (as all involved later learned,

Parker's finances were in shambles). Perhaps the extreme volatility of the post-Revolution economy had given the conservative Bostonians jitters. Possibly they realized that the fur scheme's seemingly boundless potential hinged entirely on the assurances of a single man—John Ledyard—whose stories had yet to receive corroboration. Regardless, the Bostonians got cold feet, leaving the others with a shortfall as the scheduled departure drew near.[8]

The remaining partners resolved to persevere without committing more of their own wealth. To create a new, low-budget version of the China venture, they restructured both the finances and the itinerary. Concerning the former, the partners agreed on a new allocation of shares in which Morris, Parker, Duer, and a fourth partner, John Holker, would each assume one-quarter of the expenses. As for the latter, the partners decided— to Ledyard's horror—to amputate the riskiest leg of the venture: Nootka Sound. With fur trading no longer in the plan, the fantastic trading triangle collapsed into a dull, flat segment: from New York to Canton. With the mission's scope now reduced, the experience and expertise of Ledyard became expendable. He was out.[9]

For Ledyard, the blow was psychologically searing. Desperate to keep his fur scheme alive, he sailed for Paris to locate new backers. When a partnership failed to materialize, Ledyard confronted the bleak reality that his China dream lay in ruins. At this point, the dispirited traveler stumbled into the company of Thomas Jefferson, U.S. minister to France, who sensed that the best way to cure a depressed monomaniac was to replace the old dream with a new obsession. Ledyard and Jefferson hatched a crazy scheme whereby Ledyard would become the first man to circumnavigate the globe mostly on foot: he would traverse Russia by walking toward the Pacific, sail to Alaska with Russian fur traders, hoof it down to California, and finally hike to Kentucky. Having wound Ledyard up like a mechanical toy, Jefferson nudged him out the door to start his adventure. It did not go well. The Russians, suspecting Ledyard of being a spy, banished him from the country, thus ending his quest prematurely. After this setback, Ledyard signed on with a British expedition into Africa. In Alexandria he contracted dysentery that caused vomiting spells of such a violent nature that he burst a blood vessel, went insane, and perished in a monastery in 1789.[10]

Symbol of a New Nation

With furs jettisoned from the trade mission, the remaining partners sought and found a more conservative cargo. They settled on a combination of Spanish silver dollars and ginseng. Daniel Parker had obtained reliable European intelligence to the effect that the Chinese regarded ginseng as highly beneficial to digestion, blood pressure, mental acuity, and overall bodily health. As a trade commodity, ginseng presented the partners with one further advantage: it grew wild in the Appalachian foothills. In the autumn of 1783, the partners dispatched Robert Johnson, a physician who would later serve as ship's doctor, to locate and purchase ginseng, and do so in haste. The *Empress* would need to arrive in Canton in time for the tea-harvesting season, which began in early autumn. With the temporal window closing rapidly, Johnson scoured Virginia for suppliers, eventually purchasing and shipping to New York thirty tons of ginseng.[11]

Though piles of dug-up roots lacked the romance of Ledyard's furs, ginseng perhaps offered a more appropriate cargo for the new nation's initial foray into the China trade. Indigenous to the United States, ginseng provided the first China traders with an American commodity, one that European traders could not obtain quite as easily (though the French transported Canadian ginseng to China). For this reason, ginseng functioned not only on a commercial level but on a symbolic level as well: the preponderance of this American product in the ship's hold would help accentuate the national significance of the voyage. If the *Empress* were so fortunate as to succeed in China, the victory would be an American one.[12]

In 1784 victories of this sort were in short supply. Indeed, the political and economic uncertainty of the time prompted many Americans to doubt the viability of the nation. What was needed, all agreed, was a national identity strong enough to hold together a heterogeneous populace. John Adams, looking back in 1818 on the Revolutionary period, recalled how little the thirteen colonies had in common. Since they were composed of "a great variety of religions" and "so many different nations," their "customs, manners, and habits had so little resemblance." Given this overwhelming diversity, "to unite them in the same principles in theory and the same system of action, was certainly a very difficult enterprise," an enterprise Adams described as "thirteen clocks . . . made to strike together."[13] Unfortunately, if the people lacked unity before the Revolution, the situation failed to improve in the aftermath. As historian Joyce Appleby explains, the Revolution could not provide the "socially diverse" former colonists with "the shared sentiments, symbols, and social explanations necessary for an integrative national identity." That identity, she contends, would have to emerge out of "fresh experiences and opportunistic experiments"—such as those in the commercial sphere.[14]

Enter the *Empress of China*. For Americans in dire need of a symbolic victory, what could be more timely than this American-built ship with an American cargo, American crew, and officer corps composed mostly of Revolutionary War veterans embarking for China? Indeed, the destination itself was freighted with symbolism. For over a century, the British had forced American colonists to passively consume tea and porcelain while denying them the chance to actively compete in the China trade. According to Caroline Frank, Americans had regarded this treatment by the British as emasculating.[15] Not surprisingly, many tethered the first American voyage to China to the great question of national identity that roiled the nation. "The Captain and crew," Philadelphia's *Independent Gazetteer* reported, were "elated on being considered the first instruments, in the hands of Providence, who have undertaken to extend the commerce of the United States of America, to that distant, and to us, unexplored, country."[16] The *Empress of China* was ready to sail in January 1784. After ice in New York harbor forced a one-month delay, the vessel and its forty-two-man crew finally embarked on February 22, 1784, which, appropriately enough, was George Washington's birthday.[17]

Samuel Shaw at Sea

Great expectations and patriotic fanfare surrounded the launch, but the *Empress* carried a ticking time bomb that only one man on board—Samuel Shaw—knew about. As supercargo of the vessel, Shaw had been charged to handle all commercial responsibilities in Canton: the trading of goods and the payment of customs duties and port fees. Shaw almost did not sail for China. Not the first choice of the partners, he received an offer only after William Duer pulled out. Though Duer cited the care of his wife and children as his reason, the constant squabbling and questionable scruples of the other partners probably factored into his decision.[18] It was only after Duer's withdrawal that the partners turned to Shaw, the former aide-de-camp of one of Washington's generals. However, even Shaw entertained second thoughts after initially accepting the post. Though agreeing in the end, he insisted that his close friend, Thomas Randall, accompany him.[19] Still, the myriad difficulties clearly dissipated his enthusiasm. "The mountains are giving birth to a mouse," he wrote, meaning that the once noble enterprise was now plagued by pettiness.[20]

Worse still, the mountains had yielded a snake. Along with thirty tons of ginseng, the *Empress* was slated to carry $20,000 in silver to help the supercargo make his large purchase of tea. In late January, the bill of lading, a document listing all items loaded onto a vessel before departure, indicated that all silver had been safely stowed. Yet the debt-ridden Daniel Parker, in desperate need of money, had secretly removed $2,300 without amending the bill. Shaw alone was privy to the unethical act, and Parker endeavored to comfort the anxious supercargo by assuring him that the silver, every last piece, would be safely returned before departure.

Only half placated, Shaw remained silent on the matter out of respect to Parker; that said, he spent much of the long journey fretting about the silver, which lay inside chests he could not access. If Parker had been lying, Shaw wondered as to the consequences. Would the supercargo, who was responsible for the cargo, assume liability for the shortfall? If so, would Shaw have no recourse for exculpating himself except to accuse Parker, his friend and partner? With an uneasy mind, Shaw crossed the Atlantic.[21]

Fortunately for Shaw, the wonders and horrors of the sea distracted him from his worries. He took an interest in aquatic life, filling his journal with descriptions of flying fish, sharks, albatross, swordfish, and whales. Shifting attention to the crew, he explained a rite-of-passage ceremony in which experienced sailors initiated novices to life at sea when the ship passed over into the Tropics. Shaw also witnessed the cruelty of the global slave trade when, during a stopover in Cape Verde, a Portuguese colony and depot for the transatlantic slave trade, the *Empress* established friendly relations with a French slave-trading vessel bound for America. His mind shaped by the natural rights philosophy that had suffused Revolutionary War rhetoric, Shaw castigated slavery for "trampling upon the principles of universal benevolence." "Poor creatures," he wrote of the Africans huddled on deck, "doomed to eat the bread and drink the water of affliction for the residue of their miserable lives! Good God!"[22]

After Cape Verde, the *Empress* headed south, rounding the Cape of Good Hope in May 1784. At this point, it became the first American ship to reach the Indian Ocean (in December 1783, the *Harriet*, also heading for China, had opted not to continue past the Cape after British traders, disturbed by the prospect of Yankee competition in Canton, offered to exchange the *Harriet*'s cargo of ginseng with double its weight in Chinese tea). As capable as Captain Green was, the final portion of the journey promised to present the *Empress* with the most peril. The thousands of rocky islands comprising the Malay archipelago, along with posing navigational challenges, were notorious for pirates. Yet here good fortune intervened. Before passing through the Sunda Strait, the *Empress* encountered a friendly French vessel anchored in Mew Bay. Boarding the *Triton*, Randall, Green, and Shaw were received warmly by the captain, which was not surprising given the fond relations of France and the United States after the Revolution. After the French made a reciprocal visit to the *Empress*, both parties decided that the Americans, who lacked experience in these treacherous waters, should follow the French to China.[23]

Through the Tiger's Jaws

In late August the Americans enjoyed their first view of the Chinese mainland. Making an approach south of Guangdong Province, the *Empress* dropped anchor at Macau, a port situated on the western banks of the Pearl River Delta (Figure 1.1). Administered by Portugal since the sixteenth century but under China's supervision, Macau served as a haven for European merchants when they were not trading in Canton. Here the *Empress* fired a salute and had the honor of raising the American flag in China for the first time.

In Macau the *Empress* entered China's complex system for managing its foreign trade. Historian Paul Van Dyke has described the Canton System as a "huge machine" composed of "thousands of little parts that worked independent of, but in concert with, each other to move trade forward." While new to Americans, the system had been in place for over eight decades, during which time it had received numerous modifications. In Macau

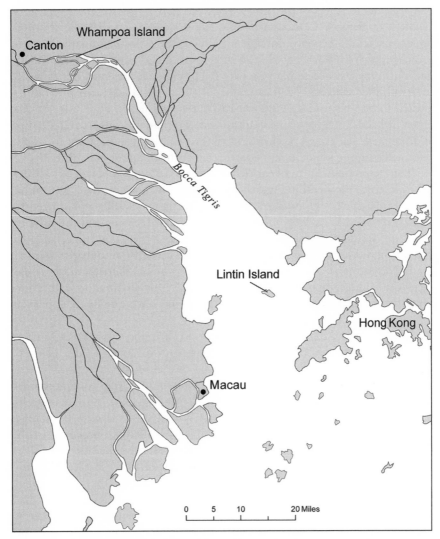

Figure 1.1. The Pearl River Delta region. *(Map by Valerie M. Sebestyen, Pennsylvania State University.)*

a Chinese official issued the *Empress* its "chop," a formal stamp affirming permission to continue. Perhaps to his surprise, Captain Green learned that his work was largely done. From this point forward, the *Empress* would not be sailing under his command as much as it would be processed by—or even absorbed into—a system under China's control.[24]

Indeed, maintaining control had been China's paramount concern in choosing Canton as its lone international port. Looking only at geography, one immediately recognizes how, from the perspective of the Qing government in Peking, Canton was uniquely advantaged to handle a group under suspicion—namely, foreigners. Unlike the other candidates for this privilege, such as Macau or Hong Kong, Canton was situated farther inland and thus was less accessible in a way the government deemed desirable. A foreign trader who had been caught smuggling contraband or who had neglected to pay his duties could not easily abscond to the high seas. At one of several checkpoints, Chinese authorities would detect his daring attempt and intercept his vessel. In the event that force became necessary to stop a fleeing vessel, the Chinese had constructed forts along the coastline.

The shallowness of the Pearl River also contributed to Canton's attractiveness. Since most trading vessels had deep drafts, the approach to Canton could prove tricky. To be sure of a safe passage, a captain would need to possess detailed knowledge of the river's peculiar features and the tides to avoid an accident. Most foreign captains lacked the knowledge, and the Chinese could justify assigning a pilot to each vessel. If an outsider were to grade Canton as a port using accessibility as the chief criterion, it would receive a failing grade. However, for Chinese officials intending to monitor foreign vessels, Canton's inland location and obstacle-course approach rendered the port ideal.[25]

The *Empress* did not itself reach Canton. The pilot, taken on at Macau, guided it to a point in the delta where the waterway constricted, called the Bocca Tigris, or "tiger's mouth." Here he debarked to visit a fort, where an official needed to see the chop before allowing the ship to continue its tortuous twelve-mile trip up the river. On August 28, 1784, six months after departure, the *Empress* anchored off Whampoa, where the crew fired a thirteen-gun salute to announce the ship's arrival to the French, British, Danish, and Dutch ships harbored there. They returned the salute.[26]

The *Empress* fired a second salute when an official Chinese boat approached. After its distinguished party boarded, Shaw met both the *hoppo*, the commissioner of the Board of Revenue, and Phuankhequa, a merchant. The *hoppo*'s primary task during the visit was to record measurements, beginning with the length and width of the vessel, which he would use to calculate port fees. While his subordinates carried out this chore, he asked Shaw to produce *sing-songs*. Noting Shaw's blank expression and empty hands, Phuankhequa interceded. Standard protocol demanded, Shaw learned, that foreigners present rare or interesting articles, such as clocks or mechanical toys, to the *hoppo*, who would later send them to the emperor. However, since the *hoppo* was forbidden from accepting gifts, Phuankhequa was expected to "purchase" the articles for him: he would suggest a price that amounted to a tiny fraction of the object's true value, which the supercargo was expected to accept.[27] Unversed in this etiquette, Shaw attempted to explain why he had arrived bereft of *sing-songs*. "We were from a new country," he stated, "and did not know that it was customary to bring such things." Apparently satisfied, the *hoppo* indicated that, next time, Shaw should bring *sing-songs*.[28]

After the *hoppo* had completed taking measurements, Phuankhequa signed a bond formalizing his acceptance of total responsibility for the *Empress*—its trade, payment of fees and duties, and hiring of servants.[29] As the hong merchant assigned to the *Empress*, Phuankhequa would work closely with Shaw in Canton. The trade, Shaw wrote, "is conducted by a set of merchants who style themselves the *co-hoang*, a word expressing our idea of a trading company." This cohong "consists of ten or twelve merchants, who have the exclusive privilege of the European . . . trade, for which they pay a considerable sum to [the Chinese] government."[30] With these few words, Shaw conveyed the essence of a remarkable mercantile arrangement: roughly a dozen hong merchants prosecuted China's entire trade with the West.

As one of his first duties, Phuankhequa secured a comprador and linguist for the *Empress*. The comprador's job was to keep the vessel in Whampoa provisioned with supplies while simultaneously tending to the needs of the supercargo residing in Canton. He would manage a staff of servants; purchase food from the market; and make arrangements for all cooking, cleaning, and laundry services. Thanks to the comprador, most supercargoes enjoyed a lifestyle in Canton that exceeded what they were accustomed to back home in terms of comfort and amenities. Of course, the comprador kept track of every expense so that he could present his client with a bill upon departure. The linguist served as a liaison between the foreign vessel and the *hoppo*. The title notwithstanding, the linguist's role had nothing to do with translating. Rather, he compiled extensive lists of each vessel's incoming and outgoing cargoes. In this way, he generated an official record of a ship's transactions so that the *hoppo* always had a current accounting of duties owed.[31]

Once a linguist had been secured, the unloading of cargo could begin. Since the *Empress* could not itself continue on to Canton, the cargo needed to be transferred onto sampans for transport to Phuankhequa's hong (his business office and warehouse). As each container passed from the *Empress* to a smaller boat, the linguist took and recorded weights and measurements. No quick affair, the unloading of the *Empress* would take place over the course of several weeks, and Shaw would oversee very little of it. Once he felt comfortable that his cargo was being handled properly, he and Randall took leave of the crew by taking a small boat farther up the river to Canton.[32]

The Foreign Factories

The *Empress* remained in China from late August to late December 1784, a four-month period that coincided with the tea season. During this time,

Shaw resided in Canton, though he did not enjoy a single glimpse of the inside of the city. Like all foreigners, he was confined to the "foreign factories," a small commercial zone on the banks of the Pearl River, situated just outside the massive crenulated walls encircling Canton. Only four hundred yards long and three hundred yards wide, the foreign compound covered roughly one twenty-fifth of a square mile. Here European men (foreign women were not allowed) lived and worked in a row of white buildings, most of which stood two stories high and possessed verandas facing the river. Their mobility severely restricted, foreigners had gathered strikingly little information about China, despite some very lengthy stays.[33] "Europeans, after a dozen years' residence," Shaw wrote from his rented rooms, "have not seen more than what the first month presented to view."[34] Though China remained a mystery, few traders cared, because their work preoccupied them. During the tea season, business consumed the better part of each day, with some traders devoting as many as fifteen hours to work.[35]

During their first days in Canton, Shaw and Randall received formal invitations to dine with Europeans. Though Shaw enjoyed these social gatherings, Daniel Parker's removal of silver weighed heavily on his mind. In late November the moment at last arrived when he could open the chests of silver, count the money, and learn whether Parker had returned the withdrawn amount. Shaw did not know that Parker had been bankrupt all along. He had been playing an elaborate shell game with creditors and partners alike, instilling confidence in these men by speaking glibly on matters of trade while surreptitiously moving money around to lend his wretched finances the appearance of solvency. When Shaw finally lifted the shell in Canton, he found no pea—he was missing $2,300. To explain the deficit, Shaw penned a formal letter in which he described the conversation in which Parker had urged him to keep the "secret from every body." Shaw stated that he had agreed out of both friendship and his personal sense of honor. Even now, he continued, he had chosen to commit his story to writing only because there was the possibility he would die before having the chance to tell the truth. Shaw presented the completed letter to French and Chinese witnesses.[36]

Moral and legal difficulties aside, Parker's pilfering had left Shaw financially handicapped at the tea-purchasing stage. Thanks to a stroke of good fortune, however, he was still able to secure a healthy cargo for the return journey. The *Empress* had arrived in Canton two months ahead of two ginseng-laden vessels from Europe, meaning that Shaw traded in a market not yet glutted with the root.[37] While doing so, he was astonished at just how easy business in Canton was. "Commerce," he wrote, "appears to be . . . as simple, as any in the known world."[38] Simplicity was exactly right, for Shaw was able to trade his silver and ginseng for tea and other goods simply by working with Phuankhequa.

Phuankhequa treated Shaw very well. To show the newcomer his hospitality, he invited Shaw to visit his estate, situated on Honam Island just across the Pearl River from the foreign factories. Here a few hong merchants maintained elaborate pleasure gardens, each one an artificial world composed of plant and animal life as well as miniature mountains, waterfalls, forests, and ponds. In these opulent settings, hong merchants entertained their foreign guests, treating them to banquets of many courses that, like Chinese scrolls, were slowly unfurled over a long evening. Having hoped to glean some information about Chinese domestic life, Shaw left his host's estate disappointed, for the party revealed nothing. Nevertheless, he appreciated the warm gesture and enjoyed strolling through the enchanting landscape.[39]

Meaningful cultural exchange between Shaw and Phuankhequa was difficult because neither man spoke the other's language. Verbal exchanges were limited to what could be communicated through Pidgin English, a trade language that had emerged in Canton to facilitate trade. Described by one scholar as a "minimum language," Pidgin amounted to little more than a small pool of words plugged into a simple syntax. Given its basic nature, foreign traders, hong merchants, compradors, shop keepers, and servants could learn to speak it in a short time. Though one could not share complicated thoughts, one could impart essential information, such as the price of a good. Though Pidgin was new to Shaw, he could understand Phuankhequa because the language's modest vocabulary was composed mostly of corrupted English words.[40]

Phuankhequa and the other hong merchants impressed Shaw. They are "as respectable a set of men as are commonly found in other parts of the world," he wrote, before listing their attributes: "intelligent," "punctual," and "fair." In lumping Phuankhequa together with his colleagues, Shaw implied their interchangeability. Nothing in his journal suggests any awareness of Phuankhequa's formidable character and storied history. If the voyage of the *Empress* brought the world's newest country into contact with the oldest, then Shaw's relationship with Phuankhequa epitomized this contrast. While Shaw measured his mercantile experience in months, Phuankhequa had entered the twilight of a long, illustrious, but infamous career that had begun back at mid-century. He was a dragon, a fearsome leader and trader who had earned the hatred of some his colleagues.[41]

Phuankhequa

The adverse conditions Phuankhequa faced justified some of his cold-blooded behavior. Though it was true that, as the only Chinese licensed to trade with the West, hong merchants could accumulate tremendous wealth, the drawbacks outnumbered the advantages. After securing a foreign vessel, they were responsible for everything associated with it—the behavior of the crew, the payment of duties and fees, and the buying and selling of cargoes. Not all transactions yielded profits. BEIC merchants were required to import annually a set quantity of woolens and Indian cotton, goods that hong merchants grudgingly took off their hands and sold at a loss on local markets—the price of doing business with the BEIC. As mediators between China and foreigners, hong merchants received no assistance from the *hoppo*, who looked after himself while lining his pockets with silver extorted from them. Since hong merchants also used silver to pay for large tea orders from the inland merchants, they faced perennial shortages of silver. Exploiting their need, foreign traders, the most active lenders in Canton's money market, charged between 18 and 40 percent annual interest on loans. Hong merchants accepted these usurious rates because they had to have tea ready to sell when foreign vessels arrived. However, they did so at great risk: those who accumulated too much debt were sometimes banished. With the profession so fraught with peril, it comes as no surprise that few hong merchants chose this career. Most were drafted into service and could retire only after paying local officials an exorbitant fee.[42]

In this precarious environment, Phuankhequa ruthlessly pursued his own self-interest. The secret to his longevity and power lay in his shrewd manipulation of the competing yet interrelated interests of the three major entities involved in the Canton trade: foreign merchants, Chinese officials, and his fellow hong merchants. He understood how to play one off the other to strengthen his position and thwart his rivals. In 1758 the death of the hong merchant Beaukeequa brought the shocking disclosure of massive debt. Hoping to avoid a similar fate, three hong merchants formed a consortium as a way to increase their leverage when bargaining and exert control over limited supplies of tea. In debt himself, Phuankhequa recognized that the consortium's advantage threatened to doom his business. To ensure his survival, he approached officials who, after Beaukeequa's death, understood that the insolvency of hong merchants threatened the viability of the Canton System. In 1760 he persuaded them to establish, with the emperor's consent, a cohong. This merchant guild, he argued, would stabilize the system by helping merchants in arrears settle their debts and preserving competitive balance among all hong merchants. Though the consortium remained, it was now forced to operate within a larger bureaucratic structure that prevented it from seizing excessive advantage. As the cohong's appointed head, Phuankhequa enjoyed certain perks. Since he had the privilege of presenting gifts to officials on the cohong's behalf, he obtained influence his colleagues lacked.[43] "His means and his connections with mandarins," observed a BEIC agent, "make him the most useful person here."[44]

A decade later, the British involved the "useful" Phuankhequa in a scheme. Viewing the cohong as an obstacle to free trade, British traders secretly offered Phuankhequa a substantial bribe to abolish it. What the British did not know was that Chinese authorities were already planning to dissolve the cohong. The recent death of Si Hungqua, the leading merchant in the consortium, had eliminated the primary rationale for the cohong's existence: the need to maintain competitive balance among hong merchants.

Phuankhequa, in other words, accepted payment for effecting a government action that was going to take place anyway. It is probably no coincidence that, shortly after the dissolution of the cohong in 1771, Phuankhequa paid officials a sum equal to the amount of the bribe to approve his retirement and transfer his business to a family member.[45]

Later in the 1770s, Phuankhequa, having been called out of retirement, faced a challenge from his archrival, Yngshaw. Yngshaw "is leader of one party here, as Phuankhequa is of the other," observed a BEIC supercargo, and "it is their jealousy and hatred of each other, which has been our great security against paying unreasonable prices for our goods."[46] Though once prosperous, Yngshaw entered financial turmoil in the 1770s after he lost some of the BEIC's business and took out loans from several European merchants. With no cohong to oversee a settlement with creditors, Yngshaw saw the ouster of Phuankhequa as the only way out of his predicament. The latter's predatory trading practices, Yngshaw believed, prevented him from reaping the profits that would enable his financial recovery.

As Yngshaw organized a cabal, he did so against the backdrop of a larger unfolding story. As the debts of multiple hong merchants began to mount, irate creditors in India urged naval officers to send HMS *Seahorse* from India to China to collect. Nervous Chinese officials, fearful that the warship would carry the complaint to Peking, pleaded with Phuankhequa and others to assume liability for the debt of their peers. As Phuankhequa prepared his response, he considered three factors: the plot to oust him, the coming British warship, and the desperation of local officials. Instead of assuming responsibility for his colleagues' debts, Phuankhequa submitted to a court the names of three indebted merchants—Yngshaw, Kewshaw, and Munqua—the chief conspirators against him. Humiliated by the public disclosure, Munqua rushed Phuankhequa with a dagger but failed to injure his enemy. As for Yngshaw, authorities took him into custody in 1780, confiscated his property (which Phuankhequa purchased), and banished him to Ili, a frozen territory in the north. With the coup crushed, no rivals remained to challenge Phuankhequa's supremacy.[47]

The debt crisis brought permanent change to the Canton System. Chinese authorities instituted a new financial mechanism, a *consoo* fund, designed to preclude debt-related crises in the future. In most transactions with a foreign trader, hong merchants would levy a small tax, which would be deposited into a chest. Hong merchants could use the accumulated wealth in the *consoo* fund to not only discharge the debts of bankrupt peers but also pay fees exacted by rapacious government officials.[48]

When Samuel Shaw met Phuankhequa in 1784, he had only recently emerged from this brutal period of infighting. Ignorant of this history, Shaw knew nothing of his counterpart's guile and failed to notice when he became the unwitting beneficiary of it. After boarding the *Empress*, Phuankhequa made a discovery that eluded the *hoppo*: this vessel hailed from a new country with no history in China. Along with noting the strange flag and the supercargo's obliviousness to *sing-songs*, Phuankhequa might have understood Shaw when he announced his national identity. Since new nations requesting trade with China were expected to pay tribute to the emperor, Phuankhequa sought to spare the Americans this expense (and endear himself to them in the process) by feeding the *hoppo* misinformation. These men were not new, he told the *hoppo*, but were rather a different variety of Englishmen who were therefore exempt from the costly ritual. Only later in his sojourn did Shaw learn of the ruse, and he took prompt action to correct the record. What was the point, after all, of making America's first journey to China only to be labeled "English"?[49]

The *Lady Hughes* Affair

Among Europeans in Canton, there was never any question as to the national origin of the *Empress of China*. Though these traders welcomed the newest entrant to the China trade, Shaw was surprised by the overall lack of sociability in the foreign community. Every Sunday evening, the Danish factory held a concert of instrumental music, but this qualified as the only example of "general intercourse" among Europeans, who were in the habit of "keeping much by themselves." In late November a major Sino-British conflict would convince Western nations, at least temporarily, to band together. Shaw would have a crucial decision to make: would he join them?[50]

On November 26, 1784, the British *Lady Hughes*, having recently arrived from India, dropped anchor at Whampoa. To celebrate the journey's end, Captain Williams invited a group of foreign merchants to dine with him aboard the vessel. As this party took its leave, Williams ordered his men to fire a parting salute, an often-repeated ritual that, by mischance, produced a tragic result. After the shots rang out, the crew saw to their horror that they had failed to notice a small Chinese boat drifting nearby. The gunner had inadvertently shot and wounded three Chinese civilians, placing one in a life-threatening condition. That night, few British sailors or officers slept, knowing that, should any of the injured die from their wounds, the consequences would be dire. Chinese authorities would move swiftly to prosecute the gunner under Chinese law, which the British regarded as capricious and cruel.

The following day, the crew's worst fears came true when the grim news arrived that one man had died overnight. Seized with terror, the gunner, though innocent as far as his intent, fled the ship. Later that day the *hoppo* and hong merchants visited William Pigou, the BEIC's representative, to insist that the British hand over the gunner. Pigou promptly directed the Chinese to George Smith who, as supercargo of the *Lady Hughes*, was responsible for handling any incident relating to the crew. Meeting with the same delegation, Smith pledged his full cooperation in resolving the matter, and the Chinese left. Not long thereafter, Smith received a mysterious message requesting that he proceed to the offices of Phuankhequa. Upon emerging from his quarters, a startled Smith confronted a line of drawn swords and was summarily taken into Chinese custody (where he was well treated). The message could not have been clearer: until the gunner was handed over, Smith would be held hostage. To solicit support, Pigou approached the representatives of Western nations. Shaw received a knock at his door.

On matters of grave importance, Pigou asserted emphatically, foreign nations must present a united front. Specifically, the British wanted Shaw to join the Europeans by authorizing the *Empress* to send an armed boat to the foreign factories to protect foreigners and their assets. Would the new nation join the others? Though all Western representatives had received the same call, only Shaw was required to think. The others needed only to adhere to the policies of their governments or, in the absence of a clear policy, follow an established precedent. In contrast, the U.S. government, which measured its existence in months, had managed to supply Shaw only with a clumsy letter of introduction. It had not briefed him on its China policy for the simple reason that it did not have one. As for a precedent, Shaw was in the act of creating one.

Shaw not only agreed to join the British; he did so with passion and conviction. While siding with the British, however, Shaw was not acting out of allegiance to them (British agents later informed him that his fondness for France had taken them aback). Rather, Shaw viewed the incident through the lens of the natural rights philosophy that had provided the ideological justification for the Revolution. The unlucky British sailor had committed a grave error but he had not intended to kill.[51] Therefore, it was a violation of human rights to place the gunner at the mercy of a Chinese tribunal whose guiding principle would be, in Shaw's words, that "blood must answer for blood" (Shaw had clearly adopted Europe's negative view of the Chinese justice system). In the same way, Shaw viewed China's seizure of Smith as "an outrage on personal liberty." Without hesitating, he communicated to the *Empress* his wish to have an armed boat sent.[52]

Alarmed by the Euro-Americans' unexpected display of unity, Sun Shiyi, the acting viceroy, realized that his nation's sovereignty was being challenged. Thinking that the best way to defeat the British was to break Western solidarity, he altered his tactics. First, he applied economic pressure on the defiant foreigners by sending forty boats to cordon off the foreign factories, bringing the international trade to a standstill. Next, he ordered hong merchants, linguists, and compradors to withdraw from the area. The message was simple: until the gunner was handed over, George Smith would remain detained, all trade would cease, and foreigners would live in isolation. Finally, he approached specific European representatives (the British excluded) to explain how they could return to trading. "The Chinese were aware," Shaw later wrote, that "if they could separate the other nations from the English, there would soon be an end of the affair."[53]

The strategy worked. On November 28, Shaw received a visit from the French consul, who informed him that some Western nations (the British excluded) had engaged in secret negotiations with the Chinese. The terms of the arrangement, which the consul advised Shaw to accept, were simple: any Western nation that agreed to remove its armed boats could resume commerce. If Shaw needed more incentive, the consul told him, "the Danes, French, and Dutch" were prepared to take China's deal. Since the united front was clearly collapsing, Shaw must have baffled the consul when he elected to stand pat, citing natural rights as his justification. "I considered the rights of humanity deeply interested in the present business," he answered. As for the armed boat, Shaw declared that he would send it back "when the English chief assured [him] that the purposes for which she had been required were answered."[54]

Later that evening, Sun Shiyi invited non-British representatives to a conference held in a pagoda. At this event he invoked "the power of the Emperor" and declared his "own determination to support the laws." While insisting that the gunner be handed over, he assured his guests that the man would receive a fair trial and repeated his earlier offer to lift the blockade once foreigners ordered their armed boats back to Whampoa. He next, according to Shaw, "presented each gentleman with two pieces of silk, in token of amity, and then dismissed us." As the exodus of European boats began, the American and British boats conspicuously avoided joining them. However, with Western solidarity broken, the British had lost all leverage. Smith finally capitulated by sending a message to the *Lady Hughes*, ordering the captain to give up the gunner. The British then thanked Shaw for his loyalty and urged him to order the American boat back to Whampoa. "Thus ended a very troublesome affair," wrote Shaw, reflecting on an unsatisfying ending in which, in his view, human greed had won out over human rights. "Had that spirit of union among the Europeans taken place which the rights of humanity demanded," he continued, "and could private interest have been . . . sacrificed to the general good, the conclusion of the matter must have been honorable."[55]

For Shaw, the "troublesome affair" had not quite reached its end. As he prepared to return to business, his linguist delivered the news that he had not received clearance. After making an inquiry, he learned that, thanks to Phuankhequa's ploy, the *hoppo* had registered the *Empress* as an English ship. Using the French as his intermediary, Shaw promptly set the matter straight with the *hoppo*, explaining "that we are AMERICANS, a free, independent, and sovereign nation, not connected with Great Britain, nor owing allegiance to her."[56] The issue finally resolved, Shaw began loading the *Empress* for the journey home.

On January 8, 1785, the foreign community learned the result of the gunner's trial: he had been strangled to death. The British, who had been expecting the defendant's outright release, expressed shock and outrage. For more than half a century, this case would fester in British memory.

Shaw did not hear the result until much later. Eleven days earlier, the *hoppo* had given the *Empress* its "grand chop," which confirmed that, since all payments had been made, the vessel was cleared for departure. On December 28, 1784, the *Empress* slowly withdrew from anchorage at Whampoa and headed home.[57]

A Ginseng Miracle?

The *Empress* sailed into New York Harbor on May 11, 1785, and dropped anchor in the East River, receiving a thirteen-gun salute. Fifteen months after departure, the journey had reached its end. Almost immediately, a mercantile house put the cargo up for sale, and Shaw later learned that the voyage earned a 25 percent net profit on the initial investment. Though this yield was not spectacular (a few years later, a ship importing pepper from Sumatra earned a profit of 700 percent), it was strong enough to afford patriotic observers the chance to celebrate a trading mission that, all along, had been linked to national identity.[58] Philip Freneau, poet of the American Revolution, composed a commemorative poem:

> *To countries placed in burning climes*
> *And islands of remotest times*
> *She now her eager course explores,*
> *And soon shall greet Chinesian shores.*
>
> *From thence their fragrant* TEAS *to bring*
> *Without the leave of Britain's king;*
> *And* PORCELAIN WARE, *enchased in gold,*
> *The product of that finer mould.*

For Freneau, the glorious meaning of the first American ship to reach China was clear. What the Declaration of Independence had accomplished in the political realm, the *Empress* had achieved in global commerce: freedom from a centralized power.[59]

One week after his arrival, Shaw sent a letter to the U.S. minister for foreign affairs informing him of his reception by the Chinese, his relations with Europeans, the *Lady Hughes* affair, and the prospects for future trade. Concerning this last topic, Shaw expressed only optimism: Americans enjoyed a wonderful opportunity to forge a mutually beneficial trading relationship with the Chinese. The Chinese "styled us the *New People*," Shaw wrote, "and when by the map we conveyed to them an idea of the extent of our country, with its . . . increasing population, they were highly pleased at the prospect of so considerable a market for the productions of their own empire." With these words, Shaw made a profound point. Just as China's immensity could cast a spell on American traders, so too could America inspire reciprocal ambition among Chinese merchants. Shaw closed his letter by announcing the friendship he had formed with the Chinese, going so far as to predict that "in a few years" Americans would enjoy "advantages equal, if not superior" to those of Europeans. The letter was passed on to a delighted Congress, which rewarded Shaw with special commendation.[60]

As for these American advantages, Shaw placed ginseng at the top of the list. Working through Phuankhequa, he had sold his entire thirty-ton cargo at the price of thirty dollars per pound. Since the Chinese had demonstrated a strong appetite for this root, Shaw believed it might offset Americans' commensurate craving for tea.[61] While Europeans are "obliged to purchase this commodity with ready money, it must be pleasing to an American to know that his country can have it upon easier terms" simply by shipping to China an "otherwise useless produce of her mountains and forests."[62] Thanks to ginseng, the American China trade promised to achieve the salutary balance that thus far had eluded Europeans. Americans would not have to wait for their China trade to enter its golden age.

In contrast to the hyperbolic Shaw, John Swift, the purser on the *Empress*, offered a sober appraisal of the future trade in ginseng. "Our Cargoe," Swift wrote to his father from Canton, "turn'd out but so so." "We brought too much Ginsang," he continued, when "a little of the best kind will yield an immense profit but all the European Nations trading here bring this Article, & unfortunately this Year ten times as much arrived as ever did before." Though not dismissing ginseng entirely, Swift went on to suggest that his brother, should he undertake a China voyage, load his ship with a diverse cargo that would include "a little Ginsang" along with other goods.[63]

As Shaw had overseen the very ginseng sales that Swift labeled "so so," we are left to speculate as to why ginseng's prospects prompted such divergent assessments. The answer perhaps lies in the target audiences of the two men. Though technically writing to his government, Shaw was also, in a sense, composing the first draft of history. He desired not only that the voyage enter the historical record as a commercial success but also that it assume some of the attributes of Divine Providence. Shaw perhaps inflated the role of ginseng in his narrative, allowing the root to come across as a blessing that God uniquely bestowed on the American people. Writing to family, Swift understood the danger of sharing anything other than a realistic assessment. Any exaggeration could ruin his brother's venture to China.

Though Swift's brother knew to trade ginseng only in moderation, other traders believed the rumors of a ginseng miracle. Though Shaw had his facts right as far as prices were concerned, he had failed to discern a flaw in his thinking. Because China had absorbed his ginseng cargo, he assumed the existence of an inexhaustible demand that would ensure stable prices in the foreseeable future. He did not know that the *Empress* had flooded the market for ginseng, a gloomy tiding that awaited the next American trader. When the *Experiment* reached Canton in 1786 with a cargo of ginseng, its supercargo learned to his chagrin that the price had fallen to one dollar per pound. Since it took months for word of this precipitous plunge to reach the United States, other merchants had—thanks partly to Shaw's robust projection—already launched their own ginseng-laden vessels. By 1790 the price had plummeted further to thirty-two cents, prompting the French consul in Canton to complain that "because of the Americans, the price has dropped so low that it hardly covers the import duties." The price of American ginseng would rebound near century's end, but Shaw's sunny forecast of an Appalachian miracle never came to pass.[64]

Defining the Shapeless Future

As his enthusiastic report indicated, Samuel Shaw, like John Ledyard before him, had caught the China bug. Fortunately, he was not predisposed to the dangerous obsessions that consumed and eventually destroyed the man who dreamed of cornering the fur trade. Still, as Shaw reflected on his historic journey, he began to discern that, through his personal agency, his nation could begin to define its promising but still amorphous China trade. He started to make plans.

Although the officers and partners tied to the *Empress* had come from a variety of backgrounds, most of them held one thing in common: membership in the Society of the Cincinnati, a fraternal order of former Revolutionary War officers. Thomas Randall, Captain Green, Dr. Robert Johnson, and Andrew Caldwell, the surgeon's mate, were members, as were Robert Morris and Daniel Parker. Most prominent of all was Samuel Shaw himself, who had played a leading role in establishing the Cincinnati. In Canton, Shaw hired a porcelain painter to emblazon the order's emblem on special sets of commemorative dinnerware that George Washington, among others, would later purchase.[65]

The prevalence of Cincinnati membership presented a unique opportunity. Shaw and Randall realized that, for a short period, their knowledge of the Canton System provided them with an early advantage over competitors. If they moved quickly to press this advantage, they could perhaps imprint the formless China trade with their own mercantile vision. In attempting to do so, they were governed by their own ideological leanings—leanings implied by their Cincinnati affiliations. What exactly were the politics of the Cincinnati and how might they shape the China trade?

The fraternity's members hewed to a set of political principles that, after maturing during the debate over the ratification of the Constitution, would coalesce into the central tenets of Federalism in the 1790s. These former war officers feared that American society would rapidly deteriorate to mob rule if the forces of liberty unleashed by the Revolution were allowed to run unchecked. Preferring order and stability, these proto-Federalists aspired to construct an American nation in which important decisions would be made not by the many but by the few—those with property, education, and gentility. This social vision sounded a lot like a European aristocracy, in which one's birthright entitled one to political power. Though the similarities were unmistakable, there was one key difference: since the United States did not possess a legally sanctioned aristocracy, the viability of this hierarchical vision depended on the voluntary consent of ordinary Americans. For the vision to win out, the small farmers, laborers, and artisans would have to defer to the "superior" leadership of the gentry on matters of political, economic, or cultural significance.[66]

When transferred to the China trade, this proto-Federalist vision promised to shape Asian commerce in a predictable fashion. One would expect to see the entire trade dominated by a small handful of large companies headed by an elite merchant class. With their fleets of vessels, rich capital reserves, and political connections, these companies would reliably carry ginseng to China and tea to America, amassing in the process greater quantities of capital, which could then be invested in the nation's emerging banking and industrial sectors. If this vision were carried to its extreme, the entire China trade would fall under the control of a single entity modeled on the BEIC. This idea had its supporters. In 1785 John Adams urged his friends in government to formally establish an American East Indian trade. However, just as the proto-Federalists were contested in politics by the Democratic-Republicans, so too was this Brobdingnagian model of trade challenged by a Lilliputian rival. Those who detested centralized power imagined the China trade as an open field of competition populated by dozens of small traders.[67]

Fearful that this chaotic model might win out, Shaw and Randall moved to impose their vision over the trade. In 1789 Randall drew up and submitted to Alexander Hamilton, secretary of the Treasury, a proposal for a government-chartered monopoly. The idea, of course, had ample precedent as European nations, without exception, created these behemoths to manage their Asian commerce. Exposed to this model in Canton, Shaw and Randall hoped to duplicate it. Since the proposed plan would centralize the China trade, Randall expected a sympathetic response from Hamilton, the architect of Federalism's economic vision. When Hamilton neglected to reply, he dashed all hope for an American East India Company. Americans would have to conduct business in China without the organization of a giant governmental superstructure—that is, unless Shaw and Randall could create a goliath of their own.[68]

While a government charter stood as their best option, Shaw and Randall had a contingency plan. In 1786 Shaw sailed to Canton not just to trade but to serve as the first American consul in China (the appointment of merchants as consuls became standard practice because it was convenient and inexpensive from the government's perspective). That same year, they established a trading company named after themselves and authorized the construction of a vessel at a shipyard in Quincy, Massachusetts. Modeled on a BEIC ship that had impressed Shaw in Canton, the *Massachusetts* surpassed the size of any ship ever built in America. Weighing in at 820 tons, it dwarfed the 300-ton *Empress of China*. With tremendous holding capacity, the *Massachusetts* could transport more cargo to and from China than any American competitor.[69]

Dimensions aside, the *Massachusetts* also functioned at a symbolic level. In this floating colossus, Shaw and Randall had translated the Proto-Federalist vision into the language of maritime architecture. With it, they planned to overawe all competitors and establish a position of unquestioned dominance in the Asian trade. As the project neared completion in 1789, all signs indicated that the imposing vessel would accomplish exactly that.[70] The ship, according to its second officer, "excited a considerable sensation" as onlookers came "to gratify their curiosity" and behold the great ark seemingly destined to win the China game as it was getting started.[71] For other traders mulling over a China voyage, the incessant sounds of hammering and sawing in Quincy must have been unnerving. If the *Massachusetts* offered a glimpse at future China trade, what did the majestic titan bode for them?

Conclusion

What shape would the inchoate China trade assume? Not content to leave the matter to chance, Shaw acted decisively to imprint the trade with his vision. On the surface, his vision appears to lack any feature one would classify as American. After all, in Canton, Shaw supported the British during the heated *Lady Hughes* affair. Back in the United States, Randall and he urged their government to mimic Europe by forming an East India company. However, this characterization of Shaw as imitative leaves out his ambition, innovation, and independent thinking. Lacking any guidance from his own government, Shaw formulated—on the spot—a unique position during the Sino-British conflict that set Americans apart from Europeans. And while he and Randall revered the East India companies, their attempt to launch a dominating trading firm existed outside the realm of possibility for most British, French, or Dutch traders, company men working within large bureaucracies. Shaw formed his own China dream, and that was a distinctly American act.

As Shaw prepared the *Massachusetts* to dominate the future, the *Empress of China* quietly passed into memory. After the maiden voyage to China, the ship entered into rapid decline. Sold in 1785 for the modest sum of $6,250, it sailed one more time to China under Captain Green, in 1786. By 1787, however, the ship had been so battered by storms as to compel the owners to cancel a planned third voyage. Its seaworthiness now in question, the run-down vessel moved from one owner to another before finally sinking off the coast of Dublin in 1791 on Washington's birthday, seven years to the day after its departure for China.[72]

As dismal as this ending was, more pathetic was the resolution of the Parker case, or lack thereof. Fearing retribution for theft, Parker absconded to England in 1784, hoping to keep himself out of reach when the *Empress* returned and Shaw reported his misappropriation of funds. When letters from America started to arrive in 1785, Parker deliberately became elusive, artfully dodging for years both his partners' attempts to recoup the missing money and Shaw's appeals to clear his name. Although Parker bore Shaw no ill will, he knew that anything he did to exonerate Shaw amounted to an admission of guilt. Shaw eventually extracted from Parker a signed statement that restored his reputation. The partners to whom Parker owed money were not so fortunate. Although this group pressed the case for years, Parker successfully evaded all pursuers until, eventually, their deaths or incarcerations in debtor's prison rendered their cause moot. In 1813, three decades after he had signed on to the China venture, John Holker, now an old man, realized that the only people still living with knowledge of the incident were Daniel Parker, Parker's agent, and himself. Why continue the chase?[73]

System Men

The Rise of Perkins and Company

As the *Massachusetts*'s departure drew near, Shaw and Randall became inundated with applications from young men, easily filling every available slot. What ambitious seaman would not want to sail on the maiden voyage of such a noble craft? Seemingly out of nowhere, however, a fortune-teller named Moll Pitcher materialized and began spewing grim prophecies before the superstitious sailors. Do not join this doomed venture, she warned, because the *Massachusetts* was destined to be lost at sea, where the crew, every last one, would perish. Spooked by the old woman's ill portent, sailors quit *en masse*, necessitating another round of hiring.

In March 1790 the day for the launch arrived. Samuel Shaw himself would be sailing with the vessel, President Washington having renewed his appointment as consul. As a large crowd cheered, the great hulk sloughed into the harbor and oozed out into the open sea. The festive departure marked the voyage's high point. Since the vessel was poorly equipped in terms of nautical instrumentation (the captain possessed neither a chronometer nor a sextant), imprecise navigation prolonged the journey. More alarmingly, the shipbuilder had used a poor-quality wood, which began to rot in the ocean brine. As seawater seeped into the leaky vessel, the lower compartments flooded, and the air, thick with moisture, became foul smelling and hard to breathe. Even more repugnant, a sickening "blue mould more than half an inch thick" invaded the hold, corrupting containers and rendering the goods unfit for sale. After the ship's arrival in Canton, Europeans marveled at the ostensibly splendid specimen of maritime architecture and asked for a tour. At this point, their nostrils alerted them to the gigantic failure that was the *Massachusetts*. Cutting his losses, Shaw sold the vessel to the Danish Asiatic Company.[1]

The most significant casualty of the *Massachusetts* fiasco turned out to be Shaw and Randall's vision of a patrician China trade. In the absence of a government-chartered monopoly, they had hoped that Americans would defer to an exclusive group of genteel traders who would manage the trade with honor, integrity, and the public welfare in mind. Americans, however, rejected this undemocratic model, and the China trade emerged as a competitive arena that beckoned anyone intent on pursuing the main chance. Between 1784 and 1814, over six hundred American vessels visited Canton. Though the lure of free enterprise attracted these men, few of them sought to preserve the free-trade status quo. Like Shaw, early China traders viewed the monopoly as their holy grail.[2]

Although these early traders were actuated by the same monopolistic goal as Shaw, they approached it in more pragmatic ways than he. Amaso Delano, who sailed with the *Massachusetts*, described Shaw as "a man of . . . considerable cultivation" who "placed so high a value on the sentiments of honour that some of his friends thought it was carried to excess." Few would use such words to describe Thomas Handasyd Perkins, the Boston merchant who pursued monopolies with zeal. Unlike the gentlemanly Shaw, Perkins never held the naive, and somewhat arrogant, assumption that other traders would or should voluntarily concede the trade to him. He knew he would need to defeat his rivals with superior organization. This Yankee would win with *system*.[3]

This chapter offers an anatomy of a single firm, Perkins and Company, that thrived in the laissez-faire environment that resulted from the virtually nonexistent official U.S. presence in China. It begins with Thomas Perkins, who, animated by driving ambition, voyaged to Canton in 1788 as a supercargo for another merchant. It was his only trip to China, but Perkins used the insights he gathered to construct the system of trade that would underpin his later success. To oversee affairs in Canton, Perkins depended on his precocious nephew John Perkins Cushing. Perkins and Cushing perfectly embodied the Yankee ethos that, with its emphasis on system and order, contributed to the prosperity of so many New Englanders in the China trade. If Perkins applied his intelligence to the *macro* aspects of trade—the movement of ships, goods, and capital through multiple ports—then Cushing concentrated on the *micro* with laser-like focus: the Canton trade. Working from the foreign factories, Cushing built and monitored the integrative machinery that connected his uncle's global system to both the Canton System and the merchant house of Houqua, the leading hong merchant.

Though these interlocking systems produced fabulous wealth, their success had a dark side. When Perkins decided to smuggle Turkish opium into China, the efficient systems within his trading empire responded beautifully to the challenge, with the result being that more of the narcotic reached Chinese civilians than ever before. That Perkins and Cushing retired with two of New England's largest mercantile fortunes shows the effectiveness of their Yankee system and the tragically lucrative nature of the American opium trade.

Derby's Debacle

No man ever learned more from a single voyage to China than did Thomas Perkins. After word of the *Empress*'s success spread, other merchants readied their vessels. In 1785 Elias Haskett Derby launched Salem's China trade when he sent the *Grand Turk* to Canton. Having profited from the return cargo of tea and porcelain, Derby made plans in 1788 for a second voyage, lining up James Magee to captain the *Astrea*. Magee already had one China voyage under his belt, having joined Samuel Shaw on his second visit to China in 1786. For his supercargo, Magee chose Thomas Perkins, then a young man in his early twenties who had recently married Magee's niece. Perkins saw the tremendous potential lying latent in the underdeveloped American economy and desperately wanted to go to sea. He stubbornly resisted his family's plans to send him to Harvard, eschewing the ivory tower in favor of the countinghouse.[4]

Perkins's education in global commerce began months before his departure. Unlike Shaw, whose responsibilities did not commence until the *Empress* reached Whampoa, the hustling Perkins lined up shippers willing to invest in the voyage by contributing cargo. With multiple shippers involved, the *Astrea* carried a diverse array of trade goods: butter, rum, spermaceti candles, codfish, iron bars, and ginseng. By playing an active role in prevoyage preparations, Perkins was able to pull back the curtain, so to speak, and examine the internal workings of global commerce. When the time came for him to launch his own trading mission, he would know how to assemble the parts.[5]

In February 1788 Perkins bid farewell to his young wife and newborn son and received final instructions from Derby. "You must endeavor to be the first ship with ginseng," Derby exhorted, "for be assured you will do better alone than you will if there are three or four ships at Canton."[6] These words would come back to haunt Derby. During the long voyage, aquatic life fascinated Perkins, as it had Shaw. Most impressive was the majestic albatross, which hovered over the waves with a wingspan exceeding ten feet. In the 1790s Samuel Tayler Coleridge, in his *Rime of the Ancient Mariner*, would bring literary fame to an old sailors' superstition concerning the crime of killing an albatross. The practical Perkins would have none of it. He shot four of the birds, retrieved three, and ate the meat. "More than tolerable," he judged.[7]

When the *Astrea* reached Canton in September, Perkins began to discharge his duties as supercargo. To his dismay, he confronted two alarming problems. First, the ginseng glut precipitated by the *Empress of China* and exacerbated by ensuing vessels depressed prices, hampering Perkins's ability to sell his ginseng. Second, the presence of twelve American ships had an adverse effect on the prices of all goods: the surplus of American goods depreciated their value, and tea prices soared as all the supercargoes bid simultaneously on a finite quantity. Perkins was stunned. The young man who had spun fantasies of a triumphant first voyage to China now faced the grim reality that forces beyond his control were conspiring against him.

There was no time for self-indulgent gloom. With Derby and the other shippers counting on him, Perkins needed to act decisively to ameliorate a bad situation. He learned that, of the twelve ships, four belonged to Derby himself, meaning that much of the damage was self-inflicted. The other three had sailed to the Isle of France (now Mauritius), off the southeast coast of Africa, where Derby's son, stationed on the island, had foolishly rerouted them to Canton. Though a clear case of mismanagement, the simultaneous convergence of four Derby vessels in Canton created an opportunity. If the four supercargoes could work together, they might find a way to forestall disaster. The group reached immediate consensus on one point: all four ships must not embark for Salem. If New Englanders were forced to absorb four large tea cargoes at once, supply would outstrip demand and the price of tea would plummet. After conferring, the Derby men hatched a two-pronged plan, the first part of which involved the sale of a hidden asset, the one American product that had not depreciated in value—their ships. After selling two ships, they next packed the remaining two with a combined six hundred thousand pounds of tea, a quarter of all tea carried out of China in American ships that year. When the ships reached Salem, Derby wisely stored the tea in warehouses, an innovation that allowed him to release it onto the market in small increments. Thanks to these measures, Derby made a modest profit on what might have been a fiasco. However, he concluded that the risky China trade was better left to others. He would not become New England's dominant China trader.[8]

A Better System

The true winner to emerge out of the *Astrea*'s troubles was Perkins himself, though his gains were not of the sort he could deposit in a bank. His yield was of the observational variety. Though he had duties to discharge as supercargo, these did not completely occupy him. His brain possessed extra capacity. In Canton he kept his blue eyes open, alertly gathering and storing data. In this way, he compiled "a fund of information," a bank of usable facts about Chinese tastes and Western trading practices that he could consult when he began "planning numerous voyages" and "directing mercantile operations."[9]

Perkins also appears to have treated the *Astrea*'s error-riddled voyage as a laboratory, a trading mission filled with instructive mistakes that his analytic mind could convert into profitable lessons. Subjecting the experience to careful study, he distilled the basic rules and strategies that would later form his system. Though Perkins did not mention this period of ratiocination in his memoirs, it must have taken place because, as the expression goes, the proof is in the pudding. In managing his own company, Perkins adhered to a system of rules that replicated Derby's wise policies, eliminated Derby's missteps, and exploited opportunities Derby missed. In this way Perkins formed the blueprints for a company that would dominate America's China trade.

First, the merchant should bring in multiple investors who could share the risk of a venture. Though Derby possessed enough resources to fund an entire venture alone, he insisted on bringing in other stakeholders. By doing so he guaranteed that a setback, such as a ship lost at sea, would not sink his company. Throughout his career, Perkins would hew to this simplest of principles: share the risk. Second, the merchant must direct trade wisely and effectively from the center. Though Derby owned an impressive record of trade, in this particular case he had unwittingly undermined himself. Derby's failure to dictate the movement of ships with a careful hand and adequately prepare his son had produced a counterproductive result. Perkins resolved never to fall prey to clumsy management. From his command post in Boston, he would assert control over his shipping ventures. And when he delegated responsibility to his agents at distant ports, he would make certain they were well versed in his system.[10]

Third, the merchant should, in most cases, spread out his ventures across time and space. The watery world was vast, and ports were numerous; thus, there was no excuse for the convergence of four ships in Canton. Along with effectively timing ship departures, Perkins resolved to dispatch vessels into different geographic regions so as to eliminate the possibility that they would meet in the same port and cannibalize each other's profits. There was one exception to this rule: if Perkins spied an opportunity to monopolize a given commodity, he could justify the deployment of multiple ships to a single port. At this port, his vessels would purchase all available quantities of the good, leaving nothing for rivals. Over the course of his career, Perkins attempted this bold gambit with at least three commodities: furs, tea, and opium. Of course, only a large merchant with a fleet of ships and abundant capital could conceive of such a strategy.[11]

Fourth, the large merchant must use his size to full advantage. Derby had failed to reap the rewards that his size ought to have brought him—indeed, his size had worked against him. Perkins resolved never to repeat this error. He understood that conditions favored the larger merchant, the one equipped with abundant resources and capital reserves. Even the cleverest merchant had to confess that irregular price fluctuations in goods like tea and ginseng prevented reliable forecasts. While a small merchant necessarily rolled the dice when he sent a ship to China, a larger merchant should not have to. Through the strategic deployment of superior resources, he should be able to exploit favorable trade conditions when they appeared and ride out the lean periods. In a cruel but realistic sense, the large merchant understood that economic downturns could work to his advantage by eliminating competitors from the field. There was, in other words, opportunity even in adversity.[12]

More specifically, Perkins resolved to establish warehousing facilities, as Derby had shrewdly done. While a smaller trader arriving in Boston with tea found himself at the mercy of a whimsical market, Perkins could store surplus tea and wait for prices to rise before releasing it onto the market. The size of Perkins's operation also allowed him to make a second innovation. Abandoning the practice of attaching supercargoes to ships, Perkins replaced peripatetic agents with a permanent employee installed in a Canton office. This company man could not only establish an advantageous relationship with the hong merchants but also purchase tea when the price was low and warehouse it until a Perkins ship arrived. In sum, the large firm, with its Canton office and warehouses, could always buy low and sell high.[13]

Fifth, family members must be used judiciously, as they present liabilities as well as assets. Derby had depended on his son who, in this particular case, had exercised judgment that could have been catastrophic. From this error, Perkins learned that a firm would suffer obvious consequences were it to assign important jobs to family members because they were family. However, the solution was not simply to look outside the family when hiring, a fact Perkins recognized when he reflected on his own motives in Canton. Though attached to the *Astrea*, he had kept his eyes open for other opportunities. When the first mate of the *Columbia*, Joseph Ingraham, told Perkins about the lucrative Northwest fur trade, the two men and James Magee made secret plans to enter that trade—plans that did not include Derby. Just months after the *Astrea*'s return, Perkins sent Ingraham to the Pacific Northwest to purchase otter skins. Perkins, in other words, lacked that loyalty that comes from family ties, so there was nothing to prevent him from pursuing his private interests once his contractual relationship with Derby had expired.[14]

So what role should family play? Perkins developed a system intended to accentuate the strength of family while suppressing its liabilities. First, he would keep a close watch on the young men in his extended family so that he could identify that cousin or nephew who exhibited desirable traits. Next, he would bring these boys into the company in their teenage years, setting them up in apprentice-like positions where they could learn the family business. Last, he would promote them to positions of responsibility should they meet his expectations. Conversely, he would prevent unsuitable family members from occupying key positions. In that the system privileged kinship relations while forcing family members to prove their worth, we might describe it with the oxymoron *meritocratic nepotism*.

In 1792 Thomas Perkins took the first step in implementing his system. With his older brother James as his partner, he established James and Thomas H. Perkins and Company, which occupied a building on the Long Wharf in Boston Harbor. In the years that followed, the firm acquired a fleet of ships and a stable of captains and sailors (in 1813 Perkins estimated that the firm had employed 2,500 seamen since its inception). Perkins also, in accordance with his system, moved to spread out his trade geographically, organizing a West Indian trade and a Pacific Northwest trade to join his Canton trade. By 1803 all three engines of trade appeared to be running on all cylinders. Napoleon might conquer continents, but Perkins would dominate the seas. The timing seemed right for a bold move.[15]

The Prodigy

In July 1803 the Perkins-owned *Patterson* embarked for China out of Providence. No routine trading mission, the ship carried a passenger whom Perkins regarded as crucial to his long-term plans: Ephraim Bumstead would establish the first American trading outpost in Canton. He was to become the first American taipan, the head of a company's Asian office. Though not related to Perkins, Bumstead had worked in the firm for years and had served as supercargo for a Canton voyage. Thus, when Perkins handpicked Bumstead for this job, he harbored no doubt as to the man's training, ability, or loyalty. Bumstead had been properly vetted. In choosing Bumstead's assistant, however, Perkins did reach into the family cupboard, selecting John Perkins Cushing, the sixteen-year-old son of his deceased sister. As Perkins contemplated the mentoring this youth would receive under the steady Bumstead, he took pride in the fact that his company's future looked strong.[16]

Just as triumph seemed near, one of the engines started to sputter. Acting on Ingraham's tip, Perkins had built an elaborate shipping operation designed to realize John Ledyard's dream. Starting in the 1790s, Perkins ships sailed regularly to the Pacific Northwest to barter for furs before proceeding to Canton. However, once rumors of large profits spread through the merchant community, rivals embarked for the Northwest coast. If Samuel Shaw's vision had prevailed, an American East India company would have controlled commercial activity in this region. As it was, overshipping resulted: only four American ships plied these waters in 1798, but by 1801 the number had leaped to twenty-one, many of them hailing from New England. "The Bostonians," wrote fur trader Sullivan Dorr, "are playing a ludicrous farce indeed." With so many Americans seeking furs, local tribes quickly became surfeited with American goods and saw no reason to part with furs except at a high price. With soaring inflation, Dorr declared in 1802 that the fur trade was "completely overdone."[17]

Making matters worse, the high demand for furs triggered overhunting in the region, which rendered available furs more dear still. In one depleted region, Ledyard's beloved Nootka Sound, vessels no longer bothered to stop. Chief Maquinna's Nootkas, feeling jilted now that ships passed them by and enraged by earlier insults, resorted to violence. In 1803 the Nootkas captured the *Boston* (not a Perkins ship) and slaughtered most of the crew.

This was not the first incident. Three years earlier, Bernard Magee, James's brother, sailed to the Northwest coast as master of the Perkins-owned *Globe*. While he was conversing with Indians, three of them abruptly seized him while a fourth landed an ax on his head. As news of these horrors reached Boston, Perkins arrived at the disappointing conclusion that conditions in the fur trade might not return to a favorable level for years.[18]

Having lost this important engine driving his enterprise, Perkins could still sleep well knowing he could depend on his other two. Or could he? At roughly the same time, the West Indian trade failed. Problems relating to the trade's entanglement with slavery compelled the frustrated merchant to "relinquish the West Indies business altogether, as it perplexes and does not pay in proportion to the vexation." Having lost two of his three engines, Perkins understandably felt less sanguine in 1804 than he had just a year earlier. Still, he did not panic because he could take comfort in his system, which was designed to handle exigencies such as these. Indeed, he could applaud the prudence behind his earlier decision to establish not one but three engines of trade—and that third engine appeared poised to dominate. "We have determined to concentrate our property in the Canton trade," he wrote, "and shall make our arrangements accordingly."[19]

In 1804 Perkins received welcome news that the *Patterson* had arrived safely in China, meaning that Bumstead had established the firm's Canton office. As other companies were sure to imitate his model, Perkins had a narrow time frame in which to maximize his advantage. Now was the time for aggressive action! He made arrangements for six ships to sail to Canton with diverse cargoes picked up from various ports: *Mandarin*, *Montezuma*, *Hazard*, *Caroline*, *Globe*, and *General Washington*. In Canton, Bumstead would load them with teas and other goods that he would have strategically purchased in high volume when prices were low. When rivals arrived in Canton, they would discover—to their collective displeasure—that the scarcity of tea had driven up prices. In this way Perkins would wreck his competitors by forcing them to contend with an adverse tea market he had created. With all six ships launched, Perkins understood that the fortunes of his firm depended on one man—Ephraim Bumstead.[20]

Then the shocking news arrived: Bumstead was sick. Though Perkins at first held out hope that Bumstead might quickly recover, he subsequently learned that the ailing taipan planned to leave his post and sail for the Isle of France on a ship captained by his brother. Even if Bumstead did make a full recovery, the Canton office would still need to function during the interim period, as someone would have to receive those six ships. That someone would have to be John Perkins Cushing, the only other company man in the region. The fate of Perkins's company—a company built on planning, perspicacity, and foresight—now rested on the shoulders of a teenage boy. How had it come to this?

What followed was an effluvium of letters, which at first streamed in one direction only: from Boston to Canton. We "shall rely upon your utmost exertions to make good his [Bumstead's] place," Perkins wrote his nephew in March 1805. "You will have a great charge on you, and such as few young men ever met with." Not mincing words, Perkins added that Cushing's "future well-being" depended on his "conduct in this crisis." Perkins also exhorted his nephew to eschew "juvenile pursuits" and resist the tendency "of youthful minds to dissipation." He even went so far as to invoke the boy's grandmother: "Let the sage counsels of y'r good grand-mother vibrate on your ear" and "sink deep into your heart." As months passed, Perkins waited anxiously for a letter, one that would convey the basic information that Cushing had taken charge of the office. Without such a letter, Perkins could not even confirm that someone could receive the six ships. No such letter arrived. "John," an increasingly distressed Perkins wrote in April, "we have been a little surprised that you have not written us since your arrival" and that you should "be so silent on the subject of business," a silence that has provoked "pain and mortification."[21]

Shortly thereafter, a letter did arrive, but it was not from Cushing. The letter recounted how Bumstead had departed Canton on the *Guatamozin*, a Perkins ship captained by his brother. While the ship was passing between Java and Sumatra, his brother had been washed overboard in a storm, a traumatic event that had triggered a fatal stroke in the frail Bumstead. Along with dashing any hope for a resumption of normality at the Canton office, word of Bumstead's demise intensified the importance of Cushing, who remained disturbingly incommunicado. Perkins put pen to paper again, and this time he did refrain from anger. "We have the extreme mortification of not having received a single line from you after the sailing of Mr. B[umstead]," he wrote, "no not a single line from you to say that Mr. B. had sailed; to give your opinion as to his sickness, to remark on the situation of the *Hazard*, or even notice the arrival of the *Washington*."[22] Cushing's silence had become excruciating. Unable to wait any longer, Perkins decided to install himself as taipan and began making hasty prepa-rations for a Canton voyage.[23]

Perkins would not embark. In May 1805 the *Guatamozin* limped into Boston Harbor with a cargo of Chinese goods. Inspecting them, Perkins de-clared that the teas had arrived "in bad order," having been poorly packed by either a sick Bumstead or an inexperienced Cushing. Unbeknownst to Perkins, events had reached their nadir, and he was about to witness a stunning rise in his personal fortunes. That same month, a letter arrived from his nephew, one that had been sent the previous year and had taken an unusually long time in reaching Boston. In content and style, the letter reflected not panic or youthful indiscretion but maturity and competence. If the letter pleased Perkins, what followed days later boosted his mood to euphoria. The *Hazard* arrived carrying teas that had been adroitly pur-chased, inspected, and packed under Cushing's supervision. As the other ships arrived, each one handled to perfection, Perkins reflected that the boy was not only adequate as an emergency stopgap measure. He possessed preternatural ability to transact company business. Perkins beamed with pride.[24]

Working within Walls

Between 1805 and 1830, Perkins and Company earned greater profits from the China trade than any other American firm. Multiple factors contributed to the company's ascension, including its ability to capitalize on the Napoleonic Wars (1803–1815). During Europe's protracted conflict, traders from belligerent nations were unable to sail through hostile waters. However, the neutrality of the United States allowed the opportunistic Perkins and other Americans to carry cargoes in and out of European ports, to such advantage that Perkins desired the war to go on indefinitely. By the war's end, Americans had surpassed the French, Dutch, and Danish in international shipping and become the second largest player in the China trade, behind Great Britain. No American firm benefited more than Perkins and Company.[25]

The firm's fortunes also benefited from Cushing's long and masterful execution of the Canton office. For nearly twenty-five years he lived and worked within the cramped conditions of the foreign factories. Inside this enclosure, he could enjoy exercise in the form of a daily constitutional, though the smallness of the space compelled him to trace the perimeter in short vectors that ended abruptly at a wall or the water's edge. For Cushing and other Americans, the experience of confinement contrasted sharply with the expansive experience of their countrymen in the United States, where free movement within open spaces provided the nineteenth century with its epic storyline. While China traders coped with a suffocating claustrophobia, Western pioneers luxuriated in the agoraphilia that defined the frontier.

China traders also tolerated extreme boredom. Robert Bennet Forbes, Cushing's cousin, employed the term *ennui* to describe his daily existence in Canton. "You say your life is without incidents," he wrote his wife. "What is mine—get up in the mornings, bathe, breakfast, compting room, dinner, walk, tea. Write, go to bed after a walk . . . same faces every day, why woman your life's a perfect wilderness of incidents compared to mine."[26] For the intellectually curious trader who wanted to know more of China, only frustration awaited. "From this country it is impossible for me to write any thing descriptive that can be interesting," wrote John Latimer, a trader from Delaware, "being debarred the privilege of going in to the Country."[27]

The tedium of Canton was well known in the United States. When James Fenimore Cooper penned his sea novel *Afloat and Ashore* (1844), Canton presented him with a conundrum. While he hoped to tell a thrilling tale, he also wanted to keep his narrative credible by basing it on published accounts of actual voyages. Canton provided the proverbial fly in the ointment because, while life there was exceedingly dull, one simply could not leave out Asia's great emporium. Cooper elected to include Canton but apologize to readers. "*My* Canton excursion *ought* to be full of marvels" explains Miles Wallingford, the protagonist. "Truth compels me to confess, notwithstanding, that it was one of the least wonderful of all the voyages I ever made." While busy "getting cargo, receiving teas, nankins, silks and other articles," he continued, "we saw just as much of the Chinese as it is usual for strangers to see, and not a jot more." The dullness does not bother Wallingford, because business preoccupies him. "It is true I worked like a dog."[28]

In contrast with the fictional Wallingford's brief sojourn, Cushing lived for more than two decades in the foreign factories, a physical edifice designed to facilitate a single activity: trade. In the typical factory building, the first floor offered large rooms suitable for the physical side of the work. Along with a storage area where Chinese goods could be kept before shipment, the first floor also often contained a tea-tasting room, a granite vault with an iron door (no banks were available), a table with weights and scales, and spacious hallways for messengers running errands and laborers moving crates. The comprador had his office on the first floor, where one would also find the kitchen and a room for the servants, valets, and cooks in the comprador's employ. On the second floor were the Western traders' bedchamber, bathing room, dining room, verandah, and—most important of all—counting room.[29]

In the counting room, traders handled the cerebral, mathematical, and paper-based side of trade. During the tea season, they started early in the morning and labored late into the night, devoting fifteen hours on average to business.[30] "The immense amount of work . . . is indescribable," wrote Osmond Tiffany, an American traveler, "and the clerks . . . seldom quit the desks before midnight, being all the time occupied in the various process of receiving and dispatching cargoes, of making out sales and interest calculations, copying letters, [and] filing away papers."[31] And always, the first and second floors exhibited parallelism; as the columns of numbers in a trader's account books lengthened, so too did the tea crates temporarily pile up one floor below at a commensurate rate. In the foreign factories, form followed function to near perfection. It was an architecture of work (Figure 2.1).

Besides architecture, other aspects of Canton intensified mercantile endeavors. Thanks to the comprador and his staff, the trader did not need to worry about housekeeping chores, because servants handled the shopping, cooking, cleaning, and laundry. "We have certainly the best servants in the world," wrote John Latimer, "and any man who gives way to indulgence here much, afterwards becomes very helpless." Latimer went on to describe the "minute attentions" of these men: "In the morning the first thing is to bring fresh water for washing—the clothes laid out on a couch, *the heels of the stockings turned*, shoes placed in front of the couch and a shoeing horn by their side—this before we rise." The servant "never leaves the house for a moment during the whole day," remains "always within call," and comes when requested with "cheerful alacrity."[32] Compradors and servants were mandatory because, from the Chinese government's perspective, they

Figure 2.1. *View of the Hongs at Canton, 1825–1835*, by Lam Qua. *(Museum purchase, 1931. A. Heard Collection. Peabody Essex Museum, Salem, Massachusetts.)*

expedited business: foreign traders freed from household drudgery would finish their trade quickly and be gone. "They wish [foreigners] to consider Canton as a kind of counting-house," wrote Toogood Downing, an English traveler, "where the merchants may transact all their business, and then retire from . . . China."[33]

For the same reason, China banned Western women and children. Alone in Canton, traders would miss their families, Downing explained, and their "thoughts" would be "constantly directed to the time when they shall leave in order to join them."[34] These men would focus greater energy on their business so as to hasten their departures. For family men, China's strategy accomplished its objective. When Forbes returned to China in 1838, he was the happily married father of a child. Though his body may have been fixed in Canton, his mind would drift to Massachusetts. "I had a dream," he wrote his wife. Standing in the office of Perkins and Company, "[I] asked where you lived." As he went searching for her, neighbors told him of "the beauty of [their] Son," who had been an infant at Forbes's departure. As the dream approached its climax, the moment when Forbes could embrace his wife, a strange voice intruded: "Seven oclock Sir." Boston evaporated, and in its place stood a Chinese servant announcing the start of another workday.[35]

For Forbes and other traders, Canton life was something to be tolerated, not enjoyed. It was exactly, in other words, what Chinese authorities had intended. By forbidding the formation of institutions, the Chinese quashed the tendency of Americans to join civic, community, and religious organizations. By forbidding Western women, they stripped traders of the twin joys of love and sex. And by offering nothing in the way of pleasurable diversions, they amplified the tedium of Canton.[36] What is more, this semitropical locale was already blessed (at least from China's perspective) with rats, lizards, snakes, centipedes, and mosquitoes. According to Downing, the flies were "still more annoying," though swatting them provided the trader with a "savage, triumphal delight."[37]

The same conditions that annoyed, bored, or depressed other traders only awakened behavioral tendencies that had slumbered deep within John Perkins Cushing. A descendant of Puritans, Cushing possessed quintessential Yankee traits. After asserting control over their own human natures, Yankees looked to extend the controlling influence to their external environments by building efficient systems. In the nineteenth century, Yankees transformed the economic life of New England by implementing systems in transportation (railroads), the textile industry (the Waltham-Lowell factory system), and, of course, global shipping. This chapter has already described Thomas Perkins's systematic approach to trade; in his nephew, he found a kindred spirit.[38]

In Canton Cushing's own mental forms took easily to the strange physical space and bizarre set of rules. Indeed, it was a frightening fit. With few distractions and with all societal and familial obligations stripped away, Cushing lived and worked in the purest business environment on earth. Here his Yankee tendencies found no opposition, and he concentrated his systematizing intelligence on trade and nothing else. "He lived for about twenty-five years almost a hermit," Forbes wrote of his cousin, "studying commerce in its broadest sense, as well as its minutest details." Cushing's achievement was to imagine global commerce as a clockwork mechanism composed of different components, each of which needed to be perfectly integrated with the whole while producing minimal friction. More specifically, he devised microsystems that successfully connected three macrosystems: his uncle's system of global trade, the Canton System, and the merchant house of Houqua.[39]

Houqua

During his only sojourn in Canton, the vigilant Thomas Perkins scrutinized Chinese customs and habits, compiling the "fund of information" that would allow him to succeed in the China trade. However, the watcher was being watched. While attending a banquet thrown by a hong merchant, Perkins attracted the attention of a young Chinese clerk who was fascinated with the Yankee. Why did this man single out Perkins? The latter might have impressed him with either his confident demeanor in the face of crisis or his inquisitive approach to his surroundings. Or perhaps the Chinese clerk, who at roughly twenty years old was plotting his own rise, saw in Perkins a mirror image of himself. Regardless, Perkins made an indelible imprint on the mind of Wu Bingjian, who would later be known in the West as Houqua (Figure 2.2).[40]

Figure 2.2. *Portrait of Houqua*, by Lam Qua. *(Peabody Essex Museum, Salem, Massachusetts.)*

After the reign of Phuankhequa ended with his death in 1788, the hong merchants limped through a period of weak or reluctant leadership. Starting his career in 1801, Houqua ascended to the paramount position around 1810 after foreign traders and Chinese authorities acknowledged his superior capabilities. In crafting his own leadership style, Houqua rejected the model of Phuankhequa. A monopolist seeking domination, Phuankhequa had been willing to tolerate, or even foment, upheavals if they crippled rivals or solidified his powerbase. In stark contrast, Houqua's leadership was informed by his Confucian worldview, which prized stability above all else. Thus, he envisioned hong merchants working in harmony to pump the nearly inexhaustible wealth from the foreign trade. Strife and discord were anathema to him because he believed that, as long as peaceful conditions prevailed, all hong merchants could imbibe the sweet nectar of global commerce.[41]

Rather than drive colleagues to ruin, Houqua endeavored to keep them afloat. In the early 1810s, a newly appointed *hoppo* demanded that all hong merchants owing outstanding duties square their accounts. Unfortunately, since seven of them, who were mostly junior members, were already deeply indebted to foreign merchants, the *hoppo*'s mandate compelled them to take out high-interest loans on top of existing loans. As hong merchants descended one after another into insolvency, BEIC officials saw a looming crisis that threatened their economic interests. If hong merchants were allowed to fail, Chinese authorities might levy higher *consoo* charges as a way to force foreigners to pay the debt indirectly. Worse, they might reinstate the cohong. Hoping to solve the problem quietly, the BEIC formed a plan for gradual debt reduction that placed the finances of the bankrupt merchants in the hands of trustees until the merchants could recover through profitable trading. The plan depended heavily on Houqua, who would supply much of the money for his embarrassed colleagues' debts on the promise that the trustee system reimburse him in the future. Were Houqua to reject the plan, the repercussions would be explosive: the debts would be revealed, the disgraced merchants would be banished, and the hong merchant system would collapse, leaving Houqua bereft of rivals. Making the choice that would define his career, Houqua elected to save his colleagues and preserve the status quo. Phuankhequa must have rolled over in his grave.[42]

Along with Confucianism, a nervous temperament shaped Houqua's behavior. As Chapter 1 explains, Phuankhequa often resorted to ruthless means to advance his interests, creating in the process enemies who unhesitatingly used ruthlessness themselves in seeking his ouster. His predecessor had thrived under adversity, but Houqua suffered from chronic anxiety attacks, and any undue stress made him sick. Given his sensitive demeanor, the Chinese playfully nicknamed him "the timid young lady." Knowing that vengeful enemies and risky investments kept one awake at night, Houqua assiduously avoided both. Seen in this light, his decision not to deliver the coup de grâce to the bankrupt seven was in perfect keeping with his character. Had he decided to abandon his colleagues, he would have not only made enemies but also created a monopoly for himself: China would have funneled its vast international trade through him alone. While such a prospect might have tantalized Phuankhequa, it filled Houqua with dread. This was pressure the timid lady did not seek.[43]

That being said, Houqua did share Phuankhequa's ambition and passion for wealth. In fact, he understood the two as linked. Of course, he coveted a large fortune because it could guarantee the security of his family for generations. Of equal importance, he knew that a fortune could fuel his personal rise in society. For Chinese merchants, the path to lofty social status was not quite as straightforward as it was for American traders. In the United States, where no natural aristocracy existed, the successful merchant did not need to concern himself with titles, because the accumulation of wealth by itself secured his place in the upper class.[44] In 1845 the author of *Our First Men*, a booklet listing all citizens of Boston whose worth exceeded $100,000, bluntly stated this point. "It is no derogation . . . to the Boston aristocracy," he explained, that its position "rests upon money." "Money is something substantial," he continued. "Birth is a mere idea, which grows every day more and more intangible."[45] In a city where prestige was tethered to money, Perkins could enjoy demigod status, even though he had shunned Harvard.

In China, however, the conversion of wealth to status was not automatic. Aside from royalty, only the mandarins—scholars who had scored high on a state examination—enjoyed the privileges of power and class. They ruled the roost, so to speak, and possessed the colorful plumage to show it: color-coded buttons or "hat spheres" made of gemstones that designated their rank. In theory, a merchant could not even claim second or third place in the Confucian hierarchy, these being reserved for farmers and artisans. The latter vocations, according to Confucian logic, contributed more to society than a merchant because, in an agrarian economy, their labor produced edible or usable things. The lowly merchant, in contrast, merely profited from the transfer of already-existing goods from one place to another.[46]

In practice, a loophole existed. To generate revenue, the government allowed merchants to purchase, at high cost, a mandarin rank. Hong merchants "who wish to distinguish themselves above the others," observed Downing, "purchase . . . the privilege of wearing *the button*."[47] Because a hong merchant had not passed the imperial examinations to enter the civil service, no real power accompanied his title. However, the honorary rank did allow an incriminated hong merchant to either receive a reduced sentence or escape punishment altogether. Instead of beating or imprisoning the offending merchant, an official might lower his rank or strip him of his title. Recognizing these benefits, Houqua paid the sum that allowed him to display a blue sapphire button, which designated him as a third-class mandarin.[48]

The Axis

With so much riding on his business dealings, Houqua practiced extreme discrimination when forming relationships with traders. He sought ties only with individuals or companies who, with reliable records of trade, promised to be steady long-term partners. Conversely, he scrupulously avoided traders whose shaky finances suggested they might default on loans. With no American East India company to oversee the trade, hong merchants dealt exclusively with private traders, some of whom left China with unpaid debts. To retrieve outstanding loans, several hong merchants, Houqua included, even resorted to litigation in American courts. In 1841 the hong merchant Consequa wrote directly to President Madison to ask for help collecting owed money. Given Houqua's conservatism, his decision in 1803 to work with Ephraim Bumstead, a trader without reputation, is strikingly curious. Most likely, his decision had to do less with Bumstead and more with the distant entity he represented. Having only recently entered the profession, Houqua kept his eyes open for traders who, though not yet established, showed promise. Perkins's decision to install a taipan probably impressed Houqua, because a company that made this investment clearly intended to conduct a high-volume trade for the long term.[49]

After Bumstead fell ill, Houqua scrutinized Cushing to determine whether the teenager could run the firm's Canton office. Liking what he saw, Houqua formed a relationship with Cushing that evolved into genuine friendship, one that would last until his death. In hindsight their compatibility makes perfect sense. After all, the world views of the Confucian merchant and the Yankee trader, though different in nearly all respects, overlapped in one key area: both prized harmony. As a system man, Cushing found contentment only when the operations under his supervision functioned smoothly and efficiently. His abhorrence of friction was matched only by Houqua's loathing of strife. Indeed, in describing Canton, Cushing could sound quite Confucian: it "was a place of business where" the trader "had more facilities and less disputes than any other he was acquainted with."[50]

As this relationship matured, something else emerged along with it, something so potent as to alter the economic landscape of the China trade: a Perkins-Cushing-Houqua axis that connected three extremely able men in an unbreakable bond of friendship, loyalty, and shared economic interest. The axis enabled the formation of a Sino-American commercial pipeline: from the American side streamed furs, silver, and later opium to China; in the opposite direction, tea, silk, and porcelain coursed toward Boston. As the goods flowed between nations, wealth underwent a rapid expansion on all three points on the axis. According to *Our First Men*, Perkins's net worth of $1.5 million ranked him as Boston's fourth-wealthiest citizen in 1845. He was outdone by Cushing, whose $2 million earned him second place. The fortunes of both were dwarfed by that of Houqua, who, worth roughly $52 million in the 1830s, was perhaps the wealthiest commoner on earth.[51]

By 1819 Perkins fully understood the splendid power of the axis. Moved to commemorate his Chinese partner, he christened his newly built vessel the *Houqua*. When the ship arrived in Whampoa, Cushing and Houqua went out to meet it. On deck, the crew honored Houqua with a ceremony that Charles Tyng, a sailor on the vessel and relative of Perkins, described. "Houqua came on board magnificently dressed in silks and satins of various rich colours," he wrote. "He was an old man, I should think near seventy." That Tyng missed by two decades (Houqua was about fifty) indicates the degree to which constant worry had taken its toll. During the festivities, Houqua "presented the ship with a beautiful set of silk flags, and a portrait of himself" and treated the crew to "a large variety of eatables." Sufficiently feted, Houqua made his departure to the booming reports of a twelve-gun salute. "It was a great time at Whampoa," Tyng recalled.[52]

For Charles Tyng, the high point of the day arrived when Cushing approached him. "This was the first time Mr. Cushing had ever spoken to me," Tyng recalled. "It brought me up a notch in my own opinion, as well as in the ship's company to have Mr. Cushing acknowledge my acquaintance. I began to feel as if I was somebody."[53] That this encounter elevated Tyng in the estimation of his peers makes one point demonstrably clear: Cushing had by this time become a revered figure in his uncle's commercial empire (Cushing's cousin, John Murray Forbes, regarded him as "many degrees higher than the pope in all his glory").[54] Of course, Cushing's fame within the New England mercantile community was directly proportional to the profits enabled by his efficient systems. In 1819 those profits soared thanks to Cushing's ability to devise a system for a lucrative commodity that could not enter China through legal channels.

Opium and Yankee System

In 1805, shortly after Cushing had taken over the Canton office, Perkins sent his nephew a complete set of Shakespeare's plays. With this gift, he hoped to broaden the mind of a young man living alone overseas. In the accompanying letter, Perkins asked Cushing to share any information he had regarding the prospects for opium harvested in Turkey. Though an English monopoly blocked American traders from carrying Indian-grown opium to China, Perkins thought there might be a market for the Turkish variety. Months later, Perkins followed up with Cushing, inquiring whether opium could be "got on shore with little risk" and, if so, how much venal Chinese officials charged for this service. Cushing's response, if it came at all, was not sufficiently enthusiastic to merit any action at this time. Perkins reluctantly dropped the matter. However, in the back of his mind, the knowledge that he was barred from trading something making the British rich nagged him.[55]

In 1815 Perkins made his move. Though we cannot be sure why he chose this moment, his appetite had perhaps been whetted by an incident that took place during the War of 1812: the Perkins-owned *Jacob Jones* happened to capture a British vessel carrying an opium cargo. When the opium was shipped to Cushing, the taipan reported that it "turned a good profit."[56] Months later, the Perkins ship *Monkey* received instructions to convey Cuban coffee and sugar to the Mediterranean, where it would take on opium for delivery to Canton. When Cushing's favorable report reached Boston, Perkins decided to take aggressive action by installing a permanent office in Smyrna, Turkey. After evaluating his young relatives, he settled on Fred Paine, a Harvard dropout who, having previously assisted Cushing in Canton, had experience managing a foreign office. Paine's primary responsibility: to provide Perkins ships with opium bound for Canton. Perkins had officially brought opium into his system.[57]

In 1817 an incident helped Perkins establish a dominant position in the Turkish opium trade. The revelation that the American ship *Wabash* had carried opium into China prompted authorities there to intensify its previously lax efforts to enforce antismuggling laws. While ostensibly a bad time to traffic in opium, Perkins spied opportunity. After the *Wabash* affair, smaller traders would conclude that "it will be very dangerous to introduce" opium. Once they withdrew, "the competition will be less . . . at Smyrna" and the price of opium will fall, thus allowing Perkins to "go very extensively into the business."[58] Certain of the soundness of his logic, Perkins instructed Fred Paine "to push it as far as we can." Though there was still the matter of heightened Chinese surveillance, Perkins had confidence in Cushing's ability to sell the cargo surreptitiously. Sure enough, when an opium-laden vessel reached Whampoa, Cushing had already made arrangements for Chinese smugglers to approach quietly and acquire their chests "alongside" the ship, before the legitimate cargo could be processed by the *hoppo*.[59]

In the early 1820s a more severe crackdown forced Cushing to develop a new smuggling system. In response to China's stern measures, Cushing advised Perkins not to "meddle" in opium unless he could ship it to Canton in a very specific fashion. He then proceeded to lay out, step by step, a sophisticated system, one based on a British model, that redirected opium around China's latest barriers. First, the approaching opium vessel should neither harbor at Macau nor take on a pilot; by bypassing Macau, a ship could avoid official processing by Chinese authorities. Second, the vessel should anchor off lonely Lintin Island in the Pearl River estuary (*lintin* literally means "solitary nail") instead of passing through the Bocca Tigris (see Figure 1.1). Third, since the Canton agent (Cushing) must be made aware of the stealth vessel's arrival, a paper communication must be sent to Canton via one of the Chinese "fast boats." However, since authorities could conceivably intercept this craft, the captain should substitute the word *gum* for *opium*. At this point, the vessel must wait at Lintin until Cushing could arrange for his Chinese clients to make clandestine visits.[60]

After this new system became operational, Cushing made one innovation. He instructed certain Perkins vessels to remain anchored at Lintin indefinitely. His plan was to use these vessels as floating warehouses, secret opium depots that could receive the opium cargoes of other ships as they arrived, store these temporarily below deck, and then disburse chests to Chinese smugglers. When Charles Tyng arrived in Canton in the 1820s, his vessel headed straight for Lintin, where it dropped anchor. "A smuggling boat would come alongside in the night," he wrote, "and bring the order, and the boxes were delivered to them." The vessel, Tyng discovered, had received this special assignment from Cushing. "I found now that our vessel was to lay where she was for some time," he continued, "as she was to receive the opium that the American ships brought from the States." For three months, the crew distributed chests illegally, their inventory being periodically replenished by newly arriving ships.[61]

As efficient as the Lintin system was, there were still kinks to work out. One problem was that a Perkins opium ship, after transferring its contraband to the Lintin storeship, was empty. How would it obtain a cargo of Chinese goods for its return voyage? In the 1820s Cushing implemented a system that solved the problem by exploiting a loophole in Chinese customs. China had historically faced rice shortages, and the government encouraged imports by reducing duties on rice by 50 percent for ships carrying a rice cargo that met a minimum weight requirement. A large Perkins vessel loaded with rice would sail to Whampoa where it would sell its cargo, preserving much of the resulting profits since it paid lower duties. In Whampoa, the crew would load the ship with as many Chinese goods as it could possibly carry, even stacking containers on the deck, for the short trip to Lintin. At Lintin the rice ship would transfer its surplus Chinese goods to a waiting opium vessel that, having unloaded its contraband, needed a fresh cargo before it could depart.[62]

In the 1820s Perkins recognized that Cushing's systems afforded him a temporary advantage over other opium traders. Following the rules of his larger system, Perkins moved to exploit his advantage by asserting total control over Turkey's opium market. Already the purchaser of half of Turkey's supply, Perkins ordered Paine to buy up all available quantities, leaving nothing for rivals. Though it was a large risk, Perkins was no stranger to mercantile brinksmanship, and he understood that monopolies were not built with conservative thinking. "You may think us acting a bold game," Perkins wrote Cushing in 1824 to explain the opium surge, "in sending so much of the drug this year, but if a certain quantity of that of Turkey must be had and we can keep the lead which we now have, we shall not be in much hazard of losing."[63] As the overwhelming crush of narcotics reached Cushing, the taipan struggled to push it through his Lintin system. Perkins, aware that he had taxed his nephew, sent a letter that approximated an apology. "As respects Opium I must take all the blame in going as far as we have," he confessed. "I tho't best to extend ourselves, to prevent intruders," yet "I am mortified that the quantity that *will go out in the spring* so far surpasses y'r wishes."[64] Though wrapped in mild regret, Perkins's core message rang clear: Cushing should brace himself because more opium would soon be on the way.

Any complaints to Perkins notwithstanding, Cushing used his opium inventory to his advantage. He developed a second system that allowed him to manipulate the price of opium and, by doing so, render the market hostile to opium speculators. "It will never answer for us to keep up the market for the benefit of occasional speculators," Cushing explained in a note to his successor. Thus, the "most advisable plan hereafter" will be to "undersell others who may adventure in it." With the price "reduced so low," these traders will look to cut their losses by unloading the unprofitable cargo. At this point, "[we can] purchase it for our own account, & when all is in your own hand . . . regulate the price as you may deem expedient."[65]

How did this system actually work? John Latimer observed firsthand Cushing's handling of opium speculators. When an opium speculator arrived in Canton, he had unwittingly drifted into an artificially controlled price chamber. As he prepared to sell his cargo, he witnessed a sudden and mysterious drop in the price of opium, "much below what the quotations just previous to his arrival led him to expect." Unbeknownst to him, Cushing had driven down the price by releasing his own opium onto the market. At this juncture, the newcomer would either "dispose of" his opium at a loss or sell it to Perkins and Company. Then, "immediately after he has sold out," the speculator would watch as "the market rises without any apparent cause." The cause, of course, was Cushing, who had pulled the lever to restrict the flow of opium, precipitating the rise in price. With this system, Latimer wrote, "the house of Perkins & Company . . . completely commanded the market."[66] Echoing this statement, a British opium dealer reported to a Parliamentary committee in 1830 that Turkish opium was "almost entirely in the hands of one American house, who have nearly a monopoly of it in China." "By holding such large quantities," he continued, "they have great command of the market."[67]

Cushing flawlessly superintended a ruthless yet elegant machine that steadily pumped narcotics into China. Like all traders, he was aware of the possibility that opium could ruin a smoker's health and finances. Though we do not know what drove Cushing to engage in a business with such serious moral implications, we can rule out simple greed, because Cushing, even while amassing his spectacular fortune, was not motivated by riches. His wealth, rather, came as a by-product of his ability to develop, implement, and monitor systems more effectively than any rival. Indeed, if we were to ask how Cushing could bring such a coldly rational approach to the opium trade, the answer perhaps lies in this very love of system.

Systems, of course, are morally neutral, and can—depending on how they are used—effect either positive or negative outcomes. In the case of Cushing, the systems were not designed to advance any moral imperative.

Rather, the proper management of his systems seems to have provided an end in itself, as the following anecdote indicates. As Cushing prepared to depart Canton in 1828, his letter to his successor reveals the extent to which his personality had become subsumed by the systems he had created. "It is of the first importance," Cushing wrote, "that every thing should be done with *system*." "It will save you much trouble & anxiety," he continued, and "render the management, & direction of your business a pleasure rather than a burthen when" all branches of the operation become "regularly *systematized*." After outlining the particulars of the taipan's responsibilities, Cushing returned to this theme at the letter's end. "I have now I believe touch'd on most subjects . . . & have only to repeat to you the importance of *system* in all your concerns . . . let every thing be done with *system*."[68] Sure enough, "every thing" was, including opium. Once the maintenance of systems became Cushing's only priority, moral considerations vanished.

Closing the Canton Office

When Toogood Downing visited Canton in the 1830s, he noticed that a small handful of traders exhibited curious behavior. "A few gentlemen have," he observed, "been known to continue residing in the place long after they would have been able to live like princes" in their native land. Why did they stay? According to Downing, these "patriarchs of the trade" had so completely conformed themselves to the Canton life that they "wish for no change from that which has become to them second nature." "Season after season have they proposed to depart," but each year they find some "fresh excuse" to stay, until they at length become "rooted to the soil."[69] Sensing that this transformation in himself was well under way, Cushing wrote Perkins in 1826 to announce his intention to come home. "We hope," Perkins replied, "that you will not have remained at your post too long, and have suffered more than you may apprehend."[70]

With this response, Perkins showed that he grasped the difficulty inherent in Cushing's return. Though possessing roughly a million dollars, Cushing paradoxically had a debt to pay. For far too long, he had transacted business in Canton, living without the affection of family and the society of Boston. As he undoubtedly understood, a reentry crisis loomed. Sure enough, when Cushing stepped onto the Boston wharf in 1828, his own sister failed to recognize him.[71] Furthermore, his health had clearly been "impaired," as a friend noted, "by too much devotion to business in a climate not favorable to 'length of days.'" And his habits, while perfectly calibrated for Canton life, did not conform to the expectations of American society. Finally, the city of Boston had changed to such a degree that he felt lost in its streets. America had become the foreign country, Cushing acknowledged, and Canton his true home. "I feel better satisfied here," he wrote of Canton, "than I ever expect to anywhere else."[72]

As Cushing struggled to acclimate himself, tragedy pulled him back to Canton one final time. Ever mindful of the future, Perkins had sent his nephew Thomas Forbes to Canton around 1820 to apprentice under Cushing. In fact, it was Forbes's rapid development that allowed Cushing to leave Canton confident that the business was in capable hands. In August 1829 Forbes learned that the *Mentor* had arrived at Lintin containing letters. Suspecting that the letter bag contained official confirmation of his China dream—that Perkins had anointed him the new taipan—Forbes set out for Lintin on his sailboat, despite an ominously blackening sky. Early in 1830 Perkins received the devastating news that Thomas had perished in a typhoon and was now buried at the Protestant Cemetery in Macau. The accident tossed the firm's future into uncertainty and prompted Cushing to sail for Canton on the *Bashaw*.[73]

Before his death, Thomas Forbes had left instructions. Should anything prevent him from discharging his duties as taipan, the firm Russell and Company was to handle all Perkins business. Cushing trusted that company's head and founder, Samuel Russell, who had turned to Cushing for advice back in 1819 when he had first come to China to represent a Providence firm. Cushing had impressed on the newcomer the importance of system, and Russell had taken this advice to heart. As a result, Cushing boasted that his protégé Russell "can get through more business" than "three men."[74] Assessing the situation in 1830, Cushing agreed to transfer Perkins's business to Russell, but only under two conditions. First, Russell and Company must add another partner to handle all Perkins ships. For this position, Cushing recommended Augustine Heard, whom he knew to be reliable. Second, Cushing requested that Thomas Forbes's younger brother, John Murray Forbes, be taken on as a clerk, with the expectation of becoming a partner before long. With this move, Cushing kept the family involved in the affairs of the company that would now handle the consignments of Perkins and Company.[75]

Having set matters straight, Cushing prepared to embark for home. However, before his departure, he shared a word of advice with his acquaintances in Canton. "He most feelingly remarked" to them, John Latimer recalled, "never to be absent more than ten years at a time or they would, like him, lose all relish for home." Cushing hoped his passionate warning would prevent others from repeating his mistake—namely, of falling into the all-consuming vortex of trade. With the paperwork signed, Cushing boarded the *Bashaw* with Samuel Russell, who had decided to follow his friend's advice and walk away from Canton after more than a decade.[76]

Back home, Cushing tried to adjust to New England. He avoided the lonely bachelor's life by taking a bride. In the 1830s he bought two properties, a home in Boston and a country estate (Belmont) in Watertown, decorating both with Chinese wallpapers and porcelains so as to remind him of Canton. The estate boasted a greenhouse that Cushing filled with specimens of Chinese horticulture. Andrew Jackson Downing, the influential landscape designer, praised Belmont as a model others should replicate. As for his Boston home, Cushing staffed it with some of the Chinese servants he had employed in Canton. Though technically retired, he expanded his fortune tenfold by making timely investments in American industry and railroads. Houqua entrusted a portion of his wealth to Cushing's management, and the hong merchant also benefited from his friend's shrewd investing.[77]

Conclusion

As the Canton office of Perkins and Company came to its end, its London-based agent, Joshua Bates of Baring Brothers, estimated that the firm handled half of all U.S. trade with China and much of Europe's tea trade. Because Russell and Company inherited this vast trade, that firm was poised to experience a dramatic takeoff. In addition to the Perkins business, a second stream shifted to Russell in the 1830s—that of Houqua. After the BEIC lost its monopoly in 1833, Houqua decided to trade exclusively with Russell and Company, establishing with the Forbes brothers, Robert Bennet and John Murray, the same close friendship he enjoyed with Cushing. On July 7, 1830, the two brothers embarked for Canton aboard the *Lintin*, with John Murray slated to start clerking at Russell and Robert Bennet tapped to manage opium operations. Lurking behind the Forbes boys, pulling the strings of their careers, remained the cagey trader Thomas Perkins.[78]

Perkins emerged as the largest winner of the high-stakes contest that had begun when the *Massachusetts* failed. In the late eighteenth century, Shaw and Randall had tried but failed to impose a European-style mercantile model onto America's inchoate China trade. In the absence of a large governmental entity, the China trade entered a volatile period in which a field of rivals vied against one another. Victory would go to the merchant in possession of the best system, with a system's worth being measured by the profits it generated. In the 1790s Thomas Perkins introduced his system, which combined Yankee organization, aggressive risk taking, ruthlessness with respect to rivals, and an internal promotional method that fused meritocratic elements with kinship loyalty.

No company man performed at a higher level than John Perkins Cushing, who exhibited in China the best and worst traits of American individualism. In the Yankee tradition, Cushing could work long hours and exhibit masterful self-control. He was also able to project his organizational genius over the Canton trade, systematizing everything under his supervision. Though his productivity became legendary, his all-consuming fixation on business came at a steep cost. In Canton he lived an existence bereft of intellectual pursuits, romantic relationships, community involvement, and civic participation. His legacy also includes his role as the architect of America's most effective opium-smuggling operation.

Though dominant, Perkins and Company did not monopolize America's China trade. That trade involved numerous other merchants and consisted of more commodities than one company could control. In the next chapter, we adopt a wide-angle lens to view not the system of a single firm but the ingenuity and resourcefulness of multiple American traders who scoured the earth in search of exotic goods that could, by appealing to Chinese tastes, provide a counterweight to Americans' addiction to tea.

All for a Cup of Tea

Finding Goods for the Canton Market

In 1793 Emperor Qianlong issued his response to King George III's request that China open up its trade with England. With striking brevity, Qianlong expressed China's position in the language of supply and demand. Since the "productions of our Empire are manifold" and "in great Abundance," China did not "stand in the least Need of the Produce of other Countries." China exhibited total self-sufficiency, he claimed, and thus did not require foreign imports. Britain was out of luck. Though refusing to acquiesce to King George's request, Qianlong did offer one consolation. Since Europe had long coveted—and China had obligingly supplied—tea, porcelain, and silk, "Warehouses" filled with these "Commodities" would remain "opened at Canton" for foreign traders to buy. The status quo, in short, would continue.[1]

It would appear, based on the dead-end nature of this exchange by sovereigns, that meager rewards awaited any American entering the China trade. The English could at least import woolens, cotton, and tin (and opium illegally). Excepting ginseng, the United States neither grew nor manufactured anything China would exchange for tea. Despite this grim economic reality, one could hardly describe the mood in American ports as glum. On the contrary, a visitor to Salem in 1804 would have witnessed a jubilant scene linked directly to the China trade. As curious spectators lined the streets, the officers of the East India Marine Society, whose membership rolls included many China traders, paraded past dressed in colorful "Chinese gowns." Joining the pretend mandarins, "negroes dressed nearly in the Indian manner" conveyed one member in an ornate "palanquin." At the head of the procession, a "person dressed in Chinese habits & mask" waved to the crowd. Salem's traders, if we are to judge by their exuberant Orientalism, had not succumbed to defeatism. They were triumphant.[2]

Later that year, the society allocated space in its building for curiosities brought back from the Far East. Part museum and part trophy case, the East India Marine Hall had strong holdings in artifacts from China, India, the East Indies, and the Pacific Islands. Though some objects horrified patrons, such as the "Embalmed Head of a New Zealand Chief," the Chinese exhibits were anything but grotesque. The luxurious tea sets, gorgeous fans, and statue of a hong merchant all presented China as a romantic land where the fortunes of Salem men were made. How could this be if China, as the emperor unambiguously stated, mostly rejected the concept of an import?[3]

The answer lies in the eclectic nature of the hall's collection. Salem sea captains acquired these artifacts along their trade routes, which meant that the objects reflected the geographic coverage of Salem's merchants. Since the collection exhibited diversity, it follows that the itineraries of Salem ships were complex. Rather than sailing directly to Canton, these vessels embarked on lengthy odysseys that included multiple stops before reaching China. To explain these peregrinations, we need only return to King George's abortive exchange with Qianlong. China's self-sufficiency compelled Salem's traders—indeed, most American China traders—to search the earth for rare or exotic goods that appealed to Chinese tastes.

This chapter adopts a macroeconomic view of the China trade. After explaining America's high demand for tea, porcelain, and silk, the chapter shifts to the traders' efforts to reduce their dependency on silver when purchasing these goods in Canton. In the early 1800s, American ships embarked on multistop voyages through the Pacific to obtain exotic goods for China: sea slugs, bird nests, sandalwood, and furs. Because this early period of the China trade involved a wide array of goods, broad geographic coverage, and dozens of merchants, we can describe it as expansive.

Starting in the 1820s, the China trade underwent a massive contraction, in terms of both the number of trading firms and the types of goods brought to Canton. As the "virtues" of Turkish opium became apparent, some traders decided to depend less on exotic goods and more on this single article as a way to finance their tea purchases. Accelerating this turn to opium, traders' ravenous appetite for furs and sandalwood depleted naturally available supplies of these goods. As many traders abandoned exotic goods, larger trading firms moved in to take their places. This trend toward greater consolidation continued when a Chinese crackdown in 1821 convinced many merchants to quit the risky opium trade, leaving it in the hands of a few large firms. While pleased with their dominant position, large traders soon discovered they had become the victims of their success. As the Chinese consumed greater quantities of opium, they lost their ability to pay for other imports. By the late 1830s, the once diverse China trade consisted mainly of three things: opium, tea, and the financial paper enabling the sales of each.

Tea, Porcelain, Silks, and Nankeens

After the success of Derby's *Grand Turk* in 1786, other New England merchants embarked for China and returned with tea. As a result of these ventures, tea consumption surged to new heights in Salem and elsewhere. Along with the beverage's delightful flavor and fragrance, Americans enjoyed its benefits as a stimulant. By reducing fatigue and sharpening focus, tea increased one's performance at work and thus facilitated upward mobility. Benjamin Rush, a physician and signer of the Declaration of Independence, extolled tea's miraculous ability to relieve stress and enhance concentration. "Men who follow professions, which require constant exercise of the faculties of their minds," often "seek relief" in "ardent spirits." They should know, he continued, "that TEA is a much better remedy" because "it removes fatigue, restores the excitement of the mind, and invigorates the whole system."[4]

How did Americans consume the Chinese wonder beverage? In the 1780s an English traveler in North America observed that "there is not a single person to be found, who does not drink it [tea] out of China cups and saucers." In the 1820s Robert Waln, a onetime supercargo, observed that a synergy existed between tea and porcelain. The two "articles" joined the list of household "necessities," achieving an "importance almost equivalent to that of bread." "There are few families in our country, however humble their situation," he went on, "which would not be greatly inconvenienced by a deprivation of this exhilarating beverage."[5] Indeed, statistics bear out Waln's contention that Americans treated tea as a staple rather than a luxury. In a typical year between 1820 and 1850, Americans consumed between ten million and twenty million pounds of tea, numbers that impress with their sheer size.[6] According to Waln, Chinese porcelain played a complementary role to tea for all classes of Americans. While "the higher & middle ranks" purchased fine porcelain, "even the poorest families" could afford to sip tea from Chinese cups because lesser ceramic wares were "procurable at a low rate."[7]

In pursuit of tea and porcelain, American traders headed to China. In Canton combined European and American demand transformed the port into a center of economic mass whose gravity continuously pulled the two commodities down from east-central China. Most porcelain emerged out of the fiery kilns of Ching-te Chen, a city in Jiangxi Province of about a million inhabitants that existed solely to produce ceramics. In 1712 a Jesuit missionary visited and marveled at the city. "The sight with which one is greeted," he wrote, "consists of volumes of smoke and flame rising in different places." At night Ching-te Chen took on a surreal aspect, as its hundreds of active kilns transformed it into a "burning city in flames." Touring the interior, the missionary discovered a system of division of labor resembling the modern assembly line. "One workman does nothing but draw the first colour line beneath the rims" while "another traces flowers, which a third one paints." Another painter specializes in "water or mountains," leaving "birds or other animals" and "Human figures" to others. "I am told that a piece of porcelain has passed through the hands of seventy workmen," he noted, adding that he saw no reason to refute this number.[8]

Most teas originated in two tea-growing regions: black teas came from the Bohea Hills of Fujian Province and green teas from the Sing-lo Hills of Anhui Province. Resembling shrubs, tea plants possess thick foliage and grow only three to six feet high, which renders their leaves easy to pick. Picked leaves undergo a complex curing process. First, the leaves are spread out on a bamboo tray where workers rub and roll them. Properly massaged, the leaves are ready for firing. In the case of black tea, the workman "sprinkles" the leaves on a red-hot iron pan and waits "until each leaf pops." He then sweeps the leaves into a drying basket that is hung over hot coals. Interestingly, the same plant can yield green or black teas since the divergence takes place in the curing process. To make the rawer green tea, the leaf should be cured over a slow fire rather than in a red-hot pan. Having been subjected to less heat, green teas can be converted into black, but the reverse is impossible. Once packed, the tea is ready for transport to Canton.[9]

Tea and porcelain traveled south along the same overland route. Since the shipping system was logistically complex and involved tens of thousands of laborers, one historian has called it a "human caravan." Containers filled with teas and ceramics were floated along rivers and lakes on small boats, pulled along other rivers against the current by teams of trackers, and portaged through the Danxia Mountains on the backs of as many as thirty thousand men. After six grueling days in the mountains, the caravan reached the Beijiang River, where boats sent by hong merchants waited to receive the merchandise and transport it to Canton. At this same juncture, the trekkers picked up a shipment of imports—cotton, tin, and salt—to haul back through the mountains.[10]

In Canton, hong merchants stored the goods in warehouses called *hongs*. Designed to accommodate the immense quantities of export goods, hongs possessed huge dimensions. When Osmond Tiffany, an American traveler, visited a hong in the 1840s, he stood inside its airy vastness, mouth agape. Later, he penned a description that could apply to a modern airplane hanger. Built right on the river to facilitate deliveries, hongs measured forty feet wide, fifty feet high, and stretched back twelve hundred feet. They "are so long," Tiffany wrote, "that at the end of one of them the human form diminishes, and we see beings engaged in occupation, and we hear no noise, for they steal along like shadows." Tiffany described one hong as "crammed almost to suffocation, with big square chests . . . piled up to the ceiling" (Figure 3.1).[11]

After a merchant made his purchase from his hong merchant, the loading of his ship left little doubt as to the relative importance of tea and porcelain. "The first part of the cargo was boxes of china," wrote Charles Tyng in 1816, describing the loading of a Perkins ship in Whampoa. "These

Figure 3.1. *Canton Factories*, by the studio of Tingqua. *(Museum purchase, 1931. A. Heard Collection. Peabody Essex Museum, Salem, Massachusetts.)*

were placed in the bottom of the ship, being much heavier [than] the rest of the cargo. They answered for ballast. Then came tea." Indeed, as all traders knew, it was tea that generated the big profits. The weightier porcelain provided the ballast necessary to keep the vessel upright.[12]

Along with their tea and porcelain, Americans also coveted Chinese fabrics. Silks, which were manufactured near Canton, arrived at the foreign factories in May, a period of low ebb as far as business activity was concerned. Since most traders timed their voyages so that arrivals would coincide with the start of the tea season in autumn, they had set sail long before silks appeared. Thus, in the silk market, advantages accrued to companies with permanent agents in Canton who specialized in silk. Nathan Dunn, representing his own Philadelphia-based company, surpassed all competitors in the silk trade. In addition to silk, the Chinese also sold Americans large quantities of nankeens. Before New England's mills began mass-producing cotton textiles, this durable yellow cloth provided an ideal fabric for men's trousers and children's play clothes.[13]

As the trades in all these goods make clear, Americans confronted in China a highly evolved system of production and distribution. As John King Fairbank points out, China's "apparent passivity," encapsulated in the emperor's blunt response to King George, "reflected the strength of its economy," not its "weakness." The teas, silks, and ceramics marked for export comprised merely the "offshoot" of a vast agricultural-industrial-commercial engine that had developed to supply goods to a burgeoning Chinese population, which had doubled in the eighteenth century. By sending ships to Canton, Americans tapped into this robust engine's enormous capacity. As Chapter 7 explains, they were able to convert Chinese goods into dollars by passing them through American markets, accumulating in the process capital they could invest in railroads and factories. In this way we can imagine the China trade as a giant transfer pump, one that steadily pumped economic power from Asia to North America.[14]

Exotic Goods

To obtain Chinese goods, American traders needed something desirable to offer in exchange. Since the emperor's proclamation of self-sufficiency was mostly accurate, finding products presented a challenge. Even without such goods, one could still conduct trade in Canton as long as one arrived with plentiful silver. Indeed, this approach offered a clear advantage in that hong merchants, ever needing capital for tea orders, gave special attention to the "rich" ships, as they called silver-bearing vessels. "The Chinese like [silver] dollars better than they do almost anything else,"[15] observed one sea captain. Silver, in short, expedited trade: a trader could arrive in Canton, pay few import duties because silver was often exempt, exchange silver for Chinese goods, and then depart for home. Between 1804 and 1808, silver accounted for 75 percent of the total value of American cargoes arriving in Canton.[16]

Despite silver's attributes, traders carried it with reluctance because it posed several problems. First, hong merchants coveted the precious metal, but so did pirates, who would lie in wait outside the Pearl River estuary like a cat crouched beside a mouse hole. Second, silver was not easy to obtain in the United States. Most silver in circulation originated in South America, where the Spanish oversaw vast mining projects in the 1700s at sites such as Cerro de Potosí, a three-mile high mountain in Peru (now Bolivia). Having extracted the silver ore, the Spanish shipped it directly to Europe. Thus, American traders hoping to obtain silver depended on European markets for their supply, markets that were highly unstable in the early 1800s. When Europe became consumed in war, which it was between 1803 and 1815, or when Spain's South American colonies revolted, which many did between 1808 and 1829, American traders faced a constriction of the silver supply. Third, a China trader wanted to do exactly what the name "China trader" implied—trade with China. If his business in Canton consisted entirely of tea purchases made with silver, the so-called trader became little more than a tea wholesaler, a middleman who bought tea from a Chinese supplier before transferring it to American retailers. Since one could enjoy profits only on the American side, most China traders deemed the scenario unsatisfactory. They far preferred the "double profit" of "exchanging goods for goods" in Canton, as well as back home.[17]

To make the coveted double profits, traders needed to locate goods that appealed to finicky Chinese tastes. Appalachian ginseng, it turned out, was the easiest trade good to obtain. The others could be had only by traders willing to send vessels on connect-the-dots missions across the Pacific Ocean, brutally long itineraries that tested a captain's navigational skill, required bartering with indigenous peoples, and lasted three years or more.

Traders could obtain one exotic product in various locations in Southeast Asia, such as Java and Borneo, but only with great exertion. High on cliffs rising straight out of the sea, swallows built nests in fissures and crevices. This species formed nests out of their own spittle, a glutinous substance cherished by Chinese epicureans, it providing the key ingredient for a variety of soup considered a delicacy. Of course, these sought-after nests were not exactly accessible, situated as they were hundreds of feet above rocky crags and breaking waves. Thus, the daring attempts to obtain them became the stuff of legend. From a high ledge, a sailor or local would descend the face of a cliff on a rope, locate his quarry as quickly as possible, and then jerk the rope to signal to the men above to hoist him back up.[18]

Captain Edmund Fanning spent much of his career trolling the South Pacific in search of goods for Canton. In his account of his voyages, he explained in detail the methods through which he obtained not only bird nests but other exotic goods. To satisfy the craving of China's elite for bêche-de-mer, "a species of marine worm," he wrote, a ship anchored near the coral reefs of a tropical region, and two men waded the shallow water in search of the slugs. When the scow that followed them was full, the men pulled it to shore and dressed the creatures by cutting them open lengthwise to remove entrails. Next they dropped their catch into a cauldron of boiling pickling water, and then they laid the scalded slugs out on a drying rack. Finally, the slugs were cured, by either sun or fire, before being boxed. "Care should be exercised," Fanning warned regarding this stage, "that after being cured it does not get wet, either by the salt or fresh water, as their arrival then at market in a prime and sound state may be prevented." Indeed, the delicate and complex method Fanning laid out presented numerous chances for error, any one of which would wreck the article's salability. All this for a cargo of tea.[19]

Fanning also conveyed sandalwood to Canton, where demand for the wonder wood bordered on insatiable. Since it was easy to carve, craftsmen made luxury items out of it, such as boxes, fans, and furniture. More importantly, sandalwood played a role in religious ceremonies because, when burned, it emits a fragrant smoke that worshippers believed could propitiate deities. Of course, since the Chinese routinely burned sandalwood, they constantly needed to replenish depleted stores, giving sandalwood a reputation as the miracle product that could balance out the West's thirst for tea. Wherever it grew, that was where Europeans and Americans were sure to be. Sadly, sandalwood, unlike tea, cannot be harvested. Since the wood derives its pleasing aroma from rich veins of oil located only at the base of the tree (the foliage and outer branches possess no value), the entire tree must be chopped down. Thus, when sandalwood mania seized the China trade, primordial forests thousands of years in the making were cut down in the space of a few years. The destructive wave rippled through the South Pacific, beginning in Fiji in the early 1800s, moving next to the Marquesas Islands in 1811, and concluding with Hawaii in 1815. In each locale, we see the same pattern: a sudden boom preceded, and precipitated, an inevitable bust a few years later.[20]

Though American ships bartered for sandalwood from all three locales, the most intense activity centered on Hawaii between 1815 and 1828. In Hawaii, American captains obtained cargoes by negotiating either with the king or his chiefs. Kamehameha I, having recently conquered the Hawaiian Islands, welcomed traders because he planned to use revenue from sandalwood sales to build up his military and maintain a firm grip on his newly expanded kingdom. After his death in 1819, his son Kamehameha II allowed his vassal chiefs to partake of the trade. Seeking easy wealth, these chiefs sent parties of up to five thousand men, women, and children deep into the mountains where the virgin forests lay. There the parties felled trees indiscriminately and hauled the logs to the coast. Addicted to short-term profits and unconcerned with long-term sustainability, traders and chieftains allowed deforestation to progress unabated.

In the early 1820s the sandalwood trade reached its peak in terms of quantities sold in Canton. In 1821 an American in Hawaii observed in horror that "sandal-wood fever" brought out the dark side of human nature. "Every one here is ready to cut his neighbors throat, truth never is spoken," and "treachery is the order of the day," he wrote, adding a summation: "I am disgusted with my fellow man."[21] In 1826 the chiefs instituted a law requiring every able-bodied man to deliver sixty-six pounds of sandalwood to authorities; the decree spurred a fresh round of chopping that precipitated a surge of imports to Canton in 1827. But the sandalwood craze could not last. By 1828 the combination of a glutted market in Canton and severe deforestation in Hawaii ended the brief and sad run of the so-called miracle product.[22]

The relentless drive of traders to locate goods for the China market yielded another ecological horror story, this time on islands populated by seals. These islands, situated off the southern part of South America, included South Georgia, the Falklands, Juan Fernández, Massafuero, San Ambrosio, and San Félix.[23] In 1849 James Fenimore Cooper imagined a fictional island for his romance novel *The Sea Lions*. In the story, a dying seaman named Dagget speaks of an uncharted island north of Antarctica on which a vast population of seals lives. The animals were numerous and trusting, and a "gang of good hands" could "kill and skin" thousands quickly, rendering profits as easy as "picking up dollars on a sea-beach."

Inspired by Dagget's tantalizing narrative, the *Sea Lion* sets sail in search of this fabulous island, and so the adventure begins. As a basis for his novel, Cooper drew from actual accounts of voyages to these islands, one of which was offered by Edmund Fanning.[24]

In 1798 Fanning's ship dropped anchor at Massafuero, off the coast of Chile. After spending ten weeks clubbing seals (with "perseverance and industry" in Fanning's words), the crew had succeeded in filling the hold of the ship with skins. Since more skins awaited packing, the men crammed additional quantities in the forecastle and cabins, leaving just enough space for the men to sleep. To make room for still more skins, they moved some provisions onto the deck. It was indeed a gory harvest. When the captain realized that four thousand skins still awaited loading, he ordered several men to stay behind and wait for the next vessel. How could they pass the time profitably? By slaughtering more seals. Fanning estimated that seal hunters took away a "little short of a million of those fur seal skins" from the island, "nearly all of which were carried to Canton, and there exchanged for China goods, suitable for the home market." The wealth derived from a single "isolated spot" presented "evidence," Fanning declared, "of the important advantage" of vigorous "American enterprise" in the Pacific.[25] As profitable as these islands were, another region held still more promise: the Pacific Northwest.

Furs from the Pacific Northwest

John Ledyard was right: the fur trade did possess almost boundless potential. Furs were abundant (at least in the early years), the Indians seemed mostly willing to barter, and the Chinese bought up the cargoes that reached them. In seeking an explanation for the fur trade's enduring strength, we should remember that fur wearers resided all over China, not just Canton. Every January, buyers from the cold northern provinces would journey to Canton to make their purchases. The fur market, in other words, was national, not regional. Given this demand, the geographically peripheral Pacific Northwest became the central arena for a high-stakes contest, one that involved entire nations and attracted some of America's largest traders— Thomas Perkins, William Sturgis, and John Jacob Astor. Many traders had read Ledyard's journal, and in their minds his prediction of an "astonishing profit" continued to reverberate.[26] Equally seductive was the prospect of securing a "triple golden round of profits," a phrase used to describe profitable trade conducted in three locations: the Pacific Northwest, Canton, and an American port. Few ambitious traders could resist this siren's song.[27]

Thomas Perkins could not. While in Canton with the *Astrea*, the everobservant Perkins had noted the arrival of the *Iphigenia*, a British vessel carrying furs obtained from the Indians of the Pacific Northwest in exchange for mere trinkets. Perkins did not miss the meaning of this vessel.

About six weeks later, he took great interest in the *Columbia*, an American vessel that had reached China by rounding Cape Horn rather than the Cape of Good Hope. After befriending the first mate, Joseph Ingraham, Perkins learned not only that the *Columbia* represented the first attempt by an American trader to realize Ledyard's dream but also that its owner, Joseph Barrel, had hatched an ingenious scheme. The large *Columbia* had departed Boston with a smaller vessel, the sloop *Lady Washington*, dismantled and stowed away in the lower compartments. After reaching the Northwest, the crew assembled the *Lady Washington*, which proceeded to trawl coastal waters collecting furs for the mother ship to transport to China.[28]

Ingraham happily shared his experiences with the eager Bostonian. He probably related the story of the *Columbia*'s encounter with two British vessels, the *Iphigenia* and *Felice Adventurer*, on the Northwest coast. The officers of these vessels had animatedly tried to downplay the prospects of the fur trade in an attempt to scare off the Americans.[29] The Indians possessed such a "Monstrous Savage disposition," one officer claimed, that "it would be maddness [*sic*]" to spend a winter with them. Furthermore, he continued, after all this time and trouble, they had acquired only a paltry "fifty skins," a fact he backed with "his sacred word and honour."[30] The British, by trying too hard to conceal their cards, had shown their hand: a bonanza awaited in the Northwest.

Not one to procrastinate, Perkins sent Ingraham to the Northwest aboard the *Hope* mere months after returning to Salem in 1790. At this same time, he and other Boston merchants commissioned a shipbuilder to construct a vessel modeled off the *Columbia*. In 1791 the *Margaret* set sail for the Northwest captained by James Magee. Like its precursor, the *Margaret* carried a smaller vessel that the crew could swiftly assemble after reaching their destination. Though equipped with a state-of-the-art vessel, the captain and crew were novices in the fur business, which meant they needed to learn how to overcome formidable obstacles before profits could be had.[31]

To obtain furs in the Pacific Northwest, unlike in the seal islands, one had to barter with Indian tribes. In the 1790s the Indians tended to want metals (copper, iron, and lead) and trinkets made of metal. However, in the early 1800s, trinkets fell out of vogue and were replaced with firearms, shot, gunpowder, textiles, alcohol, and foodstuffs such as bread, molasses, and rice. Regardless of the type of good in demand, the Yankee trader had to remain sharp because, in the space of a few years, the Indians had become adept at driving up prices by playing one trader off another. Sullivan Dorr of Boston described them as "cunning savages" who were "great Merchant traders." Any attempt to barter with inferior products was doomed to fail, he explained, because "the Indians wont have other than good." Ingraham reported that the Indians possessed "a truly mercantile spirit" and that they obstinately refused to "part with a single skin till they have exerted their utmost to obtain the best price." One captain observed that the Indians "derive all possible advantage from competition" and "will go from one vessel to another, and back again, with assertions of offers made to them, which have no foundation in truth." They were, he concluded, "well versed in the tricks of the trade." Given the Indians' sharp skills, William Sturgis instructed his firm's captains to avoid bidding wars between themselves. Instead, two captains should form a temporary partnership so as to bid as a single entity and then later divide the furs between their ships. Alternatively, two ships could part ways, with each targeting its own section of the coastline.[32]

Over time, Americans figured out how to barter effectively with Indians. Though their experience included tragedy, such as the 1803 massacre of the *Boston*'s crew, Americans enjoyed nearly four decades as the preeminent power in the fur trade. In the 1790s the vigor and enterprise of the Americans helped them wrestle the trade away from the British, a position they did not relinquish until the 1820s. Between 1788 and 1826, at least 127 American voyages reached the Pacific Northwest in search of furs.[33] According to Richard Henry Dana, whose *Two Years before the Mast* (1840) became a best seller, fur-trading missions bound for Canton enjoyed prestige among mariners. "An India or China voyage always is 'the thing,'" Dana wrote, "and a voyage to the Northwest coast . . . for furs is romantic and mysterious, and if it takes the ship round the world, by way of the [Hawaiian] Islands and China, it out-ranks them all."[34]

During these decades, Perkins's commitment to the fur trade would oscillate, rising or falling depending on factors such as the number of rival ships, prices in Canton, and the cost and availability of furs. For example, when twenty-one ships plied the coastal waters in 1801, Perkins wisely knew to withdraw temporarily from the region. Later that decade, after poor conditions had winnowed most of the competition, Perkins reentered. Free of pesky rivals, he and two other merchants, Theodore Lyman of Maine and William Sturgis of Boston, worked in concord.[35] Though overhunting had reduced populations of the sea otter (whose skin the Chinese coveted most), the capital base of Perkins allowed him to enjoy steady profits not in spite of tough conditions but because of them. Perkins could afford to place a ship permanently on the Northwest coast for collecting what remaining furs could be had. Other Perkins ships would rendezvous with this ship, receive furs, and sail to Canton, where the firm's dominance allowed it to control prices. "We have at length got the NW Trade into our own hands," Perkins informed a captain, "& you will take advantage of this circumstance to raise the Price of the articles." In 1808 Perkins instructed Cushing "to get the Price of Sea Otters up again" in time for the arrival of company ships. "We have not any doubt," he continued, "that with Your exertions . . . you will succeed."[36]

In this way, furs conformed to the same boom-and-bust pattern that defined the trajectories of most American imports to China. When the Chinese exhibited their affinity for a new commodity, the first traders to

carry it made a "killing," the "scent" of which wafted throughout mercantile circles, triggering the launch of other ventures. As the commodity
flooded the Canton market, its price plummeted, and traders failed to reap
expected profits. In some cases, the brief boom took on such a frenzied
character as to deplete naturally available supplies. As traders proceeded to
abandon their interest in this commodity en masse, larger firms like Perkins
and Company moved in to impose a rational organizational structure over
its importation.[37]

Punqua Wingchong

In the Northwest fur trade, John Jacob Astor stood as Perkins's greatest
rival. However, Perkins's nimble approach to trade prevented a direct confrontation between the titans from taking place. When the aggressive Astor
made his bold move, Perkins knew to fade and patiently wait. And when
Astor's unstoppable momentum caused him to stumble, Perkins nonchalantly stepped over his fallen competitor and revived his fur trade. On one
occasion, the two rivals joined forces because both could derive advantage
from a partnership. The strange story of Punqua Wingchong's repatriation
to China after an American sojourn illustrates the great lengths to which
traders would go to sell furs in China and tea in the United States.

In 1807 Thomas Jefferson's Embargo Act closed American ports to
international trade. The direct cause for passage of the act was the British
system of impressments, whereby British ships would intercept American
vessels and remove British deserters. However, British officers would sometimes help themselves to American sailors as well, since the Royal Navy
desperately needed men during the Napoleonic War. In 1807 an incident
involving the American *Chesapeake* and the British *Leopard* provoked such
outrage in the United States as to compel Jefferson to respond. Hoping to
avoid war with England, Jefferson elected to follow the advice of Secretary
of State James Madison by imposing an embargo. The rationale for this
policy was twofold. First, Jefferson hoped to teach England and France a
stern lesson by denying them access to America's domestic markets; if his
embargo could inflict economic pain on the European belligerents, they
might reform their relations with the United States. Second, by preventing
American ships from entering international waters, the embargo would effectively keep the United States out of Europe's internecine conflict.[38]

Despite Jefferson's good intentions, his embargo brought economic
hardship on the United States. It infuriated Perkins and Astor, who watched
powerlessly as their vessels idled at the wharf. Fortunately for Perkins, his
company could avoid total paralysis because, when the embargo took effect, several of his ships had already departed Boston for Canton. Since the
ships would have to remain harbored upon their return, Perkins instructed
Cushing to keep them busy in the Pacific: the ships could shuttle back
and forth between Canton and the Pacific Northwest carrying furs, never

stopping at a U.S. port. Aware that Americans thirsted for tea, Perkins would have loved to supply it at a high price. However, as long as the embargo remained in effect, he saw no way to import tea—that is, until Astor involved him in a scheme.

Astor had become acquainted with a Chinese man, Punqua Wingchong, who had traveled to New York from Nantucket, where he left behind a servant. Though hoping to return to China, Wingchong found himself stranded in New York by the embargo. At the urging of Astor, Wingchong applied to Jefferson for a special passport that would allow him to ship out on an Astor-owned vessel. Informed that Wingchong was a "mandarin," Jefferson granted the exception on the grounds that repatriation of a Chinese official might help the United States become "known advantageously at the source of power in China." Fearful that Jefferson would change his mind, Astor hastily prepared the *Beaver* to convey the "mandarin" home. Herein lay Astor's ruse: since the vessel was bound for Canton anyway, why not load it with furs and goods? Jealous merchants howled foul play; the gullible president had been duped, they insisted, because Wingchong was only a commoner dissembling as a mandarin.

Astor's critics were right: this was a trading mission disguised as diplomatic goodwill. However, Astor could not hatch his scheme without help from Perkins. Lacking a permanent agent in Canton, Astor inquired whether the supercargo of the *Beaver* might avail himself of Cushing's services. In exchange, Perkins would receive cargo space for the vessel's return voyage. In the end, the *Beaver* returned Wingchong to Canton where the "mandarin" opened up a fancy-goods shop; for years, he regaled customers with yarns from his American adventure. As for Perkins, he imported a cargo of tea, which he sold at an unusually high price. Sadly, the story did not end well for the servant abandoned in Nantucket. Despairing that his master would ever return, the forlorn man hanged himself in 1809.[39]

Astoria

In the fur trade, Astor enjoyed one advantage over Perkins. His sturdy supply chains, which he had steadily expanded since the 1790s, could continuously deliver into his grasp a commodity the Chinese highly coveted—furs. While all other fur traders had to send ships on long and risky missions around the perilous Cape Horn, Astor could simply load a vessel in New York with furs obtained in Montreal from the North West Company (NWC) and ship them to Canton via the much calmer route around Good Hope. "The fur trade was the philosopher's stone of this modern Croesus," wrote a contemporary. "His traffic was the shipment of furs to China, where they brought immense prices," and "the return cargoes of teas, silks, and rich productions of China brought further large profits." In selling furs to Astor, the NWC failed to realize that it was feeding the growth of a formidable rival. For Astor dreamed of building a fur-trading empire that would bring the entire fur trade under his control. Of all the China dreams imagined by Americans, few matched Astor's in grandiosity.[40]

The obsession likely took hold of Astor after the return of Lewis and Clark in 1806. In a letter to Jefferson, Meriwether Lewis explained how an American fur-trading company could conceivably, with the aid of the federal government, establish an extensive fur-gathering and fur-shipping network out West. "If the government will only aid . . . the enterprise of her citizens," Lewis advised the president, "I am fully convinced that we shall shortly derive the benefits of a most lucrative trade."[41] Newspapers published Lewis's letter, and Astor surely read it and perhaps used it to draft the blueprints for his fur-trading empire. The company's operations would work in the following manner: Trappers and hunters employed by Astor would procure furs from the wilderness of the North American interior. These men would then ship the furs west by way of the Missouri and Columbia rivers, following Lewis and Clark's route, along which Astor would place outposts at regular intervals. When the furs reached Astoria, a fortified settlement at the mouth of the Columbia River, his men would package and ship them to Canton on company vessels. In this way Astor "envisioned a complete land and sea transportation system," wrote historian James Ronda, "shifting goods, pelts, information, and employees around a global marketplace."[42]

In the years that followed, Astor moved deliberately and decisively to execute his plan. In 1808 he sought the approval of Jefferson and key members of his cabinet. Jefferson embraced the plan because he understood the relationship between trade and national sovereignty; in the wake of the *Chesapeake* affair, he was loath to concede the Pacific Northwest to British Canadians and eagerly cast his support behind this bold plan to establish an American presence in the region. That same year, Astor secured through the New York State legislature a twenty-five-year charter for the "American Fur Company." Since Astor feared that Canada's NWC and Russia's American Fur Company would encroach on his hunting and trading territory, he hammered out agreements with the two goliaths that they would respect territorial boundaries. The Russian agreement also granted Astor exclusive rights to supply Russian outposts in the North Pacific region with provisions and convey Russian furs to Canton on Astor ships. With all preparations made, Astor set his plan into motion in 1810, sending two parties to the site chosen for Astoria. One would traverse North America along an overland route, following the path blazed by Lewis and Clark. The other would reach the site by sea on the *Tonquin*, captained by Jonathan Thorn. After seeing the two parties off, Astor sensed he was on the verge of consummating Ledyard's dream.[43]

Even the best-laid plans can go awry. Poor leadership and dissension bedeviled the overland party, causing strife and unnecessary deaths. The *Tonquin* experienced an even worse fate. After dropping the men off in Astoria, the *Tonquin* was supposed to obtain furs and then proceed to

Canton, where it would pick up Chinese goods before returning to New York to report to an anxious Astor. However, on the coast of Vancouver Island, Captain Thorn's volatile nature triggered a disastrous chain of events. When a chief disputed the price of a fur, Thorn flew into a rage, physically seizing the man's head and forcing it violently into a fur. One cannot imagine a worse insult, and several days later, the chief retaliated. He and twenty others hailed the *Tonquin* to request permission to come on board. Thorn agreed, but after a second canoe brought still more men, he became suspicious—but it was too late. The Indians, who had knives and hatchets hidden in their furs, attacked and a one-sided massacre ensued. Jack Ramsey, the Indian interpreter, jumped off the vessel and swam to safety. He alone survived to tell the tale, one that did not end with the Indians' victory. While celebrating on deck, the Indians failed to detect the presence of a sailor hiding below. This lone survivor recognized that, while escape was not possible, revenge was. Locating the ship's powder magazine, he struck a flame. "Arms, legs and heads were flying in all directions," Ramsey later recalled, "and this tribe of Indians lost nearly 200 of its people."[44]

Though the *Tonquin* provided Astor with a spectacular disaster, mundane failures plagued even the easiest segments of his logistical operation. In 1812 the captain of the *Beaver*, after reaching Canton with furs, inexplicably sold his cargo at a low price to a Perkins ship, despite orders from Astor to sell only to Chinese merchants. Hearing the news, Astor was apoplectic: was not the whole point of this massive undertaking to muscle out Perkins? That same year, forces beyond Astor's control delivered the coup de grâce: the outbreak of hostilities between the United States and England. Visiting Washington in 1813, Astor urged President Madison and Secretary of State James Monroe to provide Astoria with military protection, but his efforts were in vain. After the war's end in 1815, Astor learned that a military expedition sent by the NWC had captured Astoria in 1813. Challenged by a superior force, Astor's men could only sell the settlement—including its armaments, supplies, and stores of furs—to the NWC for $58,000. Astoria was lost.[45]

In the years that followed, Astor continued his profitable trade with China. In 1815 he even followed the Perkins model by installing a permanent agent in Canton. However, the loss of Astoria wounded him deeply, and he struggled to cope with his colossal disappointment. For Astor, bygones were never bygones. Over two decades later, in 1836, he commissioned Washington Irving to chronicle Astoria's rise and fall. The eloquent Irving, Astor hoped, could capture in literary form the brilliance of a vision that the real world had so cruelly sullied. He also instructed Irving to state explicitly who deserved the blame. "It is painful at all times to see a grand and beneficial stroke of genius fail of its aim," the well-paid Irving obligingly wrote. Had Astor "been seconded by suitable agents and properly protected by government, the ultimate failure of his plan might yet have been averted." While eager to condemn others, Astor refused to accept any culpability himself. "I think it was not my fault," he wrote petulantly in 1817. "We have no settlement on the Columbia. The Northwest Company have it," along with the Russians. "They are doing that which I wish to have & wanted to do." In the 1820s Astor scaled down his business in China, divesting his interests completely by the 1830s. Manhattan real estate became his focus.[46]

Though pleased to be rid of Astor, the NWC faced an obstacle in the British East India Company (BEIC). As a part of its monopoly, the BEIC enjoyed the sole privilege in the British Commonwealth of sending ships to China, meaning that the NWC could not avail itself of the simplest and most direct route to China: a straight line between the Pacific Northwest and Canton. Of course, the NWC could ship its furs halfway around the world to London and allow the BEIC to transport them to Canton, but company officers dismissed this costly and inefficient option. Instead, the NWC formed a partnership with an American firm willing to "help" it with its problem by conveying furs to Canton for a commission. From the perspective of this firm, one could not imagine a better arrangement, as its commission included 25 percent of the proceeds from fur sales in Canton. For years, this fortunate American firm enjoyed these lucrative commissions without incurring any risk—the NWC shouldered all of that. In 1817, as Astor bemoaned the loss of Astoria, the salt hit his wound: the company pumping easy profits out of the fur trade was Perkins and Company.[47]

Assessing the Impact of Exotic Goods

To rectify the trade imbalance with China, American traders launched far-flung ventures to distant shores and remote islands. On these voyages, they exhibited resourcefulness and no small amount of rapine, sometimes pushing species to the brink of extinction. Their massive commitment to exotic goods prompts a question: what was the impact of these products on the overall balance of trade? Jacques Downs suggests it was minimal. Since the search for these products made for good storytelling, "traders, their descendents, and local colorists" exaggerated the importance of this romantic quest in memoirs and local histories. "Folklore, however, is not history," Downs warns, and "the most obvious truth is that exotic products were never very significant."[48]

James Fichter reaches the same conclusion, though employing a different logic. If traders employed silver in three-quarters of their purchases in Canton, as available statistics suggest, then all exotic products combined accounted for no more than one-quarter. To explain why traders would bother with these products at all, Fichter considers the weights and measures of the key articles of exchange. For the return voyage, traders obviously needed tea in bulk, as the beverage's popularity had spurred their ventures in the first place. However, since tea was light, it occupied a large amount of space without contributing much weight.[49] To stabilize vessels for the return voyage, traders loaded their bottoms with ceramic wares that provided ballast.[50] The material properties of silver, of course, presented traders with tea's exact opposite. As silver was "extremely compact" and "virtually volumeless," one could stow all of it in a few boxes. Though planning to trade primarily with silver, traders still needed additional cargo to steady ships and avoid the absurd scenario of hollow vessels embarking for China. Thus, traders turned to American goods that could be exchanged for exotic goods along the way.[51]

These scholars perhaps underestimate the importance of exotic products. After all, if a trader's primary objective was to fill empty compartments with ballast, he could accomplish this goal quite easily with barrels of nails, containers of butter, or piles of iron bars. He certainly did not need to establish a colony in Oregon, add dozens of months and thousands of miles to his voyages, form alliances with Hawaiian and Fijian chiefs, send teams rappelling down Indonesian cliffs, or chase slippery slugs in the ocean shallows. If we accept axiomatically that traders, taken as a group, were neither foolhardy in terms of risk nor careless with time or money, then we need to find an explanation as to why they sent ships off on far-flung errands. They clearly expected to earn large profits, but how?

By reexamining the statistics, we find profits hidden behind the numbers. Though silver did account for 75 percent of the American trade in Canton, this percentage applies only to the short span of years from 1804 to 1808; in fact, from 1816 to 1844, that percentage dropped to 65 percent.[52] Though this figure still seems high, we should remember the volatile nature of the markets for goods like furs, sandalwood, and ginseng. Affected by wars, the whims of chieftains, overhunting or overharvesting, and fickle Chinese demand, the trade in these goods was characterized by sudden surges that lasted only a few years and were followed by collapses. In other words, American traders were not filling compartments for forty years with diverse cargoes containing quantities of furs, sandalwood, and ginseng, all shipped at once in the same vessel. Rather, they would exploit one or two products until profits dried up and then move on to the next thing. For instance, during the years when sandalwood mania reigned, traders emphasized this commodity to the exclusion of others. So if we think of silver as constituting roughly 65 percent of the trade, that means that sandalwood, during its boom years, might account for much of the remaining 35 percent. In sum, for that slim time period, sandalwood played a huge role in the China trade, and the same can be said for fur during its years in vogue.

We should also remember that, though the 65 percent statistic associated with silver provides a helpful benchmark, the presence of conventional trading missions distorts the number. Some merchants, eschewing exotic products altogether, opted for a simple itinerary that pivoted on a European port, where the requisite silver was secured for the later tea purchase. In other words, if some conservative merchants based their trade mostly on silver, it follows that others relied very little on it. Not content to be mere wholesalers of tea, this latter group set their sights on the "triple golden round of profits," which necessitated at least one additional stop—perhaps Java, the Pacific Northwest, or Hawaii—to barter for the exotic goods that could replace silver in Canton. For a trader questing after this Holy Grail, exotic products formed the lynchpin of his China trade.

Even with exotic products, the scales remained tipped in China's favor. When we compare the profiles of these exotic goods with that of tea, we can see why, in the final analysis, they failed to bring balance to the China trade. Tea, after all, scores high in three basic criteria: first, since most of a growing American population consumed the beverage, demand for tea was high; second, as tea drinking was habit forming, Americans routinely replenished their supplies; and third, because tea lent itself to annual cultivation, Chinese suppliers could meet demand year after year. In contrast, each of the exotic products failed with at least one criterion. The Chinese high demand for sandalwood depleted stores rapidly; however, sandalwood production depended on the destruction of pristine forests and thus was unsustainable. The supply of sandalwood, unlike that of tea, was finite. Ginseng failed a different criterion. An American farmer could harvest the root annually, but Chinese demand remained low thanks to the presence of a superior Chinese variety. Like sandalwood, supplies of furs had limits (female sea otters have a low fertility rate). Furthermore, since Chinese consumers could wear the same fur coat indefinitely, they seldom sought replacements.[53]

One American import matched tea in two criteria and surpassed it in a third—opium. More than just habit-forming, opium might have addicted users, forcing them to waste their resources through constant purchasing. For this reason, only opium could displace silver, as a surprising claim by Perkins in the 1820s makes clear. "We have not shipped a Spanish dollar for the past *three years* to China," Perkins wrote, despite the fact that his firm carried over $1 million worth of Chinese goods to U.S. ports each year. Thanks largely to Turkish opium, Cushing bought Chinese goods without using an ounce of silver. By exchanging goods for goods and eliminating silver from the equation, Perkins and Company achieved that most elusive of all goals: it had brought balance to its China trade. In addition to opium, the firm also handled a new "product," one introduced to the China trade in 1828—bills on London (described below). As will be shown, opium and bills on London went hand in hand. Their twin success shifted the China trade, as traders moved away from exotic goods and toward bills and narcotics, products utterly lacking in romance. The China trade was becoming surreal as merchants' trading portfolios became increasingly dominated by paper and smoke.[54]

Opium

As far as opium was concerned, Americans arrived comparatively late to the scene. Historians date European importation of the drug back to the seventeenth century. By the time the Americans started carrying opium in 1804, the dragon throne had already declared its illegality many times. In 1729 Yongzheng handed down the initial proscription, which Qianlong reiterated in 1780. In 1800 Jiaqing amplified the interdiction in response to England's expanding trade in Indian opium. Not to be deterred, Britain made a simple adjustment. Since the BEIC, as an extension of the crown, must not be caught violating Qing law, Indian opium would enter China on the ships of "country traders," independent British merchants who shuttled between India and China. When Chinese authorities complained to the BEIC, the company explained (as it did during the *Lady Hughes* affair) that it could not exert control over individual merchants. At the same time, the BEIC could disingenuously point to its own stainless record of rule-abiding behavior.[55]

Ironically, Britain's monopolistic practices with respect to Indian opium produced an unintended consequence: an American monopoly in Turkish opium. In the early 1800s the BEIC enacted two measures intended to preserve its monopoly in Indian-grown opium. First, it forbade traders from other nations, the United States included, from partaking of the India-to-Canton conveyance of opium, reserving that lucrative business for country traders. Second, to protect the market for Indian opium, it prevented independent British traders from handling non-Indian opium. Though these measures kept Americans away from Indian opium, it also presented them with opportunity. If they could locate a second source for opium, they could enjoy free rein over it. They did exactly that, turning to Turkey.[56]

Philadelphia's merchants first identified Turkey as a potential supplier of opium. In early 1804 William Stewart, U.S. consul in Smyrna, left his post and returned home to Philadelphia carrying this important news, which he shared with William Waln and R. H. Wilcocks. To test the waters, the two promptly dispatched a vessel for Smyrna, where it did obtain opium. However, before consummating the venture in Canton, the traders on board lost their nerve and opted to sell the opium in Batavia. The same group's next opium ship, the *Sylph*, reached Canton in 1806, becoming the first American opium venture on record. The viability of Turkish opium attracted Philadelphia merchant Stephen Girard, who wrote, "I am very much in favor of investing heavily in opium." For fifteen years, he did exactly that. In New England, Thomas Perkins explored the opium market but did nothing more.[57]

Aware of American smuggling, the BEIC at first scoffed at the threat. Since "the Turkey Opium is held by the Chinese" as "very inferior" in quality to the Indian variety, British supercargoes assured BEIC directors, the Americans would fail to make inroads: "We do not conceive the speculations of the Americans are likely permanently to interfere."[58] Perceiving no threat, the BEIC sounded no alarm. However, at the conclusion of the War of 1812, the American opium trade gathered strength as Joseph Peabody of Salem, John Donnell of Baltimore, Thomas Perkins, and John Jacob Astor all tossed their hats into the ring.[59] Angling for a monopoly in 1818, Perkins judged Astor his greatest rival: "We know of no one but Astor we fear."[60]

Before 1821, opium smuggling mostly resembled the legal trade, though it required the cooperation of corrupt Chinese officials. Before entering the Bocca Tigris, the opium ship's captain would slip a bribe to a Chinese official, who would conveniently look the other way and allow the vessel to continue to Whampoa. Here, legal goods would be loaded onto small boats for conveyance to Canton; at the same time, Chinese smugglers would approach the vessel, purchase the opium, and handle its distribution from this point forward. Of course, the *hoppo* and his subordinates could at any time refuse to accept bribes and start enforcing the law. If so, why did opium smuggling continue unabated?[61]

According to Paul Van Dyke, pressures within the Canton System itself militated against any stoppage. One must remember here that legitimate and illegitimate goods flowed into Canton on the same ships. Thus, the trade in contraband enabled the smooth functioning of the legal trade, which generated huge revenues for Peking in the following manner: The opium trade kept foreign traders coming to Canton, where they used silver (often obtained through illicit opium sales) to purchase tea in high volume from hong merchants, paying port fees and duties in the process. Hong merchants cherished this silver because it allowed them to buy tea without borrowing at high interest rates. Since their debt had drawn the unwanted scrutiny of the emperor in the past, the *hoppo* understood the importance of keeping hong merchants solvent.

Thus, when a newly appointed *hoppo* started his three-year term, he faced a choice. If he desired, he could bring the vast machinery of international trade to a grinding halt by enforcing antiopium laws, a highly conspicuous action that would attract notice from Peking and arrest the flow of revenue into the state treasury. Or he could proceed down the well-worn path of his predecessors, none of whom had chosen to topple the apple cart. Selecting this option meant allowing the Canton System to hum along as it always had, steadily meting out profits to foreign merchants, the emperor, hong merchants, Chinese drug smugglers, and—of no small importance— himself. Indeed, if he agreed to accept the bribes that lubricated the traffic, the Canton System would continue to pump revenues north to Peking, which made for a contented emperor. Then, at the conclusion of his term, the *hoppo* could walk away from his post having won the emperor's favor while enriching himself in the process. The "choice" was really no choice at all.[62]

The *Emily*

In the early 1800s, opium traders confronted a system in Canton that mostly accommodated them. However, Chinese authorities launched a major crackdown in 1819 that brought permanent change to opium smuggling.[63] In 1821 the American opium ship *Emily* became ensnared in China's latest dragnet. Owned by John Donnell of Baltimore, the *Emily* sailed to Whampoa under the command of Captain Cowpland. Here a Sicilian sailor aboard named Terranova attempted to buy fruit from a female peddler who had rowed alongside the vessel. After lowering his money and pulling up the fruit, Terranova apparently felt cheated, and a heated argument ensued. According to a Chinese witness, Terranova hurled a ceramic jar that struck the woman on the head, causing her to fall into the water and drown. Chinese authorities ordered the immediate handover of Terranova. Fearing that Terranova would not receive a fair trial (foreigners continued to speak bitterly of the *Lady Hughes* affair, now over thirty-five years past), the Americans refused but did agree to hold a trial on board the *Emily*. The Chinese accepted this compromise, and a trial took place on the ship's deck, with the presiding Chinese magistrate completely unaware of the opium cargo lying under his feet.

The tribunal convicted Terranova, and the Americans declared the entire proceedings a farce, refusing to release the sailor. Chinese officials, however, enjoyed greater leverage, as they could—and did—shut down the entire American trade until Cowpland agreed to cooperate. For a few days, Cowpland stood his ground; however, he understood that the extreme weakness of his position prevented him from holding out for long. After all, how long could he stand defiantly on his deck, remonstrating against the unfairness of Chinese "justice," when his boat was little more than a narcotics storehouse that could, at any moment, be subjected to a search? Cowpland handed Terranova to the Chinese, who summarily strangled him.[64]

After Terranova met his end, Chinese authorities by chance captured and interrogated a Chinese bribe collector with ties to opium smuggling. The man divulged the names of people and ships involved in opium trafficking, a list that included the *Emily*. After the disclosure, the viceroy, Ruan Yuan, memorialized the emperor. Knowing he could not prevent foreigners from carrying opium to Canton, Ruan Yuan decided to target the men who enabled their trade. "The Hong merchants are so close to the foreign traders," he claimed, that they must play a role. "How can foreigners bring contraband . . . such a long distance without being assured of a market here first? They, therefore, must work hand-in-glove with the Hong-merchants."[65] Ruan Yuan's suspicions were correct. In 1817 Perkins wrote to Fred Paine in Smyrna that "our friends Houqua" and Cushing "have recommended in very strong terms the purchase of a large quantity of opium."[66] Having made his accusation, Ruan Yuan next sought the emperor's permission to punish Houqua as an example to others. "Your

Majesty's consent is requested to have his third-rank button removed," he wrote, "and see whether the hong merchants would still continue to connive in opium smuggling." Receiving approval, Ruan Yuan stripped the disgraced Houqua of his rank.[67]

After this crackdown, opium smuggling assumed an entirely new shape. A vessel arriving in Whampoa now had to post bond, which meant declaring that no opium was stowed on board. For any trader caught in falsehood the penalty was severe: "everlasting expulsion from the port."[68] The hong merchants, whom Ruan Yuan had charged with complicity, also had to guarantee that any ship they secured was opium-free. Most American traders suspected that these measures, unlike earlier ones, had teeth and therefore would bring permanent change to opium smuggling. In the mercantile calculus of Astor, Girard, and others, the risks now outweighed the rewards. They interpreted this latest crackdown as their cue to exit the opium trade.[69]

This thinking proved naive. For what neither these merchants nor Ruan Yuan understood was that, by 1821, opium importation had become an elemental force, one that assumed the characteristics of a powerful river. Thus, when Chinese officials erected this latest barrier, the opium did not so much stop as flow around the impediment, finding a new point of ingress. By 1822 foreign and Chinese smugglers had developed a new system that allowed them to circumnavigate Chinese enforcement. Since increased surveillance rendered Whampoa unsafe for opium handoffs, foreigners moved the access point out to Lintin Island. In the foreign factories, local Chinese criminal interests set up money-changing shops where Chinese buyers and foreign sellers could meet and sign contracts. A deal reached, the criminal interests sent out many-oared boats called "fast crabs" to collect their quarry from the waiting ship. Once obtained, the opium moved inland through various networks and brokerage houses. In the end, the crackdown failed to reduce the amount of opium smuggled into China. However, by scaring away risk-averse traders, it concentrated the trade in the hands of a few, such as Perkins and Company.[70]

Bills on London

While a new smuggling system was revolutionizing the physical side of the opium trade, bills on London started to lubricate the financial machinery. What exactly was a bill on London? When Robert Bennet Forbes returned to Canton in 1838 to work for Russell and Company, he discovered that these bills had become the principal medium of exchange. In a letter to his wife, Rose, he explained this mysterious new trade in paper.

It all begins, he wrote, with a British "speculator in India" who has $10,000 in his possession but wishes to buy $50,000 worth of opium. He plans to ship the opium to Canton, where his associate, "Mr. Smith," will oversee its sale. The speculator approaches Mr. Smith's agent in India, an

American trader who—crucially—enjoys strong credit with a merchant bank in London, such as Baring Brothers. That American draws up a bill on London in the amount of $40,000. This bill, which is little more than an interest-earning financial product, carries the name of its underwriter, such as Baring Brothers, whose global clout legitimizes it. A third party, usually a British merchant, pays cash for the bill as a way to invest in the speculator's debt. In exchange for the bill, this third party supplies the speculator with the $40,000 that, when combined with the original $10,000, enables him to purchase a cargo of opium, which he promptly sends to Mr. Smith in Canton. At this point, the American trader carries the bill to Canton on behalf of the bill's owner, who arranges for an associate to receive it.

The business activity next shifts to Canton, where both the shipment of opium and the bill arrive after several weeks. As bills generally mature thirty or sixty days after the arrival of the opium cargo in Canton, Mr. Smith has that long to sell the opium for silver. When he has completed the sale, the profits for all involved become manifestly clear. The third party, acting through his Canton-based proxy, presents Mr. Smith with the bill and receives back his original $40,000 plus the interest. If he owes money to a merchant bank, he can arrange to have this silver shipped to London and remitted there. Next, the original speculator, who has presumably sold his opium cargo for more than the $50,000 he paid for it, enjoys a profit far beyond what his original $10,000 would have allowed. Since he must pay Mr. Smith a commission for his services, the latter also makes money. Last, the American trader receives a handsome commission for his role in drafting the bill and conveying it to Canton. He might use his earnings to purchase a cargo of tea for the passage home.

While generating reliable profits, bills on London offered one other advantage to the American trader. Though opium lurked behind all transactions, he could play an integral role in the process without signing his name to a single document linking him to the drug. In fact, so removed was he from the foul portion of the operation that he might not, throughout his involvement, lay eyes on a single chest. Though his conscience might or might not have wrestled with the morality of his actions, as far as the legal record was concerned, he remained spotless.[71]

To gauge the impact of bills on London, we can return to the statistical record for American silver imports. Since traders carried bills in lieu of silver, we should find the two existing in an inversely proportional relationship. In other words, as bills started to gain traction in 1828, silver imports should have entered into decline at roughly the same time. Of course, the presence of other goods and trends in the China trade complicates any analysis of silver's relationship to bills. For instance, 1828 also witnessed a decline in the sandalwood trade, so we might expect to see a temporary rise in silver imports as traders reverted to this reliable medium. Even with sandalwood's bust, however, silver still underwent a precipitous drop. In 1827 silver accounted for 65 percent of all American imports to Canton;

in 1828 that number plummeted to 10 percent. Though we cannot attribute this dramatic decline entirely to the advent of bills, when we examine a larger span of years, the effect of bills is unmistakable. Between 1828 and 1838, silver constituted only 32 percent of American imports.[72]

If bills were so convenient, one wonders why they did not displace silver completely. Here we should remember that the bills were drawn up on merchant banks such as Baring Brothers, which would back only trusted traders. Thus, it behooved any American trader to establish a relationship with Baring's partners. Fortunately for firms like Bryant and Sturgis, Perkins and Company, and later Russell and Company, they knew Joshua Bates. Born in Weymouth, Massachusetts in 1788, Joshua Bates began his career in the Boston firm of William Gray. There he caught the eye of Thomas Perkins, who was always on the lookout for talent. Perkins mentored Bates until 1816, the year Gray sent him to London to serve as his agent. In London, Bates befriended John Baring, the nephew of Alexander Baring, the leading partner in the great merchant bank, and the two went into business together in 1826. By the mid-1820s Alexander Baring had become less active, and so he sought capable young men to run the bank—men like Joshua Bates. In 1828 Baring Brothers brought Bates into the firm as managing partner.[73]

Under Bates's leadership, Baring Brothers enjoyed a resurgence. The American-born financier brought a Yankee work ethic and love of system that Lord Alexander had lacked. "This is an advantage Bates has," observed a friend; "he is devoted to business and willing to labor." For his part, Bates acknowledged and criticized his own obsessive work habits. "I would rather make a quarter of the money," he confessed, "and free myself from the necessity of that day and night attention to business which becomes irksome to me." Though the desire for freedom was there, Bates did not know how to escape the iron cage of self-discipline he had imposed on himself. He spent much of his long work day processing the business of American clients and meeting these same people when they arrived in London. With bills on London, China traders connected to Bates could profit from Indian opium without actually transporting any of it in their ships.[74]

As lucrative as opium was, traders who invested heavily in it began to notice an economic downside in the late 1830s. Stated simply, as opium sales increased, all other imports declined proportionally. Why was this happening? According to Forbes, as the Chinese spent their silver on opium, they retained little "ready cash" with which to purchase legitimate goods. The only solution, he believed, was to pump silver back into the Chinese economy through high-volume tea purchases. Of course, this remedy required American consumers to do their part. "It appears to us," Forbes wrote, "that we must materially increase the consumption of tea" in the United States "before we can expect to enlarge materially our trade to China." Samuel Wells Williams, a missionary, echoed Forbes's assessment. "We have many things" that the Chinese "would be glad to get, but they cannot long pay for them in [silver] specie." The opium trade, he darkly concluded, "gradually destroys what it feeds upon." Like an incubus, opium sat on the legitimate trade, menacing it and keeping it down.[75]

Conclusion

In the early 1800s Americans introduced a fresh trading model to the world when the quest to locate goods for Canton unlocked their entrepreneurial dynamism. Acting independently, resourceful merchants established new trade routes that, while causing no small amount of ecological damage, succeeded in bringing a variety of exotic goods to China. Though Astor vigorously courted the federal government (and failed to receive its protection), other Americans flourished in the laissez-faire environment. Europe took note. According to James Fichter, free-trade advocates in Great Britain lobbying for the destruction of the BEIC repeatedly cited the astonishing success of the American model. BEIC officials countered that free trade was at best a "risky and unproven theory" that if implemented could bring disastrous consequences.[76] However, as nimble American traders identified new markets and moved goods with greater efficiency than did the English colossus, the BEIC's position grew untenable. In 1833, after America's trade in Turkish opium challenged the dominance of Indian opium, the BEIC lost its monopoly over the China trade.[77]

Ironically, the breakup of this state-sanctioned monopoly coincided with a period of consolidation within America's China trade. By the 1830s much of the trade had fallen into the hands of a few firms that dealt mostly in opium, tea, and bills on London. Russell enjoyed the largest share, thanks to the firm's inheritance of Perkins's business. Though no American firm could match Russell's might in commerce, a new company succeeded in contesting it on moral and spiritual grounds. Founded by a devout Christian merchant, Olyphant and Company conducted a profitable trade with China without conveying a single chest of opium. However, Olyphant's ships smuggled another dangerous "cargo" into China—the first American missionaries.

4

Beachhead of God

The First Wave of Missionaries

Before American missionaries came to China, there was a lone British volunteer. On April 20, 1807, Robert Morrison debarked in New York Harbor, having sailed from London. Months earlier, the London Missionary Society (LMS) had selected Morrison for a daunting undertaking: establish the first Protestant mission in China. If China was his destination, what was he doing in New York? After all, with the British East India Company (BEIC) routinely sending vessels to Canton, Morrison could presumably sail with one of these. However, China regarded missionaries as agitators, and the BEIC did not want to upset its relationship with its trading partner. Morrison would have to find passage elsewhere. Undeterred, he found support in America from a Christian merchant. Three weeks later, he embarked for China carrying a letter of introduction from Secretary of State James Madison. Arriving in Canton, a New York firm allowed him to board in the basement of its factory. Morrison had become an "adopted American."[1]

After settling in, Morrison faced a steep challenge. Since China confined Westerners to the foreign factories, he needed to invent an evangelical model that would allow missionaries to make progress without having access to the vast majority of Chinese. After a few missteps, Morrison devised a system that accepted the status quo but prepared for the great change surely coming in the future. Missionaries would study Chinese languages and translate the scriptures in anticipation of God's opening of China. Morrison next set his sights on attracting recruits. No nation filled him with more hope than did the United States, then in the throes of a religious revival. When Americans started to arrive in 1830, Morrison happily mentored those willing to learn his system. In the early years, most were.

However, Americans brought something new: Millennialism. They believed that, as instruments of God, they would help effect the Second

Coming by converting the Chinese. They collectively harbored a China dream that surpassed that of any merchant in terms of size and scope. Depending on the missionary, Millennialism could manifest itself in different ways. The first arrivals dutifully adopted Morrison's program but did so with great evangelical fervor: they supercharged his apparatus with high-voltage religiosity. Indeed, by the time of Morrison's death in 1834, his model had become their model. Other Americans rejected Morrison's model on the grounds that its emphasis on patient preparation retarded God's will. This group followed the mandate of Karl Gützlaff, a charismatic Prussian who challenged missionaries to break out of the Canton confinement. If Chinese authorities labeled them instigators, then so be it—they took orders from a higher authority. One missionary, a trained physician, developed his own model based on a loophole in Chinese law: though that law prevented him from going out among the Chinese, it did not stop the Chinese from coming to him. Believing he could save souls by healing bodies, he opened a hospital in Canton.

Though earnest and energetic, these missionaries failed to convert many Chinese. This is not to say, however, that their labors had little impact. Far removed from family and institutions, missionaries reinvented themselves in China. They tended to go off script, discover hidden talents, and develop projects independently that lacked their sponsors' approval. They generated the language primers and cultural texts that, in the years ahead, allowed China and the West to begin to understand one another. In the final calculus, the missionaries' influence flowed not out of their official evangelism but out of their intellectual, linguistic, and medical work.

The Pioneer

In Canton Robert Morrison needed to not only establish a missionary station but also invent the entire Protestant project in China. Exactly what could a missionary realistically accomplish in a closed-off country? How would he spend his hours, days, or even years? In search of a precedent, Morrison emulated the Jesuit missionaries of the sixteenth and seventeenth centuries, whose strategy had been to demonstrate to Chinese leaders the harmonious fit of Catholic principles with Chinese civilization. Modifying this strategy for Canton, Morrison elected to "go native": he ate with chopsticks, wore a long gown, tied his hair in a queue, grew out his fingernails, and studied the Cantonese dialect. By exhibiting his receptiveness to local mores, Morrison hoped to render Christianity less alien and more familiar to the Chinese. His message: we are not as different as you think.

The strategy backfired. As the awkward Caucasian with braided hair and a flowing frock groped toward unsuspecting Chinese, they withdrew in bewilderment. Who was this strange entity that, neither European nor Chinese, seemed to belong in no known category? The Chinese, in short, were reluctant to accept what they could not classify. Likewise, Western merchants rejected this bizarre amalgam of a man; an Englishman who lived with Americans and adopted Chinese customs had no place in their society. By attempting to belong everywhere, Morrison belonged nowhere, and his feeling of isolation was profound.[2] "Solitary is my situation," the dejected missionary wrote. "Today, I confine myself entirely to my room. . . . I sing a hymn, read a psalm, as in public worship, and sing again. Instead of preaching a sermon, I read the scriptures."[3] As Morrison worshipped alone in a dank cellar, singing hymns to only himself, it became agonizingly clear that he had become a marginal man. The Protestant mission was off to an inauspicious start. It was time to scrap this model.

Morrison began to methodically erect a new framework for missionary work. He was determined to set things up so that new recruits would not need to invent the wheel, as he had done, but could instead connect to his fully operational system. In developing his model, Morrison reluctantly accepted one reality: direct evangelism with Chinese people could take place only on a limited scale. China, in other words, was closed to Christ. That said, Morrison knew that a missionary must not remain idle, since inactivity would not only crush his morale but also prevent him from reaching that crucial state of readiness, because one day God would blast China open.

Certain that divine intervention was coming, Morrison devoted his time to preparatory work. Since proselytizing depended on communication, he placed the acquisition of language—written characters, spoken Mandarin, and local Cantonese—as his highest priority. By 1810 Morrison's proficiency in written Chinese enabled him to read Chinese classics. His linguistic attainments also allowed him to commence translation projects, his goal being the mass printing of religious tracts that missionaries could distribute. In 1811 he began work on the centerpiece of his translation program—a Chinese-language Bible. During these early years, Morrison was nothing short of prolific, and the reports he sent back to the LMS turned heads among directors.[4]

Americans also read about God's one-man army in Canton, thanks to Morrison's spirited letter-writing campaign. Believing that China's salvation depended on American participation, Morrison corresponded frequently with the American Board of Commissioners for Foreign Missions (ABCFM), the interdenominational organization founded in 1812 to advance Protestantism overseas. From Morrison's perspective, these letters held great strategic value because, when published in the ABCFM's *Missionary Herald*, they became a powerful recruiting tool. This point was not lost on the ABCFM's directors, who actively solicited pieces from him starting in 1820. Between 1821 and 1827, Morrison used the *Herald* as a platform to call Americans' attention to the urgent cause in China—the "perishing heathen." In 1828 he composed a special feature on China, one that consumed four pages of double-columned text. At Andover Theological Seminary, a young man studying to enter the ministry read the magazine avidly. As he did, his heart filled with fire.[5]

A Fertile Field for Recruits

In the small Massachusetts town where Elijah Coleman Bridgman was raised, dark woods, rocky terrain, and cold winters defined the physical landscape. The intellectual landscape, however, was dominated by Protestantism. Once a stronghold of Puritanism, Belchertown experienced a religious rebirth in the 1700s when the revivals of the Great Awakening swept through, offering residents an emotionally charged brand of Calvinism. Jonathan Edwards shaped the theology of the Awakening, and Millennialism lay at its core. On the basis of prophecies from the books of Daniel and Revelation, Edwards and his disciple Samuel Hopkins predicted that the world would soon enter a period of upheaval, during which old orders would crumble and the heathen would accept Christ. The world would next witness a glorious Millennium during which all peoples would coexist in harmony, speak a common language, and enjoy a unified culture. "All families, kindreds and nations of the earth," Hopkins wrote, will become "believers" in Christ "more extensively and universally, than has yet come to pass."[6]

How exactly would the world become Christianized and what form would this unified culture assume? According to New England's theologians, God had chosen America to play a central role. In his *Treatise on the Millennium* (1793), Hopkins asserted that the U.S. government would provide the framework for the new universal order and that the American people would serve as God's foot soldiers in heathen lands.[7] In 1800 the theologian Nathanael Emmons elaborated on the special role of Americans. "This is probably the last peculiar people which he [God] means to form," Emmons wrote, "and the last great empire which he means to erect, before the kingdoms of this world are absorbed in the kingdoms of Christ." This was a patriotic eschatology. Emmons added that God "will undoubtedly make use of human exertions," referring to missionaries.[8] In 1799 this prediction underpinned the establishment of the Massachusetts Missionary Society, with Emmons serving as the first president.

These theological currents coursed through rural New England, leaving Elijah Bridgman's childhood awash in the spirit of evangelism. When he was just a boy, his devout mother took him to prayer meetings intended to bring about his conversion. "My dear mother talked, prayed, and wept over me," Bridgman recalled.[9] Though this effort failed, a few years later Bridgman, now eleven, attended a revival and was born again. From that day forward, his faith never wavered. Though he idolized all Christian heroes, missionaries especially captured his imagination thanks to religious magazines such as the *Panoplist*.[10] "I remember very well" how "my good old grandfather used to call me to read to him the 'Panoplist.'" Articles on intrepid missionaries in foreign lands "first directed my attention to this subject," and "doubtless many, *many* others have been influenced by the same means."[11]

In 1822 Bridgman attended Amherst, founded the previous year to educate "indigent young men" of "hopeful piety" for the ministry. After graduating in 1826, he took the next logical step by enrolling in Andover Theological Seminary, founded in 1808 to provide a Calvinist counterweight to Harvard Divinity School, captured by liberal Unitarians in 1805. In a letter home, Bridgman described his daily routine:

> Rise at five . . . exercise till six—study till seven—then to prayers . . . from prayers to breakfast in commons—coffee, milk, cold white and brown bread & c.—from eight read Greek and Hebrew—from 11 o'clock recitation one hour—then exercise till dinnertime, half past twelve in commons again—roast beef, baked beans, puddings, etc.—till half past on read newspapers & c.—and then Hebrew, study and recitation till half past 4 o'clock—then prayers . . . then suppertime—tea, milk, biscuit & c.—I spend the evening in reading, writing, & c.—at ten retire—thus the time passes.

With this demanding schedule, Andover tried to inculcate self-discipline, a distrust for idle time, and the value of hard work. Bridgman also took an entire "course on *self denial*." However, if one was supposed to suppress one's self, what, or more appropriately, who would take the self's place? Andover taught students to emulate Christ. "I *hope* and *profess* to be a Christian," Bridgman wrote, "to *feel* like Christ—to *act* like Christ—to *be* like Christ—and to *live* like Christ." How, he asked, "did Christ *feel* and *act* and *live*?" The answer: "Christ *wept* over sinners—though they were his enemies."[12]

One looking to shed tears for sinners could find plenty in heathen countries. While studying at Andover, Bridgman continued to consume religious magazines, poring over the accounts of heroic missionaries in fields like Bombay, Ceylon (Sri Lanka), Hawaii, Turkey, Palestine, Malta, Syria, and China, home of the great pioneer, Robert Morrison. In fact, these engrossing articles, when combined with a curriculum steeped in Hopkins theology, produced a powerful synergy. The farm boy from remote Belchertown began to imagine his life as playing out not in the margins but rather at the center of God's Millennial plan.[13]

Though the ABCFM expressed great interest in supplying Morrison with recruits, the costs and logistics appeared formidable. No one understood this more than Morrison himself who, to fund his own mission, had accepted employment with the BEIC, which needed a translator (in the 1820s, only a small handful of people could speak both English and Chinese). Looking for a way to reduce the ABCFM's financial burden, Morrison formed relationships with Christian merchants who backed the Protestant mission. From this group, one pious trader stepped forward to pledge more than just a small monetary contribution.[14]

Passage to China

D.W.C. Olyphant harbored a holy purpose that transcended his material activity of buying and selling goods. In a letter to Morrison, the merchant wrote modestly that he knew "something of the love of God in Christ" and felt an obligation "to extend the knowledge of it." He then penned the magic words: "I hope you will make use of me if I can . . . serve you in the blessed cause."[15] Morrison did not need an epiphany to recognize the complementary interests of the pious merchant and the ABCFM: the board had volunteers but could neither transport them to Canton nor lodge them once there; Olyphant rented space in a Canton factory and had ships at his disposal but lacked a connection to missionary networks. Stepping in as intermediary, Morrison brought the two together: Olyphant would provide the material necessities for the ABCFM's spiritual enterprise.[16]

With a conduit to China in place, the ABCFM faced a momentous decision: who would go first? Actually, there would be two. Working in conjunction with the ABCFM and the Seaman's Friend Society, Olyphant agreed to send two missionaries, one to assist Morrison in Canton and the other to preach to sailors in Whampoa. In September 1829, two men were interviewed in New York: David Abeel, a graduate of the New Brunswick Theological Seminary, and Bridgman from Andover. As both men were judged suitable, the societies decided that both should go. The result showed, Abeel wrote, that the "Lord repays to us *double* our feeble at-tempts to serve him."[17] Returning to Belchertown one final time, Bridgman was officially ordained. During the ceremony, one clergyman urged him to "attack the prince of darkness in his most imposing fortress."[18] Another or-dered him "to go to the proud, bigoted and fornicating pagan in his distant pagoda . . . and let [him] learn the glad song of salvation."[19]

Returning to New York, Bridgman received his instructions from the ABCFM. Since he was the first, the board exhorted him to seek out Morrison immediately. It next spelled out his priorities, which it based on its limited knowledge of Morrison's operation: the "acquisition of the Chinese language" and the "distribution of tracts and books." As for direct evangelism, the board urged caution. Since the "Chinese government will not tolerate the public preaching of the Gospel," Bridgman must exercise his "judgment in order not to . . . shut the door." Though effective in America, direct evangelism would surely arouse the suspicions if not the anger of Chinese authorities and, in doing so, imperil Christian missions in China. Bridgman, in short, must keep a low profile and emulate the unob-trusive Morrison.[20]

But what missionary, brimming over with Millennial zeal, wanted to be told to hold back? Though the ABCFM certainly appreciated fervor, it also understood that China remained closed and that the opening might not take place for some time. Given this reality, the board prepared Bridgman for the worst. "It may be long . . . before you will see much fruit of your labors," the ABCFM letter soberly warned. "Even if you should arrive at old age . . . you may never . . . be permitted to preach a sermon publicly within the limits of the empire." Should this be the case, Bridgman must not consider his life wasted. "Do not feel that you will live in vain if you accomplish nothing more than to open the field" for "your successors" because "obstacles . . . must be removed" and "preparatory work must be performed." To avoid dampening the young man's zeal entirely, the board balanced its gloomy scenario with an optimistic one. Elsewhere in the world, signs of the Millennium were starting to appear. God was on the move as of late, and he might "soon open a wide and effectual door" into China.[21]

On October 14, 1829, the Olyphant-owned *Roman* set sail from New York. The long passage presented Bridgman and Abeel with the watery side of creation, which neither had seen before. They observed whales, sharks, and tremendous storms filled with thunder and lightning—God's pyrotechnics. Bridgman, ever the dutiful Protestant, felt a pressing need to impose structure over his idle time. "I need more system," he goaded himself, "and close application." Toward this end, he rose early; performed various acts of devotion; exercised on deck in the fresh sea air; returned to his quarters to study Chinese, Greek, and Hebrew; and then read the Holy Scriptures. While sticking to his regimen, he indulged occasionally in Millennial fantasies, dreams in which he, a mere speck in the universe, played a major part in God's cosmological scheme. "*Small as I am*, my conduct will, no doubt, affect many, perhaps all China, nay, perhaps *the whole world*."[22]

A Panorama of Cantonese Life

Arriving in February 1830, the new recruits moved into a block of rooms in the American factory that soon became jestingly known as Zion's Corner.[23] When Morrison revealed himself to be a caring mentor, both men felt relieved. However, as crucial as Morrison was, the two Americans also looked to each other for support. "I find in him a warm friend," Bridgman wrote of Abeel, "with whom I can take sweet counsel." Such warmth was welcome because China itself struck them as being alien and forbidding. Outside "all is dark as midnight," Bridgman wrote, as "the whole city is given to idolatry . . . of strange gods."[24]

Before converting the Chinese, one needed to understand them. During the day, the public square between the factories and the waterfront afforded the two men a panorama of Chinese life. "As the morning opens upon this scene," Abeel wrote, "silence retires and the ears of the stranger are assailed" by an "inharmonious concert" composed of human and animal voices. The square quickly becomes animated by "multitudes of natives," who gather daily "to transact business, gratify curiosity, or murder time." Abeel enjoyed watching vendors peddling meat, fish, pickles, vegetables, fruits, and pets; "quacks" hawking remedies for maladies; barbers cutting hair and shaving beards; gamblers organizing games of chance; and "idlers" who gathered around jugglers, sword swallowers, and storytellers. The square also attracted Chinese who had come to gawk at the foreigners for whom they harbored "insatiable curiosity." When Abeel strolled among them, the Chinese would freeze their bodies in a manner "approaching to statues" and then "continue to stare as though riveted by a magic spell."[25]

As Abeel extended his gaze to the Pearl River, a new sight seized his attention: the "water population." Thousands of Chinese passed their lives on floating domiciles, seldom touching land. Other Chinese classified these aquatic citizens as "low, alien people" and "refuse[d] to intermarry with them."[26] Yet the boat people were nevertheless remarkable, able to maneuver about on their boats quite adroitly. Mothers carried infants on their backs as they worked. When a child learned how to crawl, the mother would attach a cork-like flotation device to the toddler's back; if the child fell overboard, the mother would nonchalantly scoop the bobbing boy or girl out of the water and resume work.[27] Amazingly, these people enjoyed "every convenience of land." In addition to "edibles," one could find barbers, theatrical productions, religious shrines, and "flower boats," or floating brothels, which provoked Abeel's outrage. To feed this evil industry, the girls were "early sold, by their inhuman parents . . . to perpetual infamy and wretchedness."[28]

Of course, all this amateur ethnography served a larger purpose: the conversion of the heathen. To help the newcomers understand the nature of their adversary—namely, Satan—Morrison led Bridgman and Abeel into evil's sanctuary. Crossing the Pearl River by boat, the three reached Honam Island, the site of a Buddhist temple, where Bridgman counted 150 priests and almost as many "huge and ugly" idols. Buddhism's unfortunate partnership with Satan notwithstanding, Bridgman judged their hosts to be accommodating. After the conclusion of the guided tour, a priest served refreshments and engaged Morrison in conversation. "We thanked and rewarded him for his hospitality, and left him as we found him," Bridgman wrote, "a miserable idolater." Morrison's temple tour confirmed for the Americans the entrenched nature of Chinese religions. However, it also gave them a chance to see their mentor in action, and he impressed them with the ease he had conversed in Mandarin with the priest. If the Millennium were coming (and this they did not doubt), then the Morrison model offered the best means to prepare for China's opening. It was time to study.[29]

Learning Language

In the early months, Bridgman's life revolved around books. Under his mentor's guidance, Bridgman spent his days poring over volumes borrowed from either the BEIC's library, to which Morrison had access, or the latter's private collection. Morrison also made arrangements for Bridgman to receive clandestine lessons from a Chinese tutor, who agreed to the arrangement despite its inherent danger: any Chinese citizen caught teaching language to a foreigner risked incurring the death penalty. For a period, Morrison's program became so engrossing as to compel Bridgman to lay aside other activities, such as letters home. "I hope that my friends will not think that I have forgotten them," he wrote in his journal. "I need the whole of my strength . . . for the acquisition of the Chinese language." Though eager to begin "distributing books" and "conversing with individuals," he understood that "very little can be done until considerable proficiency is made."[30]

Following Morrison's advice, Bridgman elected to study the spoken Cantonese dialect in addition to Mandarin, a decision that was not obvious. Across the country, the Chinese wrote and read the same ideographs; from the missionaries' perspective, this universality meant one could distribute the same tracts in all regions. Unfortunately, China's spoken languages amounted to an audible jigsaw puzzle, as dialect was determined by geographic region and ethnicity. Thus, when a missionary chose to learn a given dialect, he could hear, figuratively speaking, the creaking open of one door and the slamming shut of many others. For example, if he chose Cantonese, he could communicate with people living in his immediate vicinity but nowhere else. Needing practice, Bridgman appreciated the Chinese people's boldness. "The common people will come right into the house" and ask your age, your reasons for coming to China, and the status of your parents. "They are great talkers."[31]

The small missionary cohort enjoyed a special relationship with one Chinese man. In March 1830, Morrison introduced Abeel and Bridgman to Liang Afa. Converted in Malacca in 1816 by the British missionary William Milne, Liang presented several assets that rendered him indispensable to the missionary operation. Trained as a printer and proficient in English, Liang could not only operate a printing press but also perform the translations required to generate fresh tracts. Moreover, as a Chinese citizen, he could rove outside Canton with his hand-cranked press, distributing tracts in areas other missionaries could not reach. A courageous and devout man, Liang made a deep impression on Bridgman and Abeel. As the four men bowed their heads, Liang led them in prayer.[32]

An Infrastructure of Exchange

Bridgman's rapid progress allowed him to launch in the 1830s a series of writing and translation projects. For a couple of reasons, his earliest publications targeted children. Given the rudimentary nature of his language abilities, a work intended for Chinese children made practical sense because the undertaking did not require a large vocabulary. In addition, Bridgman believed that missionaries must not neglect children, given the malleability of their minds. It was for this reason that he adopted several Chinese children, a group that included the son of Liang Afa, who wanted his boy to learn English from a native speaker. For his first publication, Bridgman translated a short English collection of biblical verses, *Scripture Lessons for the Young*. After Morrison checked it for errors, Liang Afa printed it, and Olyphant absorbed the costs.[33]

To introduce American children to the plight of the Chinese, Bridgman composed *Letters to Children*. "Now, children," Bridgman begins, as if present in their Sunday school, "if you will look on your maps, you will see that China is situated . . . directly opposite to the United States." In China, he stated, millions of children grow up without the Gospel. "But O, what do you think will become of all these poor heathen children," he asked, "who have no Bibles, and who have never heard of the name of Jesus?" These unfortunate souls were sure to fall under the "wicked" stewardship of Taoist and Buddhist priests and priestesses. Frighteningly, priestesses—"witches"—professed to drive away demons and speak to the dead. Along with false religions, opium inflicted damage on Chinese society. Bridgman cited an anonymous American merchant who claimed that opium "is doing more . . . to open the country to foreigners, than all the efforts of missionaries." Bridgman countered that opium mainly caused crime: "Stubborn facts compel me to believe, that *of all the causes of crime*" among Chinese, "OPIUM . . . *is the greatest*." Despite these discouraging problems, Bridgman found positive developments to report. For example, Liang Afa, whose son "now lives with me," bravely distributes *Scripture Lessons for the Young* in remote places. However, in Bridgman's view, his young American readers offered the greatest cause for hope: "I desire that some of *you* may come here . . . for hundreds are now needed to preach the gospel to these heathen. Say, will you come?"[34]

By 1834 Bridgman's advances in language allowed him to tackle more difficult translation projects. To his sorrow, just as he began to step out of Morrison's shadow, an ill Morrison slid into the world of shades. On August 1, 1834, Morrison passed away, leaving Bridgman in a profound state of grief. "Death of Dr. Morrison. At 10 o'clock this evening," he recorded empirically in his journal, before an upwelling of emotion seized his pen: "O LORD THOU GAVEST & THOU HAST TAKEN AWAY & BLESSED BE THY HOLY NAME." Morrison's death marked a turning point for Bridgman, who drew strength, energy, and conviction from the event. After a period of mourning, Bridgman picked up the mantle of his fallen comrade and began to advance Morrison's vision with renewed vigor. In 1835 he accepted a prominent role on a team assembled to revise Morrison's great work—the Chinese-language Bible.[35]

That same year, Bridgman brought together missionaries and merchants who shared his concern for Chinese children. This effort culminated in the Morrison Educational Society, a charitable organization formed to establish Christian schools in China.[36] In 1838 Olyphant traveled to New Haven to ask Yale faculty to recommend a suitable teacher for the society's first school. This group suggested Samuel Robbins Brown, a young man from Connecticut. Brown's commitment was never in doubt; indeed, he claimed that from "early childhood" he had resolved "to be a missionary to some heathen people." However, since Olyphant's *Morrison* was scheduled to depart in twelve days, Brown had that long to pack, bid farewell to family, and—most challengingly—convince his wife to accompany him "to the ends of the earth." Elizabeth Brown agreed, and the two set sail. Arriving in 1839 the Browns established their school in Macau.[37]

Bridgman also targeted China's ignorance of the outside world. He knew that, if missionaries could topple this barrier, information from Europe and America would rush in, erode China's intellectual and religious structures, and prepare the way for the Millennium. A "diffusion of knowledge," Bridgman prophesied, "shall . . . purify the sources of authority," "prevent . . . unlawful punishments," "save this empire from destruction," and allow it to assume "its proper rank among the nations."[38] As this final phrasing indicates, Bridgman firmly believed China could become a progressive Christian nation—but only if its people could engage in the free interchange of ideas. Knowledge, in other words, provided the skeleton key that opened all doors in China.

Inspired by this idea, Bridgman initiated a series of remarkable publishing projects. Starting in 1837, he edited the *East-West Examiner and Monthly Recorder*, a Chinese-language periodical designed to educate readers about the outside world. In covering history, the *Recorder* placed China's past in juxtaposition with that of the world. Along with drawing parallels, Chinese readers would, he hoped, discern that "the rewarding of good and punishment of evil is the universal way of Heaven." In addition, the *Recorder* introduced Chinese readers to Western science with essays on zoology, botany, and astronomy. Articles described the topography of the moon, listed the objects of the solar system, and explained why the seasons changed. The *Recorder* also included articles on progressive Western institutions, such as European courts and penal systems, in the hope that these could provide models for reform. Last, Bible stories appeared in predictable profusion, as did Millennial theology. For instance, the first issue claimed that recent storms in England and China suggested that God had begun to punish sinners in preparation for his Son's triumphant return.[39]

Since God had chosen Americans to help usher in the Millennium, Bridgman believed the Chinese should understand his homeland. He composed *A Brief Account of the United States of America* to describe American governmental, scientific, and religious institutions in the hope that these might inspire Chinese reformers. Through the application of science, rational thought, and Christian principles, the United States had improved the condition of its citizens. The Chinese would achieve similar results, Bridgman asserted, were they to adopt the American model. Allowing the United States to put its best foot forward, Bridgman de-emphasized subjects that undermined his overall thesis of progress, slavery being the prime example, and instead packaged America's brief history and most compelling ideas into a concise book.[40]

When China and the West were finally ready to talk, each side would require a textbook with which to study the other's language. To address this glaring need, Morrison had earlier compiled his *Grammar of the Chinese Language* (1815). Though useful, this text offered Mandarin instruction only, not Cantonese, and targeted Western rather than Chinese learners. In 1835 Bridgman got to work on a textbook that would complement his mentor's publication by focusing on Cantonese. In 1841 he unveiled his *Chinese Chrestomathy in the Canton Dialect*, which combined language instruction with literary passages. While users learned to speak Cantonese, the *Chrestomathy* would simultaneously teach them about Chinese civilization. Intriguingly, the textbook possessed one other dimension. Since Bridgman designed it "to assist native youth in acquiring the English tongue," the Chinese could use it to learn English. With this innovative two-way textbook, Bridgman hoped to open up a portal between China and the West, allowing each to access the other's language and culture.[41]

The larger meaning behind Bridgman's labors emerges when one examines his publications collectively. In methodical fashion, he constructed the infrastructure for China's coming intercultural exchange with the West. Indeed, "exchange" is the operative term, for Bridgman believed that knowledge streams must flow in two directions. Of course, the Chinese stood in dire need of Western thought and religion—the pressing cause to which Bridgman had devoted his life. He also maintained, however, that the West ought to study China. Since Bridgman never deviated from this principle, his portfolio reflected a wonderful symmetry. His *Scripture Lessons for the Young* (for Chinese children) was balanced by *Letters to Children* (for American youth); his *Brief Account of the United States* found its English-language doppelganger in his *Description of the City of Canton* (1839), the only part of China Bridgman knew well. The *Chrestomathy*, aimed at Chinese and Western students alike, achieved balance by dint of its own interior gyroscope. Even the *East-West Examiner and Monthly Recorder* had an English-language counterpart: the *Chinese Repository*.

Launched by Bridgman in 1832 and published in Canton on a printing press obtained by Olyphant, the *Repository* had a clear mandate: to inform the West about China. In explaining the rationale for the periodical, Bridgman pointed out that China and the West, though adept at trading material goods, had enjoyed "so little commerce in intellectual and moral commodities." With the *Repository* Bridgman sought to rectify this imbalance, and its articles covered a diverse array of topics, many of which were secular. In fact, with merchants constituting half of the circulation, Bridgman obligingly supplied content on trade-related issues and Chinese policies affecting foreigners. To help with this, he excerpted material from the *Peking Gazette*, the official Qing organ. Since China preferred to keep foreigners in the dark on internal matters, this mildly subversive practice occasionally drew the ire of Chinese authorities. They were not the only ones voicing disapproval. In the opinion of the ABCFM, the information-rich

Repository existed outside the parameters of standard missionary work and, thus, siphoned off Bridgman's valuable time and energy. Instead of writing about Confucius, Bridgman ought to be securing converts, of whom, the board pointed out, there were too few.

At the crux of the board's criticism lay an even deeper concern. Bridgman was reinventing himself in China, an act that required him to question previously accepted certainties. By 1832 he had shed much of the crude provincialism that had colored his earlier view of China as Satan's stronghold. More fascinated by Chinese civilization than contemptuous of it, he argued that China offered the "most interesting field of research under heaven." The *Repository* reflected this enlightened view. However, while his opinion of China was evolving, that of the ABCFM remained static, and therein lay the conflict. "I really fear very much that you do not understand China," Bridgman wrote in response to the board's criticism.[42] Though lacking his sponsor's support, Bridgman nevertheless brimmed with optimism on the eve of the inaugural issue. Readers would encounter a feature article written by an international celebrity causing a sensation in the Protestant world—Karl Gützlaff.[43]

The Transgressor

Karl Gützlaff refused to wait for God's signals. Born in 1803 in Stettin, Prussia, Gützlaff received an education until turning thirteen, at which point his family abruptly shunted him onto the artisan's track. Feeling his intellect thwarted, Gützlaff and a friend hatched a scheme. Upon learning that King Frederick William III would be passing through the city, the boys composed welcome verses in the hope that an impressed King Frederick would offer them royal patronage. When the day came, the two thrust themselves before the startled monarch and handed him their poem. Sensing they had crossed a line, the boys scampered away to hide, certain they had committed a tragic error. Or had they? Frederick read the poem, appreciated the boys' gumption, and dispatched messengers to locate them. Standing before the king, the boys learned of his willingness to sponsor additional years of education. For Gützlaff, the lesson was simple: God favors the bold.[44]

Securing sponsorship from the Dutch Missionary Society (DMS), Gützlaff was sent to Batavia, a Dutch settlement on the island of Java. Arriving in 1827, he met Walter Medhurst, who for ten years had proselytized under the auspices of the LMS. As the raw recruit watched the veteran in action, he found himself impressed by the latter's method. Medhurst daily went out among the common people, explaining Christianity to them in their native tongue, reading Bible verses, singing hymns, and distributing tracts. Gützlaff realized not only that he wanted to engage in the same work but also that he wanted to start immediately. Instead of immersing himself in a comprehensive language program, Gützlaff made only a cursory study of the local dialect before venturing out. "It is delightful and amusing to see him conversing with the people," a colleague wrote. "Though yet a novice in the language, he presses onward regardless of difficulties. The people laugh at his blunders, and he, good humouredly, laughs with them. And when they observe him in straits, they kindly help him out, by supplying the words." Amiable, charismatic, hyperactive, and lacking in self-consciousness, Gützlaff established an easy rapport with the local population.[45]

Though he had found his missionary style, Gützlaff felt restricted by the smallness of his missionary field. Writing to God from the tiny island of Bintan in 1827, Gützlaff expressed frustration. "Lord, send me wherever thou wilst," he offered, before apprising the Almighty of his true request: "[if] I must remain on Bintan, this will sorely oppress my heart" when "I could have access to millions of Chinese." Dutch islands were small potatoes, in his estimation—China loomed as the big prize. For three years, Gützlaff paced restlessly in his pen, his otherwise intolerable confinement brightened only by romance. In 1829 he married Maria Newell, the first single woman to be deployed in Asia by the LMS.

In 1831 a tragedy simultaneously rocked Gützlaff and infused his life with urgency. Maria died giving birth to twins. Though his sorrow rendered him physically ill, he gained a valuable insight: life was too short to be spent waiting for a distant bureaucracy to grant his transfer request. His destiny lay in China, and to China he must go. When a Chinese friend offered him passage on a junk to Canton, Gützlaff donned the garb of a Chinese sailor and set sail, knowing full well the DMS would cut off his funding. Gützlaff no longer cared. God, after all, favored the bold.[46]

The junk, as it turned out, did not sail directly to Canton. Instead, it plied the Chinese coast, stopping to trade in towns as far north as Manchuria before returning south. Along the way, Gützlaff distributed tracts and dispensed medicine to a Chinese populace that, surprisingly, seemed receptive. In December 1831 an ecstatic Gützlaff stepped off the junk in Macau, eager to share his amazing discovery with his new colleagues: China was more open than previously thought. In Canton and Macau, however, he confronted a missionary operation dominated by the Morrison model. Morrison himself came out to greet the Prussian and attempted to assimilate him into the missionary culture Morrison had created. It did not take. "He would not work well, I fear, with others," Morrison wrote the LMS, since "he would be insubordinate" and "domineering."[47]

Morrison's prediction proved to be mostly, but not entirely, correct. Gützlaff could suppress his ego for the betterment of the group—provided that doing so advanced his personal goals. For example, he contributed to the *Repository* because, read in Europe and America, it could generate publicity for his missionary work. No longer funded by the DMS, Gützlaff depended on donations from Christian organizations, and so he needed to promote himself more than other missionaries did. Gützlaff also performed translation work, joining the team revising Morrison's Bible, but he did so mainly because his evangelical model required access to a ready supply of tracts.

What exactly was the Gützlaff model? Inspired by his eye-opening voyage of 1831, Gützlaff believed that a missionary must ignore Chinese injunctions restricting him to Canton and bravely seek out the millions of unsaved souls populating the coast and the interior. The missionary must not, as Morrison had done, accept that China was closed and wait passively for God to open the door. He must force the door open himself.[48]

In the early 1830s Gützlaff made several coastal expeditions that, when publicized, captivated the Protestant world. He also accepted offers to serve as interpreter for illegal expeditions organized by the BEIC and the Scottish firm of Jardine Matheson. Driven by economic concerns, these expeditions attempted to gauge Chinese demand for English textiles, access the secrets of tea production, or sell opium directly to coastal populations. Gützlaff joined them for one reason only: they offered effective vehicles for evangelical penetration. Of course, his employers paid him to communicate with the Chinese, not distribute tracts. Specifically, his job was to pacify, bribe, or intimidate suspicious Chinese officials, as the following example illustrates.[49] In 1833 the captain of a Jardine Matheson opium ship described Gützlaff's encounter with a party of Chinese officials who approached to learn the intentions of the vessel that brazenly sailed in forbidden waters. "Dressed in his best," Gützlaff went to meet them "accompanied by two boats made to appear rather imposing." Striking an indignant pose, Gützlaff "demanded their instant departure and threatened them destruction if they ever in future anchored in our neighbourhood." The "Mandareens" departed in haste, "saying they had anchored there in the dark by mistake. We have seen nothing more of them."[50]

Thanks to these opium voyages, Gützlaff distributed thousands of tracts and secured large donations from the British as his payoff. In the process, however, he had become a prime lubricant in the opium machine, prompting a troubling question: was he really accomplishing God's work or had he made a Faustian pact with Satan? The possibility undoubtedly occurred to him when he received a letter from William Jardine, requesting his presence on the *Sylph*, an opium ship preparing for a coastal voyage. It is "our earnest wish that you should not in any way injure the *grand object you have in view*," Jardine wrote, referring to Gützlaff's evangelical goal, by participating in "what by many is considered an immoral traffic." However, it is this "traffic" that generates the profits for any given expedition; "the more profitable the expedition the better we shall be able to place at your disposal a sum that may hereafter be usefully employed in furthering the *grand object you have in view*." As Gützlaff pondered the strange letter that ended where it began, he did not miss the meaning of its circularity. The ends justified the means; vice made virtue happen. Though he wrote of "a conflict in my own mind," he signed on with the *Sylph*.[51]

Two Poles

In 1832 Gützlaff dropped a bombshell. "My most sanguine expectations have been far surpassed," he proclaimed, as "*China is not shut.*" How did he know for sure? His coastal voyages had proved it, at least to his satisfaction. After recounting his triumphs in the *Repository*, he closed with a stirring call: "I have weighed the arguments for and against" and have resolved "to publish the gospel to the inhabitants of China Proper." Death, he acknowledged, was a distinct possibility. However, if it was his fate to be "blotted out from the list of mortals," he far preferred annihilation to the alternative: to grow old waiting in Canton for God's cue. "This lively hope of China's speedy deliverance from the thralldom of Satan," he continued, "prompts me to action."[52]

With these words, Gützlaff unveiled a bold new missionary model that, by spurning inaction, posed a direct challenge to the Morrison model. Missionaries could no longer afford "to wait quietly," he wrote, referring to Morrison, "deterred by the numerous obstacles which seem to forbid an entrance into the country."[53] Indeed, Gützlaff had a point. Was the Christian community really to believe that opium traders could breach Qing defenses but that disciples of Christ could not? Clearly, missionaries were not trying hard enough. Having thrown down the gauntlet, Gützlaff listened for a response. He did not have long to wait.[54]

In the United States, where years of stasis in the China field had lulled Protestant organizations to sleep, Gützlaff's rallying cry roused many to action. "The attention of the whole Christian world is turned extensively toward China," announced the *New York Observer*. "Gutzlaff declares that the nation received him with open arms," reported the *Missionary Record*. "Blot out from your missionary publications that China is shut." With his declaration of an open China, the Prussian garnered immediate and generous support from American institutions—far more than Bridgman had been able to muster. For unlike the scholarly Bridgman, the vigorous Gützlaff captured the zeitgeist of America in the 1830s. He came across as a man of the people in the age of Andrew Jackson, a bold Byronic hero in the Romantic period, and a rugged pioneer in the era of manifest destiny. If James Fenimore Cooper were to set an adventure story in China, he might model his protagonist on Gützlaff—the missionary action hero.[55]

Presented now with two models, new American missionaries had a choice to make. For some, the charismatic Gützlaff proved irresistible. When Jehu Lewis Shuck, a Baptist from Virginia, and his wife, Henrietta, arrived in Macau in 1836, he based his missionary identity on Gützlaff. "My present determination under God," he wrote, is "to get farther into this vast empire of darkness." In 1837 he left his wife with Gützlaff's second wife and chartered a boat for Hainan Island off the coast, but two pirate attacks forced him to turn back. In 1835 Gützlaff's accounts of his adventures inspired a second Baptist, Issachar Roberts of Tennessee. Upon reaching China, he became Gützlaff's right-hand man.[56]

Also cut from Gützlaff cloth, Edwin Stevens demonstrated a willingness to court danger. Trained in theology at Yale, Stevens arrived in Canton in 1832 to replace the ill David Abeel. For Stevens, the choice between the kinetic Gützlaff and the stationary Morrison was really no choice at all. While respectful of Morrison, Stevens had not traversed oceans to proselytize inside a cramped space.[57] In 1835 he eagerly joined Gützlaff on a British expedition organized to infiltrate the tea districts. Returning to Canton, Stevens judged the mission a "failure" because the men faced stiff armed resistance. After progressing up the Min River, the men found themselves under direct bombardment from soldiers firing from both banks. One ball blasted through the side of the vessel, whizzing by a prostrated Gützlaff. "The interior of China," Stevens concluded, "cannot be traversed with impunity by foreigners." Though this revelation discouraged Stevens, the Chinese people filled him with hope. When Gützlaff and he entered villages carrying boxes of tracts, friendly Chinese mobbed them. When the two returned to a village previously visited, their eyes met with a pleasing sight: "the people were in their houses reading the books." The hearts of the people swung wide open, Stevens discovered, even if the government insisted on keeping the empire shut.[58]

As for Bridgman, he was intrigued by Gützlaff but never seduced. For a brief period, he entertained hope that the two models might coexist in a state of synergy. "There are pleasing signs amid the darkness," he wrote after Gützlaff's remarkable 1831 voyage. "The long, patient, persevering efforts of one individual in acquiring and promoting an intimate knowledge of the language," he wrote, in reference to Morrison, have been joined by "the bold, adventurous voyage of another," meaning Gützlaff.[59] However, as Bridgman learned more about Gützlaff's role in opium trafficking, ambivalence crept into his tone. In 1833 he labeled Gützlaff's most recent opium junket as "disastrous but most interesting." By 1835 Bridgman's skepticism had darkened to pure negativity. Gützlaff was bad news.[60]

Making matters worse for Bridgman, the Christian world failed to see through Gützlaff's boastful bluster. Bridgman resented the charismatic Prussian for commanding the world's attention at the expense of the unostentatious Morrison. "We may not extol one course of conduct because it is novel and striking," he wrote, "nor undervalue a different one because it is humble."[61] Indeed, not lost on Bridgman was the fact that a juxtaposition of the models always worked to the Prussian's advantage. Gützlaff was active; Morrison passive. Gützlaff defiantly broke rules; Morrison obediently followed them. Gützlaff lived by the motto *Carpe diem*, or "Seize the day"; Morrison hewed to the lesser-known (and less inspiring) *Ammitte diem*, or "Let the opportunity pass." While Gützlaff, the swashbuckling Christian privateer, attacked the heart of heathenism on daring coastal raids, the scholarly druid Morrison sat in his study translating texts.

Bridgman knew that these exaggerated caricatures missed the subversive nature of his and Morrison's work. After all, when God opened China,

Westerners and Chinese alike would look in awe at their accomplishments. Right under the noses of Chinese authorities, the two had built the infrastructure for intellectual, cultural, and linguistic exchange—a fully operational system that could enable the frictionless flow of ideas between West and East. When that glorious day came, Bridgman would be ready—that is, as long as Gützlaff did not foul up the works. Though irked by Gützlaff's flamboyance, Bridgman mostly worried about the consequences of these reckless voyages to the interior. Gützlaff's disrespect for boundaries might provoke retaliatory measures from the Chinese that would adversely affect *all* missionary activities.

Sure enough, by 1835 all signs indicated that authorities had detected the unwanted presence of a Prussian bull in their China shop. That year, Peking issued imperial edicts ordering local officials to deploy military units to thwart all such incursions. The ambush on the Min River that Stevens reported had been the direct result of this crackdown. In the United States, news of these troubles gradually trickled into Protestant churches. A disenchanted David Abeel, now stateside, informed a congregation that Gützlaff had given the false impression that missionaries could rove freely. Also problematic, Gützlaff's optimistic forecasts, when printed in religious magazines, had generated unrealistic expectations with respect to converts. Not only did the tally remain low, but more to the point, Liang Afa—not Gützlaff—had secured most converts. In America disillusionment set in, interest in China subsided, and the number of donations plummeted. Like the sandalwood trade, the Gützlaff-inspired boom was followed by an inevitable bust.[62]

The Perfect Partner

Fortunately for Bridgman, at least one capable recruit fell into his orbit. In the early 1830s Bridgman began to complain of fatigue. "Learning, teaching, writing, printing," he wrote his parents, "have kept me very busy." The last item on his list, printing, taxed him most because he lacked the necessary skills. In letters to the ABCFM, he asked for a "devout" and "pious" printer, a request that, when coupled with Olyphant's financial guarantee, was granted. In 1833 the *Morrison* arrived carrying Samuel Wells Williams, a twenty-one-year-old printer from Utica, New York. Given the close quarters in which he and Bridgman lived and worked, Williams expressed relief on discovering that his partner was not a "freaky, impulsive man!" "Blessed be God for Bridgman's example and influence." Indeed, Williams conformed beautifully to Bridgman's "example." Like his mentor, he had been shaped by a strong mother. According to family legend, one Sunday in 1831, Sophia Williams had found herself bereft of money as the collection plate drew near. On the plate, she placed a slip of paper that pledged two sons to God's service.[63]

His mother's religiosity notwithstanding, Williams loved science above all else. In his teenage years, he had imagined a career collecting specimens, not souls, and dreamed of studying science at Yale. Unfortunately, his father, a printer, harbored other plans. He arranged to have Samuel learn the trade, under the expectation that his son would succeed him. Though adroit with a printing press, Williams lacked business sense, and his father reluctantly sent him to college—not Yale but a newly opened scientific college, the Rensselaer Institute. Since the Rensselaer lacked Andover's prestige and theological curriculum, Williams's tendency in Canton was to defer to Bridgman, especially on matters relating to theology and writing. That said, Williams complemented Bridgman because his expertise lay in areas where Bridgman was weak: printing and science. Along with operating Olyphant's press, Williams wrote articles for the *Repository* on China's natural history.[64]

In every way, Williams showed his willingness to inhabit Bridgman's missionary architecture, just as Bridgman had done three years earlier with Morrison. Bridgman especially enjoyed William's review of Gützlaff's *China Opened* in the *Repository*, which exposed the Prussian's grand seduction of Protestants. "Calculated to attract notice," the book broadcast the thrilling message "that China was open." Unfortunately, China chose "obstinately" to remain "shut." The hastily prepared book had other problems as well; it was sloppy, inaccurate, self-contradicting, and, in some parts, clearly plagiarized. A trained scientist, Williams eviscerated Gützlaff's natural history chapter. The devastatingly critical review closed with the following summation: "With this brief notice we dismiss *China Opened*."[65]

China was not open in the 1830s, and that was exactly the problem. Though the refutation of Gützlaff had been necessary (even satisfying, from Bridgman's perspective), it left Bridgman and the others back at square one—staring at the grim reality of a closed China. However, in the latter half of the decade, a new arrival succeeded in restoring some hope by experimenting with a novel tactic, one so simple he perhaps wondered why more missionaries had not tried it before. If a missionary could not venture out among the Chinese, could he not coax the Chinese to come to him?

Body and Soul

During the early 1830s, Bridgman repeatedly asked the ABCFM to send a physician. "He should be a first rate oculist," Bridgman advised. "While he heals the sick, & opens the eyes of the blind, he will find plenty of opportunities for distributing books." At first paying little heed to these requests, the ABCFM made an unexpected about-face in 1833 to Bridgman's delight. The board's change of heart, however, had nothing to do with Bridgman and everything to do with Gützlaff. The year 1833 marked the high point of Gützlaff mania. As donations rolled in, the ABCFM found itself in a position to grant requests that, at other times, might have fallen on deaf ears. The end result: Dr. Peter Parker would be sailing for China.[66]

Peter Parker grew up in a devout farming family in Framingham, Massachusetts, before attending Amherst in 1827. If his background sounds familiar, it should: the early curvature of Parker's life arc bears a strong resemblance to that of Bridgman. Indeed, as Clifton Phillips explains, the small agricultural villages of rural New England and western New York, with their evangelical fervor, presented a fertile field for the recruitment of missionaries, one that far surpassed that of the cosmopolitan coastal cities.[67]

Unlike Bridgman, Parker did not stay at Amherst long enough to earn a degree. Convinced that the school failed to recognize his intellectual gifts, Parker decided to drop out and continue his studies elsewhere. "I am going to leave," he informed a friend, as "the Faculty do not notice or appreciate me." "Now mark my word," he continued, revealing the white-hot ambition that glowed at his core, "you will all hear from me and regret that Peter Parker's name is not among the graduates of Amherst College." Mulling over Harvard as a potential destination, Parker was attracted to its prestige but repulsed by its Unitarianism. He preferred the stronger stuff—specifically, the Millennial theology of Hopkins. For anyone so inclined, Yale presented the best choice, and so Parker applied and was admitted in 1830. Not coming from affluence, Parker received aid from benevolent institutions and worked at a nearby school in exchange for his room and board. He also met Edwin Stevens, whom he would later join in Canton.[68]

At Yale Parker aimed for perfection. Like Bridgman, he structured his days without leaving any time for rest or play, as a letter home reveals:

> I arise at half-past five in the morning, and attend prayers in the Seminary. From this till breakfast, at half-past six, study Hebrew or Greek. From eight to ten, again study Hebrew or Greek. From ten to eleven, attend Dr. Ives' lecture on the theory and practice of medicine. From eleven to twelve I am engaged in Miss Hotchkiss' school. From twelve to one, attend Dr. Knight's lecture on anatomy. From two to three p.m., a recitation to Professor Gibbs in Hebrew or Greek. From three to four I have a class in chemistry, or Paley's Theology, then one hour for exercises, and the remainder of the day for study and attending meetings.[69]

In Parker personal ambition combined with the Protestant work ethic to form a potent internal motor. This motor powered him through what may have been the most rigorous course of study undertaken by a Yale student at the time: Parker simultaneously pursued two degrees, theology and medicine.[70]

The demands of the dual academic program pushed Parker to his limits. The Protestant work ethic, sturdy structure though it was, started to buckle under the stress he placed on it. At one point, Parker confessed to himself that he had disregarded his devotional chores to focus on medicine. The resulting anxiety waylaid him, leaving him temporarily incapacitated. "As I was upon my knees before God," he wrote, "the conviction struck my mind that I had deliberately . . . neglected my Savior . . . with a secret presumption that I might do it till I had accomplished a given end (i.e. my Medical Lectures)." Parker had forced Christ to wait while he studied medicine, and for this he experienced paralyzing guilt.[71]

Though under great strain at Yale, Parker discovered that his education provided him with a unique set of qualifications that intrigued the ABCFM. Parker's first encounter with the board took place in 1831, when Yale hosted Rufus Anderson, the board's chief secretary, who made a deep impression on him. By this time, Parker had begun to read the same religious magazines that had inspired Bridgman.[72] "If I am not deceived," Parker wrote, "there is no subject which so much interests my whole soul as the condition of the heathen. May it not be that the Great Head of the Church does intend me for this benevolent cause?"[73] In January 1834 the final piece fell into the puzzle when Parker met in New York with Olyphant, who offered passage to China later that spring. Galvanized by the prospect, Parker rushed back to Yale to accelerate his progress in both degree programs. Upon receiving his diplomas, he wrote the ABCFM to announce his readiness to depart for China.[74]

Though Yale's medical instructors passed Parker, they identified gaps in his training that they urged him to address. Specifically, they stressed his need for clinical experience. In making this recommendation, Parker's professors revealed a remarkable aspect of his medical preparation: it had included neither a clinical nor a laboratory component. Today, society would label unethical any institution granting degrees to students who had not handled a scalpel. The purely academic nature of Yale's program, however, was standard for the time. With cadavers being difficult to obtain (there was a black market for exhumed bodies), most students passed through medical school without performing a dissection. Some schools taught anatomy with papier-mâché mannequins, crude teaching props that cost less than wax models imported from Europe. As for surgery, students learned the various procedures entirely through textbooks, such as John Dorsey's *Elements of Surgery* (1813). Indeed, it was this compelling need for higher standards that provided the impetus for forming the American Medical Association in 1847.[75]

The Medical Magnet

As Parker prepared to embark, the ABCFM provided him with instructions. Unlike the instructions given to Bridgman, which had been based on the Morrison model, Parker's set reflected Gützlaff's growing importance. "Your first business," the authors wrote in deference to Morrison, "will be to acquire both the written and spoken languages," which "may require two or three years of close and unremitted study." Partway through the letter, however, Morrison's influence recedes, and his rival's vision asserts itself: "It is the wish of the Committee that you . . . take a station . . . within the limits of China" that is "recommended by Gutzlaff."[76]

The letter also revealed the board's awareness of the inner conflict that had troubled Parker at Yale. On this matter of spiritual versus medical goals, the letter not only dictated his priorities but also issued a stern warning. "The medical and surgical knowledge you have acquired, you will employ . . . in relieving the bodily afflictions of the people," the authors explained. "But these, you will never forget, are to receive your attention only as they can be made handmaids to the gospel." Though the "character of a physician" is "respectable," you must never allow it "to interfere with your character of a teacher of religion." These words turned out to be prescient; they would haunt Parker in Asia. However, in June 1834, the medical missionary possessed only optimism as his ship set sail.[77]

On board the *Morrison*, Parker read Gützlaff. The Prussian's inspirational example, he wrote, stoked the fires in his heart. Arriving in Macau in October, Parker found the Protestant missions in flux owing to the recent death of Morrison. Bridgman, the logical inheritor of the Morrison mantle, had yet to assert his leadership, perhaps in deference to the deceased missionary's son, John Robert Morrison. The younger Morrison, however, found himself in no condition to carry his father's torch, having contracted a serious illness. Samuel Wells Williams, also a member of this camp, would become a major intellectual force, but in 1834 he remained raw in terms of experience. The Morrison model, in other words, was in the process of becoming the Bridgman model, but the transition was not complete.

In contrast, Gützlaff's star neared its zenith, and Parker found himself irresistibly pulled into the Prussian's orbit. Though Parker was fresh off the boat, Gützlaff advised him to embark again immediately. Parker must sail for Singapore, where overseas Chinese would teach him their Hokien dialect without interference from Qing authorities. Though Gützlaff was correct on this point of safety, his advice was calculated to advance his own agenda. Spoken in Fujian Province (the site of Gützlaff's coastal junkets), Hokien afforded a missionary no practical benefit in Canton. The decision to study this dialect, therefore, was tantamount to choosing the Gützlaff model. Placing his trust in the Prussian, Parker sailed for Singapore in December, mere weeks after his arrival.[78]

For a reason Parker had not anticipated, Singapore failed to offer the desired language laboratory. A new force, one that would apply constant pressure on his missionary career, intruded on his plan of study: the endless river of sick. Of course, Parker had always intended to treat the ill; however, he had planned to devote no more than one hour each day or, alternatively, one day per week to seeing patients. In Singapore he discovered how naive these expectations were. As patients lined up outside his door,

Parker found himself shirking his language lessons.[79] When he did, the anxiety he had felt at Yale reared its head. "I read last evening my instructions from the Board," he wrote in March 1835, "and not without grief to find that, in the deep-growing interest I have felt for the sick and dying among the Chinese, I have . . . deviated from those instructions." To his personal horror, Parker found himself "involved in medical and surgical practice" without any way "to extricate myself." Deciding to abort the plan, Parker returned to Canton that summer.[80]

Though a failure as far as language study was concerned, the Singapore sojourn boosted Parker's confidence by providing him with the real-world medical experience he had lacked. His self-confidence soaring, Parker prepared to make his mark. On November 4, 1835, he opened the Canton Ophthalmic Hospital in a factory space rented from the hong merchant Houqua. As the hospital anchored him in Canton, the move shows he had broken free from Gützlaff's orbit and had accepted the reality of a closed China. For Parker, however, a closed China did not preclude direct evangelism, because he possessed the power to cure. Patients would come with medical problems, but they would leave with the Gospel. As the hospital's name indicates, Parker intended to specialize in eye disorders—that, at least, was the plan. Since a physician could treat cataracts with surgery, Western doctors enjoyed a substantial advantage over Chinese healers, who favored nonsurgical remedies, in ophthalmology.

Given this declared specialty, Parker had a difficult choice to make on December 27, 1835. "As I was closing the business of the day," Parker wrote, "I observed a Chinese timidly advancing into the hospital leading his little daughter, who, at first sight, appeared to have two heads." The thirteen-year-old girl, whose name was Akae, was "sadly disfigured" by a bulbous sarcomatous tumor that extended from her right temple down to her mouth (Figure 4.1). "Excited into action" four years earlier by a smallpox infection, the tumor had recently swelled, much to the distress of her parents. With nowhere to turn, they sought out Parker. Would he help their daughter?[81]

After preliminary inspection, Parker concluded that he could remove the tumor. However, before agreeing to perform the surgery, he considered the ramifications of his decision. On the one hand, his Yale training had not included a clinical component; though he had performed small surgeries in Singapore, he had never attempted a tricky operation like this. Making matters worse, Parker could not even consult an authoritative text on surgical oncology, for the simple reason that one did not exist (John Collins Warren's pioneering *Surgical Observations on Tumours* was not published until 1837).[82] Anesthesia had not yet been introduced, and he wondered whether Akae could bear the excruciating pain. Finally, he recognized the dire consequences of failure. Should the risky surgery end with Akae "dying under the knife," as he admitted was a distinct "possibility," Chinese authorities might shut down his hospital, ending his career in China. On the

Figure 4.1. Akae, patient of Dr. Peter Parker, by Lam Qua. *(Peter Parker Collection, no. 1. Harvey Cushing/John Hay Whitney Medical Library, Yale University.)*

other hand, Parker interpreted the case as "presented in divine providence," meaning that God himself had thrust the child into his path. Should he turn her away, the tumor would likely "terminate the life of the child." Parker stood as her last and only hope. "I resolved upon the undertaking."[83]

In an eight-minute operation, Parker removed the tumor from the face of the courageous girl. The surgery was a success, and Akae's life was transformed. As word of the miracle rippled through Canton, the sick and injured began to line up outside the hospital before dawn. To handle the influx of patients, Parker devised a system, which Samuel Wells Williams described. At street level, a porter handed each arrival a numbered piece of bamboo, which helped Parker treat arrivals in order. The bamboo serving as a "passport," a patient climbed to the second floor, where a staff member created a card containing all pertinent information: the patient's name, the time and date of admission, and the nature of the illness. After meeting with the patient, Parker could add new information to the card, such as a prescription or the need for a second appointment. If instructed to stay, the patient moved to a large room able to hold two hundred people. Since patients recovering from surgery required several days of bed rest, the hospital could accommodate forty overnight patients. "No branch of mission work in the East is . . . more universally successful than this," Williams observed. "Its direct use in spreading the gospel among all classes . . . has been inestimable." Using a loaded term, he credited Parker with effecting "a new opening" to China.[84]

Williams also noted that Chinese authorities and foreign merchants kept a close watch on the hospital. The former eyed with "suspicion" any missionary who had extensive contact with ordinary Chinese. The latter, fearing that a botched surgery would attract unwanted attention from angry locals and punitive officials, viewed the hospital as "hazardous."[85] After mere months, Parker converted nearly all skeptics into supporters. On Wednesdays he invited foreigners to observe surgical operations, which Robert Bennet Forbes described. "I stood by 5–6 cataract operations," he wrote, "one totally blind for twenty years." In graphic detail, Forbes explained how Parker skillfully maneuvered a needle "just under the ball of the sightless orb" of a woman. After "the film which had shut out the day was displaced," Parker "told her to look into his face which she did with great joy." The Chinese, Forbes noted, rate Parker as "little short of a deity." Houqua, recognizing the hospital's value, stopped collecting rent.[86]

Chinese authorities reached the same conclusion as Houqua. Often they favored the hospital's continuance for the simple reason that they could avail themselves of its services. One official visited with a severe case of cataracts. Though his condition appeared hopeless, a friend had told him of a doctor who had journeyed from a distant land. In the words of a lengthy ode he composed after regaining his sight, which Morrison's son translated:

A fluid, darksome and opake, long time had dimm'd my sight,
For seven revolving weary years, one eye was lost to light;
The other darken'd by a film, during three years saw no day,
High heaven's bright and gladdening light could not pierce it with its
*   ray. . . .*
O'er tens of thousands of miles of sea to inner land he's come;
His hope and aim, to heal men's pain, he leaves his native home.

When the surgery was complete ("The fragile lens his needle pierced; the dread, the sting, the pain"), Parker removed the bandages: "There came one ray—one glimmering ray, I see—I live again!" This example illustrates an important point. Though Parker regarded cataract surgery as routine, the patient with restored vision viewed it as miraculous. In this case, the cured official even tried to obtain a portrait of Parker, so that he might "bow down before it." Parker politely refused. His purpose, after all, was to inspire the worship of Christ, not himself.[87]

For cases involving large tumors, Parker sought volunteers from the merchant community. Answering the call, William Jardine and Forbes provided regular assistance. With anesthesia still years away (Parker first used ether in 1847), surgery subjected patients to several minutes of excruciating torture—and they knew it. Often, a patient would lose his nerve when he reached the operating table and beheld the tray of razor-sharp knives. As a tussle was sure to ensue, Parker could count on Forbes and Jardine to ignore the desperate caterwauling, subdue the patient, pin him onto the table, and apply the physical restraints.[88] Chinese also worked in the hospital. To ensure the hospital's continuance after his departure, Parker trained Chinese youths in the methods of Western medicine. "There are two promising youths now with me," Parker wrote in 1837, "wishing to become doctors themselves." "One of the lads is a brother of Lam Qua, a painter," who "is a great lover of the medical profession, and regrets that he is too old to become a doctor himself."[89]

As a young artist, Lam Qua had the good fortune to meet George Chinnery, an English painter who had moved to Macau to flee mounting debt and a failing marriage. Though the language barrier blocked meaningful communication, Lam Qua observed Chinnery's techniques and later became the most accomplished Chinese artist who painted in the Western tradition. Fascinated by Western medicine, Lam Qua visited the hospital with his charcoal and sketch pad. He later converted these sketches into oil paintings, producing a remarkable series that documented Parker's toughest cases. In 1838 Forbes sent a set of Lam Qua's paintings to Dr. John Collins Warren, America's foremost authority on surgical oncology, who had taken an interest in Parker.[90]

Lam Qua's rendering of Leäng Yen dramatically shows Parker's impact on individual Chinese (Figure 4.2). A married woman, Leäng Yen suffered from a massive growth clinging to her right hand. While portraying the

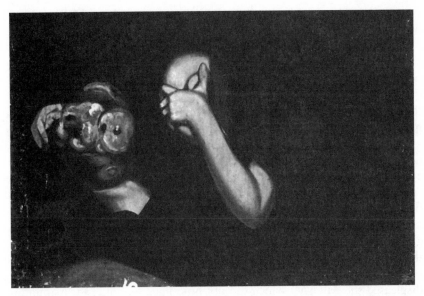

Figure 4.2. Leäng Yen, patient of Dr. Peter Parker, by Lam Qua. *(Peter Parker Collection, no. 5. Harvey Cushing/John Hay Whitney Medical Library, Yale University.)*

physical deformity itself, Lam Qua also captured the patient's traumatized psychology. As the subject obediently raises her right hand to bring the abnormality into view, her profound sense of shame compels her to shield her face from the intensity of the scientific gaze.[91] From Parker's record of the case, we know too that, when she learned of his intention to amputate her forearm (he felt certain the "disease" had penetrated the bone marrow), Leäng Yen pleaded, "No cutting!" She doubted she could endure either the painful sawing or life without her limb. She also feared her husband would abandon her, leaving her alone in world. At one point, she agreed to the surgery on the condition that Parker give her $200, a strange attempt at bargaining that left him nonplussed ("She quite misunderstood the kindness that had been shown her"). After weeks of delay, Parker performed the surgery, which he judged a success: "The prospect is that she may live for years, and enjoy good health."[92]

Conclusion

Parker transformed Leäng Yen's life, but did she accept Christ? For surgical patients, his policy was to broach the subject of religion only after a patient had recovered. While discharging Leäng Yen to her husband's care, he somewhat hastily urged the couple to consider "their obligations to the living God."[93] With Akae, Parker enjoyed a more meaningful exchange. During a follow-up visit, he "made known to her . . . the name of the Savior who died for her." "When on earth," he explained, Jesus had been fond of "taking little children in his arms & blessing them." After he asked her "if she would like to see Jesus," Akae "replied with much animation in the affirmative." "I can ask for her nothing more," Parker wrote after bidding her farewell.[94]

With other patients, Parker enjoyed even less opportunity to proselytize. With a hundred patients lining up on some mornings, he found time to introduce the Gospel only in a superficial way, if at all. For a while, he arranged for Liang Afa to distribute tracts to patients in the queue. Yet despite his best effort, Parker conceded that the ABCFM's worst fears had come true: the bodily needs of the Chinese people had utterly engulfed his spiritual goals. As late as 1839, he could not claim a single convert and frequently complained of exhaustion.[95]

The others did not fare much better. In 1835 Bridgman reported a grand total of fourteen converts for the Canton mission, a low number that seems even less impressive when one considers that the tally included Liang Afa, his wife, two children, and servant. The glaring paucity of souls displeased the ABCFM, which did not hold back its criticism. Astounding reports out of Burma inflicted further damage on the Canton group's reputation. There the stalwart Adoniram Judson famously baptized hundreds of people a year. The Canton mission, in the board's view, appeared "feeble" in contrast. With such meager results, missionaries had become demoralized by 1838. In storage rooms Christian tracts piled up, providing food for cockroaches but not nourishment for souls. Williams, who had never been ordained, began to wonder if there was any point in pursuing this goal. Frustrated by the stagnant situation, the group considered moving the operation to Singapore. American missionaries had tested three different models—those of Morrison and Bridgman, Gützlaff, and Parker. Not one had worked.

Or had they? Parker, Bridgman, and Williams influenced China in a fashion that cannot be measured by a simple conversion count. During his two decades in China, Parker would treat over fifty thousand patients, an extraordinary achievement for one man. Bridgman, with his manifold publications, built an infrastructure that would allow China and the West to communicate and understand one another. "Bridgman led the American discovery of China," Fred Drake observed, "not the maritime passages that would develop into avenues of commercial exchange, but of the broad range of elements that comprised Chinese culture and civilization."[96]

This insight applies equally to Williams. While adroitly handling the printing press, Williams spent the 1830s quietly absorbing vast amounts of information on China. In 1848 he would publish the nineteenth century's definitive book on China. In sum, the very activities the ABCFM viewed as distractions formed the core of the missionaries' legacy in China. The yield was medical, linguistic, educational, and intellectual—if not evangelical.

The board's opinion notwithstanding, all missionaries agreed that the true cause of their low conversion numbers was a closed China. When would God force open the gate? Though accepting that it was not for them, the Lord's humble servants, to ask him to expedite his holy schedule for their benefit, divine intervention is exactly what each yearned for. Just as their collective will started to falter, they saw unmistakable signs of divine activity in 1839. God was finally on the move in China, and the day for which they had devoted years of patient preparation would soon be at hand.[97]

5

Rising on Smoke

Opium and Identity in Canton

How could a doctor concentrate amid so much commotion? As Peter Parker prepared to remove the growth from Leäng Yen's hand on December 12, 1838, he tried to block out the noisy ruckus outside the hospital. Days earlier, two coolies caught with opium had, when interrogated, pointed to the American ship *Thomas Perkins* as the source. In a deliberate provocation, the viceroy had ordered the execution of a Chinese opium dealer in front of the American factory—directly beneath the Stars and Stripes. The planned strangulation, however, did not go smoothly. After irate American traders and, later, boisterous British sailors intervened to disrupt the proceedings, word of the altercation spread through the local population. Thousands of enraged Cantonese armed with rocks and bricks streamed into the square, and a melee ensued. A square that had enjoyed a century of peace erupted into bedlam. As passions flared violently on the square, within the hospital Parker coolly reported that "all was quiet" and "the operation was performed."[1]

By deciding to perform the surgery despite the tumult outside his window, Parker made a statement. If traders would only relinquish their sinful opium trade and instead treat the Chinese as he did—that is, with Christian charity—Canton would be transformed: foreigners would earn the trust of Chinese officials, the xenophobia within the local population would subside, and commerce and evangelism could prosper unhindered by ugly scenes such as this. Parker, however, recognized the wishful nature of his thinking. Merchants were too invested in opium to relinquish the trade voluntarily. They would bow only to a superior force.

This chapter explains the vast importance of opium to Americans in China. By the late 1830s, all Americans either defined themselves, or were defined by others, according to their relationship to the narcotic. The majority of traders dreamed of becoming self-made men; they regarded opium, or rather the wealth derived from it, as fueling their rise in the world. Anticipating critics, these men steeled themselves against attack by developing justifications for their controversial import. Sure enough, those aspiring to join the *moneyed aristocracy* received a challenge from a vocal cadre of Christian merchants who used opium to effect a different form of upward mobility. Having forsaken opium's easy profits, they claimed exclusive membership in a *moral aristocracy* based on their opposition to the drug. In sum, one group sold opium and another protested its sale; yet all Americans viewed opium as indispensable to their plans to self-actualize.

Within the foreign factories, these two factions coexisted in a state of uneasy tension. However, the *Thomas Perkins* incident signaled the beginning to the end of the stalemate. As opium streamed into China and silver leaked out, the emperor recognized the unsustainable nature of the economic status quo. After first flirting with legalization, he sent Lin Zexu to Canton in 1839 to abolish the trade. For the plaintive antiopium faction, Lin's arrival brought true catharsis; they saw him as a deliverer sent to reward the virtuous and punish the wicked in what amounted to Judgment Day in Canton. However, the British dashed their hopes for a satisfying resolution by vacating Canton and preparing for war. Adding salt to the moral faction's wounds, opportunistic American traders took advantage of Britain's temporary absence to seize control of shipping. The sinners, in other words, had found a way to benefit from the crackdown. As for the missionaries, the strange unfolding of events filled them with horror and wonder. Though appalled by Britain's unjust war, they discerned the hand of God forcing China open.

Rise of an Opium Trader

No American handled as much opium as Robert Bennet Forbes. His career illustrates the powerful role the drug could play in an individual's self-invention. By the time Forbes reached boyhood, his father had already failed in life. Thomas Perkins, recognizing his sister's predicament, took a special interest in her sons. After a period of observation, Perkins concluded that Forbes had a sharp mind and adventuresome spirit. One fateful day in 1817, Perkins took his thirteen-year-old nephew on a seemingly innocent stroll along the wharf. On the deck of the *Canton Packet*, Perkins abruptly presented the boy with a loaded (and probably premeditated) question: "Well, Ben, which of these ships do you intend to go in?" Unbeknownst to Forbes, his answer would determine the trajectory of his life. "I am ready to go on this one," he replied eagerly, referring to the *Canton Packet* itself. To the boy's delight, Perkins ordered him to inform his mother that he would soon be shipping out.

Though starting out as a cabin boy, Forbes benefited immensely from his family ties. When the *Packet* reached Canton, he enjoyed the privilege of living and working with John Perkins Cushing. Impressed with his cousin,

Cushing wrote Perkins to say that Forbes was "without exception, the finest lad I have ever known." Imagining Forbes as his eventual replacement, Cushing urged him to remain in Canton to learn the trade. Forbes, however, planned on becoming a sea captain, and he chose to return to his ship. Before Forbes's second voyage to China in 1819, Perkins presented him with a box of silver dollars, instructing him to "invest it in such articles as you may think will answer." Forbes would learn the China trade by trying his hand at the buying and selling of goods. "Attend to my wishes," Perkins admonished, "and you may be sure of my support and patronage." With his powerful uncle putting wind in his sails, Forbes rapidly climbed the nautical ladder, serving as second mate for his third voyage to China and as first mate for his fourth. In 1824, one day after his father's death, Forbes embarked on his fifth voyage—this time as the captain of the *Levant*, his uncle's favorite ship. He had recently turned twenty.[2]

For Captain Forbes, the voyage of the *Levant* revealed the machinery of his uncle's opium business. After reaching the Pearl River Delta, he learned that Cushing had special plans for the vessel: it was to anchor at Lintin and become the firm's opium storeship. Deeming Forbes too young to administer opium sales, Cushing transferred him to another vessel. A seed, however, had been planted. In 1826 Forbes returned to Canton, where he presented Cushing with a novel proposal: if Cushing would lend him a vessel, he would ferry opium traders along the coast of China. Cushing agreed, and Forbes took great delight in guiding a vessel on this exciting mission. "This was one of the earliest trips," Forbes later wrote, "made up the coast by an American vessel." In 1828 Forbes captained the *Danube* to Smyrna, Turkey, carrying a little silver, some coffee, and a large bill drawn on Barings. The coffee turned out to be a bogus cargo, included to give an opium voyage a veneer of legitimacy. In Smyrna, Forbes unloaded the coffee and used his credit with Barings to purchase opium.[3]

By the late 1820s opium had taken hold of Forbes's imagination, grafting itself onto his dreams. After the drowning of Bennet's brother Thomas Forbes in 1829, just as he expected appointment as taipan, Bennet was offered the post. Though acceptance would have cinched his fortune, he declined because he had become wed to a different vision of self-actualization. "I had looked forward to the command of the Lintin station-ship as the summit of my ambition." When a propitious moment presented itself, Forbes hatched his plan. In 1830 he took a trip to New York to inspect the *Milo*, which he intended to establish as the new Lintin storeship—pending, of course, his uncle's approval. Returning home in a mail coach, Forbes was passed, purely by happenstance, by a coach conveying Thomas Perkins and William Sturgis, one of America's largest traders. To Forbes, who described himself as driven to "accomplish the destiny to which God and my uncles had con-signed me," this coincidence seemed fated.[4]

His "destiny" beckoned, and he had to act fast. "I felt that my fate depended on catching them," Forbes wrote, "and I immediately made sail in pursuit." Perkins and Sturgis stopped in Walpole to pass the night, and Forbes did too. Dusty from the trip, he "went to a hair-dresser's, and had a wash, bought a new collar and a tooth-brush," before reaching their lodging house. He then nonchalantly strode inside and expressed disingenuous surprise at meeting Perkins and Sturgis. As he had hoped, the two invited him to dinner. Later and in private, Forbes laid out his plan to Sturgis, whose vessel the *Tartar* currently occupied the Lintin station. Receiving Sturgis's blessing, Forbes next approached his uncle. Though Perkins admired his nephew's gumption, he predictably shook his head, informing Forbes that "Sturgis now has control at Lintin." After Forbes informed his uncle of Sturgis's prior consent, Perkins not only embraced the idea but agreed to furnish a brand-new vessel, one superior to the *Milo*. "I do not recall any night of my life," Forbes wrote, "when I have been blessed with more happy dreams of prosperity." Destiny had opened a window, and Forbes had leaped through. Shortly thereafter, a shipyard began to build the aptly named *Lintin*.[5]

Did Forbes's opium scheme yield the quick fortune of his dreams? After spending just eighteen months selling opium on the *Lintin*, Forbes accumulated enough wealth to last a careful person a lifetime. As long as he avoided foolish investments and extravagance, he could afford to purchase a fine home, start a family, and dedicate his free time to his passion— the building and sailing of boats. As Forbes prepared to leave China in 1832, his future appeared incandescently bright. "His horizon is now so cloudless," wrote a friend, "that he fears there must be a dark day in store for him."[6] His instincts proved correct.

An Opium Scourge?

This story of a young man taking the initiative to realize his dream puts a smile on one's face—that is, until one remembers that the *Lintin* existed solely to pump narcotics into China. Forbes's rise, in other words, required that scores of anonymous Chinese become users. Decades later, while composing his memoirs, Forbes revisited his involvement in the opium trade. He did not, when young, question the morality of his actions because the people, companies, and countries he revered were also importing the drug. "I considered it right to follow the example" of the British East India Company (BEIC), European nations, and New England's merchant families.[7] With these paragons of global trade casting their combined luminescence on the opium trade, could one really expect an impressionable young man to question the morality of the trade?

In his memoirs Forbes reflected on the legality of the opium trade and the drug's effect on Chinese people. Concerning the legality, he claimed not to have violated a single law. Because Chinese law extended only as far as territorial boundaries, opium selling was a "legitimate business" so long as "the drug was sold on the coast, outside the professed jurisdiction of China." The onus for breaking the law, Forbes implied, rested on the Chinese smugglers who carried opium into China and the corrupt mandarins who accepted bribes. Turning to opium's "effect on the people," Forbes admitted, "There can be no doubt that it was demoralizing," adding the qualifier "to a certain extent." He then claimed opium "had a much less deleterious effect" than rice liquor.[8]

In comparing opium to alcohol and citing the limits of China's jurisdiction, Forbes offered the standard pair of exculpatory arguments that traders used to defend their business. It is "a fair, honorable and legitimate trade," wrote Forbes's friend, Warren Delano of Russell and Company, no worse than "the importation of wines, Brandies & spirits" into the United States.[9] Another Russell employee, William Hunter, pushed the comparison further. "Compared with the use of spirituous liquors in the United States," he argued, "the evil consequences" of opium were "infinitesimal."[10] That China traders parroted one another suggests they had developed, in anticipation of probing questions, a set of rehearsed answers.

Were Forbes and others downplaying opium's destructive influence to sanitize their chosen pathway to wealth? Our knee-jerk reaction is to doubt their veracity because their likening of opium to alcohol is inconsistent with the commonly held assumption that opium smoking inevitably caused physical and financial ruin. However, some historians have contested the opium-as-scourge thesis. According to R. K. Newman, nineteenth-century missionaries exaggerated opium's harmful physiological effects to advance their reformist agenda. They publicized a highly sensationalized depiction of the opium addict as a "degenerate creature" with "shrivelled limbs, tottering gait, sallow visage, feeble voice and death-boding glance of eye." Though the scientific evidence is not conclusive, Newman finds that it does not support this portrayal. Why then has the opium-as-scourge thesis gained such wide acceptance? Historians adopted it because it fit perfectly into a larger indictment of Western imperialism.[11]

Jonathan Spence neither endorses nor refutes the thesis in his study on opium smoking in China. He moves beyond the stereotypical image of the tragic junkie by cataloging the diverse motivations behind opium consumption. Soldiers smoked it to alleviate the boredom of military life. Opium afforded those in power a temporary refuge from the pressures of governance. For low-level literati and officials, it offered an escape from a disappointing or vexing career. Merchants used it to sharpen mental acuity during business dealings. Similarly, students believed it enhanced their powers of concentration during examinations. For the affluent with abundant leisure, an opium habit pleasurably filled empty hours. Poorer classes of Chinese—such as coolies, boatmen, or chair bearers—took opium to ease their pain after strenuous labor. Chinese of all classes used it medicinally to treat illnesses, and most considered it an aphrodisiac. What was the physical effect of opium usage on these users? According to Spence, those "who ate regularly and well did not show physical deterioration resulting from their addiction." That said, he did not consider opium benign. The poor in particular suffered because they devoted scarce resources to opium that might have been used to buy nourishment.[12]

Even if we do not know for certain what the impact of opium was, we do know that retired opium traders regarded their careers as problematic. Later in life, they were loath to reflect on their opium businesses, as Forbes discovered in the 1870s. Intending to write a history of Russell and Company, he contacted over a hundred former associates to solicit their recollections. The response was underwhelming. His old friend Warren Delano sent only a skeletal outline of his career that left out any mention of opium. This ranked as one of the better submissions; the others provided less or nothing at all. Why had these ex-traders adopted a close-lipped policy? In the 1870s these men headed prominent families and enjoyed reputations as elite citizens. With their collective silence, they sent Forbes an unmistakable message: nobody wanted to revisit the controversial past. Their determined reticence prompted Forbes to rethink his project. "The only thing I fear," he admitted to Delano, "is that in giving a sketch of the causes and effects of the opium traffic . . . I may say too much." Forbes abandoned the project, and in his memoir the usually candid Forbes opted to repeat the standard justifications for the trade.[13]

However, back in 1839, Forbes's youthful idealism had worn off but the self-protecting tendencies of affluence had not set in. Only this middle-aged Forbes could offer an unvarnished opinion of the matter, which he did in a letter to his wife from Canton. "I will tell you something about" the opium trade so "that you may speak learnedly." The trade, he frankly admitted, has been "demoralizing the minds, destroying the bodies, & draining the country of money." Though not expressing remorse, Forbes acknowledged opium's ill effects. He closed the letter by reminding his wife that his "first fortune" (which he subsequently lost) had come through opium sales, which complicated his message. Opium had damaged China— that much was sure. However, since it had expedited Forbes's rise, his wife should tread gingerly if the topic came up.[14]

Opium and Competencies

Not all opium traders pursued personal fortunes. As Forbes's correspondence illustrates, opium could also play a role in the less ambitious plans of traders. In middle age, Forbes saw himself less as the risk-taking captain and more as the risk-averse family man. Content in his life as a husband and father, he grudgingly returned to China in 1838 to secure not a fortune but a competency, or earnings sufficient to allow his family to live without financial worry. Though competencies differed in amount, most hovered between $100,000 and $200,000. Writing to his wife, Forbes expressed his wish "to stay only long enough to get my Competency," which he set at $180,000, and not "an hour after."[15] Like all traders chasing this financial goal, he measured the distance between Canton and Boston in neither miles nor months of sea travel. Home lay $180,000 away.

When we recognize that many traders sought competencies, we can understand opium's seductive power. The drug beckoned the lonely trader counting his earnings until he could head home. Confined to the foreign factories, these men longed for a more open China that would allow them to sell American goods in several ports and purchase tea not through hong merchants who took a cut but directly from inland merchants in the tea districts. The Canton System, in other words, retarded their progress toward that glimmering goal—earning the competency that would allow them to rejoin their families. During the seven years in Canton of Ned Delano, Warren's younger brother, four of his five sisters died. Is it any wonder he would refer to Canton as a "vile hole"? Frustrated by Chinese regulations, he looked favorably on any commodity, even an illegal one, that could hasten his return from exile. For him, the opium trade sped up profit making, thus counteracting the artificial slowdown imposed by the Canton System.[16]

To explain the almost irresistible allure of opium, William Hunter of Russell and Company drew a parallel between its sellers and consumers, both of whom nursed addictions. For the "foreign *exile*" opium offered an "easy and agreeable business" that allowed him to erase debts and accelerate profits. Before long, this trader acquired a psychological and economic dependence on opium that eerily resembled the physical dependence of Chinese smokers. "His sales were pleasantness and his remittances were peace," Hunter wrote. "Transactions seemed to partake of the nature of the drug; they imparted a soothing frame of mind."[17]

No trader pursued a competency with more dogged determination than William Low. In the company of his wife, Abigail, and his niece, Harriet, Low sailed for China in 1829 with a clear objective: to earn $100,000. Debarking in Macau, Low spent only a day making living accommodations for Abigail and Harriet before departing for Canton to head the Russell office. Time, after all, was money. In the early 1830s Low struggled to process the relentless flow of paperwork resulting from Russell's recent absorption of the Perkins trade. With office resources severely strained, need compelled Low to hire anyone with basic business skills, a group that included William Wood.[18]

William Hunter described William Wood as a Romantic drifter. "He was a person of great versatility," Hunter wrote, who "abounded in wit, was well read, and of no fixed purpose."[19] In describing Wood as lacking a "fixed purpose," Hunter no doubt referred to the dilettantism that prevented Wood from mastering a vocation. John Perkins Cushing he was not. In rebuttal Wood might have argued that he did have the ability to concentrate but only on things that mattered in life, such as writing, science, and art. His talents converged in *Sketches of China* (1830), a book he wrote and illustrated that covered Chinese culture and natural history. Highly opinionated, Wood also launched two newspapers in Canton, including the *Canton Register* in 1827, the port's first English-language newspaper. These newspapers provided vehicles for his strong views on the Canton System, BEIC, and opium trade, all of which he despised.[20]

Canton's Renaissance man struggled as an accountant for Russell, a tedious job that demanded long hours and attention to detail. Bored by his work, Wood allowed his mind to wander. One day a client entered the office requesting bills on London. As Wood drew these up, his attention drifted to a group of sea captains discussing Chinese furniture. After finishing the bills in mindless fashion, Wood dropped them off in Low's office for signatures. From that office came a roar of laughter, which was followed by Low. "I doubt if Baring's will accept this," Low said as he showed Wood the bills, which designated "lacquered ware boxes" rather than silver dollars as their unit of currency. Low's good-humored response aside, the office chief was growing irritated by the inefficiency of the distracted William Wood.[21]

Making matters worse, Low learned in 1832 that Wood was wooing his niece. Attractive, charming, and one of the few unmarried Caucasian females in Macau, Harriet also had a free spirit that infatuated Wood. In 1830 she caused an international incident by infiltrating the foreign factories disguised as a man. Detecting her presence, Chinese authorities brought the entire Sino-American trade to a standstill pending her removal. Though the brazen act left her uncle aghast, it captivated Wood. Making frequent visits to her home, ostensibly to provide drawing lessons, Wood fell madly in love, and she reciprocated his affections. Since most men in the region cared only for money, Harriet appreciated Wood's fertile imagination and the noble stands against injustice he took in his second newspaper, the *Courier*. In 1832 the firebrand Wood provoked a confrontation with the rival *Register*, accusing it of being a tool of the BEIC. His honor offended, the *Register*'s editor challenged Wood to a duel. Never one to back down, Wood accepted, a move that paid off twofold. Not only did his opponent withdraw but his act of bravery impressed Harriet Low.[22]

Sensing the imminence of a marriage proposal, William Low moved to intervene. He strongly disapproved of a match that would join his sparkling niece to someone he viewed as a mere instigator, utterly lacking in prospects. No mere stodgy killjoy, Low sincerely worried about the financial future of Harriet, whose father had failed as a merchant. Low had promised to look after her, and he felt obliged to sever the attachment. In the fall of 1832 he pressured Harriet to abandon Wood. Though she reluctantly complied, the separation caused great anguish, as her journal entries make clear. "Oh *romance*, where dost thou dwell? Our dearest and fondest hopes are often dashed for the want of the *filthy lucre*," and "even our affections have . . . to be sacrificed." Hoping to cheer up his disconsolate niece (and unaware of her "filthy lucre" comment), Low took Harriet on an excursion to Lintin, thinking that a few days aboard a floating narcotics depot might help her forget her antiopium lover. It reminded her of him more.[23]

If Low had miscalculated Harriet's emotional state in planning the Lintin vacation, the error was understandable owing to the tremendous pressure under which he labored. As he processed the paperwork side of Russell's trade, much of which involved opium, Robert Bennet Forbes handled the genuine article on the company's Lintin storeship—the goose that laid silver eggs. To Low's displeasure, Forbes kept most of these eggs for himself, allowing precious few to roll toward the Canton office. "The ship is supported mainly by our opium, our patronage & our exertions," Low griped in a letter to the retired Cushing. "We can see no reason why we should continue to labour for the individual interest of Cap[tain] F[orbes]."[24]

Low had little time to grumble about Forbes. At Russell's understaffed office, the overwhelming cataract of trade continued to pummel him. Working continuously, Low stopped only for meals, for sleep, and for brief visits to Macau to check up on his wife and niece. Each night, as his head struck the pillow after another seventeen-hour workday, he perhaps contemplated the role of opium in his life. By expediting the attainment of his competency, and thus enabling his entry into the respectable class, was opium making the man? Or was it, by pushing him to the brink of physical exhaustion, killing the man?

A healthy human being can sustain such a pace for quite a while, assuming that all other areas in his life remain stable. Unfortunately, such was not the lot of William Low. In 1830 he learned to his horror that his wife's brother had been indicted in the murder of a Salem sea captain. After the courts found his brother-in-law guilty and hanged him, Low helplessly watched as his wife descended into depression, withdrawing almost entirely from Macau society. On top of the emotional strain placed on his family by the tragedy, Low also contended with the financial fallout: he was now obligated to support her entire side of the family. Of course, it did not help matters that the penniless Wood was courting his niece. The weight from these combined burdens proved more than even the sturdy constitution of William Low could bear. On September 9, 1833, he returned to Macau, in the words of Harriet, "looking like death." The family sailed for home in November, but Low would not live to see America. He passed away in Cape Town.[25]

Moral Ascension

Low, Forbes, and dozens of others hitched their personal ambitions to the opium trade. For a smaller group of traders, however, opium enabled upward mobility of a different sort. By refusing to traffic in it, and by broadcasting their opposition, these merchants established themselves as Canton's moral aristocracy. The most vocal members of this faction worked for D.W.C. Olyphant, known in Canton as "Holy Joe." A missionary in merchant's garb, Olyphant first worked in the New York firm of Thomas Smith. He might have switched careers in 1826, when Smith's spectacular gamble to control New York's tea market ended in bankruptcy. "I suspect Holy Joe's time has really come," wrote Benjamin Wilcocks, an opium trader from Philadelphia. "The best thing he can do next is to take up Morrison's trade"—missionary work. Wilcocks spoke too soon. Olyphant emerged from Smith's wreck prepared to launch his own firm, Olyphant and Company. He and his partner, Charles Talbot, prospered to such a degree that, in the 1830s, the company could fund the assembly of much of the missionary apparatus.

That decade, Olyphant, the merchants in his employ, and the missionaries he supported formed a God squad. A thorn in the side of all opium traders, Olyphant and Company had an especially antagonistic relationship with Russell and Company. In a memo, John Murray Forbes advised his colleague Augustine Heard to remain "on your guard" with respect to Olyphant. "Ye gods great & small, protect me from the all hallowing influence of holy Joe," whose ships are "commanded by J-C [Jesus Christ]," "officered by Angels & manned by Saints." An Olyphant ship, Forbes jested, plies the seas with "omnipotence," "flies instead of sails," and becomes "regenerated."[26]

In the 1830s Olyphant and Talbot groomed Charles W. King, the son of Olyphant's cousin, to head the Canton office. Precocious and ambitious, King made his first voyage to China in 1829 at the age of twenty. Taking King under his wing, Olyphant helped him resist the temptation to sell opium. "Happily, the wise and Christian guardianship" of Olyphant, King recalled, "kept me aloof from the seductive traffic."[27] Inspired by America's temperance movement, King launched vigorous antiopium campaigns in Canton. In 1837 he urged all merchants to pledge to abandon a trade "fraught with evils commercial, political, social, and moral." After King called a public meeting to discuss his proposed pledge, the *Canton Press* commented that "we do not know of *any one* permanently established here who could possibly give the pledge—*all* being more or less interested in the drug." King met with defeat. "It is scarcely necessary to add," he wrote, "that the call for a public meeting failed."[28]

On the opium question, King summoned evangelical fervor that, paradoxically, even missionaries could not match. American missionaries exhibited a careful reserve on the subject, at least publicly, that requires explanation. Since they did not generate revenue themselves, and since the ABCFM funded only some of their operating costs, missionaries depended on donations. Who in Canton had money to spare? Missionaries solicited aid from the largest opium traders—William Jardine, James Matheson, and Lancelot Dent. To avoid offending these donors, Bridgman and Williams adopted a guarded approach when discussing opium in their *Chinese Repository*, decrying the trade without naming names. Beholden to no master other than his Lord, King refused to compromise his language.[29] Showing no fear of ruffling feathers, he reminded perpetrators, past and present, of their sin. In 1838 King raised the topic of opium in Robert Bennet Forbes's presence, hoping to get under his skin by making insinuations about his "former life at Lintin." Forbes found the sanctimonious King insufferable.[30]

The Quaker

Not all opium objectors had backgrounds in mainstream Protestantism. Nathan Dunn was born in 1782 to a farming family in Salem County, New Jersey. His father died shortly after his birth, and his widowed mother remarried and became a Quaker minister. In 1802 Dunn moved to Philadelphia, where he learned business by apprenticing to a merchant. Feeling confident, he and a partner launched their own company in 1805, the same year that the Quaker Monthly Meeting of Friends received him as a member. However, over the course of the next decade, Dunn incurred an alarming level of debt. In 1816 the Monthly Meeting expelled him on the grounds that he had become "embarrassed in his affairs." Though adopting a harsh tone in its dismissal, the Monthly Meeting held out the possibility of future reinstatement: "We desire that he may experience a qualification to be rightly restored." To redeem himself, Dunn would need to engineer a moral as well as a monetary recovery (the two were linked), and that is what he set out to do.[31]

The city of Stephen Girard, Philadelphia presented numerous examples of men who had thrived in the China trade. While planning to enter it himself, Dunn lacked the start-up capital needed to prepare a vessel. For assistance, he turned to his friend and creditor, John Field, who had previously traded in Canton. "I proposed this voyage to him," Dunn wrote, "and though he at the time had no intention to make another voyage to China, he finally acquiesced on the condition that" all profits help "liquidate a debt I owed him." In 1818 Dunn embarked for Canton as supercargo of the aptly named *Hope*.[32]

In Canton Dunn faced a quandary. Like all traders, he pursued a financial goal; unlike them, however, he adhered to a strict Quaker code that forbade him from seeking wealth in an immoral fashion. Somehow, Dunn had to get rich quickly *and* play by the rules, a feat few had pulled off. Out of this conundrum, innovation was born. Dunn identified a pocket of hidden demand that his peers had overlooked. "I soon found . . . that there was an opening for . . . different kinds of British goods," Dunn recalled, "and that by procuring them . . . better calculated for the Chinese wants" he could secure "a fair profit." Hoping to capitalize on his insight, Dunn sailed to England where he located manufacturers willing to supply him with English goods modified for Chinese tastes. This task complete, he set into motion his triangular enterprise. His vessels would carry American goods to England where the cargoes would be sold, the profits then purchasing these specialized English manufactures. The ships would then embark for

RISING ON SMOKE • 121

Canton, where Dunn, permanently stationed, would exchange British wares for Chinese goods for the American market. Exchanging goods at three ports, Dunn could not only achieve the elusive "triple golden round of profits" but do so without selling opium.[33]

For the next eight years, Nathan Dunn resided in Canton, becoming rich through his triangular trade. During this time, he remained an outspoken critic of the opium trade. "Opium is a poison," Dunn believed, "destructive alike of the health and morals of those who use it habitually." The trade in opium, therefore, "is nothing less than making merchandise of the bodies and souls of men." Though Dunn amassed a fortune without opium, he could not have accomplished his next objective without it—or rather, without the controversy opium sparked. In the late 1820s Dunn assembled a collection of Chinese artifacts that, at the time, possessed no equal in the West. Indeed, the BEIC had tried but failed to obtain a Chinese collection of its own, this despite the vast resources at its disposal.[34]

How did Dunn achieve such a remarkable feat? Like everyone in Canton, Dunn accepted the sad but obvious truth that opium possessed value because one could exchange it for silver. Unlike most others, Dunn figured out that antiopium views could also function as a tradable commodity, something that could be exchanged for special favors. Dunn forged friendships with Chinese officials who appreciated both his interest in Chinese culture and his outspoken opposition to opium. These men, along with a couple of hong merchants, helped Dunn obtain artifacts from all over China. Dunn also benefited from his friendship with William Wood, who shared his views on opium. Wood contributed to the effort by training Chinese agents to find, handle, and bring back specimens of natural history for the collection—plants, animals, fish, fowl, and insects.[35]

With his colossal collection packed away, Dunn departed China for good in 1831. Though heavily in debt when he had left Philadelphia more than twelve years earlier, he returned home one of the city's wealthiest citizens, able to pay creditors and restore his good name. In 1838 he opened the Chinese Museum, which offered Americans their first comprehensive exhibition of Chinese culture. Dunn had not only won redemption but also realized his dream to re-create China through objects. He had used opium, or rather the opium controversy, to effect a stunning personal transformation.[36]

The Failed Legalization Movement

According to one source, word of Nathan Dunn's stand on opium traveled all the way to Peking, where the Daoguang emperor took note.[37] If true, the monarch must have regarded Dunn as a pleasing anomaly, because most of the intelligence he received pegged foreign merchants as the root cause of a vast problem. By 1836 both the state treasury and the overall economy of China had begun to suffer noticeably from the outflow of silver. That year, the emperor held opium conferences at which he asked trusted advisers to present solutions. By this time, he had become convinced of the ineffectiveness of a trade embargo. An embargo would precipitate a dramatic showdown with Britain, which China could win only if backed by a strong military—something the emperor knew he did not have. Thus, when the opium debate began, he was inclined to listen to advisers within the pragmatist camp who favored the legalization of opium.

A leading advocate of this policy, Ruan Yuan received a summons to present the case for legalization. The former viceroy of Guandong and Guanxi Provinces (1817–1826), Ruan Yuan had experience dealing with opium smuggling, which he did not believe could be stopped. He endorsed a proposal for legalization previously submitted to the Qing court. If opium were legalized, advocates asserted, the government could generate revenue by taxing it. Furthermore, to stop the hemorrhaging of silver, a new law might require the implementation of a barter system in all opium transactions; instead of silver, Chinese opium dealers would purchase the drug using tea or silk as their medium of exchange. Finally, China might consider harvesting its own opium, which would prevent profits from fleeing the country on foreign ships. Deng Tingzhen, the current viceroy, sent a letter declaring his support of legalization. In Canton, Charles Elliot, Britain's superintendent of trade, received the welcome news from an informant that the emperor was on the verge of legalizing opium.[38]

Later in 1836, however, the emperor abruptly abandoned legalization. A rival political faction, the Spring Purification circle, had dissuaded him from following the course recommended by pragmatists. According to the historian James Polachek, the Spring Purification circle was composed mainly of activist literati whose disappointing careers had left them feeling disaffected. Though starting out as a fringe movement, this faction infiltrated the emperor's inner core of advisers. From this privileged position, it brought to the emperor's attention intelligence gathered in Canton—intelligence that cast the pragmatists in an unfavorable light. During the Terranova affair (the sailor hanged for murder in 1821), Ruan Yuan had uncovered evidence linking Houqua to the opium trade. Though he had publicly humiliated Houqua, he had opted not to prosecute the case further, choosing instead to use his evidence to gain leverage over the merchant. Predictably, Houqua proceeded to make large "philanthropic" donations in support of Ruan Yuan's initiatives, funding among other things an academy that educated students according to Ruan Yuan's realist school of statecraft. Ruan Yuan, in sum, had used money linked to opium to secure his legacy.

When Spring Purification officials presented their evidence, the emperor regarded it as damning. Unaware of what had transpired up north, Deng Tingzhen waited anxiously in Canton. As the official most directly affected by the emperor's decision, he wondered how his letter favoring legalization had been received in the Qing court. In the fall of 1836, he received devastating instructions from the capital. Instead of laying the groundwork for legalization, Deng was ordered to begin devising ways to stop opium trafficking. Having no choice but to comply, Deng responded vigorously to any infraction involving opium, as his handling of the *Thomas Perkins* affair demonstrates.[39]

The *Thomas Perkins* Affair

On December 3, 1838, Chinese authorities apprehended two coolies carrying suspicious boxes that turned out to contain opium. When interrogated, the frightened men explained how they had come by the contraband. Hwang Aseën, a Chinese merchant, had approached James Innes, a Scottish trader, with silver for an opium purchase. Innes had ordered the two coolies to secure opium for Hwang from the *Thomas Perkins* (not named after Thomas Handasyd Perkins), consigned to the American Charles Talbot. The hong merchant Punhoyqna, who secured the vessel, had already certified the ship as free of contraband. After reviewing the case, Viceroy Deng indicted Talbot, Innes, and Punhoyqna. While condemning Punhoyqna to the pillory, Deng used the occasion to rebuke all hong merchants for their complicity. "Being owners of these factories," how was it that they "have neither seen nor heard anything of such transactions?" As for Talbot and Innes, Deng expelled them from Canton forever. Refusing to turn himself in, Innes holed up in his factory, compelling the hong merchants (who needed to demonstrate their toughness before the viceroy) to threaten to "pull down the house in which he lives."[40]

Talbot chose not to hide. A Christian trader with impeccable antiopium credentials, he knew that somebody's mistake or lie had ensnared him in China's latest dragnet. Professing his innocence in a letter to Deng, Talbot insisted that the *Thomas Perkins* had brought only rice. Learning that neither Talbot nor Innes admitted guilt, Deng responded with outrage. From his perspective, he had demonstrated "great leniency," and so the foreigners ought to consider themselves "fortunate in so escaping the net" after committing such a heinous crime. Instead of expressing gratitude, the guilty ones spoke of the "false evidence" presented against them. "This is the perfection of stupidity," he fulminated, "most worthy of detestation!" Deng ordered all trade suspended until he could take the two men into custody.[41]

To demonstrate his resolve, Deng also arranged for a drug dealer to be executed in front of the American factory. By staging the execution at this location, he hoped to lay the opium problem, literally, on the doorstep of American traders, since one of their ships was thought to have brought the opium. The move, however, proved to be too incendiary. After the executioner arrived with Ho Laoukin, a drug dealer (who bore no relation to this case), and began setting up the strangulation apparatus, William Hunter and several other traders challenged the proceedings: they knocked down the tent, trampled on the poles, and demanded the execution take place elsewhere. At this point, a gang of British sailors on shore leave physically assaulted the execution party. Throughout the scuffle, Ho Laou-kin, who had been sedated on opium, watched with glazed-over eyes.[42]

As word of the altercation spread through Canton, an enraged mob of local Chinese streamed into the square. Soon the square teemed with rioters who pushed and shoved, swung fists, and hurled rocks and bricks. "There were without doubt eight or ten thousand of the vilest of the population," Hunter recalled, "seemingly bent on the destruction of the 'foreign devils.'" Making matters worse, Chinese authorities vacated the square, abandoning the foreign community to "the mercy of the mob," which began to use a battering ram to force its way into foreign residences. Hunter knew it was time to act. Taking to the roofs, he and a fellow American traveled by sprints and leaps to the factory of Houqua. Finding the old man in a state of "trepidation," they urged him to call for help, which he did by sending a messenger to the magistrate. Shortly thereafter, soldiers burst into the square, banging gongs and cracking whips to disperse "the rabble."[43]

After the riot, C. W. King renewed his antiopium crusade, urging foreigners to view the incident as a sign of dark events to come. King also defended Deng's deliberate provocation, insisting that it was not intended as "a disrespect to the flags," as many thought. Instead, Deng was trying to teach a lesson by "holding up before the eyes of the introducers of opium . . . one of the wretched victims of their seductions."[44] For his part, Deng mostly agreed with this interpretation of his demonstration. "It was designed to strike observation," he insisted, "to arouse careful reflection, and to cause all to admonish and warn one another."[45]

Unfortunately for Deng, he had acted on flawed evidence. In the riot's wake, the hong merchants uncovered fresh information after conducting an investigation. An interview with Innes, who truly was connected to the confiscated opium, revealed that a different vessel had conveyed it, not the *Thomas Perkins*. Learning of these new findings, Deng saw fit not just to vindicate Talbot but to commend him: Talbot "has acted the part of an upright foreigner." Unfortunately for Deng, his days as viceroy were numbered. His reversal on Talbot's status, though the right thing to do, made him appear to have bungled the case. More importantly, Deng belonged to the losing political faction. An ally of Ruan Yuan, he was on record for favoring legalization when the emperor had shifted to the hard-line policy of the Spring Purification circle. Someone loyal to that movement would handle China's opium problem.[46]

Enter the Commissioner

For information on the *Thomas Perkins* incident, the foreign community turned to the *Repository*. Williams and Bridgman composed a chronological account of the standoff that included the full texts of all pertinent documents: the viceroy's proclamations, the hong merchants' messages to foreigners, Talbot's letter of defense, and the viceroy's exoneration of the

Christian trader. As useful as the journal was, Bridgman had almost been forced to suspend operations before the incident. Earlier in 1838, Rufus Anderson of the ABCFM, who viewed the *Repository* as a distraction to evangelism, stunned Bridgman by ordering him to step down from his editorial post. In an affront to Bridgman's dignity, Anderson had the gall to announce the decision in the *Missionary Herald* before informing the missionary himself. Apoplectic, Bridgman returned fire. The article in the *Herald* has "given the impression" that "you have stopped it," he wrote Anderson, when the ABCFM could not possibly discontinue the *Repository* for the simple reason that it lacked the power to do so. Olyphant, King, and Talbot are the "chief supporters," Bridgman reminded Anderson, and "they will not withdraw their support." "I shall do all I can . . . to keep it in circulation," warned Bridgman, drawing a line in the sand. Realizing he was treading on sacred ground, Anderson backed off.[47]

In Anderson's defense, Bridgman did ask a lot of the board. If one were to select at random one of Bridgman's publications—choosing from among the dictionaries, language primers, Bible translations, Christian tracts, and cultural periodicals—and examine this text individually, one would struggle to comprehend how it advanced Christianity in China. To properly appreciate Bridgman, one had to look at his entire output holistically; only in this fashion could one behold the linguistic and cultural highway he had built. Even then one had to get past the disconcerting fact that, at present, no one traveled on these barren roadways. They had all been built, at great expense in terms of time and money, in anticipation of China's opening, that elusive event that always seemed to recede further into the future as the years advanced. That is, until 1839.

The previous year the emperor received three memorials from Lin Zexu. The viceroy of Hunan and Hubei Provinces claimed to have orchestrated effective opium-suppression campaigns in areas under his jurisdiction. In these memorials, Lin described his method, which paired leniency with severity. He began by demanding publicly that all users and dealers surrender their opium; as long as they cooperated, he promised not to prosecute their cases any further. However, should a smuggler refuse to comply, Lin turned merciless, sentencing resistors to death. Greatly impressed, the emperor ordered Lin to eradicate opium at its source by employing a modified version of this method in Canton. After making a grand entrance, Lin would bring commerce to a halt until traders handed over their opium and signed a binding agreement preventing the opium menace from rearing its head again. Of course, the emperor understood that behind Lin's blustery show of force lay military weakness. The hope was that the British, reeling from the shock of the sudden loss of trade, would hastily settle with Lin on China's terms so as to resume normal business activity. Lin, in short, would be bluffing.[48]

When Commissioner Lin descended on Canton on March 10, 1839, several foreigners stepped forward to introduce themselves as allies:

C. W. King, Samuel Wells Williams, Peter Parker, and Elijah Bridgman. Though all pledged their support, Bridgman offered something of immediate utility. Shortly after his arrival, Lin encountered a problem that had nothing to do with opium. Since neither he nor his staff spoke English, how would he communicate? Compounding the problem, he also faced a gaping cultural divide. Lacking basic knowledge of Western civilization, Lin had no way to understand the mind of his adversary. To his relief—and astonishment as well—Lin discovered that a fully operational system for intercultural communication already existed.

Lin wasted no time availing himself of Bridgman's infrastructure. That all of it violated Chinese law did not concern the commissioner, who understood that opium was his priority. In desperate need of a bilingual interpreter, he employed Liang Ateh, the son of Liang Afa, whom Bridgman had raised and educated. Liang worked closely with Lin, serving as not only interpreter but also cultural informant, sharing his knowledge of Western culture, values, and religion. As useful as Liang was, Lin wanted to read about the West himself. After making this wish known, he found his arms cradling, to his stunned delight, copies of the *East-West Examiner* and *A Brief Account of the United States*. It was almost as if he had willed them to existence.

Bridgman also helped Lin surmount one final obstacle. Deciding to send a letter to Queen Victoria to explain his position and solicit her support, Lin confronted a problem. Since China had never formalized its relationship with Britain, Lin did not have a channel for diplomatic communication. How could he get the letter to London? With no other recourse, Lin awkwardly sought a volunteer among British traders, the very group his letter excoriated. No one stepped forward. Recognizing Lin's predicament, Bridgman presented a solution. After Peter Parker finished translating the letter into English, Bridgman and Williams printed the letter in the *Repository*, which enjoyed a substantial circulation in England. Though Lin did finally locate a merchant willing to carry the letter, the Foreign Office in London, when apprised of the letter's contents, refused to open it. With this abortive result, the *Repository* provided the only means through which British royalty, officials, and subjects could access Lin's message. Given the recent exchange with Rufus Anderson, Bridgman must have found Lin's utilization of his infrastructure enormously gratifying.[49]

The letter's translator, Peter Parker, understood the physiological effects of opium better than anyone, having treated addicts in his hospital. For this reason, he viewed Lin as a deliverer. In June 1839 he composed a letter to Lin that extolled the latter's virtues and introduced himself as someone sympathetic to the antiopium cause. "As I have witnessed the wide desolations of opium," Parker wrote, "[I have often wondered] whence shall the power come to stay the deluge?" Certainly, the West had supplied some of the requisite power, and here Parker credited Olyphant, King, and others who "raise a cry against the opium evil." More importantly, however, the emperor himself had taken the necessary step to cleanse China of the opium scourge by dispatching Lin.[50]

Receptive to Parker's overtures, Lin recognized the value of the famous missionary physician. However, wishing to keep all contact indirect, Lin communicated with Parker by either passing messages through Houqua or sending underlings to the hospital. Having heard of Parker's medical miracles, Lin asked the physician to supply him with a cure for opium addiction, a single "prescription that would answer for all opium victims irrespective of age & sex and the various other diseases with which it might be complicated"—a tall order, to say the least. After replying that no such miracle cure existed, Parker proceeded to outline a treatment program of incremental reduction of opium consumption over a prolonged period. Only by weaning the patient off the drug, Parker informed Lin, could a physician rid the addict of dependency. Parker assisted Lin in other ways. For example, several members of Lin's staff appeared at the hospital requesting that Parker treat an anonymous patient suffering from a hernia. Parker obligingly fitted a truss for the mysterious gentleman, who happened to share the stout Lin's bodily dimensions.[51]

Breaking with the British

To the collective delight of missionaries, Lin came down hard on the traders. Unlike earlier crackdowns, this one appeared to have real teeth. Though friendships between specific missionaries and merchants were not uncommon (think of Forbes assisting Parker), missionaries reviled traders as a group for one reason—opium. "What chiefly increases the enormity of this modern evil," missionaries wrote the board in 1839, "is the notorious fact that foreigners, enlightened nations, Christian people, have been the chief agents in providing . . . this drug." Though missionaries labored to offset the crimes of merchants, their efforts had been futile. "Alas, even the little that is good here is spoken evil of" by the Chinese, who no longer believe "that any good thing can come from foreigners."[52] The actions of traders, in other words, tarnished the reputations of all foreigners, missionaries included. Nathan Dunn made the same point succinctly: "Opium and the Bible cannot enter China together."[53] In his private correspondence, Williams vented his anger. Merchants are "wicked men" who form "active guerilla parties of the evil one," aiding Satan in his plans to subvert "the holy commands of God's law."[54]

As Lin began to implement his tough measures, missionaries salivated in anticipation. One week after his arrival, he issued a decree ordering traders to hand over all supplies of opium. At the same time, he drew up a bond for foreigners, a formal document in which the signer solemnly pledged never to import opium under penalty of execution. To expedite acceptance of his terms, Lin suspended all trade: he arranged for a cordon of junks to prevent anyone from exiting or entering the foreign factories (Figure 5.1)

Figure 5.1. *Blockade of the Factories by the Chinese during the Opium Crisis of 1839. (Peabody Essex Museum, Salem, Massachusetts.)*

and ordered all compradors and servants to remove themselves. The entire foreign community had been placed under house arrest.[55]

Aware of the hong merchants' close relationships with foreigners, Lin had them placed in iron chains. His hope was that the lugubrious sight of hong merchants dragging chains like Marley's ghost would affect traders emotionally and hasten their compliance. With Robert Bennet Forbes, the strategy proved effective, at least at first. "I had the infinite mortification of seeing my old friend," he wrote, referring to Houqua, "with an iron chain about his neck."[56] However, after feeling the chain's surprising lightness, Forbes "could not help thinking this was a farce."[57] Even if the chains were not onerous, the stress on Houqua certainly was. Aware that his friend suffered from anxiety, Forbes made frequent visits to Houqua's quarters during the standoff. "I found the old Gent almost exhausted & the very picture of despair," Forbes wrote, he having "hardly slept for a week, his feet & legs much swollen." A couple of nights later, Houqua dropped in on Forbes at midnight. Learning that Forbes was doing his own cooking, Houqua arranged for food and a cook to be smuggled in.[58]

After several weeks, the stalemate broke. Led by Charles Elliot, the British agreed to forfeit their opium, but refused to sign the bond that would have allowed the British trade to resume. They next removed themselves to Hong Kong, a mountainous island dotted with small fishing villages. Most Americans, in a dramatic break with the British, signed two bonds, the second of which contained strong and explicit language regarding China's right to execute foreigners.[59] Before departing, Elliot accosted Forbes, the head of Russell, to implore him to join the British exodus. "If your house goes," Forbes recalled Elliot stating, "all will go, and we shall soon bring these rascally Chinese to terms." As China's second-largest trading partner, the United States could force China to its knees, Elliot claimed, by joining Britain's walkout. Forbes had other ideas. Obliged to serve the interests of Russell's clients and eying his own competency, Forbes replied that he had come to China not for "health or pleasure" but for money. Therefore, he intended to "remain at my post as long as I could sell a yard of goods or buy a pound of tea." The Americans relinquished their opium, and most of them signed Lin's bonds, making possible the resumption of trade in late May.[60]

A group of American traders also agreed that Forbes should draft a letter apprising Congress of the situation in China and explaining their split with the British. The letter, signed on May 25, 1839, held Britain mostly accountable for the crisis, as its opium trade had drained nearly $35 million in precious metals from the Chinese economy over the previous five years. Aware that most Americans regarded the opium trade as sinful, Forbes acknowledged that it "has been productive of much evil and of scarcely a single good to the Chinese." Perhaps in a nod to the missionaries, Forbes added that opium trafficking had "degraded the foreign character" in the "estimation" of the Chinese. This being the case, the letter reassured Congress that Americans had chosen the high ground: "We have no wish to see a revival of the opium trade" and have "signed a voluntary pledge" guaranteeing that "we would in future abstain from dealing in the drug." Though most traders signed, Forbes noted they followed different rationales in doing so. While some viewed the opium question "in a moral and philanthropic light," he and others were motivated by "commercial" concerns: they wanted to start trading again. For reasons explained below, C. W. King refused to sign the letter.[61]

With their largest competitor sidelined in Hong Kong, Americans enjoyed a brief period of profiteering, a fact the pouting British pointed out. "They are very annoyed," Forbes delightedly informed his wife, because "we Yankees . . . intend to remain here & do all the business." By late June, just one month after the resumption of trade, Russell had earned $50,000, recouping all money lost in opium seizures ($25,000) and clearing profits to the same amount. By the end of August the British, tired of watching the steady traffic of fully laden American ships from Hong Kong, decided to resume their trade. However, since their ships remained banned, British merchants were compelled to ship their goods in and out of Canton on American ships, much to Forbes's satisfaction.[62]

The Fall to Earth

While Forbes made hay while the sun was shining, C. W. King eyed a prize so vast that it dwarfed Forbes's pursuit of a competency. He believed his moment had at last arrived. For years, while opium traders greedily amassed their unholy wealth, the noble King had been accumulating moral credits by opposing the sinful trade. The time had now come to cash in his chips. If everything worked out, Lin's intervention would prove to be nothing short of transformative—for China, for the United States, for Europe, and above all, for King.

Shortly after Lin's arrival, King initiated a correspondence with him. His plan was to use his spotless antiopium credentials to secure preferential treatment—treatment that would provide him with commercial advantages over Forbes and others. The commissioner, while opting not to confer this special status on King, did offer something of value to the antiopium faction. "Now that the Heavenly Court has banned opium," Lin informed them, "you people who have not sold opium in the past and who will . . . never think of bringing it in the future, must do more than that." Merely abstaining from evil no longer sufficed, Lin explained, as the virtuous trader must now actively advance the good. "You must persuade the foreigners of every country to devote themselves . . . to legitimate trade," Lin continued, "and not seek to enrich themselves in defiance of the ban." With this pronouncement, Lin granted King a license to lecture the grubby opium traders on their sinful ways. For King, who had nursed a grievance for so long, Lin's mandate amounted to a total validation of the identity he had worked so hard cultivate.[63]

Equally gratifying, Lin invited King and Bridgman to join a select group of spectators for the climax of the drama—the destruction of confiscated opium. After arriving at Chinkow on June 17, 1839, the Americans beheld a staggering sight: pyramids of opium chests about to be flushed into a river that flowed to the ocean. Standing on platforms, Lin's men broke open the chests, crushed the opium balls, and then used their feet to push the opium off the platform and into waiting vats.[64] Here more men mixed the narcotic with salt and lime, producing a "foetid mud" that was dumped into dugout channels that led to the river. When a desperate addict attempted to steal a pail of opium, soldiers killed him on the spot. For King, the great opium flush was cathartic. However, it was also laced with irony. While "Christian governments are . . . farming the deleterious drug," how unexpected it was that the "pagan monarch" should "nobly disdain to enrich his treasury" through the resale of confiscated opium.[65] Indeed, the value of the destroyed contraband—which included 20,000 British chests and 1,400 chests from Russell—was substantial, given that a single chest could satisfy eight thousand users for a month.[66]

As the pollution flowed out to sea, Lin issued a heartfelt apology to affected marine life. Fish, however, were not alone in their intoxication. As King realized that he enjoyed a level of access to Lin denied to others, his mind flooded with visions of self-grandeur. When Lin invited King and Bridgman to pay him a visit, King decided to press his advantage. Walking through "piles of broken opium boxes," the two reached Lin's temporary residence. They bowed their heads respectfully before the seated commissioner, and the talks commenced. After dispensing with formalities, King produced for Lin's inspection a paper of proposals, according to Bridgman, "with a view to remove existing evils, to guard against their recurrence, to preserve peace, and to extend commerce."[67]

Specifically, King made four requests: first, that three additional ports be opened to foreign commerce; second, that families of merchants be allowed to reside in trading zones; third, that foreign ministers enjoy the right to establish offices in Peking; and fourth, that a foreigner accused of a crime stand trial before his own consul, who would render a verdict in consultation with local authorities. King's plan was bold. It not only called for the end of the Canton System but also provided the blueprints for a new system to replace it. King knew that, were he to succeed, he would have achieved through his own personal agency what had thus far eluded the mightiest governments on earth. A modern-day Moses, he, C. W. King, would have single-handedly opened China.[68]

Unfortunately for King, he had grossly overestimated his influence with Lin. The commissioner accepted the curious paper, provided no comment, and then proceeded to take none of the requests into consideration. Instead, he redirected the conversation toward topics that advanced his interests. Which hong merchants, he asked King, were law-abiding and which complicit with opium traders? King politely declined to answer. Lin next inquired about the strength of British naval power. In fielding this question, King was perhaps tempted to remind the commissioner that acceptance of his proposals, by forestalling war, would render the point moot. Instead, however, he described the destructive power of British war vessels for Lin, who responded by knitting a "frown on his brow."[69]

When the interview concluded, King walked away empty-handed. After returning to Canton, he absorbed another stinging blow. There he beheld the flourishing commerce of his unscrupulous peers, the very men who should have been punished but were not. If anything, Forbes and the others had been rewarded. Jilted by Lin and disgusted by the unrepentant American traders, an embittered King vented his frustrations in a letter to the *Repository*.[70]

King versus Forbes

Letters to the editor are usually short. This one spanned thirty-two pages. In his retelling of events, King spared no one. According to his version, Lin had been on the verge of exempting traders from all bonds as a way to keep the British at the bargaining table. "This release had been virtually promised to an American resident," King wrote, referring to himself, who witnessed "the destruction of the opium."[71] Unfortunately, when the

Americans signed the bond, their act set in motion a disastrous sequence of events: Lin could no longer make such an offer, the British began their mass exodus, and war now loomed as a likely outcome.

King also singled out the American resident merchants, who he claimed had recklessly placed all foreigners at the mercy of China's criminal justice system. In their haste to resume trade, they had, King contended, agreed to the outrageous clause consigning guilty parties to capital punishment. To "add the character of meanness to error," the American resident merchants placed the entire onus on sea captains, not on themselves. Even though the resident merchants had been the "chief encouragers of the traffic," should a vessel be caught with opium, the death penalty would apply to the captain, not the resident merchant. "Why then this unfair substitution?" In answer, King pointed an accusatory finger at Houqua. The "wily head of the co-hong," conniving with men like Forbes, wanted "to have a victim" ready to hand over to authorities. Resident merchants had also undermined the British position with their insatiable lust for profits. Superintendent Elliot had hoped to exercise coercive power over Lin by denying China access to English markets. However, when the "leading American houses," King wrote, referring unmistakably to Russell, agreed to carry the cargoes of British merchants in and out of Canton, China experienced no discernible reduction in its trade with England.[72]

The letter left no doubt that King had soured on Lin Zexu. He described the "interview with his excellency" in which he had submitted his "earnest petition" urging Lin to start "liberalizing the laws regarding foreign inter-course." "Unhappily," King reported, "the advice was not taken." In a complete reversal of the opinion he had expressed at the opium flush, King now found the "pagan" Lin "wanting in that strict integrity, that unde-viating veracity, which Western nations owe solely to their Christianity." Reaching the end of the lengthy screed, readers encountered not King's name but the cryptic initials "C. R."[73]

Forbes was not fooled. "I shall send you per first direct ship the last Chinese Repository," he wrote his wife, "the article signed CR which means Charles King is a most libelous & atrocious one." Forbes added that, "as one of the vilified Americans," he had been compelled to sub-mit his response to the *Repository*.[74] In his considerably shorter rebuttal, Forbes refuted his adversary's arguments one by one. Introducing himself with the pseudonym "Non Sine Causa" (not without cause), Forbes began by addressing King's tone since this, he argued, leads to the author's true character. Beneath the veil of "Utopian ideas" and "Christian spirit" lurked something far less noble. "There is a spirit of jealousy stamped in every line," Forbes asserted, "there is a degree of self-esteem and arrogance in the language of the article."[75]

Forbes next addressed the bond controversy. He wondered how King could fault Americans for signing an agreement that would allow trade to resume when he, King, was at the same time engaged in private dealings with Lin to secure the same result through preferential treatment. King "cherished the idea with characteristic vanity . . . that he individually would be the favored one." While ordinary traders were forced to sign bonds, "the *pure*, the *uncontaminated*" King would "proudly hold up his head, and say, 'Lin knows whom to trust.'"[76]

Nothing rankled Forbes more than the charge that Houqua and the resident merchants had conspired to rig the new system to allow them to enjoy opium's profits while captains incurred the risk. "I pronounce this to be neither more nor less than *most atrocious intimation*," Forbes fulminated, "conceived in malignity, and born with falsehood stamped upon its face." Forbes then turned the issue back on King, who had also signed the first bond (but not the second). If the Chinese would have allowed either resident merchants or captains to assume liability, and if King considered it "mean" to sign a bond that placed the burden on captains, then "*why did he do it?*"[77]

The answer: King had acted in his own economic self-interest. He had assented to sign the first bond when "he had a ship to load" but had protested the second when "he had no ship unsecured." Forbes did not regard such behavior shameful. Indeed, he candidly admitted that he and others had signed bonds not "*to prove their sincerity in abjuring* the opium traffic" but rather "*because their duty to their constituents and their own interests demanded it.*" What made King so reprehensible was that he cloaked the pursuit of profit in the rhetoric of high-minded Christian idealism and then zealously imputed sinful behavior to others. Forbes closed by asking King to probe deeply "into his own heart," to refrain from "holding his head too high," and to adopt greater "lenity towards the faults and foibles of his fellow men."[78]

Deus Ex Machina

Something had gone terribly wrong. During the ominous lull that followed the departure of the British, American missionaries contemplated the sad state of affairs. Lin's tough measures had failed. C. W. King, though on the side of angels in their view, sat sulking while Forbes, the former *Lintin* captain, raced gleefully toward his competency. Worse still, Britain seemed likely to send a naval force to protect its foul opium trade. In September 1839 missionaries expressed their sunken mood in a letter to the board. "In view of what has transpired here," they wrote, "we confess we have sometimes been both distressed and perplexed." To ease their troubled minds, they reminded themselves that the ways of God were "mysterious and dark . . . even to the righteous." Since God's plan eluded their comprehension, they confessed that faith alone allowed them to stave off "despair."[79]

In January 1840 Bridgman published a gloomy assessment of the Sino-British conflict in the *Repository*. As war loomed, Bridgman's conversations with the Chinese revealed their tragic naivete on military matters, they evincing a foolish fondness for the motto "To join battle we fear not." They should fear it, Bridgman believed. "Not aware of the advantages which modern science" has given "the western warrior" and "believing their cause to be just," the Chinese showed almost no desire to "prevent collision." Events had progressed "from bad to worse," Bridgman summarized. "Instead of light, there has come darkness; instead of order, confusion."[80]

Six months later, the fog enshrouding God's plan suddenly lifted. When British expeditionary forces reached Guangdong in June 1840 and immediately commenced bombarding coastal forts, Bridgman expressed not anger but relief. Finally, a drama that had seemed exasperatingly incapable of resolving its own internal problems was witnessing a deus ex machina—a powerful outside force that could blast the plot out of demoralizing paralysis. "The gauntlet has been thrown," Bridgman wrote excitedly, "forts and batteries demolished" and "men left dead and dying on the battlefield." A peaceful man who generally abhorred bloodshed, Bridgman made an exception for this conflict because he sensed God's will at work. In the Old Testament, God takes the form of a pillar of fire to aid his chosen people; intending now to open China for his missionaries, God had chosen the British military as his battering ram. "We are on the eve of a new era," Bridgman declared, when "the God of nations is about to open a highway for those who will preach the Word."[81]

Samuel Wells Williams also discerned the "hand of God" in the strange events. "I am happy," he wrote his brother late in 1840, because the British "expedition was no doubt sent here to advance his [God's] kingdom among the Chinese." When the proud Chinese "feel the tremendous power of foreign nations," they will become filled with the "wholesome dread and fear" that is a precondition of salvation. "As a nation, this people are inconceivably conceited & proud," and thus "cannon balls are a mean of disabusing them of some of . . . their traits of character." On top of the drugs, greed, guns, and blood, Bridgman and Williams superimposed the shimmering overlay of God's plan, and when they did, the ostensibly foul conflict made perfect sense.[82]

Conclusion

His competency earned, Forbes made immediate preparations to embark for home in 1840. Though longing to see his family, he found it difficult to part with Houqua. Paying his friend one final visit, Forbes struggled "to keep the show of feeling down." After Houqua inquired when Forbes expected to get back, Forbes fumbled for an appropriate response, since he had no intention of returning. Just before departure, Forbes visited the grave of his brother Thomas, who had perished ten years earlier in a storm. He then departed on board the *Niantic*, exulting in his regained wealth. Thanks largely to the opium trade, he had invented himself in China not once but twice. Also satisfying, in a war of words Forbes had trounced

Charles W. King, a religious crusader who had tried to convert his anti-opium activism into personal power and glory. "Just think of it," Forbes exclaimed in a letter to his wife, "leaving China for home, crowned with success—well in health, in a good ship with good company."[83]

The "good company" to whom he referred was Peter Parker. Having grown weary of single life, Parker planned to find a wife back home. Secretly, however, he harbored a much larger ambition. He predicted that the Sino-British conflict would dramatically alter the status quo in China. Like Bridgman and Williams, he did not view this change negatively, since the environment in the 1830s had been hostile to missionaries, with two large entities thwarting their efforts. The Canton System restricted their movement and rendered language acquisition difficult. British and American traders, by flooding China with opium, taught the Chinese to distrust all things Western, even Christianity.

Even though Lin Zexu's crackdown had failed, Parker nevertheless spied a ray of hope. For the first time, a Chinese official had acknowledged both the good intentions of American missionaries and the value of their linguistic, cultural, and medical knowledge. The Chinese, he suspected, might be receptive to a representative from the United States if he came in friendship, did not support the opium interests, and could mediate between China and Britain. From the voyage of the *Empress of China* until now, the U.S. government had played an insignificant role in China. If Parker had his way, that was about to change.

6

Formal Ties

The Caleb Cushing Mission

arker and Forbes made themselves useful on the *Niantic*. When the captain and half the crew fell seriously ill early in the voyage, Parker treated the sick while Forbes, an experienced captain, took the helm. After the crisis passed, the two friends spent their idle time at sea discussing, among other topics, matrimony, because Parker planned to find a wife. While receiving some helpful advice from Forbes, Parker also absorbed no small amount of ribbing from the sophisticated Bostonian, who amused himself by listing the many uncouth habits retained by the New England farm boy: "he eats always with his knife," "uses his fingers to blow his nose," and "gulps at [the] table." Though Parker was "full of the milk of human kindness," Forbes found him surprisingly lacking in "good manners" for someone who had lived in cosmopolitan Canton for six years. Forbes also made sport of Parker's fear of storms. "Whenever the wind . . . is at all threatening," Parker "sleeps but little & asks a thousand silly questions." "I feed his fears . . . for amusement," Forbes devilishly admitted, "by predicting squalls."[1]

Though Parker had not shed all of his rustic ways, he was becoming a global citizen. During the opium standoff, Parker had discovered not only that he enjoyed the diplomatic arena but also that his fame as a medical missionary provided him with access to this game. Along with treating Lin Zexu for a hernia, Parker had undertaken two important translation projects. He had created an English version of Lin's letter to the queen and had translated into Chinese sections of Emerich de Vattel's *Law of Nations* (1758), the legal handbook consulted by Europeans. In his translation, Parker took the liberty of adding exclamatory sentences—lines that do not appear in Vattel's original—so as to amplify any point strengthening Lin's hand. For example, Vattel explained the legal justification for a nation's decision to ban a given import. To this, Parker added, "Let it be understood, when a nation establishes a prohibition, it has a purpose!" Parker's translation apparently influenced Lin, as he proceeded to adopt the exact plan of action recommended in the text: Lin declared the illegality of opium, ordered its confiscation, and solicited Queen Victoria's aid in ending the drug traffic. For Parker, this was truly gratifying.[2]

Watching Parker's drift into international affairs, the circumspect Houqua cautioned the missionary to stick to what he knew: "Trade you not understand. Opium ships you not understand."[3] However, Parker insisted that he did have a broad understanding of this pivotal moment in Sino-Western history. After all, he had received a degree from Yale in not just theology but medicine. Though he valued the Gospel, he understood it as part of a larger cultural wave about to sweep across China:

> The barriers will all be taken away and civilization will scatter its blessings through the land, traversing her territory with roads— railroads probably; her harbors and rivers will be navigated by steamboats; her laws will be modified by that foundation of all laws, the Bible; the female sex will be elevated, and treated not as the slaves but as the . . . companions of man. The time is coming when her people will be delivered from their burdens of perpetual disease, and when they will no longer be debarred the privileges of education and the pleasures of intellectual life, and when, under the rule of Jesus, China will be wonderfully different from the China of to-day.[4]

Though all missionaries dreamed of China's opening, Parker understood the great event as offering so much more than the mere chance to preach freely. As he lay in bed at night, this glorious vision of religious-scientific-technological-social progress fired his imagination. He was a Christian missionary, to be sure, but his interaction with Lin convinced him that he was meant to play a larger role: he was a bringer of Western civilization. Arriving in the United States, Parker immediately began to convert his fame as a medical missionary into political influence.

Parker hoped to convince his government to play an active role in China, something it had conspicuously avoided doing. Specifically, he believed that a U.S. envoy might mediate the Sino-British conflict. As this chapter shows, Parker's proposal, purely by chance, fell into alignment with Daniel Webster's grand vision for American dominance in the Pacific. In 1843 this vision culminated with Caleb Cushing's mission to China. Its chief purpose: to secure a treaty granting America the same rights Britain had won through war. As a secondary objective, Cushing planned to promote American military technology before Chinese leaders, who were expected to be receptive after losing the war. Arms, he hoped, could replace opium as a profitable American import.

Cushing left China with a remarkable treaty, one that pleased traders, delighted missionaries, exceeded the expectations of Congress, and transformed China's relations with the West. Since the treaty was secured during an official government mission, one might be tempted to attribute the success to federal power and assume that the era of American individualism in China had ended. This was hardly the case. Following its launch, the mission suffered several catastrophic setbacks that appeared to doom it to failure. Cushing pulled the mission back from the brink, and he did so not by dutifully following his official instructions but by deviating from them. The first Sino-U.S. treaty, in other words, came as the result of an individual's perseverance and willingness to improvise.

The Doctor and Daniel Webster

In January 1841 Parker journeyed to Washington, D.C., to make the case before policy makers for American involvement. New at this game, Parker naively started at the top, calling on the White House. Surprisingly, Martin Van Buren agreed to see him. As outgoing president, Van Buren explained that he was not in a position to provide much assistance. He did, however, redirect Parker to someone eager to hear his ideas. Daniel Webster, the appointed secretary of state to the incoming President Harrison, would be shaping foreign policy for the new administration. On January 22, Parker spoke privately with Webster, who liked what he heard. "I was well received," Parker wrote, "and he requested that I would submit to him my views in writing."[5]

Parker did not waste time. One week after the meeting, he placed in Webster's hands a series of proposals. In the document, Parker urged the federal government to assert itself in China, something it had historically avoided. Despite the high volume of its China trade, the United States had been represented only through a merchant asked to act as consul to handle official business, if there was any, while conducting trade. The complex nature of the times, Parker argued, demanded a more substantial American presence.[6] Specifically, Parker urged the United States "to send *a Minister Plenipotentiary direct, and without delay, to the court of Taou Kwang.*" As his primary purpose, this minister would mediate the dispute between China and Britain, helping the two sides reach an agreement that would end hostilities, allow commerce to resume, and effect "the cessation of the opium traffic." The United States enjoyed the moral authority to assume this role because it "stands higher in the confidence of the Chinese than any other nation," owing to its traders' "limited traffic" in opium. Moreover, these merchants had recently taken a "stand against" the illegal trade "and ha[d] exerted their influence . . . to rouse the moral sense of Western nations against it."[7] Had traders in Canton known what Parker was saying about them in Washington, the majority would have been pleasantly shocked. Though the signing of Lin's bonds had been an expedient measure for many, they were now being cast—by a missionary, of all people—as exemplars of morality.

Parker's call for federal action appealed to Daniel Webster. Through pure luck, Parker happened to approach Webster as he was beginning to imagine the links of his "Great Chain" across the Pacific. Through a methodical, determined, and energetic foreign policy, the United States would form official relationships with Pacific countries and islands that would render these locales hospitable to American traders. The metaphor of the chain originated in Webster himself, who in 1851 would refer to Japan as "the last link in the chain." Webster would officially forge the first link, Hawaii, in 1842, when drafting the Tyler Doctrine, which would define the islands as within the American sphere of influence. A formal relationship with China would constitute the second link, which would lead to a trading outpost in the Oregon Territory, a third link that recalled John Jacob Astor's dream.[8]

Indeed, as the mere mention of Astor suggests, Webster's vision of American empire was intended to advance the nation's mercantile pursuits. In this sense, it was the sort of vision one might expect from a New Englander. Born in New Hampshire and trained in law, Webster shrewdly bolstered his political base by cultivating alliances with New England's merchant elite. As a lawyer, he defended these men in the courtroom; as an elected official, he represented their interests in the Senate. Webster enjoyed especially warm relations with Thomas Perkins, who early on detected talent in the aspiring politician. In 1817 Perkins invited Webster, then age thirty-five, to spend a day at the shore in Gloucester, Massachusetts. As the two discussed national affairs, their carriage reached a spot overlooking the water where they enjoyed a prolonged view of a sea monster spiraling through the water. One does not soon forget that sight, nor does one forget the indomitable Thomas Perkins, who would remain close to Webster throughout his political career. Indeed, when Perkins contemplated the nation's manifest destiny, he thought not of land but water, not of farmsteads but trade routes, and not of the pioneer's covered wagon but the mariner's vessel. Webster's Pacific chain, in other words, was the sort of foreign policy Perkins embraced.[9]

In the early 1840s President John Tyler agreed with Webster as to the efficacy of sending an envoy to China. However, the United States' strained relations with Britain forced them to shelve the idea temporarily. The two countries were embroiled in a heated dispute regarding the border separating Canada and the United States, with Oregon being the most contested territory in the squabble. In 1842 Webster negotiated a treaty with his British counterpart, Baron Ashburton, establishing the northern boundary for the eastern states. Though the Webster-Ashburton Treaty said nothing about Oregon, leaving that for another day, it eliminated the main obstacle blocking a mission to China by mending relations with Britain.[10]

That same year, the First Opium War concluded with the signing of the Treaty of Nanjing, which opened four new ports to British trade: Ningbo, Shanghai, Xiamen, and Fuzhou. When this news reached Washington,

Webster returned with urgency to the idea of an envoy. He feared that Britain might be poised to control China's markets to the detriment of other trading nations. President Tyler arrived at the same conclusion after receiving an ominous letter from Caleb Cushing, a Massachusetts congressman. British forces in Asia, Cushing warned, would next proceed to Japan to force that nation "to open its ports to the commerce of England." Already well positioned in the Pacific Northwest, Britain would only have "to seize" Hawaii "to have a complete belt of fortresses environing the globe," much to the "peril" of "our vast commerce on the Pacific." Instead of Webster's Great Chain, an ever-tightening British belt threatened to choke American commerce. Three days after reading this letter, Tyler urged Congress to allocate funds for a China mission. It was now vital to U.S. interests that an envoy secure a comparable treaty.[11]

Who would go to China? In his proposal, Parker recommended the selection of a senior statesman nearing the end of a distinguished career. His choice: John Quincy Adams. Adams, however, had disqualified himself in 1841 by delivering a lecture that left him politically radioactive on the subject of China. In the controversial speech, Adams blamed the Opium War on Chinese arrogance, not British greed. With Adams eliminated from contention, Tyler and Webster chose Edward Everett, a former Whig congressman and governor of Massachusetts now residing in London as the U.S. ambassador to Britain. After Congressman Adams steered both the appointment of Everett and the funding for the China mission through Congress in 1843, Everett—who had never agreed to any of this—announced his intention to remain in London. As a last-minute substitution, Webster tapped Caleb Cushing. Since the congressional session had ended, the Senate could not debate the merits of the selection until the start of the new session, by which time Cushing would have departed.[12]

Caleb Cushing

Quite possibly, Webster had favored Cushing all along, as Cushing's biographer John Belohlavek suggests. To expedite the proposal's movement through Congress, Webster had cleverly named Everett, whose reputation almost guaranteed confirmation in the Senate, knowing full well that Everett would decline the appointment. If so, one can easily see why Webster would view the lesser-known Cushing as an attractive choice. An ambitious young congressman, Cushing had made the tactical decision to hitch his political fortunes to Webster's star. He dined with Webster once a week and even loaned his mentor money, apparently without charging interest. Of course, this alliance carried an implicit quid pro quo. To enjoy the fruits of Webster's power, Cushing was expected to advance Webster's agenda. For Cushing, such loyalty involved no sacrifice in integrity because, as a lawyer, a New Englander, and a fellow Whig, he already sympathized with Webster's initiatives.[13]

As for the Pacific chain, Cushing's views exceeded mere sympathy—he offered passionate support. Indeed, Cushing had closer ties to New England's merchants than even Webster. His cousin was none other than John Perkins Cushing, the legendary former taipan of Perkins and Company. His father, John N. Cushing, a merchant invested in the Oregon trade, often urged his son to use his political influence to convince Washington to challenge the British in the North Pacific region. The government should sponsor a settlement in the Oregon Territory, the elder Cushing insisted, to facilitate America's Far Eastern trade. Sure enough, Caleb Cushing emerged as a vocal advocate in the House for an aggressive Oregon policy.[14]

Along with filial responsibility, expansionist ardor fueled Cushing's advocacy of a stronger American presence in the Pacific. "I rejoice in the spectacle of the Anglo-American stock extending itself into the heart of the Continent," Cushing gushed in 1838, "taking the place of the wild beasts and roaming savages of the Far West." Though some politicians embraced manifest destiny to win votes, Cushing would back his rhetoric with action, volunteering for military service during the Mexican-American War (1846–1848). Much like Peter Parker, Cushing believed that the United States owed its rise as a nation to a unique ideological synergy: no other nation, past or present, had successfully harmonized Christianity, science and technology, and democracy. The country's mission, therefore, was to spread its civilization across the continent and throughout the world. In Britain, however, the young nation faced a formidable foe. A confirmed Anglophobe, Cushing believed that the British, wary of American dynamism, planned to hem in the rising power by limiting its territorial growth and thwarting its overseas trade.[15]

In particular, Cushing deplored British policy in China, a point he made perfectly clear in the House chamber in March 1840. Cushing learned of a possible covert agreement in which the United States and Britain would "join heart and hand" to "obtain commercial treaties from . . . China." Speaking before the House, Cushing demanded that the chairman of the Committee on Foreign Affairs, Francis Pickens, dispel the ugly rumor. Before Pickens could respond, Cushing launched into a passionate diatribe, the content of which suggests he had studied Forbes's letter to Congress. The "Americans at Canton," he asserted, "have manifested a proper respect for the laws . . . of the Chinese empire, in honourable contrast with . . . the English." "God forbid," he stated in closing, "that I should entertain the idea of co-operating with the British Government in the purpose . . . of upholding the base cupidity and violence . . . in the seas of China. I disavow all sympathy with those operations. I denounce them most emphatically."[16] Stunned and perhaps overwhelmed, Pickens assured Cushing that no such plan was afoot.

Given Cushing's desire to spread American values and defy Britain's containment strategy, the China mission provided the ideal outlet for his energies. On June 17, 1843, Cushing attended a dinner held at Faneuil Hall in Boston, the occasion being the dedication of a monument on Bunker

Hill. The list of distinguished guests included Daniel Webster, President Tyler, and Thomas Perkins, without whom the towering granite obelisk would not have been possible. Perkins had constructed a railroad, one of the country's first, connecting the construction site to a quarry in Quincy, Massachusetts. Though Perkins happily commemorated New England's spirited defense against a British siege, patriotism explains only part of his philanthropy. Showing uncanny foresight, Perkins predicted that stone would replace brick as the chief building material of Boston homes; with controlling shares of both the Quincy quarry and the Granite Railway, he had positioned himself to corner that market.[17]

When Cushing stood to deliver his speech, his intention was to explain the historical significance of the China mission. Civilization, he asserted, had progressed in circular fashion. Starting in ancient China, it had moved through Europe before finally reaching America, where it had blossomed in the areas of science, religion, and government. With China now opening after the Opium War, Americans could complete the circle. "Knowledge is being rolled back from the West to the East," he announced, such that "we have become the teacher of our teachers." While not denying the importance of his diplomatic and trade-related objectives, Cushing also viewed the mission to China as didactic.[18]

An American Arms Bazaar

If America was to become China's teacher, technology would dominate the curriculum. In the 1840s new technologies in communications, transportation, and agriculture were transforming American life and commerce. In industry Cushing's home state boasted mills that produced cotton textiles with an efficiency surpassed only by those in England. The United States was also becoming a leader in the manufacture of firearms with the recent establishment of Samuel Colt's factory in Hartford. If Americans were willing to sell modern weapons, Cushing predicted they would find eager buyers in China. He attributed the Opium War's lopsided outcome to Britain's technological superiority, as did most observers. "The world has seldom seen," wrote Samuel Wells Williams, "a more conspicuous instance of the superiority of a small body possessing science, skill, and discipline, over immense multitudes of undisciplined, ignorant, and distrustful soldiers." Cushing assumed—incorrectly, as it turned out—that the Chinese shared this interpretation of the war. If the American opium trade was dead, as Cushing (mistakenly) believed that it was, might not the transfer of arms take the drug's place?[19]

Making the same incorrect assumption, American arms manufacturers began to fill orders China had never made. Before departing, Cushing received letters from manufacturers asking him to promote their product lines in China. One shipbuilder provided Cushing with a letter addressed to the emperor. "Your Majesty will readily perceive the immense advantage to be derived from this invention," he said of his armed steamship, "enabling your seamen to cope with those of other nations who are farther advanced in naval tactics and architecture." The vessel places an "overwhelming power in your hands," he continued, one capable of destroying "the most powerful ships built, without endangering the safety of your crew." To give the emperor a demonstration, he offered to send the vessel piecemeal to China along with a team of workmen who would reassemble the craft in Peking. Similarly, an armory in Philadelphia expressed its willingness to establish a factory in China.[20]

Cushing also had technology in mind when he assembled the team of young men who would form his legation. Of course, politics and need dictated most of his selections. For his secretary, he chose Fletcher Webster, the son of Daniel Webster; Elisha Kent Kane would serve as doctor; and George West, a skilled draftsman, would provide a pictorial record of the mission. Answering a request from Daniel Webster, a consortium of New England China traders advised Cushing to include scientific drawings; models of steamboats, railroads, and cannons; and a trained engineer. The Chinese harbored "a great fear of the encroachment by other foreign nations," this group explained. Thus, if the United States could "contribute anything to their means of defense against further aggression, it would open the eyes of the emperor to the value of an alliance with us." The traders, in sum, conceived of a Sino-American alliance based on the transfer of technology that would improve the positions of both sides in relation to the British.[21]

In May 1843 Cushing received a letter from a young man who seemed able to fill this technological need. "My profession is that of a Civil Engineer," wrote John Peters Jr., who offered to help the mission by "conveying, exhibiting and explaining models" of machines and mechanical inventions.[22] No mere shot in the dark, Peters had been endorsed by the American Institute, an organization founded in 1829 to spread scientific and technological knowledge. A few years earlier, Samuel Morse had unveiled his telegraph at the institute.[23] Along with his training, Peters had one additional point in his favor: his father was a personal friend of President Tyler.

Cushing submitted and Tyler approved a long shipping list of books, tools, and models. For his technology showcase, Peters could present firearms, a telegraph system, and working models of a steam excavator and a war steamer. Though the list initially included a miniature locomotive, Tyler nixed the idea, penciling in "Will require too much time to prepare."[24] The absence of a railroad notwithstanding, the inventory of objects had the potential to dazzle the Chinese. As the one expected to make everything function properly, Peters worked tirelessly to prepare his models as the departure drew near.[25]

Onward to China

His son's position secured, John Peters Sr. began to take an active interest in the China mission. Writing to Cushing in July 1843, he shared an important piece of news that had come from the president himself. Cushing would enjoy "the glorious opportunity of proceeding direct to China in the most complete and splendid steam ship in the world"—the USS *Missouri*. Fully armed and equipped with the latest steam-propulsion technology, the vessel was "superior to any British steamer." The addition of the *Missouri* to the mission raises a question: if this was to be a peaceful diplomatic mission, why did the United States deploy such a fearsome vessel?

The Tyler administration felt certain that British forces had conditioned the Chinese to fear and respect armed steamers. The Chinese "attribute the frightful power of the British to their use of steam power," the elder Peters wrote, reflecting the administration's view. Therefore, "is it not infinitely important that you should arrive in the most imposing manner?"[26] Cushing could enjoy greater leverage during negotiations if his steamer convinced China that the United States matched Britain in terms of military technology. Of course, since the United States had neither the intention nor the capability to apply real force (the *Missouri* was the navy's only ship of this kind), Cushing's strategy was to present a facade. What mattered was not actual power but China's perception of power. For this same reason, Cushing received a splendid uniform, complete with embroidered blue coat, gold-striped pantaloons, and a plumed hat. Finally, Tyler promised to provide an impressive letter to present to the emperor.[27]

As Cushing prepared to depart, he thought he had a clear objective (to obtain a treaty comparable to the Treaty of Nanjing) and the props necessary to execute his strategy—a presidential letter, warship, and uniform. Fate would strip him of both the objective and the props before he reached China. The first prop, the impressive letter, never materialized; this is not to say that Tyler neglected to write a letter, but rather that the letter he composed failed to impress. Tyler, as Belohlavek points out, presented the emperor with an elementary-school book report:

> I hope your health is good. China is a great empire, extending over a great part of the world. The Chinese are numerous. You have millions and millions of subjects. The twenty-six United States are as large as China, though our people are not so numerous. The rising sun looks upon the great mountains and great rivers of China. When he sets, he looks upon rivers and mountains equally large in the United States.[28]

If the goal was to leave no doubt in Chinese minds that the United States belonged on the international stage, this was not the letter to present. As it turned out, Tyler's expository shortcomings constituted the least of

Cushing's problems. Disaster befell the mission before it even took to the high seas. As the *Missouri* chugged up the Potomac River to meet Cushing, it grounded on a bank. In an effort to refloat the vessel, fifteen sailors and an officer perished.[29]

Finally, on July 31, 1843, the firing of guns from the *Missouri* announced Cushing's departure. According to Daniel Webster, one could not overstate the significance of the China mission. "I consider it a more important mission than ever proceeded from this Country, & more important than any other, likely to succeed it, in our day."[30] In all, four vessels comprised the mission: the *Missouri*, *Brandywine*, *St. Louis*, and *Perry*. According to his logistically complex itinerary, Cushing was to cross the Atlantic on the *Missouri*, harboring temporarily in Gibraltar before taking the overland route to the Red Sea. However, this plan collapsed when another catastrophe befell the doomed *Missouri* in Gibraltar. On the night of August 26, a sailor accidentally ignited a turpentine container, causing a raging fire (Figure 6.1). Though Cushing salvaged his diplomatic papers, most of his personal possessions, including his uniform, perished in the flames. For four hours, the fire blazed uncontrollably, reducing the vessel to a charred skeleton. As Cushing watched the smoldering remains slowly sink, he realized that he must now meet the Chinese bereft of props of power. It was a massive setback, but Cushing never contemplated turning back. After all, he had an objective of vital importance to execute.[31]

Or did he? His objective was next to vanish. In his instructions to Cushing, Webster had outlined the mission's priorities, chief among them

Figure 6.1. Burning of the *Missouri* in Gibraltar. *(Naval History and Heritage Command, Washington, D.C.)*

access to the treaty ports "on terms as favorable as those which are enjoyed by English merchants." As a lower priority, Webster considered an interview with the emperor "desirable" but added that Cushing should press for one only "if practicable." Were Cushing fortunate enough to obtain this meeting, he must under no circumstances agree to perform the kowtow, a ritualistic sequence of kneeling and head knockings, because compliance with this custom would signal his country's acceptance of its subordinate position. The United States intended to negotiate as China's equal.[32]

Thinking his objectives etched in stone, Cushing arrived in Macau in February 1844. While establishing a residence for his legation, he received a communication from Edward Everett in London that carried, paradoxically, a disappointing piece of "good" news. In the supplementary Treaty of the Bogue (1843), Britain had demanded, and China had conceded, that Europe and the United States receive most-favored-nation status. Cushing had yet to make contact with a single Chinese official, and already American merchants enjoyed the right to trade in the treaty ports. The mission no longer had a purpose. It was redundant.[33]

Observers were quick to make this point. An American trader in Macau expressed a view apparently held by many of his countrymen. As he watched Cushing trying to look "imperial" with "spurs on his heels," he recognized the danger posed by this envoy, now rendered superfluous. "I most heartily wish he [Cushing] were anywhere else but here and am, as well as every other American merchant here, in great fear." "As Americans we are now on the very best of terms with the Chinese." Cushing "cannot make us better off," but if he continues to put on "important airs," he might make us "hated by the Chinese, and then we lose all the advantages we now have over the English."[34] Once a vocal constituency calling for an envoy, American merchants now believed that Cushing's presence placed Sino-American relations in a precarious position. The British derived great pleasure from his predicament. "Laughter has already begun at the appearance of two Ambassadors," wrote the London *Times*, referring to Cushing and a French envoy, sent "to gain a purpose which was granted before they appeared." With "no grounds for negotiation," they must return to their countries "to be laughed at."[35]

As Cushing hunkered down in Macau, he confronted the unpleasant fact that the mission had turned into a fiasco. Sixteen men were dead, his country's greatest naval vessel lay rusting off Gibraltar, his mission had been rendered obsolete, the English had begun to mock him, his own countrymen wished he would disappear, and the Chinese had yet to acknowledge his presence. Faced with such grim prospects, many envoys would have aborted the mission. From where would Cushing summon the will to press onward?

The answer perhaps lies in a portrait of Cushing painted before he departed for China (Figure 6.2). The portrait depicts a man determined to make his mark in the political world but who has yet to do so. In the 1820s and 1830s, Cushing made several congressional bids, all of which ended in

Figure 6.2. Caleb Cushing. *(Historical Society of Old Newbury, Newburyport, Massachusetts.)*

Engraved by T.Doney.NY.

bitter defeat. Though he did eventually gain a seat in the House, his entry required the unexpected withdrawal of a congressman, which had opened up a seat for special election. Thus, when Cushing arrived in China, he had not yet proved himself. In this way, he presented a microcosm of his nation which, though young and showing promise, had not demonstrated conclusively that it belonged on the international stage with Europe. The personal aspirations of the envoy mirrored his country's hopes for a rapid ascendancy. In China the driving ambition of the young man from the young nation pushed the seemingly futile mission forward.

Chess Match

In Macau Cushing found himself in need of advisers who understood Chinese languages and customs. He took advantage of the American missionaries, attaching Bridgman, Williams, and Parker to the mission. Hoping to negotiate with his Chinese counterpart using the official language of the imperial court, Cushing passed the dead time studying Manchu (not realizing that Manchu was in decline even among Qing officials). Fletcher Webster, representing the mission in Canton, studied Mandarin—that is, until his tutor abruptly quit. That man had initially agreed to offer lessons on the condition that the doors remained locked; however, even this precaution failed to calm his frazzled nerves. "Dr. P[arker] says that heads come off very easy," Webster informed Cushing, and he "does not deny that there may be real grounds for alarm."[36]

As his most pressing task, Cushing needed to find a new purpose for his mission. Hypothetically, had Britain never negotiated the supplementary treaty, Cushing could have returned home a hero simply by securing a near replica of the Treaty of Nanjing. Now that the diplomatic terrain had shifted under his feet, Cushing could only justify the mission, and convert disaster into victory, by obtaining privileges above and beyond those granted to Britain. As he reread Webster's instructions, Cushing realized what he had to do. He would elevate in importance the trip to Peking, which Webster had characterized as desirable but not mandatory. The United States would make history, Cushing resolved, by negotiating directly with the emperor.

Waiting in Macau for official recognition from the Chinese, Cushing started to feel ignored. Unbeknownst to him, the Chinese were taking him quite seriously and had been for some time. Several months before his arrival, Keying, the Qing official who had negotiated the Treaty of Nanjing, learned through the U.S. consul in Canton, Paul S. Forbes (Robert Bennet's cousin), that the Americans were sending an envoy who intended to visit the capital. The news alarmed Keying, who knew the emperor's wishes on this matter: foreigners must never be allowed to violate the inner sanctum of the Chinese court. "Why go to Peking," Keying asked Forbes, "when the imperial commissioner [himself] is already at Canton, and when the Americans have already been given all the advantages . . . conceded to the English?" Keying urged Forbes to turn back the Cushing mission, which Forbes was not empowered to do.[37]

Keying next placed this new information in context with the British treaty, which automatically granted to Britain any concessions given to another nation. He logically concluded—mistakenly, as it turned out—that the Americans and British were in cahoots: through force, the British had secured rights which were subsequently extended to all Western nations; in the next phase, the United States would repair to Peking to establish the right to negotiate directly with the throne, a privilege that would automatically redound to Britain. Hoping to intercept Cushing before he could proceed to Peking, Keying remained in Canton as long as he could. When the mission failed to materialize by the end of 1843, Keying departed, forcing Cushing to work with Viceroy Ch'eng Yu-tsai.[38]

In a formal communication to Ch'eng, Cushing announced his intention to proceed to Peking. Ch'eng took nearly one month to respond, a delay Cushing attributed to either disrespect or apathy. What he did not know was that he had inadvertently tripped a wire, causing alarms to sound from Canton to Peking. Far from inactive, Ch'eng used the time to obtain instructions from Peking. Indeed, between the north and south, messages flew with frequency, as Ch'eng kept the emperor apprised of any move Cushing made. By heading to Peking, Ch'eng wrote, Cushing intends "to follow the example of the English barbarians and further to surpass them." Though Cushing's intentions were certainly cause for concern, Ch'eng reassured the emperor by noting the pattern of past American behavior: since they had always been "peaceful," it was "not likely that any disorderly thing will happen." To handle the situation, Ch'eng promised to "keep the barbarians under restraint at present" and then "gradually proceed to control them." When he finally responded to Cushing, Ch'eng did not deny the request as much as he did explain the long delays involved with such an extraordinary proposal.[39]

As weeks passed without progress, Cushing grew frustrated. Though the Chinese were taking him seriously, Ch'eng's stalling lent the opposite impression. Predictably, Cushing's next move was to repeat and amplify his demands. "Coming here . . . to tender to China the friendship of the greatest power of the Americas," Cushing began, "it is my duty . . . not to omit any of the tokens of respect customary among Western nations." Though this seemed cheery enough, Cushing's message darkened ominously in the following sentence. "If these demonstrations are not met in a correspondent manner, it will be the misfortune of China, but it will not be the fault of the United States."[40] This vague threat had the desired effect of unnerving Ch'eng. "Although we are still stopping him," a less-confident Ch'eng wrote the emperor, "we are afraid that he will not obey our orders." Since Cushing had "come to China after a long voyage," he cannot be expected "to sail home if we did not exercise some benevolent control over him." Cushing, in other words, could not be pacified without the royal treatment. Unsure what to do, Ch'eng told Cushing to wait patiently for further instructions.[41]

By this time, however, Ch'eng had exhausted Cushing's patience. Once described by a colleague as "brilliant and cold as an icicle,"[42] Cushing made the decision to escalate what, up until this point, had been a tense but peaceful standoff. He deployed his best (and only) chess piece—the *Brandywine*. With the *St. Louis* and *Perry* still en route to China (and the *Missouri* destroyed), Cushing ordered his lone vessel to proceed to Whampoa and pay the viceroy a "courtesy call."[43] Not amused by the warship, Ch'eng responded that Cushing, who claimed to be an ambassador of peace, had chosen a strange way to express himself. The viceroy ordered the war vessel to back away. For his next move, Cushing sent the *Brandywine* back to Whampoa, this time to treat Ch'eng's eardrums to a twenty-one-gun salute. As provocative as this move appeared, Cushing could do little more than rattle his saber, a point he privately acknowledged. Without the *St. Louis* and *Perry*, "it would be idle to repair to" Peking "in any expectation of acting upon the Chinese by intimidation."[44] Cushing was only bluffing.

The strategy worked. In early May Ch'eng informed Cushing that Keying was on his way to Canton, posthaste, to enter into negotiations. The emperor's assignment of Keying held far more meaning to the Americans than it did to the Chinese. As the United States had hoped to use the mission to demonstrate its ascendance as a world power, the consummation of this hope required something from the Chinese that, up until now, Ch'eng had refused to offer: respect. Indeed, the importance of respect to Cushing is underscored by the frequent appearance of words like *honor* and *disrespect* in his communications with Ch'eng. Thus, he was enormously gratified to learn that he would be negotiating with the same official who had worked with the British. Word of Keying's deployment also prompted relief, because it meant that the Chinese had failed to discern that his belligerent antics were not backed by real power. After a series of devastating setbacks, a blade of light broke through the gloom.[45]

Negotiations

On June 18 Keying arrived at Cushing's residence in a sedan chair surrounded by a retinue of soldiers. After formal greetings, Cushing, Keying, and their underlings commenced the preliminary round of negotiations. Like Ch'eng, Keying entered these talks determined to block an expedition to Peking. However, unlike the viceroy, the skilled negotiator knew how to use charm to manipulate his counterpart. "We shall take each other by the hand," he told Cushing through a translator, "and converse and rejoice together with indescribable delight." The envoy dropped his bellicose posturing and quickly warmed to Keying's gracious overture.[46]

He did not, however, abandon his Peking plan. While direct talks with the emperor were attractive in their own right, Cushing also believed that, by dangling this possible course of action before Keying, he could gain leverage. Nor was he bluffing this time around; with the *St. Louis* and *Perry* having joined the *Brandywine* in early June, Cushing could now order an expedition to the capital, should negotiations falter. If "matters do not go smoothly with [Keying]," Cushing wrote, "the legation has now the means of proceeding to and acting at the North." To gauge Cushing's thinking on this vital question, Keying casually mentioned the impossibility of such a trip, only to learn that the American still intended to head north. Alarmed, Keying resolved to find some means to dissuade Cushing from pursuing such a course.[47]

In memorializing the emperor, Keying revised his earlier view that the Americans and British were working together. He now surmised that the magnetic pull of Peking had nothing to do with an Anglo-American partnership and everything to do with an Anglo-American rivalry. Showing uncanny perception, he also discerned Cushing's predicament. At first, Cushing had merely "hoped to trade according to the English barbarians' new regulations." However, "on hearing that the English barbarians had a supplementary treaty," Cushing now needed "to emulate and outdo them." Hitting the nail squarely on the head, Keying explained that Cushing sought Peking mainly to "show off before the English barbarians." Confident that he had exposed Cushing's true motivation, Keying attempted to anticipate his adversary's plan. Judging Cushing to be a "crafty man," he predicted that Cushing would press for a "speedy signing of the treaty" before proceeding to Peking, treaty in hand. Cushing, in other words, aspired to execute a double coup by obtaining both a superior treaty and an interview with the emperor! Determined not to "fall into his trap," Keying formulated a strategy of his own.[48]

Pushing aside Peking, Keying inquired whether the United States sought territorial acquisition, like Britain had with Hong Kong. Cushing assured him his country had no such ambition. A pleased Keying then removed from his finger a ring, a family keepsake, that he presented to a surprised Cushing. He then asked Cushing to submit a draft of his ideal treaty, and the members of the legation and Keying's staff would meet to hammer out its details.[49] While negotiations shifted to this lower level in late June, Keying continued his friendship offensive. "It is a source of regret that we do not understand one another's language," he wrote to Cushing, "and that we cannot directly express our most private views." He also explained the rationale behind China's resistance to the Peking expedition. If the emperor were to bestow on the Americans an audience, that would set a dangerous precedent. Every foreign nation would demand the same.[50]

On June 30, as the treaty neared completion, Keying made his move. He informed Cushing that the emperor had empowered Keying, and him alone, to negotiate an American treaty. Thus, should Cushing depart for Peking to work with officials there, the throne would interpret this act as a total rejection of Keying. Of course, if Cushing's orders obliged him to proceed north, humiliating his new Chinese friend in the process, he was free to do so. However, such an action would have serious consequences: Keying would be forced to tear up the existing treaty, which was highly advantageous to American interests. Cushing would have to start from scratch in Peking, where success was not guaranteed. The choice, Caleb Cushing, is yours. Reluctant to forfeit the favorable treaty, Cushing uttered the magic words: Peking was off the table. Delighted and relieved, Keying promptly shepherded negotiations toward completion.[51]

The Treaty of Wanghsia

On July 3, 1844, Cushing and Keying met in the Temple of Wanghsia, each man backed by a small retinue. Formally attired for the occasion, Cushing and his men suffered from the sweltering summer heat. Seated at a stone table, the two men signed eight copies of the first Sino-American treaty (four in each language), which repeated and reinforced many of the articles from the supplementary treaty, the most important of which granted Americans access to the treaty ports. Duplication aside, the Treaty of Wanghsia contained several original privileges, some of which reflected the active role of missionaries during the drafting stage of the treaty.[52]

For Parker and Bridgman, treaty negotiations had afforded an opportunity that, just two years earlier, would not have entered their wildest fantasies. They found themselves not just present at the founding of the official Sino-American relationship but also in a position to define this relationship in its embryonic stage. They could add specific articles to the treaty draft with every expectation that these would appear in the final version. Taking advantage, Parker and Bridgman composed two articles to facilitate evangelism. According to Article 17, U.S. citizens would have the right to lease land from Chinese property owners to build churches, hospitals, and cemeteries. Article 18 stipulated that Americans studying Chinese could hire native teachers, who would not face punitive measures from their own government.[53]

Though Keying did not contest most American requests, his first inclination was to reject these two provisions. However, when Cushing provided arguments in their favor, Keying agreed to reconsider. Cushing assured Keying that the impact of Article 17 would be negligible since Americans were not numerous. Furthermore, if the "living" cannot "pray for blessings" in churches and the "dead" cannot "find places of burial," Americans in China would become "lost in an abyss." Though Keying relented, he privately resolved "to publish a prohibitive law forbidding any compulsory leasing."[54] Though an American might theoretically enjoy the right to build on Chinese property, he would first have to secure a lease from a Chinese landowner, who reserved the right of refusal. As for Article 18, Cushing reminded Keying that Chinese tutors had been secretly teaching foreigners for decades; the treaty, therefore, would merely legalize a de facto practice. Keying, who had seen Bridgman's system with his own eyes, acknowledged that enforcement of this prohibition was "impossible." He allowed both articles to enter the treaty.[55]

Interestingly, Keying opted not to challenge Article 21, "extraterritoriality." According to this provision, American citizens who "commit any crime in China" shall be tried according to the "laws of the United States" and, if necessary, punished by the American consul, not Chinese authorities. Though Keying made no objection, he asked that the treaty include one exception: China must exercise jurisdiction over cases involving opium (Article 33).[56] By readily agreeing to the opium exception, Cushing impressed Keying, who reported the laudable American position to the emperor. Lingering in Keying's memory, the Treaty of Nanjing mentioned opium only once and not in a favorable context: the treaty forced China to reimburse Britain for destroyed opium to the sum of six million silver dollars. When the emperor's councilors subjected the treaty to a rigorous review, they also approved of extraterritoriality coupled with an opium exception. The former, they reasoned, would "prevent controversies between (native) persons and barbarians" from arising, and the latter would "guard against smuggling."[57] History also offered a clear precedent: the

Sino-Russian Treaty of Kiakhta (1727) stipulated that Russian authorities would oversee the punishment of offending Russians.[58]

Extraterritoriality did not appear in Cushing's mind out of thin air. Foreigners spoke frequently of the need for this form of legal protection just in case, through accident or stroke of bad luck, they found themselves at the mercy of the Chinese justice system. The *Lady Hughes* affair, though long ago, and the more recent Terranova affair continued to resonate with them. Since an execution ground lay not far from the foreign factories, foreigners had witnessed the grisly remains of decapitations. Fletcher Webster, writing to Cushing, described the rotting heads. Having also witnessed such grue-some sights, C. W. King, in his 1839 proposal to Lin Zexu, recommended that the U.S. consul try Americans charged with a crime.[59] Similarly, Robert Bennet Forbes in a letter to Congress stated that an accused American should not receive punishment until his guilt had been "fairly and clearly proved" by an American authority.[60]

Extraterritoriality did not remain hypothetical for long. Before the ink had dried on the treaty, an outbreak of violence allowed Cushing to test the article. Back in May, Paul S. Forbes had installed an arrow-shaped weather vane on his roof. This innocent act sparked a firestorm. As the region was in the throes of a terrible drought, area residents applied the principles of feng shui to the arrow, holding it responsible for bringing evil. The arrow, an anonymous public posting declared, "shot towards all quarters . . . causing serious impediment to the felicity and good fortunes of the land."[61] Realizing that local Cantonese had ascribed supernatural powers to his weather vane, Forbes immediately removed the offending fixture, but he was too late. A mob of Cantonese broke into the foreign factories and smashed flower pots as they hunted for the "charmed" arrow. As far as Forbes could tell, their purpose was not to destroy the arrow but rather to possess its otherworldly power. When Americans fired warning shots into the air, they were greeted with a "shower of stones." Eventually, the viceroy sent in two hundred troops to disperse the mob. On another day, however, a second mob materialized, this time to demand the immediate removal of the American flagstaff. When it too began to destroy property, foreigners resorted to force. In the ensuing tumult, a Chinese man, Hsu A-man, was shot and killed.[62]

The viceroy viewed the case as clear-cut: since an American had caused the death of a Chinese civilian, the United States must hand over the guilty party. When the Americans refused to surrender the man, the standoff in Canton pushed the case to Keying and Cushing in Macau. In writing to Cushing, Keying described local Cantonese as having a "temper" that is "overbearing and violent." He further explained that the region was beset by "fiery banditti" who, being "destitute of employment," gamble, steal, and "interrupt peace between this & other countries." That being said, Keying insisted that the Americans bore the blame: "I judge reasonably . . .

that the merchants of your country causelessly and rashly took life away." Invoking extraterritoriality, Cushing asked that an American official (himself) try the accused man. Keying deferred.

After hearing testimonies, Cushing conveyed his verdict to Keying. He began by reviewing the facts, as he understood them. Americans had not intentionally given offense to locals when they found themselves "attacked by hordes." As the rabble grew in number, "the police greatly neglected its duty" by allowing the "riot to go on." With "showers of brickbats and stones" descending on the foreigners, "one of them fired a shot, which killed" a rioter. Was the American who pulled the trigger guilty of murder? In answer, Cushing explained that American law distinguished between "justifiable" and "unjustifiable" homicide. As the defendant had clearly fired in "self defense," Cushing rendered a verdict of "not guilty" in the first case tried under Article 21.[63]

In a letter to Paul S. Forbes, Cushing articulated a philosophical justification for extraterritoriality. Aware of the precedent set by Europeans in the Ottoman Empire, Cushing declared the intrinsic difference between Christian and non-Christian nations. When a Christian nation apprehends a foreigner from a fellow Christian nation, no issue of jurisdiction exists: the host nation simply tries the accused party under its own laws. However, in cases involving Christians accused of crimes in Muslim countries, Europeans have invoked "a different principle": the accused party receives an "exemption" from the eye-for-an-eye justice system of "local authorities" and instead receives a trial from a "minister" of "his own government." "In my opinion," Cushing concluded, the policy employed by Europeans in "Mohammedan countries . . . is to be applied to China."[64]

Cushing understood the issue within a religious framework, classifying nations as either Christian or non-Christian. However, as William Donahue points out, he might have reached a more nuanced understanding had he instead distinguished between countries that favored individual rights and those that valued collective security. Shaped by Confucianism, Chinese authorities concerned themselves less with the fairness of the defendant's trial and more with the restoration of social harmony. When Keying urged the Americans to hand over the shooter, his frequent references to disaffected elements around Canton strongly suggest that his primary aim was to forestall social unrest. The execution of an American, by balancing the death ledger, would pacify angry locals and restore order. Yet Caleb Cushing, setting the rights of the individual as the highest priority, refused to condone the execution of a man who had acted out of self-defense. At its root, the controversy had less to do with Christianity and more to do with cultural differences.[65]

The Failed Exchange

Criminal justice aside, Cushing exhibited a surprising degree of openness to Chinese civilization. Naturally curious, he subjected Chinese culture to as rigorous a study as his short sojourn would allow. As he walked the streets of Macau, he jotted down notes about Chinese customs, architecture, and street life. He acquired an appreciation for Chinese art and manufactures and admired the overall creativity and work ethic of the people. If the Chinese rose in his estimation, some Westerners underwent a concomitant decline. The same traders he had lauded on the House floor for their admirable conduct during the opium crisis appeared to him now as "money grubbing traders" who sought fortunes selling "contraband."[66]

If Cushing manifested a curiosity for China, the Chinese failed to reciprocate, despite Cushing's best efforts. He tried to engineer the great technology transfer that various China watchers in the United States had predicted would play a central role in the mission. After closing negotiations, Cushing broached the subject to Keying:

> Your Excellency is doubtless aware that all the modern improvements in the arts of war & navigation are . . . practiced in my country quite as . . . extensively as in Europe. That if your government is desirous of books on . . . engineering, ship-building, steam engines, discipline of troops, or manufacture of arms . . . I shall be happy to be the means of placing them in your hands. I also tender to you models for the construction of the instruments of war as now used in Europe and America. Also the services of engineers skilled in these arts.[67]

The moment John Peters Jr. had prepared for had at last arrived. Unfortunately, his hopes evaporated when his technology showcase failed to have the same effect on the Chinese as a similar exhibition would have on the Japanese a decade later. As a part of Commodore Matthew Perry's expedition (1854), John Williams, Samuel Wells Williams's brother, would captivate the Japanese with models of locomotives and telegraphs. The ensuing Meiji Revolution, though not the direct result of this demonstration, would include a sweeping modernization program.[68]

In the immediate aftermath of the Opium War, the Chinese had shown genuine interest in American technology. Mere days before the Treaty of Nanjing, a Chinese official tasked to explore options for the navy apprised the emperor of an "American model." A U.S. vessel had been obtained and dismantled, he reported, so that its construction could be analyzed. Impressed with the strength of the wood and the impenetrability of the craft's thick lining of iron, copper, and leather, he asserted that "even large cannon balls could hardly shatter it." The vessel also had formidable cannons that "could shoot a great distance, thus causing people to be very afraid of them." At roughly the same time, a different official reported to the throne that a "prominent citizen" of China had, at his own expense, engaged an American ballistics expert "to concoct explosives." A "torpedo built by him is particularly ingenious and efficacious," wrote the official, who had already "sent men to him to learn his skill." Intrigued, the emperor demanded that the torpedoes be sent to Peking for inspection.[69]

Given this level of Chinese interest, why did Peters's technology transfer fail to materialize? According to James Polachek, Chinese officials and literati disagreed as to the meaning of the Opium War. Astoundingly, one faction did not even concede that the Chinese had lost the war at all. After the war, a myth emerged that, in Guangdong Province, paramilitary forces composed of civilians and led by literati had dealt the British several defeats, with the most decisive being the Sanyuanli incident. Believers of the myth attributed these successes not to Qing forces but to these local militias. This myth of a victory in the south gained a surprising degree of traction among enough officials to prevent the government from initiating a reform movement that would have included Western learning and technology. An alarm that might have sounded failed to go off, and China saw no need for John Peters Jr.[70]

One other explanation exists. At some point during negotiations, Cushing presented President Tyler's letter to Keying. The "superlatively beautiful" prose, the tactful Keying responded, was so "full of thought and elegant expressions" that he could not "restrain his spirit from delight and his heart from dilating with joy."[71] Keying later offered the emperor his advice as to how the monarch should first interpret and then respond to the letter. As he read a translation of the letter, Keying fixated on Tyler's apparent use of the character "*ku*" in reference to himself. "In feudal usage," Keying reminded the emperor, "*ku* is the word employed by the head of an inferior state, vassal to a higher imperial overlord." Of course, Keying was reading too deeply into a single character that had originated not with Tyler, of course, but with the letter's translators, Bridgman and Parker, whose knowledge of Chinese characters lacked nuance. That notwithstanding, Keying proceeded to make a far-reaching extrapolation based solely on the term. Tyler's "use of this character clearly indicates," he proudly explained, his "belief in China's traditional position as the apex of a world hierarchy, which was not destroyed by the Opium War."[72]

A Sino-centric world view also permeates Keying's recommendation that the Emperor adopt a "rather simple style" in his response. "Of all the countries," Keying began, the United States is "the most uncivilized and remote." The Americans "hope for the Imperial favor," in the form of recognition from China through this imperial letter, and "we have . . . commended . . . their determination to turn toward culture." China enjoyed a total monopoly on culture, in other words, and America's crude attempt to learn from China was, though childlike, encouraging. Finally, Keying reminded the emperor that the United States was "an isolated place outside the pale, solitary and ignorant," and thus, "if the meaning be rather deep they would probably not even be able to comprehend."[73]

If Keying's memorial comes across as condescending, we should remember its context of China's tributary system, which projected the Confucian concept of family onto Asia. At the head of a family, the father presided over his wife and children, all of whom respected him and understood their role within the clearly defined hierarchy. According to the tributary system, China and nearby Asian states—Korea, Thailand, Vietnam, Burma, and at one time Japan—behaved much like a Confucian family. As the "father," China radiated a civilizing influence from its privileged position. Subordinate nations expressed their deference to the patriarch by traveling to the Forbidden City to perform the kowtow. The emperor would acknowledge them by lavishing the visitor with gifts. Much like this ritual, China's overall relationship with its vassal states was reciprocal: China preserved harmony in the family and "civilized" the children by teaching them Confucian values and statecraft; in exchange, the latter adopted the Chinese calendar and paid periodic tribute to the Son of Heaven.

How did China comprehend nations outside Asia? For such countries, China employed the term *barbarians*, which, though ostensibly insulting, simply meant that the country in question had not yet been Sinicized. From this outer position, it presumably awaited assimilation into China's orbit. That, of course, would require China's tutelage, which the Middle Kingdom was pleased to offer. However, the difficulty with Western states, as China had already discovered with Britain, was that they sought a relationship of equals. Indeed, Daniel Webster had instructed Cushing not to kowtow for this very reason. Furthermore, the West harbored its own vision of a "family of nations"—one that implied the member states' shared belief in open markets, scientific progress, and Christianity—which was antithetical to China's patriarchal model.[74]

When we juxtapose Keying's memorials to the emperor with Cushing's speech at Faneuil Hall ("We have become the teacher of our teachers"), we can easily understand why no transfer of technology took place. The Sino-American relationship resembled a one-room schoolhouse occupied by two teachers and no students. With both sides eager to offer a lesson but neither side humble enough to receive one, John Peters Jr. never had a chance. Though disappointed, the young engineer promptly set his sights on a new China dream. As Cushing prepared to depart, Peters informed him that he, Peters, would remain behind. He had begun collecting Chinese art and objects, which he planned to ship to Boston. There he would open a Chinese museum that surpassed Nathan Dunn's earlier museum in size.[75]

Conclusion

In August 1844 Caleb Cushing departed Macau on the *Perry*. Though his mission had not gone according to plan, he could take pride in his ability to improvise when confronted with setbacks. After Britain's supplementary treaty stripped his mission of its primary purpose, he acted decisively to reconfigure his objective. He also engaged in some daring brinksmanship that, risky though it was, convinced the Chinese to deploy Keying, with whom Cushing formed a bond of friendship. After negotiations, the two exchanged portraits and agreed to maintain a correspondence. Cushing later named a family vessel the *Keying*.[76]

Though Cushing failed to interest the Chinese in American military technology, he could claim victory in other ways. Most importantly, he proved that the Americans belonged on the international stage with Europeans. In fact, his mission secured privileges beyond what Britain had obtained through war—an accomplishment Cushing relished. "English newspapers have commented rather boastfully," he wrote to the secretary of state, that "English arms had opened the ports of China to other nations." Those same papers had "ridiculed" him for attempting "to do that which . . . had already been done wholly by England."[77] However, since Britain automatically received any privilege granted another nation, the same British observers who had savored Cushing's predicament found themselves compelled to accept fresh concessions gained by him. Of all the articles, extraterritoriality surprised Britain the most. Though the Treaty of the Bogue had included a form of this protection, the British regarded Article 21 as "superior." In the "vigilant protection of their subjects at Canton," a high-ranking British authority admitted, the United States has "evinced far better diplomacy . . . than we have done."[78]

Since the State Department had not asked for extraterritoriality, Cushing composed a long memorandum at sea justifying its inclusion. According to legal scholar Teemu Ruskola, this single article had far-reaching consequences. While Cushing had hoped to shield Americans from rigged trials and hasty decapitations, immunity from Chinese law had the unintended effect of encouraging foreigners to behave in the domineering fashion associated with imperialism. China, having forfeited the right to enforce its laws in expatriate communities, could not stop their aggressive behavior. Inadvertently, Ruskola contends, Cushing erected the "legal architecture" for the "semicolonial" status that would define China in the decades to come.[79]

Foreseeing none of this, Cushing considered himself a friend to China. Arriving in New York on the last day of 1844, he received a hero's welcome. In January the treaty sailed through the Senate by a unanimous vote. Cushing next launched a lecture tour, speaking before audiences throughout the Northeast.[80] Typically, Cushing would begin by confessing that, upon first arriving in China, everything had appeared strange—the costumes, sounds, and customs. However, if one were to accept this "cursory view" and fail to penetrate beneath the surface, "injustice will be done to a great and polished people." Cushing would next extol the virtues of the Chinese, emphasizing their diligence, ingenuity, and courage. It was true, he conceded, that China's failure to modernize its military left the nation vulnerable. However, to judge the Chinese solely on their performance during war was to miss the genius of this civilization.[81]

Cushing's respectful lecture suggests his awareness that a momentous event was taking place: the entry of China into the family of nations. For any new inductee, a set of requirements accompanied membership. China would be expected to embrace Christianity, modern technology, and free trade. However, the coerced nature of China's induction complicated things. "With the sword at their throat," William Hunter wrote, the Chinese "became members of what is facetiously called the 'Brotherhood of Nations!'" Forbes made the same point: "I have always contended that the Chinese would never get into the list of civilized nations until fairly flogged." Given China's forced entry, Western observers speculated as to the nation's initial status: would China come in on par with a European nation or would it receive an inferior rank? In his lectures, Cushing broke from most Europeans by emerging as an advocate for high status. As Chapter 9 shows, Anson Burlingame would go much further. As the American minister to China, he would attempt to build equality into the permanent diplomatic machinery of China's relations not just with the United States but with all Western powers.[82]

Centrifugal Force

The Spread of People, Goods, Capital, and Ideas

Imagine the energy pent up behind those walls. By applying constant pressure, the Canton System had managed to contain three forces within the foreign factories: evangelical fervor, commercial ambition, and intellectual curiosity. Expansive by nature, each of the three yearned to spread out, conquer geographic space, and penetrate Chinese markets, minds, or hearts. Confinement, in other words, thwarted their intrinsic tendencies. Compelled by one of these forces, an American would periodically locate a weak spot in China's shield and exploit it. In 1826 Robert Bennet Forbes sailed a vessel along the coast to test markets for opium. In 1835 Edwin Stevens escaped Canton with a British expedition to the tea districts. However, the Canton System mostly succeeded in holding the three forces captive—until the Opium War liberated them.

This chapter explores the American experience in China during the three decades following the war. Unlike previous chapters, which describe American activity as concentrated within a single location, this chapter presents the theme of dispersal. As the Canton System crumbled, we see American vectors shooting out of Canton and coming to rest at the treaty ports.

In the new era, missionaries established stations in each of the treaty ports. The first to mobilize, David Abeel founded a settlement on an island off the coast of Amoy (Xiamen). He experienced firsthand the possibilities afforded by an open China when an inquisitive official approached him to learn about the West. Despite this auspicious start, the missionary movement fractured when a translation project intended to unify the dispersed missionary population revealed the presence of a deep theological fissure. After the squabbling translation group failed to reconcile its differences, the missionary movement itself splintered into factions. The U.S. government further undermined missionary cohesion by pulling two stalwarts, Williams and Parker, away from evangelical work to handle its official business.

Like missionaries, merchants moved swiftly to take advantage of China's new openness. While establishing offices in all treaty ports, most merchants chose Shanghai as their new headquarters, effectively ending Canton's dominance. In an era of commercial change, American traders also revolutionized transportation, whether to and from China or within the newly accessible Chinese interior. Clipper ships, by achieving record times on ocean voyages, allowed Americans to rival the British in terms of cargo-carrying tonnage. Steamship lines established by enterprising American firms stretched up the Yangtze River and along the coast. As traders extended their reach into new markets, opium inevitably followed. Viewing resistance as futile, Chinese authorities pragmatically decided to legalize the drug so as to at least generate customs revenue from it.

Developments outside China also contributed to dispersal. After the discovery of gold in California in 1848, thousands of hardy Cantonese men embarked for San Francisco, dreaming of quick fortunes. This migratory stream intensified in the 1860s when railroad and industrial projects in the American West attracted those seeking wage-labor positions. Railroads also diffused capital previously concentrated in New England and New York. Most notably, John Murray Forbes channeled the wealth of China traders into railroad construction, creating an east–west U.S. railway system. Forbes succeeded partly because he repurposed the system first developed over a half century earlier by his uncle, Thomas Perkins, for the China trade.

David Abeel in Kulangsu

"We seem to be on the eve of a new era," David Abeel wrote on January 1, 1842, "when the barrier against ingress to this empire must fall."[1] Back in 1830 Elijah Bridgman and he had been the first American missionaries to set foot in Canton, so he had waited twelve years for this moment. Itching to explore territories long denied to him, Abeel boldly sailed up the coast of Fujian Province in February, six months *before* the signing of the Treaty of Nanjing. His goal: explore Kulangsu, an island under British control off the coast of Amoy, as a possible site for a missionary station.[2] William Boone, an Episcopal bishop from South Carolina, joined him on the venture. Five years earlier in the United States Boone had argued that China presented the greatest of all missionary fields. "We have in China 360 millions of men, who are civilized and intelligent" Boone wrote, "whose spiritual necessities demand from us obedience to our Saviour's command." Backing words with action, Boone volunteered that year to become a missionary.[3]

Though Kulangsu looked promising, Abeel spent the early days of his sojourn fighting off despair. After Boone headed back to Macau, Abeel found himself alone. Though no stranger to loneliness, he was not psychologically prepared for the blow contained in a letter from home: his mother had passed away mere months after the death of his father. With the news intensifying his feelings of "aloneness," Abeel comforted himself by recalling that his mother had found spiritual solace in Psalm 23—"Though I walk through the valley of the shadow of death." However, it was Abeel who beheld a landscape of death and ruin, having witnessed on this trip the destructive power of British forces.[4]

The ravages of war also affected a Chinese official with whom Abeel was about to become acquainted. In 1840 Xu Jiyu had arrived on the Fujian coast with orders to strengthen coastal defenses in anticipation of British attack. Harboring a Sino-centric worldview, Xu was convinced that China had nothing to learn from Western barbarians. However, after observing the ease with which British forces blasted coastal fortifications and sank war junks, Xu underwent a conversion. "I can neither eat nor sleep," he wrote, "trying to think of ways to help." No longer dismissing the West as inferior, Xu resolved to uncover the source of its incredible power. In 1843 Peking appointed him financial commissioner of Fujian Province, a post that required him to oversee commerce in Amoy. Here his curiosity led him to the doorstep of David Abeel.[5]

"He is the most inquisitive Chinese of a high rank I have yet met," remarked a pleasantly surprised Abeel. During their meetings, Xu asked Abeel "many questions about foreign countries," so many in fact that the missionary "proposed bringing an atlas" to show him their positions in relation to China.[6] Since the demands of work limited Xu's hours with Abeel, the official would often send underlings in his place. "I gave him books," Abeel wrote of a young staff member, "which he has examined with great care." This "heathen" youth exhibited "such brilliance and grasp of mind" that Abeel asked God to "save him" and "direct his noble powers to the conversion of his countrymen." Neither Xu nor any of his staff converted to Christianity.[7]

Abeel had, however, planted a seed. Five years later, the first fruit appeared. In 1848, while on furlough in New York, Samuel Wells Williams published *The Middle Kingdom*, America's first comprehensive study of Chinese civilization.[8] That same year, Xu published the mirror image of Williams's work in China, *A Short Account of the Maritime Circuit*. If Williams's publication explained China to Americans, Xu's introduced the West to Chinese readers. Though Xu covered European nations, he devoted a disproportionate number of pages to the United States, partly because he respected the Americans for defeating Britain in the Revolution. Might this new nation, he wondered, provide a counterweight to British power in China?[9] Xu held George Washington in the highest regard, rating him the single greatest Western figure of modern times:

> He governed his state with reverence. . . . He did not esteem military achievements; he was very different from [the rulers] of other states. I have seen his portrait. His bearing is imposing and excellent. Ah! Can he not be called a hero? . . . *Of all the famous Westerners of*

ancient and modern times, can Washington be placed in any position but first?[10]

Xu drew heavily from Bridgman's *Brief Account of the United States*, given to him by Abeel. Indeed, Xu's book represented a triumph for the Bridgman operation, which produced the texts the Chinese official had mined for information. Though Lin Zexu had earlier consulted Bridgman's library so as to know his adversary's mind, Xu's inquiry still constituted a new development. He was the first Chinese to study the West because Western knowledge was valid in its own right.[11]

The Term Question

After David Abeel's pioneering settlement in Amoy, other missionaries followed by establishing stations in Ningbo (1844) and Fuzhou (1847).[12] In 1847 Bridgman sailed to Shanghai to evaluate it as a possible site for a northern mission. "I have, to use a military phrase, commenced reconnoitering this stronghold of the great adversary," he reported to Rufus Anderson of the American Board of Commissioners for Foreign Missions (ABCFM), and soon "you shall know all that I can learn about . . . Shanghai."[13] Located at the mouth of the Yangtze, Shanghai could provide energetic missionaries with a launch pad for forays to the towns and villages situated along the river. Liking what he saw, Bridgman moved his family to Shanghai, where his wife, Eliza, opened a school for Chinese girls.[14]

As missionaries spread out geographically, not one among them questioned the overall unity of the group. First, they believed that their shared objective, to save Chinese souls, transcended all differences. Second, they had proved their unity to their collective satisfaction during the years of their Canton confinement. Though Gützlaff and Morrison had put forward different methods, their disagreement had not been so severe as to threaten the overall tranquility of the group. Indeed, the fact that collegiality had always prevailed—despite very real differences in the missionaries' education, nationality, and denomination—had lulled the group into a false sense of security. In the 1840s, however, a project intended to keep the missionary community unified during this time of geographic dispersal yielded acrimony and ultimately schism.

In 1843 missionary leaders gathered in Hong Kong to discuss a new translation of the scriptures. In subsequent meetings, the group agreed on a three-phase plan that would involve nearly all missionaries. In the first phase, the Bible would be broken into sections, which would be farmed out to the several mission stations: Ningbo, Fuzhou, Canton, Amoy, Macau, Hong Kong, and Shanghai. After each station had translated its portion, phase two would circulate drafts among participating stations. Once errors had been flagged and corrections made, each station would send an amended draft to a general committee that, during phase three, would assemble a final version. If any disagreements arose, these would, theoretically, be resolved amicably by the general committee.[15]

Early in the process, participants encountered an obstacle. Before work could start in earnest, all parties had to agree on the answer to a most basic question: what Chinese term should translators use for *God*? As missionaries debated the Term Question, a previously hidden fault line revealed itself. The American camp, represented by Bridgman, favored the term *shen*; the British, led by Walter Medhurst, advocated for *shang di*. Interestingly, both sides agreed on three essential points: first, that the Chinese language did not have a term that captured the monotheistic sense of the "one true God"; second, that *shang di* was a deity who appeared in classical Chinese texts; and third, that *shen*, loosely translated as "spirit," did not enjoy such a precedent. According to the British camp, the Chinese people's fond familiarity for *shang di* would expedite their acceptance of monotheism. However, to the Americans, *shang di*'s association with older "pagan" religions was exactly why the term must now be shunned.[16] "Jupiter and Zeus," Williams argued, "were never regarded by the Jews, or Apostles, or Christians" as "designating the true God." *Shang di* was no different.[17]

With both sides refusing to budge, what had begun as an honest difference of opinion deteriorated into pompous posturing and destructive discord. "I rejoice to acknowledge in the *Shangti* of the Chinese Classics," declared the Scottish James Legge. William Boone countered, "He, who shall worship *shang-ti* . . . is guilty of breaking the first and chiefest of the commandments of God"—namely, that "you shall have no other gods before me." Bridgman succinctly expressed the dire nature of the situation: "*Pray for us.*"[18] As translation work went forward at several mission stations, the contentious atmosphere within the general committee crushed any hopes for compromise. In 1850 the group decided to leave blank all places in the translation calling for *God*, thus allowing Christian organizations to fill in gaps as they chose. After this unsatisfying conclusion, participants went their separate ways harboring the sad knowledge that the quarrel had irrevocably divided the missionary community.[19]

For Bridgman, the affair brought profound disillusionment. An ardent Millennialist, he had staked his entire career in China on his belief that spreading knowledge and truth would ultimately create the global unity that was the precondition for Christ's return. Given his total commitment to this single idea, the Term Question, which showed that knowledge could divide as well as unite, introduced troubling doubts into his once-ironclad faith. If Christians in China could not agree on a single set of doctrines, a single version of the Bible, or even a single name for God, how could they convince the Chinese to adopt "the one true religion"? After the opening of China, Bridgman had imagined himself standing at the threshold of the Millennium, when the world would move rapidly toward divine unification. In the Term Question's wake, he saw evidence only of fragmentation. This was disheartening, to say the least.[20]

Williams's New Role

Though the controversy also disturbed Williams, the indefatigable missionary responded by beavering away at his work. After all, what other way of life did he know? "I find myself to have exceeded my strength latterly, and that my head is crying out from overstraining," he wrote a friend in 1850, "yet I see little prospect, short of the grave, of being relieved. Nor in fact do I desire to be." Preferring to keep busy "as long as life lasts," Williams forged ahead with his printing, translating, and studying. In 1853 he marked his twentieth year in China.[21]

That same year, Williams experienced a strange and novel physical sensation, one he had not felt once over the previous two decades. He had gotten sick. In the back of his mind, Williams had noted but thought little of his remarkable strength and stamina. In the Canton printing office, he quietly amazed himself by easily lifting boxes that two assistants struggled to hoist off the floor. During a recent furlough in the United States, he had traversed the Northeast and Midwest on the lecture circuit, written America's authoritative book on China (*The Middle Kingdom*), and successfully courted Sarah Walworth, all in the space of two and a half years. As he took to his bed under Parker's care, Williams recognized something else about himself—he had an iron constitution. Over the years, he had mourned the deaths of many friends and colleagues: Robert Morrison in 1834, William Milne in 1834, Edwin Stevens in 1837, John Robert Morrison in 1843, David Abeel in 1846, and Karl Gützlaff in 1851. Only recently, in 1851, the homeward-bound Olyphant had died on the Suez Pass. Robert Bennet Forbes, the former *Lintin* captain, had comforted the antiopium crusader during his final moments. While so many had succumbed to death, Williams had not suffered so much as a sniffle.[22]

Along with this changing of the missionary guard, two other developments convinced Williams that God was shifting him into a new role. First, with no ceremony, Williams printed the final issue of the *Chinese Repository* in 1851. After Bridgman's move to Shanghai, Olyphant's death, and a decline in circulation caused by the dispersal of the English-speaking population, Williams decided that the journal's time had come. Second, Commodore Matthew Perry, upon arriving in Hong Kong in 1853, stunned Williams by asking him to serve as interpreter for his expedition to Japan. Knowing only a little Japanese (he had learned what he could from a shipwrecked Japanese sailor), Williams explained to Perry his unfitness for the post. Perry insisted, however, and Williams relented. By impressing Perry in Japan, Williams inadvertently opened a new doorway in his career. Aware for the first time of the steady, able, multilingual Williams, the State Department wasted little time in putting him to use.[23]

By serving Washington, Williams would follow in the footsteps of Peter Parker. After the Cushing mission formalized Sino-American relations, the U.S. government was required to maintain an official presence in China.

Each time a new commissioner arrived in Canton, Parker offered his advice. When an outgoing commissioner's departure left the office temporarily vacant, Parker reliably filled in. His eagerness for diplomatic work placed added pressure on his already strained relationship with the ABCFM. For years the board had skeptically tolerated Parker's hospital, believing that it saved bodies but not souls. When Parker accepted the position of U.S. commissioner in 1846, it was the last straw. Williams, then stateside on furlough, traveled to Boston to lobby for Parker but to no avail. The ABCFM severed ties in 1847: "Resolved,—That the connection of Dr. Peter Parker with the Board [is] terminated." For Parker, who viewed the board as a "venerable parent," the verdict detonated like a bomb.[24]

In 1855 Williams felt the same tug that had pulled Parker into the diplomatic sphere. When Robert McLane resigned as commissioner after just fourteen months, the State Department asked Peter Parker, then on leave in the United States, to return to China to occupy the post. After Parker fell ill, Matthew Perry presented President Franklin Pierce with his personal endorsement of Williams as substitute. When the offer came, Williams somewhat reluctantly accepted. In the space of a few years, he had gone from serving God as a printer in Canton to serving his government in his new home, Shanghai.[25]

If Williams needed further evidence that the center of gravity had shifted northward, he received it in 1856. In December a conflagration in Canton reduced the foreign factories to a charred ruin. Because both the missionary press and the Ophthalmic Hospital were destroyed, Williams and Parker interpreted the event as a clear sign from God. For Parker the fire signaled the end of his career in China. In 1857 he and his wife returned to Massachusetts, where they planned to live comfortably on their savings, the management of which they entrusted to John Murray Forbes.[26] Predictably, Washington turned to Williams to substitute for Parker. Recognizing the irresistible pull of secular affairs, Williams wrote Rufus Anderson to tender his resignation from the board, explaining that the "burning of the printing-office seems to direct me." Anderson had never approved of the press's intellectual publications, and Williams took this opportunity to explain how hard it had been to labor without the board's "confidence." "I have had the feeling," Williams wrote candidly, "that you did not altogether like the way in which it [the press] was conducted." This disapproval had often left him feeling "depressed."[27]

This sadness could not compare with what followed. After an uneventful trip to the United States in 1860, Williams; his wife, Sarah; and his daughter embarked for China out of New York. As the vessel left the harbor, Williams waved good-bye to his son, Wally, who was staying behind to attend school. After arriving in Hong Kong, the first mail ship brought the devastating news that Wally had died from an illness. "My Dear Bridgman," the disconsolate father wrote to Shanghai, "the news of the death of my boy Wally has . . . drawn my thoughts away from every thing save what is associated with him."[28] When the reply from Shanghai came, it brought not the spiritual solace from an old friend but news of more tragedy. Elijah and Eliza Bridgman had contracted dysentery; though Eliza had recovered, Elijah's condition had worsened until, on October 15, 1861, he too had died.[29] "From the day I reached Canton, in 1833," Williams wrote Eliza, "to the day—so sad a one—when I learned of his death, there was no interruption to our friendship."[30] The death of Bridgman confirmed what Williams already knew: a new chapter in his personal China saga had begun.

Legalizing Opium

In tending to matters of state, Williams spent precious little time on the issue that had consumed his attention in the 1830s—opium. In June 1858 the British pushed for opium's legalization when negotiating the Treaty of Tianjin at the conclusion of the first stage (1856–1858) of the Second Opium War. China, however, held firm its prohibition policy, despite the ban's notorious fecklessness. Indeed, opium traders faced scant resistance when their ships arrived at the treaty ports to funnel the contraband into well-established smuggling networks. In 1857 American traders accounted for a fifth of the 32,000 chests smuggled into Shanghai, much to the consternation of the U.S. commissioner, William Reed.[31]

As for the official U.S. position, nothing had changed since Cushing's treaty, which declared the illegality of the opium trade. Indeed, Reed's instructions from the State Department had been explicit on this matter: "The United States does not seek the legalization of the opium trade, and will not uphold its citizens in any efforts they make to introduce the drug."[32] What raised Reed's ire was the alarming disparity between official U.S. policy and the everyday practices of American traders. How could he be expected to parrot Washington's antiopium line when, outside his window, American vessels unloaded opium in open defiance of U.S. law? Were not these traders making a mockery of him, in his role as representative of the United States? As angered as Reed was by the traders, he recognized that his own government bore most of the blame. It had placed him in this intolerable situation by conferring on him the authority to speak for his nation while withholding the power to enforce its laws. Though he despised the opium trade ("No one doubts it is very pernicious and demoralizing"), he found the weakness of his position more deplorable still.[33]

When a letter outlining a possible solution floated into the exasperated Reed's office, it found him in a receptive mood. The letter, written by an American merchant in Shanghai, drew Reed's attention to a minor article buried in the Treaty of Tianjin that allowed for a periodic revision of the tariff system. Might Reed work with Chinese and British officials to include opium on the list of taxable goods processed by Chinese customs? If successful, the ploy would de facto legalize opium.[34] Of course, Reed knew that, by advancing the scheme, he would not be in compliance with instructions from Washington. To him, however, the decision was justified: if the foul trade could not be stopped, legalization would at least end the "masquerade."[35]

But would the Chinese cooperate? Reed felt certain they would. In a letter to Britain's Lord Elgin, Reed noted that Chinese customs officials in Shanghai had already begun to collect duties on opium, surreptitiously of course. From their perspective, all attempts to stymie the trade had failed, so why not at least generate income from it?[36] In 1858 this tripartite alignment of interests yielded the following words in the revised tariff code: "Opium will henceforth pay thirty taels per picul Import Duty. The importer will sell it only at the port. It will be carried into the interior by Chinese only."[37]

For Williams, legalization ended a prolonged struggle that had absorbed much of his energy. He judged the result to be at best bittersweet. On the positive side, he found some relief in making opium a taxable import and having at least removed criminality from the stigma attached to Westerners. "Legalization," he commented dryly, "is preferable to the evils attending the farce now played." That said, Williams ultimately viewed the watershed moment as unsatisfying because evil had won. "So the opium war of 1840 has at length ended in an opium triumph," he wrote, "and the honorable English merchants and government can now exonerate themselves." In 1839 Williams had interpreted the First Opium War as the trigger event for setting in motion a cosmic sequence that would end with the Second Coming. Two decades later, the older and wiser Williams still believed the "millennium will come in good time." He, however, had given up "hope of seeing it."[38]

Though no longer a political issue, opium continued to frustrate American missionaries. After legalization, an increase in opium consumption undermined the efforts of missionaries. "God knows how often and often is our message of peace and salvation," complained a missionary in Fuzhou, "contemptuously thrown back in our face with the scornful remark, 'You destroy us with your opium, and now you insult us with your offer of peace and salvation.'" Our "best efforts as missionaries," the exasperated missionary continued, are "rendered abortive . . . by the knowledge that we belong to the country which forces the opium traffic upon China!" No solution was in sight.[39]

The New China Trade

Along with legalization, other forces were transforming the China trade. By the 1850s the shift of Western trade to the north was well under way. The large commercial houses had transferred their headquarters to Shanghai by 1856, and the conflagration that consumed the foreign factories that year served mainly to provide the Canton era with a fiery coda. Though Canton receded in importance, the China trade continued unabated, still defined by the parallel streams of incoming opium and outgoing tea. If the goods had not changed, starting in the mid-1840s traders could avail themselves of a more efficient means of conveying cargoes.

For ten years, clipper ships dominated the China trade. These sleek vessels ruled the oceans well into the 1850s, when steamships started to register superior times between New York and Shanghai. Since American shipbuilders constructed the finest clippers, the United States enjoyed a brief but substantial edge over the British in shipping. Though British firms easily outnumbered American firms, and though England conducted trade in a higher volume than did the United States, American clippers still managed to carry half of all merchandise in and out of the treaty ports.

In a comparison of the clippers with their predecessors, the advances in nautical architecture stand out in bold relief. Recall that the 360-ton *Empress of China* had required six months to sail from New York to Canton in 1784. In 1847 the 900-ton *Sea Witch* required just eighty-one days for its Canton-to-New York voyage, despite sailing against the gale-force winds of a monsoon. With a black Chinese dragon as its figurehead, the *Sea Witch* commanded respect when it sailed into harbors, as did many clipper ships. Able to carry greater tonnage than their predecessors and post miraculous times, these rakish vessels not surprisingly acquired names that connoted speed or magic: *Flying Cloud, Flying Arrow, Comet, Spitfire, Witchcraft, Wizard, Racer, Ariel, Antelope,* and *Race Horse*.[40]

Bucking this trend, some merchants chose names that harkened back to the China trade's recent, but already storied, past. A year after Houqua's death in 1843, Abiel Abbot Low (William Low's nephew) launched the *Houqua*, one of the first streamlined vessels of the clipper era. "We never saw a vessel so perfect in all her parts as this new celestial packet," rhapsodized the *New York Herald*, which noticed with amusement that "her figure head is a bust of Houqua." Similarly, the *Tingqua* (named after another hong merchant), *Derby, Joshua Bates, R. B. Forbes,* and *Samuel Russell* all made voyages to China in the 1850s. When taken collectively, these vessels commemorating the giants of the previous era spoke to the changing nature of the trade. Gone were the swallows' nests and sea slugs that had infused the trade's early days with romance. In the new era, many traders concentrated less on the goods themselves and more on control over the infrastructure through which the goods flowed.[41]

By 1850 the major American firms in China had largely removed themselves from high-risk speculations on trading voyages, which raises a question: If "trading" houses such as Russell, Augustine Heard, and Olyphant no longer traded commodities, what form of business were they in? Answer: the commissions business. In exchange for healthy commissions, these firms provided services that allowed clients in Europe and America to access the China market. For example, if a New York–based merchant were considering investing in a China voyage, Heard and Company would supply him with the market data necessary to estimate the proposed venture's profitability. If the client decided to proceed, Heard would help him transfer capital from New York to Shanghai; for clients known to be reliable, Heard would also extend credit, using silver from its own vaults to purchase tea for the client, trusting that a remittance would come later. Much of Heard's silver reserves had come by way of the opium trade. Though the firm itself did not speculate in opium, it owned the infrastructure—two receiving ships, an opium warehouse in Hong Kong, and a network of Chinese brokers—that allowed the firm to process the opium shipments of others.

Opium aside, New York merchants benefited most from Heard's assistance with tea. In the Canton era, the tea trade was simple: a trader submitted an order to his hong merchant, who secured the tea for him. The dissolution of that system, however, brought complexity to tea buying because a trader had to find and form a relationship with one of the many inland suppliers. In hiring Heard, the client could benefit from the firm's relationships with several tea dealers, its willingness to bargain on the client's behalf, its expertise in inspecting and tasting the product so as to ensure quality, its transportation and warehousing facilities, and finally its ability to write insurance policies protecting the client from losses at sea.[42]

For each service rendered, Heard received a commission. From the partners' perspective, the commissions business presented an obvious advantage: since the client bore all the risk, the commercial house would receive its payment even if a venture lost money. However, the commissions business offered challenges as well, as the example of tea purchasing illustrates. In the Canton era, merchants had complained about the monopoly of the hong merchants; these critics yearned to trade directly with the inland tea merchants under the assumption that, by doing so, they could obtain lower prices. Though foreign merchants got exactly what they wished for, they discovered that tea purchasing, complex process that it was, required a Chinese agent willing to serve as an intermediary. They needed, in short, someone to act in a capacity similar to the hong merchant's. To meet this need, foreign firms turned to a set of men with whom they had worked before—the compradors. In the foreign factories the compradors had overseen not the trade itself but everything ancillary to the trade: shopping, cooking, cleaning, and laundering. Conversing with foreign merchants daily, a comprador learned how to communicate effectively with them. They trusted him, and he grew comfortable with them. In search of a new go-between in the treaty port era, foreign firms turned to the compradors, who replaced the hong merchants as the chief brokers of the Sino-Western trade.[43]

For the American commercial houses, capable and honest compradors proved indispensable. Speaking both Pidgin English and the local dialect, these men established relationships with inland suppliers on behalf of the foreign traders. Often, American firms sent their compradors into the tea districts to make large purchases, entrusting them with hundreds of thousands of dollars. "Huge amounts of money went into the country in

February . . . and did not come back in the shape of teas till May," recalled Augustine Heard Jr. "It was a great risk to run." If a comprador chose to steal the money, nothing could stop him from doing so; he could easily return empty-handed and claim to have been robbed. Despite the risks inherent in this practice, Heard claimed that compradors never once betrayed the trust of an American firm. "I doubt if there is another country in the world where such an experience is possible." Compradors also brought Chinese business to American firms. Since Heard, Russell, and Olyphant offered banking services, they attracted Chinese merchants looking for secure places to keep their money hidden from corrupt officials. Houqua's family, for example, placed huge sums with Russell, treating the company like a Swiss bank. In sum, almost every service rendered by American firms depended on compradors. Recognizing this, Heard remarked, "It would be easier to tell what the comprador did not do than what he did."[44]

Steamships on the Yangtze

Though all treaty ports allowed foreign merchants to participate in a coastal trade, Shanghai offered an extra dimension. Positioned at the mouth of the Yangtze River, Shanghai provided foreign merchants with access to China's largest artery of inland commerce. Sensing the huge potential, Heard ordered a steamship from a builder in New York in 1859. With this acquisition, the firm hoped to open up a lucrative transportation business between Shanghai and Hankou, a commercial hub in China's interior. In April 1861 Heard's *Fire Dart*, its wooden side-wheel churning water, steamed out of Shanghai on its five-hundred-mile maiden journey. When the steamer returned to Shanghai in May, an ecstatic Albert Heard shouted, "We've opened up the Yangtze!" In the early 1860s the *Fire Dart* proved quite profitable, filling the void left by Chinese junk owners who were unable to venture into rebel-held territory during the Taiping Rebellion (see Chapter 8). Though Heard took the first step, Russell and Company would dominate steamship transportation. One might be tempted to view Russell's monopoly as the triumph of a large, capital-rich firm; however, the steamship lines originated in the dream of one man, Edward Cunningham, and owed their success to his dynamism.[45]

In 1861 Cunningham, the managing partner of Russell's Shanghai headquarters, returned to China after a honeymoon in Egypt and Europe. Perhaps inspired by the pyramids, he expressed his wish to build something big in China. Russell, he informed the partners, ought to invest resources in steamship lines. As Cunningham was known to be brilliant but quixotic, his more conservative partner, Warren Delano Jr., who controlled the firm's funds, viewed with skepticism any bold proposals presented by the firm's radical member. Why take massive risks, Delano asked, when partners could steadily enrich themselves through commissions? Even if Delano had responded positively, Cunningham knew the burden of locating capital would fall on his shoulders for the reason that Russell possessed surprisingly little of it. Primarily a commissions business, Russell kept on hand only the small amount of capital it needed for tea purchases. Money earned through commissions flowed into the accounts of partners, not into the firm's reserves.[46]

Despite his firm's tepid response to his idea, Cunningham could not rid his mind of steamships. He believed that American steamships, which had for decades plied American rivers, were perfectly suited for the Yangtze. "Deep draft boats," he wrote, would encounter difficulty navigating the Yangtze, notorious for its "shoals, ill defined channels & sunken rocks." However, there were "scarcely any passages that could not be passed by a Mississippi boat." On the Yangtze, "no boats in the world . . . can compete an hour with the boats that navigate the Western rivers of America." Deciding to forge ahead without his firm's support, Cunningham hunted for investors willing to buy a stake in his transportation company.[47]

Cunningham looked first in the most obvious place—the Forbes family. Paul Forbes, a Russell partner now in New York, possessed ample capital thanks to the shrewd and timely railroad investments made on his behalf by John Murray Forbes. However, the Forbes cousins saw no reason to invest their money in Cunningham's distant and risky venture when domestic railroad stocks paid handsome dividends. In a letter to Paul, John Murray confessed he was "a confirmed *croaker* as to steam in China," meaning that he viewed the economic viability of steamship lines with pessimism. Though John Murray passed on the opportunity, Paul Forbes agreed to serve as Cunningham's purchasing agent in the United States. If Cunningham could transfer capital to New York, Forbes would purchase steamships and have them disassembled for shipment to Shanghai. Though buoyed by Forbes's offer, Cunningham still lacked capital. How could he find American investors when railroads, factories, and telegraph projects absorbed so much of the available capital?[48]

Failing to find investors in the United States, Cunningham turned to Shanghai. After forming a joint stock company, he lined up investors from the local community. In particular, he targeted small British and American traders who, lacking the facilities to transport and store goods themselves, eagerly sought partial ownership in a company that did exactly that. More impressively, Cunningham sold stock to Chinese merchants, three of whom had formerly worked as compradors for Russell. In a move calculated to earn their trust, Cunningham purchased a wharfage site for his company right next to the city's Chinese section. The gesture impressed Chinese merchants, convincing them that Cunningham's company would take their interests to heart. On March 27, 1862, Cunningham formally established the Shanghai Steam Navigation Company (SSNC) as a subsidiary of Russell and Company. American, British, and Chinese stockholders gathered at the Russell building to pop champagne corks and toast the future success of their enterprise.[49]

After a period of intense competition between 1862 and 1867, the SSNC emerged victorious on the Yangtze. Its rivals—Dent, Heard, Olyphant, and Jardine, Matheson—all capitulated in one way or another. Some sold their fleets to the SSNC, and others relocated their steamers to more promising coastal routes. By 1868 Frank Blackwell Forbes, John Murray's cousin and the SSNC manager, reported that the company's biggest problem was not competition but the lack thereof. To appease a Shanghai public growing anxious over the firm's monopoly, he adopted measures designed not to crush a small British firm but to keep it alive. "Feeling that public opinion in Shanghai required an opposition," he wrote, "we made no attempt to crush the Union Co.," but instead "made an agreement with them to keep freights up . . . so long as they behaved themselves." With the Yangtze as the SSNC's focus, the company also established lines between Shanghai and the other treaty ports.[50]

John Murray Forbes

When John Murray Forbes declined to invest in the SSNC, his decision effectively doomed Cunningham's efforts to raise money among his former Russell colleagues. Forbes oversaw not just his own investments but the portfolios of many prominent China traders. Consolidated in this way, the traders' aggregate wealth became a vast sum of capital, a dynamic force capable of transforming America's economic landscape. Though Forbes channeled this capital in several profitable directions, he invested much of it in Western railroads. To build and monitor these railroads, Forbes developed a system modeled on that of his uncle. The similarity with Thomas Perkins, however, ends here. In contrast with his fearless uncle, Forbes attracted other people's wealth by impressing investors with his cautious approach to life and money.

In personality, the careful John Murray bore little resemblance to his risk-taking older brother, Robert Bennet. John Murray, for example, would never have concocted anything like Bennet's daring *Lintin* scheme; nor for that matter would he have agreed to live on a shadowy vessel, illegally handing opium to Chinese smugglers. The two brothers also adopted very different lifestyles in Canton. Whereas the energetic and athletic Bennet entered sailboat races on the Pearl River and reveled in his victories over British rivals, the reserved John Murray shunned the camaraderie of others, choosing to spend his free time grumbling about the humidity, mosquitoes, and greed of traders. In 1833 John Murray happily departed Canton (he thought for good) to settle down in Boston and start a family.

If John Murray Forbes loathed Canton, why did he return in 1834? More curiously, why did he embark mere days after marrying Sarah Hathaway? Shortly after his wedding, Forbes confronted the unnerving fact that he now bore responsibility for a family of dependents (he planned to have children). Should he fail to meet these obligations, the consequences promised to be severe—a point he knew all too well. Into his mind crept unpleasant childhood memories of a hapless father who failed in life before dying in debt. Fortunately, the family patriarch, Thomas Perkins, had stepped in to rescue the family and oversee the training of the boys. As John Murray examined Bennet's character, he saw the same foolhardy carelessness with money that had wrecked their father. Bennet too would need help. Ridden with anxiety, John Murray concluded that the only way to find marital bliss, paradoxically, was to ship off for China during what ought to have been his honeymoon. After all, he needed a career right away, and his training applied to the China trade and nothing else, or so he thought. On March 7, 1834, he bid farewell to his bride and shipped out, just two weeks after his twenty-first birthday.[51]

While working for Russell and Company, Forbes cultivated an approach to business that stressed prudence. Though he revered his uncle, he lacked the killer instinct and thrill of conquest that defined Perkins's aggressive style. Antithetical to Forbes's nature were the bold gambles intended to control markets and destroy competitors. In character, he more closely resembled Houqua, who had amassed his fortune with sagacity, foresight, careful planning, and—above all else—constant worry. True, Houqua's timid demeanor masked a deeper ambition. Though the hong merchant pursued wealth and status, he did so with a strong sense of Confucian propriety: the merchant house and trust fund he created could support family members long after his death. Similarly, John Murray Forbes saw a controlling interest in Russell as a way to guarantee that his dependents would never suffer. In this way, the young New Englander's sense of tribal responsibility mirrored the old hong merchant's Confucian belief in familial obligation. Both adhered to the same code of honor.[52]

In the 1830s Houqua sought an American he could trust. For two decades, his close relationship with John Perkins Cushing had worked toward their mutual enrichment. After Cushing's departure in 1828, Houqua maintained a correspondence with his friend, who continued to receive his tea shipments in Boston. However, with Cushing scaling back his business activity, Houqua needed someone to fill his shoes. When Cushing returned to China in 1830 to handle the crisis caused by Thomas Forbes's death, he introduced Houqua to John Murray. Houqua "at once took me as Mr. Cushing's successor," John Murray recalled, "and gave me his entire confidence." In John Murray, Houqua recognized the mirror reflection of his own finest traits. Here was a careful man who could be trusted to handle his assets responsibly. To provide John Murray with leverage within Russell, Houqua declared his intention to give that house his exclusive business, provided it place John Murray in charge of his account.[53]

Confident he could now provide his family with economic security, Forbes sailed for home in 1836. While en route, a tragic accident affected Forbes deeply and confirmed his conservative approach to life. Forbes had befriended a chronically ill boy whose father had sent him to sea hoping that the salt air would restore his health. Since the father could not afford the passage, the boy was technically a sailor; though, because of his frailty, he spent most of the voyage in his berth. Taking a liking to the "gentle, kindly boy," Forbes brought him books and sat by his bedside to boost his spirits. To the delight of all on board, the boy regained his strength enough to assume minor responsibilities. Then tragedy struck. Hearing a loud thump late one night, Forbes hurried to the deck, where he found the boy cradled in a sailor's arms, having fallen to his death from the mast.

Later, in his cabin, Forbes broke down. In his journal he fixated on the poverty of the boy's family. "Poor fellow," he wrote. "I was much touched . . . to find that his clothes were coarse as any of the crew's, and that he had spent his little earnings in buying at Canton . . . velvet slippers and a box of gay fans . . . for his father and mother." It was not just the boy's touching affection for his parents that lent the episode its poignancy; it was rather that this love had flourished despite the parents' inability to protect their son. The next day, the atmospheric conditions surrounding the funeral prompted Forbes to revisit this theme of the vulnerable child in a cruel world. As the teary-eyed crew slid the small body, wrapped tightly in a sheet, down the gangway and into the sea, Forbes noted that "the sky was black." In a cold universe indifferent to human life, fathers needed to protect their children. Later in his life, when one of Forbes's own children fell ill, he would hold the child throughout the night, humming lullabies and pacing the floor. At daybreak, the sleepless father would trudge to the office to manage the business that kept his family secure in an unkind world.[54]

Arriving home in 1837, John Murray received a double jolt: the economy had collapsed, and his worst fears regarding Bennet had come true. Through excessive generosity and unsound investments, his brother had squandered his entire fortune—money supposed to last his lifetime. "I had not acquired the art of saying 'No,'" Bennet recalled, "lived always . . . for the present [rather] than the future," and "made several bad 'specs.'" In the worst of these speculations, Bennet had bought part of an iron foundry that manufactured inferior nails.[55] To save his brother from his creditors and himself, John Murray seized control of Bennet's finances and ordered him back to Canton to earn a competency. "I shall never feel that I am rich," he wrote sternly to Bennet, until "I see you" practicing "rigid restriction of . . . expenses clearly within your income."[56] Bennet found it humbling to be treated like a child by his younger brother, but what choice did he have? "If I had stayed at home," he later wrote, "I should have sunk under the load or become a melancholy & morose old man at 35." After handing his troubled finances over to "the hard labor of [John's] brain," Bennet sailed for China.[57]

In Boston, John Murray entered a new stage of his career, one that did not involve voyages to Canton. Along with fixing Bennet's finances, he managed Houqua's investment portfolio. "Remember, security is my first object," Houqua wrote to John Murray in 1838; "I desire to run no unnecessary risks."[58] Pleased with Forbes's management, Houqua entrusted over half a million dollars to his care. To simplify the buying and selling of securities, Forbes created the "American Stock Investment," under which he consolidated Houqua's U.S.-based assets.[59] Forbes also oversaw the American side of Russell's business, earning a handsome, if not spectacular, income in the process. Since these responsibilities did not tax him excessively, he prepared to salt away his many remaining years in a comfortable state of semiretirement. Though he had not yet turned thirty, he felt sure the excitement of life was behind him. He did not see his massive new role coming.[60]

A Conduit of Capital

China had changed Forbes in ways he only partly understood. Once believing that his skills as a China trader applied nowhere else, his second stint in Canton convinced him otherwise. In performing duties for Russell, he said, "[I] acquired a confidence . . . that would enable me to undertake any business in any part of the world."[61] In Canton, Forbes managed the accounts of merchants and bankers from Boston, New York, Canton, Calcutta, and London, stitching together in the process a formidable network of investors. These individuals not only knew Forbes but believed in his probity, honesty, and prudence. After he returned to Boston, they continued to trust him when he apprised them of sound investment opportunities. Similarly, Baring Brothers held Forbes in such high regard as to grant him access to its financial services and investment capital. Not by design, the semiretired Forbes controlled the spigot of one of the largest private capital flows in the world.[62]

Where would he direct all this capital? By the mid-1840s, Forbes had shifted most of his clients' investments out of trade, which fluctuated too much for his liking, and into the stock market. "I am rather inclined to Sell out my shipping, & turn my attention to Stocks," he wrote. "In fact every day there are openings for investment."[63] Able to summon capital at will, Forbes did not need to scour the economic landscape in search of investment opportunities. They found him.

In 1846 John Brooks approached Forbes, hoping to convince Boston's broker to invest in Western railroads. A trained engineer from Massachusetts, Brooks had headed west to capitalize on the railroad-building craze. In the 1830s the demand for internal improvements had prompted state governments to build railroads. Organized by "people's governments" rather than private enterprise, these projects had been financed by state debt. Under ordinary economic circumstances, this state system might have succeeded. However, the panic of 1837 pushed these public enterprises into bankruptcy, leaving railroads lying abandoned in states of partial completion. Thinking specifically of the Michigan Central Railroad, Brooks spied a possible solution. Might Forbes be persuaded to revitalize this moribund project by infusing it with fresh capital?[64]

Intrigued, Forbes approached the moneyed elite within his personal network. To gain access to New York's stores of capital, Forbes contacted John Green, Russell's one-time head, who had married the daughter of George Griswold, a wealthy New York China trader. Harboring deep reservations about something as speculative as railroads, conservative New Englanders and New Yorkers agreed to put up capital on one condition: Forbes must assume the presidency of the Michigan Central. If he agreed to stake his time, reputation, and money on the risky venture, they would invest. Partly to satisfy them, Forbes assumed the presidency. However, he had a hidden motivation. "I only accepted the office to get the thing going," he wrote, and to "keep it *warm* for Bennet." Forbes planned to hand the office to Bennet, who could draw a reliable salary from it for many years. At least, that was his initial idea.[65]

In the years that followed, however, railroad management would consume not less but more of Forbes's time. "Little did I dream of the load I was taking when I accepted the office of president." True, Forbes did *not* dream, and that is precisely what makes him exceptional among Americans in China. Starting in 1783, ambitious arrivals had believed they could consummate their dreams in China. Ironically, it was this man of modest aspirations who ended up making, arguably, the largest impact on the world of any American in China in the nineteenth century. While supervising the Michigan Central, Forbes mastered railroad management and learned of other industrial projects requiring fresh capital. "Whenever any coal mines are to be made accessible," he wrote in 1847, "or ill managed Rail Roads made available, or indeed any scheme that requires Capital & intelligence they come to Boston for help."[66]

The presidency also taught Forbes that a railroad line, like a trade route, needed to be protected. The Michigan Central existed alongside rival lines, each of which aspired to become the chief artery of the Midwest by tapping into large markets and population centers. Thus, the responsible railroad man could not simply build a line and walk way, assuming the long-term viability of his enterprise. Only constant vigilance and preemptive action could ensure the sustained relevance and profitability of a line. For this reason, the company's "temporary" president constructed auxiliary lines to feed into the Michigan Central, keeping it connected to as many cities as possible. This object in mind, Forbes organized and funded new railroad projects in Michigan, Illinois, Missouri, Indiana, and Iowa.

In the 1850s Forbes found himself overseeing something that had never previously entered his imagination—a *system* of interlocking lines. Understanding the importance of westward migration, Forbes envisioned his transportation system as facilitating and propelling this epic demographic shift. From the East, a man could travel to Niagara Falls along various rail lines (financed by John Perkins Cushing and William Sturgis) before connecting to Forbes's system, on which he could ride to Detroit, Chicago, or as far west as the Mississippi River. "We are bound to use every exertion to make our road a link in the great chain of communication between the East and the West," he boldly wrote, sounding less like himself and more like Thomas Perkins, the China trade's system man.[67]

Indeed, Forbes came to understand that railroads and the China trade were not so different. To impose a rational order over Western railroads, Forbes implemented much of his uncle's system.[68] First, he never shouldered any financial burden alone, choosing always to "share the risk," as Perkins liked to say. Excessive caution, however, could prevent one from seizing opportunities; for this reason, the usually risk-averse Forbes acted out of character by embracing a second Perkins principle. A "certain amount of boldness," Forbes came to realize, "is *true* prudence."[69] For example, he knew that economic downturns favored aggressive action, even if one's instincts dictated caution. "I don't believe the world is coming to an end," Forbes wrote in 1854 during a recession, "& consider this check up good . . . as it reduces labor & shuts off competition."[70] A recession, far from being a time to panic, worked to the benefit of the railroad man who was rich in capital. Along with providing leverage over labor, it swept weaker players off the field.

Third, the railroad builder, like the China trader, needed to contend with the geographic dispersal inherent in his industry. With investors located in London or Canton, and with Brooks supervising construction on-site in Michigan, Forbes provided his far-flung enterprise with a command center in Boston. Fourth, Forbes intended to continue Perkins's practice of grooming capable young family members. Though he did prepare Charles E. Perkins, the grandnephew of Thomas Perkins, for the railroad industry, Forbes, by his own admission, fell short.[71] "I think the mistake we have made . . . was in not bringing up youngsters we know something about as foremast hands," he wrote, making the nautical analogy explicit. "[We missed] the chance of picking our good mates and captains just as the old-fashioned shipowners used to do." With more reliable men at his disposal, Forbes might have achieved what one historian has called a "coast-to-coast system."[72]

Unlike his uncle, Forbes never intended to monopolize anything. According to a former partner at Russell, he was motivated not by "acquisitiveness" but by "constructiveness." Forbes took pride in "building up things" that could benefit humanity and advance civilization. He saw his railroads as bringing progress to the western territories by attracting industrious "workmen and settlers."[73] During his trips to Michigan, Forbes became impressed with the spirit of Western settlement, which contrasted favorably in his mind with the "absurdity of the slave institution." Ultimately, Forbes hoped to use railroads to claim the West for his vision of civilization: the energetic and free North, not the lazy and exploitative South, must shape the continent. In 1854 when the Kansas-Nebraska Act opened these territories to "squatter sovereignty," Forbes contributed to the New England Emigrant Aid Society, which funded the activities of armed Northern settlers in what became "bloody" Kansas.[74]

During the debate over slavery, Forbes did not forget the hardworking Chinese. In 1856 he convinced himself of the efficacy of a scheme that would have imported contracted Chinese laborers into Florida to work on plantations. By presenting the South with an agricultural model based on nonslave labor, Forbes hoped to deliver a blow to the slave system. The Chinese experiment, however, never advanced beyond the drawing table because a friend persuaded him to abandon the politically explosive scheme. Railroad building would remain the chief vehicle through which Forbes could influence his country.[75]

Chinese Migrations

That Forbes could count on the availability of Chinese labor suggests another manifestation of our theme of dispersal. Along with missionaries, traders, goods, and capital, Chinese people began to spread out in the new era. In the 1830s two China traders went to great lengths to smuggle a single Chinese woman out of China; her exhibition in the United States caused a sensation because few Americans had ever seen a Chinese person. As late as 1847 the owner of the Chinese junk *Keying*, which had sailed from Hong Kong to New York, could promote his Chinese crew as exotic rarities. By 1856, however, Forbes could imagine the Chinese not as individuals but rather as a migratory flow one could direct to a location of one's choosing.[76]

What accounted for this change? One factor was that the Chinese government lost the ability to control borders after the Opium War.[77] If a subject wanted to go overseas, the government could not stop him. Along with loose borders, repellent forces within China—economic, agricultural, and demographic—combined to dislodge thousands of men from their ancestral villages. To pay the large indemnity owed to Britain after the Opium War, the Qing government placed stringent taxes on Guangdong's peasant farmers, forcing many off their land. This tax exacerbated an ever-worsening agricultural crisis caused by a demographic surge: the province's population grew from sixteen million in 1787 to twenty-eight million in 1850. "The population is extremely dense," wrote a foreign observer. The "means of subsistence, in ordinary times, are seldom above the demand, and, consequently, the least failure of the rice crop produces wretchedness." "No one will wonder at the emigrating spirit now alive in China" when one considers the widespread "misery" and "starvation."[78]

Dreams of California gold also inspired the "emigrating spirit." One month after the discovery of gold at Sutter's mill in January 1848, two Chinese men who had accompanied a China trader to San Francisco ventured to the site in search of a quick fortune.[79] In October the sensational news reached Canton. "Good many Americans speak of California," a Cantonese man wrote to his brother in Boston. "Oh! They find gold very quickly. . . . I think I shall go to California next summer."[80] Many Chinese made similar plans. "The stories we hear are wonderful," Samuel Wells

Williams wrote from Canton in 1849. The "El Dorado seems at last to have been found," and the Chinese "resort to California in large numbers."[81] In 1852 alone, twenty thousand embarked for California; by decade's end, the Chinese constituted one-quarter of all miners.[82]

Though gold provided an early magnet, other opportunities for gainful employment also attracted the Chinese to California. After a man opened the first Chinese laundry in 1851, his success inspired others. By 1870 California had nearly three thousand Chinese-owned laundries. Other enterprising Chinese set up commercial fishing operations in California. Those from farming villages brought their agricultural techniques, growing and selling produce to miners. Chinese merchants opened stores in San Francisco that sold the standard Chinese goods to the white population (tea, silk, and porcelain) and ethnic foods and mining supplies to Chinese prospectors. In the late 1860s a Chinese man could find work on the transcontinental railroad.[83]

American shippers sought to capitalize on this migration. To profit from Chinese who could not afford sea passage, they instituted a credit-ticket system. Either the shipper or a broker would lend ticket money to the migrant on the condition that he use his earnings in California to pay off the loan plus interest.[84] To entice potential travelers, shippers posted signs in and around Hong Kong and Canton. "Laborers are wanted in the land of California," one poster read. "Great works to be done there, good houses, plenty of food. . . . The ship is good."[85] Another advertisement preyed on people's dreams for a better life:

> Americans are very rich people. They want the Chinaman to come and make him very welcome. There you will have great pay, large houses and food and clothing of the finest description. . . . It is a nice country, without Mandarins or soldiers. All alike; big man no larger than little man. There are a great many Chinamen there now, and it will not be a strange country.[86]

While American shippers had previously profited only from the transport of Chinese goods, they now carried a new "cargo": Chinese people.

As ridiculous as these portrayals of California were, they fueled the collective imagination of the Cantonese, who began to refer to California as the "Gold Mountain." Though many Chinese met with hard times in the New World, the success stories of a few returning prospectors provided enough fuel to sustain the Gold Mountain mythology.[87] Lee Chew, who grew up in rural Guangdong, recalled being dazzled at age sixteen by one returning traveler. "The man had gone away from our village a poor boy" but returned with "unlimited wealth." He purchased a massive plot of land, walled it off, and proceeded to construct "paradise"—a "palace" surrounded by an elaborate pleasure garden. Just as the Canton trade had powered the upward mobility of many Americans, so did California fuel this man's rise from poor peasant to wealthy landowner. Lee Chew later immigrated to America.[88]

Nearly all those who ventured to California exercised free will in making this choice. According to William Speer, a missionary in San Francisco, the Chinese he saw had not been "brought over by capitalists and worked as slaves . . . against their will."[89] However, some American shipping companies did engage in the coolie trade. In Hong Kong or one of the treaty ports, a shipper would coerce, cajole, or trick several hundred Chinese men into signing long-term labor contracts. The company would next herd these unwilling migrants onto ships bound for plantations in Cuba, Peru, or Hawaii. Like Africans on slave ships, the coolies were inhumanely packed below deck, flogged by the crew, and provided with inadequate food and water. Many died along the way, a few committed suicide, and attempted mutinies were not uncommon. Between 1847 and 1859 American shippers carried an annual average of six thousand Chinese to Cuba alone.[90]

In 1852 Peter Parker adjudicated a mutiny case involving the American *Robert Browne* while filling in as commissioner. Fooled into thinking the ship was bound for San Francisco, 410 Chinese in Amoy signed on to the voyage. Discovering the deception just south of Taiwan, the Chinese organized a mutiny that succeeded in killing the American captain and most of his crew. After two surviving officers reported the mutiny, American and British vessels rounded up twenty-three mutineers and placed them before Parker.[91] After hearing accounts from both sides, Parker acknowledged that the crew had abused the Chinese; nevertheless, he accepted the testimony of the surviving officers. In reporting the matter to Chinese authorities, he charged seventeen of the men with "aggravated piracy" and recommended the death penalty. After a lengthy investigation, Chinese authorities mostly rejected his findings. They executed one man, imprisoned another, and set fifteen free.[92]

Parker came to regret his performance in this case. In siding with those who profited off the coolie trade, he had come across as "gullible" and "harsh."[93] To atone for his error in judgment, Parker raised the issue of the coolie trade with the State Department in 1855. The "traffic in Chinese coolies, as carried on in vessels of the United States," he claimed, "is replete with illegalities, immoralities, and revolting and inhuman atrocities." Parker continued to denounce the coolie trade after retiring in 1857.[94] In 1862, after U.S. Commissioner John Ward repeated Parker's plea for federal action, Congress passed the Prohibition of Coolie Trade Act. Before an American ship could depart a treaty port with Chinese subjects aboard, an American official needed to sign a permit guaranteeing passengers' voluntary emigration.[95]

Conclusion

The First Opium War and the treaties that followed triggered the rapid dispersal of people, goods, capital, and ideas once restricted to a single location. The war also created, with the treaty ports, fresh "contact zones," or loci of Chinese and American encounters.[96] To these encounters, each side often brought a pressing need that only his counterpart could satisfy. In Amoy, David Abeel, after enduring twelve frustrating years in Canton, craved direct engagement with the Chinese. In Xu Jiyu, he met someone equally driven by need: the official hoped to unlock the secret of British power. Similarly in Shanghai, Edward Cunningham, in desperate need of capital for his Yangtze steamship line, solicited investment from local merchants. The Chinese greeted his overtures favorably because they stood to benefit from the partnership. Of course, Sino-American encounters did not always work to the mutual advantage of both parties. Contact zones could foster relationships that were exploitative in nature, like the coolie traffic. As the next chapter shows, an encounter could also result in an explosion, such as mass civil war.

Heavenly War

Americans and the Taiping Rebellion

The zeal that propelled Edwin Stevens to China (see Chapter 4) also caused his frustration in Canton. Driven by evangelical fervor, Stevens had willingly given up what promised to be a comfortable life in the United States and accepted a harder existence in China. However, when he started studying Chinese in 1832, he discovered that he lacked linguistic gifts. Bridgman phrased the point charitably when he characterized Stevens's progress as marked by "accuracy" rather than "rapidity."[1] Unable to contribute to Bridgman's translation projects, Stevens sought other outlets for his energy. His sponsor, the Seaman's Friend Society, expected him to tend to the spiritual needs of sailors, and so he made regular trips to Whampoa to preach on merchant vessels. Unfortunately, this was an unrewarding job if ever there was one. Captains often turned him away, and sailors expressed a clear preference for strong drink over strong religion. After delivering a sermon, Stevens noted glumly that "no one seemed deeply affected."[2] Inside, a personal crisis began to brew. Had he journeyed all the way to China for this?

Stevens craved direct contact with the Chinese. Predictably, he gravitated toward Gützlaff, who took him on an expedition to the tea districts. More than even Gützlaff, Liang Afa impressed Stevens. His clandestine tract distribution evinced greater subtlety than did the intrusive expeditions of the Prussian. By 1834 Liang had begun to employ a new tactic: he proselytized outside the examination hall to civil service candidates within the walled city of Canton. If he could influence a few future officials, they might one day lift the draconian restrictions impeding the spread of Christianity.[3] Though Liang exercised caution, Chinese officials detected his presence in 1834 and subjected him to intense persecution. This disturbing development, coupled with the death of Morrison, greatly distressed Bridgman, who wrote of the "dark clouds" that have "come over us" and "caused us great anxiety." After missionaries smuggled Liang out of China, Stevens stepped in to take his place.[4] In 1836 a man who was almost certainly Edwin Stevens donned Chinese garments, infiltrated Canton, and distributed a tract written by Liang to examination candidates, a group that included Hong Huoxiu.[5]

Seemingly insignificant at the time, this single transmission held enormous consequences. It set in motion a sequence of events that culminated in the bloodiest civil war in human history—the Taiping Rebellion (1850–1864). Along with Stevens, two other Americans played important parts in this story. Hong used Liang's tract to interpret a vivid dream, convincing himself that he was God's son. Eager for spiritual guidance, Hong sought out a second American, Issachar Roberts, a rogue missionary whose aberrant behavior caused his estrangement from the missionary community. After leaving Roberts, Hong launched a traveling ministry to spread his unorthodox religion. When subversive elements glommed onto the movement, Hong found himself at the head of an armed rebellion. Militarily successful, Taiping armies wrestled huge swaths of territory away from Qing control. From his palace in Nanjing, Hong summoned Roberts, who believed it his personal destiny to usher in the Millennium by influencing the Taiping ruler.

The third American to influence this story did so not with Western religion but with Western military techniques. A career adventurer, Frederick Townsend Ward convinced two Chinese elites in Shanghai that, by raising a small army, he could protect their assets during a Taiping invasion. Achieving startling success in battle with an army of Chinese troops, Ward inspired both the fear and the admiration of Qing officials. To control the fiercely independent American, the Qing moved to absorb him into its own bureaucracy. Ward accepted Chinese citizenship, a Chinese title, and a Chinese wife before a bullet took his life.

These three Americans played crucial roles in igniting, nourishing, and then suppressing the Taiping Rebellion. That said, one does not want to overstate their importance by claiming either that the rebellion would not have happened without Stevens and Roberts or that it would not have been crushed without Ward. More accurately, one can state that the uprising, though inevitable given the widespread discontent with Qing rule, received its quasi-Christian coloring from the two missionaries. And Ward, while he should not be credited with defeating the Taipings, demonstrated the military effectiveness of a novel combination—Chinese soldiers trained according to American military methods. The stories of these three men also highlight the role of American individualism in China. Stevens acted on his own initiative when he infiltrated Canton; Roberts lacked institutional sanction in heading alone into Taiping territory; and Ward formed his paramilitary force in defiance of U.S. neutrality. Each man, in his own imagination, cast himself as a solitary bringer of change to China.

A Single Tract

It began with a single tract. Though the tract emerged out of the missionary operation, it was written not by Morrison or Bridgman but by Liang Afa. Born in 1789 in a farming village outside Canton, Liang studied the major Confucian texts in school before his parents' poverty forced him to drop out. In 1804 he moved to Canton, where he learned woodblock printing while leading a dissolute lifestyle involving gambling and alcohol. In 1813 he began handling printing jobs for Robert Morrison and William Milne. Under their influence, Liang came to see Christianity as the antidote to vice. After reforming himself, he received his baptism with great joy in 1816. The power of the Holy Spirit, he believed, had miraculously cleansed his life of moral dissipation.[6]

What was good for one man could also better society. That was Liang's rationale as he composed *Good Words to Admonish the Age* (1832). Because it was written by a Chinese missionary, *Good Words* possessed qualities that set it apart from all other Christian tracts. By filtering Protestant theology through his Chinese consciousness, Liang rendered it palatable to its target readers. Liang also modeled *Good Words* on Confucian morality books, which stressed the cultivation of the individual. Most missionaries regarded Confucianism as a rival philosophical system that a potential convert must jettison as a precondition to accepting Christ. Bucking this trend, Liang held that filial piety, a key Confucian concept, was exactly what Chinese society needed. The problem with Confucianism, however, was that it did not stress filial piety enough, a shortcoming Christianity rectified. According to Liang, Christianity pictured the world as governed by a "Heavenly Father" who "loves mankind as a parent loves his children." In return for his fatherly love, humanity must, like dutiful sons and daughters, obey God by leading lives of moral devotion. Christianity, in other words, offered an intensified version of filial piety. It was more Confucian than Confucianism.

Liang also believed that Chinese society had grown so sinful that only a strong, monotheistic religion could regenerate it. Confucianism no longer presented a viable vehicle for reform, having grown stale and corrupt. Liang also rejected Daoism and Buddhism because, in their pantheistic portrayals of the cosmos, they dispersed divine power among multiple deities, tragically weakening it in the process. Compounding the problem, these religions mistakenly diluted purity by encouraging the worship of "lifeless images." Only Christianity concentrated divine power in a single entity, God the Father, and so it alone could bring the drastic reform China needed.[7]

Liang also dismissed both Confucianism's explanation for evil and the remedy it prescribed. According to that philosophy, evil might temporarily tempt one to wander down an immoral path, but one could always take corrective measures by cultivating virtue. As Liang surveyed society, the prevalence of sin convinced him beyond doubt that this characterization woefully underestimated evil's power. Far more persuasive was the Christian account, which centered on the fall of man in the Garden of Eden. In that story, the serpent wields substantial power, enough to seduce Adam and Eve into disobeying God the Father. In Liang's retelling, original sin becomes humanity's first act of filial impiety. "If everyone in the country believed in God and followed His commandments," Liang admonished, "the poor would be peaceful and the rich good and virtuous. . . . Fathers would be merciful and sons filial; officials would be uncorrupt and the people happy." Instead of locking doors at night, humanity could live in a world that was "peaceful, bright, and good."[8]

In crucial spots, *Good Words* offered vagueness when precision was needed. Preoccupied with China's degeneration, Liang cited biblical antecedents for rampant immorality, such as Sodom and Gomorrah and Noah's ark. When civilizations sink to these nadirs, Liang ominously claimed, God always responds in one of two ways: he either afflicts them with "disasters" so as "to warn us" or orders "other nations to attack us." In the 1840s a reader of *Good Words* could only assume that this reference to foreign invaders referred to the Opium War. Somewhat confusingly, however, Liang infused God with ambiguity, characterizing him as not just vengeful against sinners but infinitely merciful: he destroys corrupt peoples but also sends his Son to redeem humankind. Muddying the water further, Liang failed to present a coherent timeline for Christ's term on earth. Though Liang knew that Jesus had come and gone, the temporal indeterminacy of his text left the point susceptible to misinterpretation. A reader not familiar with Christian theology could easily misconstrue Liang's writings and think that rampant sin heralded the coming of the redeemer. The Son of God had not yet appeared on earth, but he would be arriving soon, perhaps in China.[9]

First Spark

Hong Huoxiu had taken, and failed, the civil service examinations once before. A member of the Hakka minority, Hong had grown up in a village in Hua County, thirty miles north of Canton. His parents, though not rich, supported Hong's studies in the hope that he would become the first in the family to pass the examinations. Since this financial assistance did not cover the living expenses of Hong and his wife, he took up work as a schoolteacher. When Hong arrived in Canton in 1836, he carried the weight of his family's dreams on his shoulders.

As Hong milled about with other candidates near the examination hall, a foreigner approached him. Speaking through a Cantonese translator, the man informed him that he would "attain the highest rank." The next the day, the same man handed Hong a copy of *Good Words*. Hong gave the tract only a glance, since he was more concerned about the examination, which he proceeded to fail. After recovering from the disappointment, he resumed his study in anticipation of the next year's test. *Good Words* sat on his shelf forgotten. Hong would never again see the mysterious foreigner, who was probably Edwin Stevens. While visiting Singapore in 1836, Stevens was waylaid by a sickness that punished him with a high fever and excruciating headaches before it killed him.[10]

After Hong learned he had failed the examination a third time in 1837, the crushing blow was more than he could bear. Becoming ill, he took to his bed. Believing that death was near, he called his family members to his bedside and apologized for his inability to win glory. "O my parents! How badly have I returned the favour of your love to me!" he exclaimed. "I shall never attain a name that may reflect its lustre upon you."[11] After acknowledging filial failure, Hong entered into a feverish sleep that produced a remarkably lifelike dream.

In the dream, Hong ascends to heaven in a sedan chair. When he reaches the gates, a group of attendants wearing dragon robes cuts him open and removes the black impurities of the earthly world. He is next brought before his father, a man with a golden beard, who informs him that the people have lost their "original natures" because "demon devils . . . have led them astray." Hong volunteers to fight the demons, who are led by Yan Luo, the king of hell. As Hong prepares for battle, he learns that he has an older brother, who intends to join him in the demon war. When battle commences, the two brothers and their celestial army roll through the evil hordes, slaying demons one by one. At one point, Hong even holds the slippery Yan Lou in his grasp when, unexpectedly, his father commands him to release their ancient foe. If captured, the demon king might disguise himself as a serpent, contaminate the heavens, and consume human souls. Thus, at the close of battle, the cosmos is not entirely cleansed of evil. The father instructs Hong to change his name and return to earth to exterminate the demons that remain.

While deep in slumber, Hong startled his family members by physically acting out the events of his dream. "Slash the demons," he called out as he jabbed an imaginary sword in the air, "one here, one there." After waking, he formally requested that all family members call him by his new name, Hong Xiuquan. Though they obliged, many suspected he had gone mad. Shortly after the strange dream, normalcy returned to Hong's life. Still entertaining hopes of passing the examination, he returned to his books and began to teach school again. His amazing dream continued to intrigue him; however, since he lacked the means to interpret it, it remained a colorful enigma.[12]

In 1843 Hong worked up the nerve to take the examinations a fourth time. This effort too ended in bitter failure. In frustration, Hong hurled his books and launched a tirade against the Qing officials who had administered the examinations. Months later, Hong's cousin noticed *Good Words* on the shelf and asked to borrow it. After reading it, he urged Hong to do the same. The latter discovered—to his astonishment—that the tract offered the key to decoding his dream! The golden-bearded man was God the Father. The brother with whom Hong fought was Jesus. The various attendants were angels. Yan Lou was Satan. As for Hong himself, he was none other than the brother of Jesus, or God's second son. "If I had received the books without having gone through the sickness, I should not have dared to believe in them," Hong later remarked to another cousin, Hong Rengan. "If I had merely been sick but not also received the books, I should have had no further evidence as to the truth of my visions." When combined, the book and vision formed a mandate from God: "The will of Heaven rests with me."[13]

Hong moved to proselytize. After converting family members and villagers to his version of Christianity, he passed the next few years engaged in a traveling ministry in Guangdong and Guanxi Provinces. In 1846 an acquaintance of Hong's learned during a trip to Canton of an American preacher, Issachar Roberts, who had established a mission within the walled city. Locating Roberts's Chinese assistant, the acquaintance shared the news of Hong's mystical dream. Certain that Roberts would want to meet this visionary, the assistant sent a message to Hong urging him to visit Canton.[14]

Bitter Baptists

Issachar Jacox Roberts baffled almost everyone he knew. His aberrant personality presented an amalgam of traits one seldom saw bundled together. Those who strongly disliked Roberts—incidentally, the clear majority—cited his stubborn disposition, uncouth mannerisms, boorish behavior, unsanitary slovenliness, and ugly selfishness. In China Roberts stepped on many toes, always remaining oblivious as to how his actions affected others. Before we dismiss Roberts as a Bible-toting Sasquatch, we must complete the portrait. Roberts was also motivated by a driving ambition to change China and by a passion for the Gospel that even his harshest critics conceded was genuine. Roberts set lofty goals for himself, which he doggedly pursued, often in the face of danger or against the wishes and warnings of others. He also possessed a high degree of cunning that most observers failed to detect, hidden as it was beneath an unrefined exterior. This wily streak, when combined with his innate gift for histrionics, allowed him to escape predicaments, most of which were of his own making.

Born on a farm in Tennessee in 1802, Roberts received only a fragmented education at various country schools. He did not graduate from college, though he did study at Furman Academy and Theological Institute in South Carolina for several months. In the early 1830s, while perusing a Baptist periodical, Roberts encountered Gützlaff's passionate appeal to the Christian world. Something stirred deep within Roberts, and his life's purpose emerged from a fog: he must join Gützlaff. After hastily assembling required documents, he sent his application to the Baptist Board in Boston, which, following standard review procedure, contacted the references he had listed. When the responses came, red flags jumped off the paper. "His talent as a preacher is not above mediocrity," observed the most favorable evaluator, who found his personality "vexious." "His native talent is moderate," replied a second, "though unfortunately he seems not to know it" since there was in him "a deficiency in his apprehension." A third, who had seen Roberts conduct church services, reported that "as a preacher, I must say, he is not popular here." Though none disputed Roberts's physical health and Christian piety, they nevertheless judged him unfit for missionary work. The board rejected Roberts's candidacy.[15]

A hard blow like this would have sent many spiraling into self-doubt. Not Roberts. The rejection merely glanced off the armor of his self-confidence, which was surprisingly resilient given that he had received so few accolades in life. Undeterred by one closed door, Roberts forced open another. He founded the China Mission Society, mortgaging his own farm in Mississippi to fund it. As its first action, the society appointed Roberts its missionary to China. Before sailing, Roberts installed as president a man named William Buck, who wrote to Gützlaff to inform him of Robert's plans. Gützlaff replied that he was "moved to tears" by Roberts's willingness to sacrifice all earthly possessions "upon the altar of the Lord." He and Roberts must not limit themselves to the "outskirts" of China but rather must "with *iron perseverance* attack the stronghold of Satan."[16]

When Roberts arrived in Macao in 1837, five months after the death of Edwin Stevens, he moved into Gützlaff's residence. Having groomed Stevens, Gützlaff welcomed a new American who shared Stevens's appetite for high-risk evangelism. Roberts discovered he was not the first American Baptist in China; that distinction belonged to a married couple from Virginia, Jehu Lewis and Henrietta Shuck, who had arrived in 1836. Though Roberts and Jehu Lewis Shuck did not agree on much, both favored the Spartan Gützlaff's intensely physical model of evangelism over the Athenian Bridgman's cerebral variety. As for Bridgman's circle, Shuck and Roberts felt certain they were not wanted there.

Nor were their impressions ill founded. The highly educated New Englanders regarded the southern Baptists as ill-mannered country cousins. Shuck and Bridgman sparred over the issue of baptism, with Shuck embracing the dramatic immersion-in-a-river technique and Bridgman advocating the more delicate sprinkling of drops on the head. Bridgman and his clique, Shuck vented to his board, "have no converts, no churches and no extensive Militant missionary operations, yet they regard it as interference for Baptist missionaries to come to Canton or Macau. Interfere with what?" While Bridgman battled Shuck, Peter Parker unleashed a torrent of scorn on the character of Roberts. The Tennessean was an "illiterate" and "indiscreet man," who appeared childlike in his pathetic understanding of "human nature & the world." Speaking more generally, Parker characterized the arrival of Baptists "as one of the greatest calamities that have befallen this mission since its establishment." In the gilt triptych of Bridgman, Parker, and Williams, there was no room for Baptists. Shuck and Roberts felt this snub acutely.[17]

The grumbling Shuck simply went about his business, though carrying a chip on his shoulder. For Roberts the disrespect of fellow missionaries provided more grist for the motivational mill. As Shuck came to realize, Roberts's outward appearances deceived. Deep inside the gruff and inarticulate man, outrageous visions of self-grandeur glowed white hot. As these visions had never received corroboration in the real world, they bordered on delusional in Shuck's opinion. Roberts was propelled by a "desire to glorify himself," Shuck remarked, that amounted to a "monomania." How did Roberts propose to earn undying glory? He would personally bring about the conversion of China.[18]

As long as the Mississippi property continued to generate revenue, Roberts could afford to ignore Shuck. When that source of funding sputtered, as it did in 1841, Roberts abruptly found himself in dire need of support from the Baptist Board, the sponsor of Shuck. To persuade the board to fund his work, Roberts arranged for his China Mission Society to send an appeal to Boston. Though the board had denied Roberts once before, it was prepared to reconsider his candidacy now that he had found his way to China. Only one stumbling block remained: Shuck. When the board wrote Shuck to gauge his willingness to accept a new colleague, he doused its hope for a Shuck-Roberts partnership. "It is my duty to assure you that he understands the *principles* of no language," Shuck wrote of Roberts's communications skills, "not even the English." Worse still, "his egotism and forwardness would never permit of his working with another."[19]

As adamant as Shuck was, he was about to be bamboozled. Roberts was not willing to let his China dream slip away solely on account of Shuck's personal dislike. Roberts had the hidden talent of being able to summon at will seemingly heartfelt feelings of contrition. In Shuck's presence, a visibly distraught Roberts not only confessed the errors of his ways but also, in a dramatic show of penitence, fasted for ten days. Convinced of the sincerity of Roberts's self-reproach, Shuck reversed himself. "A number of circumstances . . . have wrought wonderful changes in Mr. R's mind, feelings, opinions and ideas," Shuck reported to the board. "My heart has been drawn endearedly toward him." With Shuck's endorsement, the board agreed to sponsor Roberts and promptly sent him to Hong Kong. Shuck belatedly discovered he had been fooled.[20]

In Hong Kong Roberts found misery. As the people were mostly illiterate, they could not read his tracts. That, when combined with his own inability to speak Cantonese, precluded any meaningful exchange from taking place. Worse still, his mission—little more than a hovel—was situated a half day's walk from the nearest English settlement. In sum, Roberts found himself living alone in an isolated outpost on China's fringe when the consummation of his dream required that he penetrate the interior. Just when Roberts needed a way out, his only friend in China reappeared.[21]

The Canton Mission

Gützlaff had returned. During the war, the British made good use of the Prussian's linguistic abilities, deploying him as translator on military expeditions to the north. After the fall of Ningbo in 1841, the British installed him as magistrate of the city where, according to a widely circulated rumor, he enjoyed two concubines. In 1842 he moved to Hong Kong, where he planned to reinvigorate his mission with a bold plan designed to capitalize on China's openness. At great expense, he intended to dispatch hundreds of native colporteurs to distribute tracts in every province. He proposed, in essence, to blanket China with paper-based Christianity. The Prussian impresario also invited Westerners to join his grand enterprise, as long as they were willing to don Chinese garb.[22]

Roberts, of course, was. While almost everyone found Roberts repugnant, Gützlaff's belief in him never wavered. Finding Roberts languishing in Hong Kong, Gützlaff urged him to disobey the board and make history by founding the first Protestant mission inside the walled city of Canton. He promised to help support the mission with money and manpower. Eager to escape Hong Kong, Roberts needed no coaxing. Roberts "acts almost entirely under the influence of Mr. Gutzlaff," Shuck observed, a man of "strange, not to say doubtful piety."[23]

Because Protestant missionaries had occupied the foreign factories since 1807, the short move past the wall might not appear significant. However, there was a reason missionaries hesitated to venture into the city: Canton was a hornet's nest of virulent xenophobia. The city's residents had not forgotten the atrocities committed by British soldiers during the war. One British unit had broken into local tombs so as to study Chinese embalming practices. A local newspaper recounted multiple instances of foreign soldiers "lewdly plundering" temples, "opening graves," and "scattering the bones about." If the desecration of graves was not enough, Sepoy troops (Indians serving in the British military) had raped village women, an outrageous crime that inspired angry Cantonese to mobilize against British soldiers in the Sanyuanli incident. As Roberts prepared to hang his shingle, these violations continued to smolder in the collective memory of local Cantonese.[24]

Though obtuse, Roberts did understand the inherent danger of his planned Canton mission. So too did his three Chinese assistants—Chun, Chow, and Cheng—who dreaded the move. In April 1844 Roberts held a ceremony designed to steel their resolve, bolster their courage, and bond them to the holy task before them. After leading them through a series of rituals, Roberts arrived at the "great question." "I was indeed afraid to ask because I knew it would present to them a cross" that they might prove unable to bear. Turning to Chun, the oldest, Roberts asked, "Will you go with me to preach the gospel in Canton?" "Yes, most assuredly!" Chun called out. After Chow and Cheng followed suit, Roberts moved forward with his plans.[25]

Though early success encouraged Roberts, trouble began to brew in 1847 when he built a chapel in the poorest section of the city. The strange new structure attracted the attention of the local population, who eyed it with suspicion. Jittery shopkeepers, who viewed Canton as a powder keg lacking only a spark, expressed to Roberts their uneasiness over his provocative structure. Undeterred, Roberts installed a gong. "I am now considering," he wrote one day, whether "to commence beating the gong" to call locals to worship. "Oh Lord, direct me." Somewhat nervously, Roberts banged the gong, and to his relief, nothing untoward transpired.[26]

Hong and Roberts

That same spring, two men from a small village appeared at the mission. They had come "for the sole purpose," Roberts exclaimed, "of being instructed in the gospel!"[27] One of them had received a "vision of angels" that "showed him things" he did "not know the meaning of" until later reading *Good Words*.[28] This amazing story, Roberts wrote, "affords the most satisfaction of any Chinese experience I have ever heard."[29] Hong Xiuquan had reached Canton, and for one month Roberts tutored him. Hong returned home and then made a second journey to Canton to continue his training.

After two additional months under Roberts, Hong expressed his wish to be baptized, and his teacher agreed he was ready. The baptism, however, never took place. Roberts's assistants had jealously noted the attention their employer heaped on the new recruit. One of them, fearing he would lose his salaried position to Hong, plotted sabotage. Appearing to act with good intentions, he advised Hong to ask for financial assistance from Roberts. When the trusting Hong made this request, it caused his undoing.[30] To prevent those lacking in pure motives from joining the church, Roberts told Hong, baptisms were never accompanied by guarantees for "employment" or "pecuniary emolument." Roberts halted the ceremony, and Hong fell into despair. "I know not what will become of me," he cried, as "I am poor" and "have no living." "The baptism was postponed indefinitely," Roberts wrote, "and I saw him no more."[31]

A decade later, Roberts revisited the encounter in an article he wrote for *Putnam's Magazine*. Hong, he recalled, had experienced acute shame after failing to receive the holy sacrament, feeling much as he had following his four unsuccessful attempts to pass the state examination. However, with the advantage of hindsight, Roberts could discern the hand of God in both the aborted baptism and the failed examinations. "We must believe that an all-wise Providence overruled in both instances," Roberts wrote. Had Hong passed the examinations, his ambition would have expressed itself within Qing bureaucracy. And had Roberts dunked Hong in a river, he would have aspired only to become Roberts's assistant. God, in his infinite wisdom, had thwarted both of Hong's early dreams, Roberts claimed, so as to keep his life unfulfilled in anticipation of a much larger role.[32]

Turmoil

Like Hong, Roberts met with setbacks in pursuit of his dream. After Hong departed, he resumed work on his chapel. If the gong had not been provocative enough, Roberts next set his sights on a belfry. After completing the steeple in May 1847 and installing a mammoth bell, Roberts received a visit from his landlord, who informed him that a "conjurer" was busily inciting unrest among the locals by pointing out the steeple's poor feng shui. "It was not a good thing for my bell-steeple," Roberts learned, "to be in its present position with regard to the Queen of Heaven's temple." Roberts had been warned, but he refused to revise his plans. This time he paid a price. One day, a "rabble" accosted Roberts in an "abusive manner." Returning from an outing later that evening, he discovered that his chapel had been ransacked. The thieves had stolen everything he owned—furniture, files, books. The bell was gone.[33]

When it rains, it pours. Over the next few months, Roberts absorbed more blows, nearly all of which were self-inflicted. He began by repelling Francis Johnson, a new Baptist missionary who wrote the board specifically to complain about him. Churches must select "men of *knowledge*" and "of *good education*," Johnson exhorted. If they send just "*any man*" with "hot zeal" they "will *inevitably* do *positive* harm." "As to the prospects" of the mission, "they are as dark as darkness." Fearing that Johnson would jeopardize his mission, Roberts moved to perform the same act of alchemy that had worked on Shuck: to transform the lead of scornful criticism into the gold of ardent approval. After speaking with Roberts, Johnson mystified the board by recanting. "In a letter written by me last year, I wronged my Bro. Roberts," a penitent Johnson wrote. "I have had words with my Bro. Roberts" and "he has accepted my confession of Sin."[34]

The crisis averted, Roberts struggled to cope with the isolation of his Canton life. For a brief while, he held out hope that a new Baptist, George Pearcy, might offer companionship. Pearcy, however, developed an acute dislike for Roberts. After refusing to allow Roberts to share his living space ("Brother Pearcy . . . thinks we can love each other better apart!"), Pearcy moved to Shanghai, partly to escape Roberts.[35] Though Pearcy's exit again left Roberts alone, he found a silver lining. Acting on his own authority, Roberts absorbed Pearcy's congregation, assuring the confused Chinese that Pearcy had approved of the merger. He then burned all paper records associated with his rival's church.

Though Roberts had doubled the size of his congregation, the problem of loneliness persisted. "Days, weeks, and months without a living soul to bear me company," he wrote. "It is not good for a man to be alone." Back in the board's good graces, Roberts addressed his isolation by making an odd request. "The favor desired," he wrote, is that "the Board will send me a suitable female of sound health."[36] Roberts wanted a wife, and the board, astonishingly, initiated a search. However, before its selection, Harriet Baker, could reach Canton, the impatient Roberts had taken Chun to the United States to locate a wife on his own.[37] Though he successfully wooed Virginia Young of Kentucky, he also created more trouble for himself. On board a Mississippi steamship bound for New Orleans in 1849, Roberts physically and verbally abused Chun before a group of shocked passengers who felt obliged to intervene. Unluckily for Roberts, the witnesses included a Baptist minister who reported the incident to the board. "You may rely on it," this man wrote, that the victimized "servant" was "superior to his master" in terms of "natural intelligence, humility, gentlemanly deportment and Christianity." Its patience nearly exhausted, the board resolved to terminate its sponsorship if Roberts made another misstep.[38]

The board did not have long to wait. In 1850 Roberts, his wife, and Harriet Baker moved into a Canton residence with James Bridgman, Elijah's cousin. To Elijah's concern, James exhibited disturbing symptoms of depression. "I did all I could to cheer and encourage him," Elijah wrote. Nothing seemed to work. As James's melancholy deepened, he increasingly withdrew from society.[39] One Sunday morning, after Roberts had gone out to preach, Harriet Baker and Virginia Roberts heard a scream. Rushing to the source, they found James bleeding profusely, having just slit his throat. In a panic, they sent for Peter Parker, who raced over, and Issachar Roberts, who did not. Instead of coming in person, Roberts sent a note that baffled and horrified Baker. "He must be deranged," she said, as she repeated Roberts's one-sentence reply: "Let the dead bury their dead, but I must preach the gospel." Though Parker made a heroic effort, he had arrived too late to save James. When the board learned of the suicide and Roberts's incomprehensible indifference to it, it was apoplectic. To refuse to offer aid to a dying man was not just negligent and not just unchristian—it was *inhuman*! The board dissolved its relationship with Roberts.[40]

Realizing the magnitude of his error, Roberts took measures to save himself. Needing respected individuals willing to vouch for him, Roberts targeted Peter Parker. Who, after all, could provide a better character witness than the renowned physician who had also played a role in this particular case? Obtaining Parker's support, however, presented a stiff challenge. Parker had earlier maligned Roberts as a blight on Protestant missions. More recently, he had judged harshly Roberts's callous response to James's suicide. Not surprisingly, Parker went into their meeting determined to reject Roberts's plea. Like others before him, he had grossly underestimated Roberts, who again summoned that strange power that allowed him to turn the toughest critic into the staunchest ally. After the interview, Parker—as if under hypnosis—sent the board a lengthy defense of Roberts. "It is self-moved that I now address you," Parker began, before portraying Roberts as a "self-denying servant of Christ." Though Roberts had flaws, Parker attributed these to "his not having enjoyed all those early advantages of education and acquaintance with the world which others have." As for the suicide, Parker assured the board that Roberts had spent the previous night with the spiritually lost man, "uniting with him . . . at a throne of grace."[41]

Roberts convinced others to rally behind his cause. U.S. consul Paul Forbes backed Roberts, as did other missionaries. In Kentucky Peter Buck drummed up support by publishing the board's correspondence with Roberts in the *Western Recorder*, a Baptist periodical Buck edited. As a result of his public relations strategy, many readers came to view Roberts as a sympathetic figure, a man of deep religious conviction who had been wrongly ousted by his own board. "He is violently assailed," wrote one irate reader, "not by infidels or anti-missionaries, but his own brethren! Baptists!" Despite Roberts's efforts, the board refused to reverse its decision. Only a miracle could save Roberts's China dream. A miracle is what he got.[42]

Summoned

After the failed baptism in 1847, Hong returned to the region of his birth to fine-tune and promulgate his message. He printed an expanded version of his vision in which he added an episode involving Confucius. As the story now went, the Heavenly Father presides over a hearing in which he charges Confucius with misguiding China for centuries. Realizing his predicament, Confucius flees to join the devils of earth, only to be tracked down by Hong himself, who drags the false sage back to heaven where angels flog him. Confucius pleads for forgiveness, which the Heavenly Father grants, on the condition that he never again venture to earth.

In the late 1840s the movement attracted followers. One convert, Xiao Chaogui, impressed Hong with his ability to channel Jesus Christ while in a trance. Mostly though, Hong appealed to subversive and disaffected elements—bandits, river pirates, landless peasants, ethnic minorities, and members of secret societies—who brought their antidynastic orientation to the movement. By 1849 Hong and his followers had identified the demons of his dream: the Qing rulers. By 1850 the movement had gained military capability, with the inevitable clashes with Qing forces beginning in 1851. On January 11 of that year, Hong proclaimed the founding of the Kingdom of Heavenly Peace ("Taiping Tien-kuo") and commanded all to call him the "Tien Wang," or Heavenly King.[43]

Though dimly aware of the expanding rebellion, Roberts had remained oblivious to his own connection to it. On a trip to Hong Kong in 1852, Roberts happened to read Taiping documents left behind by Hong's cousin,

Hong Rengan. The moment yielded an amazing discovery: the movement's leader was his former student! The revelation activated a latent megalomania, and Roberts's imagination ran wild. "The chief, having been already taught by the missionary," Roberts wrote, referring to himself, "will, I presume, be accessible and teachable." Hong "will learn the truth fully as it is in Jesus," and then, "co-operating with the missionary," he will become engaged "in communicating the same to his people." The plan Roberts hatched was simple: he would teach Hong, and Hong would teach the millions of Chinese under his control. China would be Christianized, and Roberts, as Hong's chief adviser, would stun the world and silence his critics by having triggered the Millennium.[44]

In 1853 a messenger from Nanjing, now the Taiping capital, fueled Roberts's megalomania. He carried a letter sent—to Roberts's indescribable joy—by Hong himself. "Though it is so long since we parted, yet I constantly cherished a remembrance of you," Hong began, before getting to the point:

> I have promulgated the Ten Commandments to the army and the rest of the population, and have taught them all to pray morning and evening. Still those who understand the Gospel are not many. Therefore, I . . . request you, my elder brother, to [come and] bring with you many brethren to help to propagate the Gospel and administer the ordinance of baptism.[45]

The Heavenly King had summoned Roberts to Nanjing. As Roberts digested the information, he could not have failed to note that real life had begun to conform to his fantasies. After sailing to Shanghai, Roberts planned to reach the Taiping capital by taking a boat up the Yangtze River. "Never were the prospects for usefulness, with God's blessing, brighter," a euphoric Roberts wrote. "They almost dazzle!"[46]

Two obstacles stood between Roberts and Nanjing. First, Qing forces had erected a blockade between Shanghai and the rebel stronghold. Second, the United States, with its official position of neutrality, could not grant the request of any citizen seeking permission to travel to Nanjing. The trick, which Roberts failed to realize, was not to ask. "I'll hang you if you attempt it," responded the irascible U.S. commissioner Humphrey Marshall to Roberts's application. In truth, Marshall wanted Roberts to venture to Nanjing so he could obtain intelligence. "Why could not the infernal ass go without saying anything to me about it?" Humphrey vented. "Of course I had to tell him 'no.'" Roberts would have to wait.[47]

For seven years Roberts looked for an opening. Returning to the United States, he launched an aggressive public relations campaign to drum up support for his mission. Not surprisingly, he boasted frequently of his special relationship with the Taiping leader. As for Hong, he made inquiries about Roberts to foreign dignitaries, such as Britain's Lord Elgin, who paid him visits. Finally, in 1860 a series of developments allowed Roberts to depart for Nanjing.[48] First, the Second Opium War (1856–1860), which pitted British and French forces against the Qing, ended with the Treaty of Tianjin, which granted foreigners the freedom to travel anywhere in the empire. Second, Roberts, for once, had money, having successfully won, after a prolonged legal dispute, a suit for damages to his Canton chapel from exhausted Qing authorities. Third, the Taiping capture of Suzhou, a city just to the west of Shanghai, simplified the logistics of travel to Taiping territory. Meeting with Taiping representatives in Suzhou, Roberts received a horse, servant, and guide.[49] As he approached Nanjing, he believed that his "wonderful vindication" lay tantalizingly near. God had chosen Roberts, William Buck wrote, as his "honored instrument in bringing about this revolution."[50]

The Dream Collapses

When Roberts stepped inside the palace of the Heavenly King, his thoughts probably drifted to personal redemption. This, after all, was to be the transformative moment of his life. If it went well, it would retroactively cleanse his muddy past, converting all the hardship, rebuffs, and acrimony into the heroic trials of God's loyal servant on his inexorable path to glory. Unfortunately, things got off to a rocky start. Before Hong made his entrance, court attendants instructed Roberts to kneel in subservience before their ruler. Roberts refused on the ground that such deference was reserved for God alone. However, when a voice commanded all to bow before the "Lord," Roberts dropped to his knees, only to realize that his obeisance honored not God but Hong.[51]

To Roberts's disappointment, the hierarchy implied by this symbolic moment structured the interview that followed. Though Roberts had come to Nanjing to fix the egregious theological errors propounded by the Taipings, Hong had other ideas. Believing that the erstwhile teacher must become the humble student, Hong intended to convert Roberts to the Taiping faith, which was based less on the Scriptures and more on Hong's revelations. Roberts would then go out into the world as Hong's apostle. Over the course of the interview, Hong also offered to provide Roberts with three concubines and a position as director of foreign affairs. Declining both wives and title, Roberts did accept living quarters, a stipend, and a yellow robe. With Roberts's purpose left vague, the interview ended.[52]

What exactly was Roberts expected to do? Yung Wing, a Yale graduate who had studied in Macau under Samuel Brown, visited Nanjing and beheld Roberts "dressed in his yellow satin robe of state" and "clumsy Chinese shoes." Trying to pin down Roberts's position, Yung speculated that he was "a religious adviser" or "secretary of state" but admitted, "I was at a loss to know." Yung's inability to define Roberts's role reflected the nebulous nature of his position.[53] For a while, Roberts entertained the hope that, by influencing Hong, he might rid Taiping theology of its monstrous aberrations. Hong, however, offered no hint he could be swayed. "Add to your faith," Hong wrote Roberts. "I am the one savior of the chosen people. Why do you feel uncertain of the fact of divine communications to me?" Making matters worse, Hong was becoming inaccessible. In the early 1860s the reclusive leader withdrew into an inner sanctum, granting audience only to intimate friends and family members. Roberts could not influence a man he could not see.[54]

Roberts recognized the intractable nature of his predicament: the Taipings would never amend their faith, and he, Roberts, would never preach their blasphemy. Exacerbating his troubles, the outside world, both his supporters and critics, eagerly awaited his report from Nanjing. Since Roberts had staked his entire reputation on his special relationship with Hong, he found himself in an unenviable position. Should he continue to profess the great promise held by the movement, despite his own apostasy? Or should he impart the tragic truth and lose all of his supporters?

It was a terrible dilemma, and Roberts handled it as best as he could. His solution was to split his self into private and public halves, privately maintaining integrity while publicly propagating a lie. Inside Nanjing, Roberts resolved to preach Christianity correctly, as he saw it, even if his street sermons placed his life in danger. To the outside world, however, he would send optimistic reports urging fellow missionaries to rally behind the Taiping cause. He would, in other words, *Robertsize*, a verb coined by other missionaries and meaning to describe something as "entirely different from what it really is."[55]

Accepting Roberts's call in 1861, T. P. Crawford, an American Baptist, visited Nanjing and later returned to Shanghai to share his gloomy assessment. It was "unwise and useless" to plant missionaries in Nanjing, he reported, in direct contradiction to Roberts's glowing reports, which he dismissed as a desperate man's pathetic attempt "to humbug the world." The picture painted by Roberts and the reality in Nanjing were as different "as night is from day." Roberts held "no power or influence" over the Taipings, "except in his own vain imagination." Most shockingly, the man had degenerated physically: he lived in a "miserable old dirty room," wore the "cast-off robes of the chiefs," and was "the dirtiest, greasiest white man I ever saw." In Shanghai, Crawford's account exposed Roberts's grand deception. Skeptics who had long doubted Roberts's veracity pounced. "The fanatic Roberts," gloated the pro-British *North China Herald*, "must be looked on as a most untrustworthy witness" through whose "blatant folly" the "English public were deceived as to the motives . . . of the rebellion." Roberts was a "foolish old man . . . crowned with a tawdry tiara."[56]

The China dream of Issachar Roberts lay in shambles—nothing could save it now. It remained to be seen only how his Taiping saga would end. Roberts continued to preach the Gospel in Nanjing, delivering provocative sermons that mercilessly assailed Taiping doctrines. These incendiary rants, according to Josiah Cox, an American missionary who visited Nanjing in 1861, rapidly earned Roberts the enmity of Taiping leaders. Given their hatred of him, Cox asked Roberts why they allowed him to stay. Cox learned, to his astonishment, that God had endorsed Roberts in Hong's presence; controlled by "superstition," Hong had convinced himself that "calamities would follow Mr. Roberts's removal."[57] Roberts, in short, was a protected species. When a merchant for Heard and Company returned from Nanjing, he included Roberts in the list of sights enjoyed during his tour. "We did the Porcelain Tower," he reported, "the Heavenly Palace—old Roberts—and the Tartar City." To ensure the safety of the charmed missionary, Hong Xiuquan ordered Hong Rengan to provide Roberts with protection.[58]

Hong Rengan had met Roberts before. Back in 1847 he had journeyed to Canton with Hong to meet Roberts. After this trip, Rengan lost touch with his cousin's movement, only to rejoin it in 1859 when he managed to infiltrate the Qing blockade and reach Nanjing. Overjoyed to be reunited with Rengan, Hong dubbed him the "Shield King" and appointed him prime minister, charged with overseeing economic, religious, and military reform. When ordered to guard Roberts, Rengan regarded the assignment as fraught with peril. Once other officials recognized that Rengan's protection allowed Roberts to continue battering Taiping beliefs, they would stop supporting his reform program. However, if Rengan were to permit these men to kill or evict Roberts, his failure to protect Roberts would attract his cousin's fury. Rengan's position appeared hopeless.[59]

What if Roberts were to leave Nanjing on his own accord? On January 13, 1862, an incident, one perhaps orchestrated by Hong Rengan with that end in mind, succeeded in driving Roberts out. According to Roberts's account, Rengan "stormed" into his quarters and went berserk. After hurling invective at the missionary, Rengan became violent. He threw "a cup of tea in my face," "shook me violently," and "struck me on my right cheek." Far worse, the enraged Rengan turned on a servant boy, whom Roberts "loved like a son," and murdered him with a sword. "After having slain my poor, harmless, helpless boy, he jumped on his head most fiend-like, and stamped it with his foot."[60] Fleeing Nanjing, Roberts jumped aboard a British warship and immediately began to describe the incident in a letter later printed in the *North China Herald*. He also renounced the entire movement and the "crazy man" at its head. In a postscript, Roberts charged Rengan with theft, in addition to homicide. Roberts had been in Shanghai "ten days," and still Rengan had not sent his things. "Heathen cannibals," Roberts closed, "could not act with more cruelty."[61]

If the account sounds sensational, one should remember that stories were all Roberts had left. In describing the bloody encounter, Roberts had hoped to garner some sympathy from a public that now discredited him. Even that meager hope was dashed when word reached Shanghai that the victim of Rengan's "murder" had made a full recovery. Disgraced by the disclosure, Roberts wrote the newspaper to retract his murder indictment;

a boy whom he had thought killed had merely been severely flogged. In the same letter, Roberts sheepishly admitted that his belongings had arrived safely.[62]

Shanghai's Defender

The one thing that did not return from Nanjing intact was Roberts's dream. As Roberts licked his wounds in Shanghai, he perhaps reflected on how agonizingly close he had come to consummating his dream. If Hong had only been teachable, the Taipings would have disseminated correct Christian doctrines, which might have resulted in the mass conversion of China. What Roberts never realized was that theology hardly mattered at all. The Taiping movement had gathered steam not by meeting people's spiritual needs but by serving as a magnet for disaffected elements in China who saw an opportunity to topple the Qing government. This strong anti-dynastic sentiment also attracted capable military men such as Li Xiucheng, a peasant farmer who rose rapidly through the ranks to command Taiping forces as the Chung Wang ("Faithful King").[63]

To strengthen their armies, the Chung Wang and his generals capitalized on the availability of Western arms. Sensing potential in the chaos, opportunistic American and British arms dealers, acting independently of their governments, supplied Taiping clients with modern weapons of war: muskets, carbines, cartridges, heavy artillery, and powder kegs. One American dealer, who carried a passport signed by the Chung Wang himself, moved freely through Taiping-controlled waterways in his vessels, floating arms bazaars from which he peddled modern weaponry. As these purchases lent Taiping armies a decisive advantage on the battlefield, the Qing were painfully learning the lesson John Peters Jr. had hoped to teach in 1844.[64]

In Peking the Qing military's failure to contain the uprising prompted panic. Making matters worse, the Taipings did not constitute the only threat as, in the 1850s, two other groups entered into open rebellion: the Nien in the north and the Muslims in the southwest. Their dynasty on the verge of collapse, the Qing turned in desperation to China's regional armies for help. Unlike conventional Qing forces that were led by the Manchu ruling class, these armies were headed by Chinese officials of the Han ethnic majority. They were composed of not career soldiers but local peasants who were paid and whose loyalties belonged not to the Qing but to the official who recruited them. Chief among these men, Zeng Guofan led his Hunan Army into battle against Taiping forces. Zeng placed his protégé Li Hongzhang in command of the Anhui Army. Thanks partly to Zeng's military success, the Taiping Rebellion stalled in the late 1850s. Hoping to rejuvenate it in 1860, Taiping leaders targeted Shanghai for an all-out assault. The capture of Shanghai would allow the Taipings to secure supplies, seize armed steamships, and forge relations with the several thousand foreigners who were expected to greet the "Christians" with open arms.[65]

In anticipation of an invasion, the foreign residents of Shanghai placed their military forces on high alert. But who would protect Chinese property, assets, and lives? This question vexed Wu Hsü, Shanghai's circuit intendant, in charge of military defense and tariffs, and Yang Fang, a wealthy banker. Realizing that they could rely on neither the Qing, whose military had proved only its ineptitude, nor the foreigners, who could be expected to look after only themselves, Wu and Yang sought outside help. When a brash American, age twenty-nine, proposed to recruit, train, and arm a unit of foreign soldiers in exchange for money, he found a receptive audience in Wu and Yang.[66]

Frederick Townsend Ward was born in 1831 in Salem. Though Ward's father, an experienced mariner, trained his son for the sea, he lacked the resources to place his son in a promising position. Lacking prospects but possessing nautical skills, Ward became a roving adventurer. Intrigued by soldiering, he applied unsuccessfully to West Point before heading out into the world. A true soldier of fortune, Ward materialized in any hot spot where men were hired to fight. For him, the justness of the cause mattered less than the thrill of battle, chance for glory, and promise of pay. In 1853 he fought alongside William Walker during his attempt to invade Sonora, Mexico, to establish his own colony. Having grown disenchanted with Walker, Ward next appeared in the Crimean War but got in a dispute with the French military and was discharged for insubordination. Though the facts are murky, some sources place Ward in Mexico in 1858, fighting under Benito Juárez, and in Texas that same year with the Texas Rangers. True or not, the restless Ward clearly gravitated toward any army in need of a hired gun, which is why Shanghai beckoned in 1860.[67]

China's civil war offered Ward something other conflicts lacked. Ward's first biographer stated bluntly that "what he craved was power,—not the semblance of power." After Wu and Yang placed the defense of Shanghai in his hands, Ward enjoyed the chance not just to fight but to lead a militia into battle. By doing so, however, he acted in defiance of his country's official position of neutrality, which made him an "outlaw," a "desperado," and a "dangerous man" in the eyes of British and American expatriates. To these slurs Ward paid little heed, focusing instead on recruitment. Days after receiving his commission, he began to scour the waterfront looking for men. Since as many as three hundred vessels harbored in Shanghai at any time, Ward easily rounded up volunteers from among the vagabonds, navy deserters, fugitives, and ruffians who washed up on China's shore. Though these men—white Europeans and Americans, without exception—handled firearms with dexterity, they lacked discipline. For this reason, Ward and his two lieutenants, Edward Forester and Henry Burgevine, relocated the troops to a training camp, a deserted plot of muddy land twenty miles southwest of Shanghai.[68]

After three weeks of drills, Wu and Yang grew impatient. They reminded Ward that they had, at great expense, equipped the Foreign Arms

Corps, as the unit was called, with modern weaponry. The time to engage the enemy had come. In June 1860 Ward reluctantly marched his men to Sung-chiang, a walled city recently captured by the rebels that held strategic value owing to its proximity to Shanghai. Since Ward lacked the heavy artillery that could blast through the city's outer gates, his only hope was to mount a surprise attack under the cover of night. However, when his men became loud and drunk while waiting in the tall grass (they had brought alcohol), Taiping sentries detected them, and a bloody fiasco ensued. After sustaining heavy casualties, Ward's militia was forced to retreat. Those who survived were paid for their service and dismissed. Ward was disgraced.[69]

He regrouped quickly. In assembling a second corps, he recruited mostly "Manilamen," Filipinos famed for their battle ferocity. Determined to take Sung-chiang, Ward led this second iteration of the Foreign Arms Corps, along with several pieces of heavy artillery, back to the walled city for a nighttime siege. After his large guns blasted an opening through the gate, the Manilamen poured through, only to find a second wall and gate. Undeterred, Ward ordered his men to ignite sacks of gunpowder under the gate. After a terrific explosion, Ward spied a small hole just large enough for the Manilamen to climb through. Once inside, they engaged Taiping soldiers in hand-to-hand combat armed with machetes. They also seized control of a battery of howitzers, which they swiveled toward the interior of the city to rake the rebels with unremitting fire. At daybreak, as surviving Taiping soldiers fled the city, Ward declared Sung-chiang captured.[70]

Though this victory restored the confidence of his financial backers, a devastating setback followed. In August, Ward laid siege to Ch'ing-p'u, another walled city. In anticipation of the assault, Taiping defenders, led by a British blackguard known as "Savage," had prepared an ambush. As Ward's men began to scale the walls, Savage ordered his surprise attack, to which Ward had no answer. In mere moments, Ward sustained five wounds, the most serious of which, a musket ball that penetrated his face, impaired his ability to speak. Just ten minutes into this one-sided battle, Ward scribbled "retreat" on paper. The *North China Herald*, which viewed Ward as a rogue, gleefully reported his defeat: "This notorious man has been brought down to Shanghai, not as was hoped, dead, but severely wounded with a shot in his mouth, one in his side, and one in his legs."[71]

A Mystical Modern Military

Though the defeat injured both Ward and his reputation, he recovered quickly and began to plot his return. Three factors contributed to his resurgence. First, he maintained the loyalty of Yang Fang, with whom he enjoyed a close friendship. Formerly, Yang had worked as comprador for Jardine, Matheson, and Company, and so he enjoyed an easy rapport with Westerners. He harbored a special fondness for Ward, a frequent visitor to his business office. His faith in Ward was so strong that in 1862 he allowed Ward to marry his daughter and become his son-in-law.[72]

Second, by the early 1860s most foreigners had downgraded their initial opinion of the Taipings. During the previous decade, Westerners might have officially professed their neutrality, but they were in fact disappointed in the Qing, who they felt had not lived up to their treaties. Thus, the possibility of a Taiping victory intrigued them. They were also tantalized by the reform plan of Hong Rengan, who in 1859 called for the construction of railroads, post offices, and banks patterned on Western models. When Rengan's plan fell out of favor in 1860, the collective turning away of Westerners had already begun. Missionaries returning from Nanjing expressed their disillusionment. More importantly, new concessions granted by the Qing after the Second Opium War convinced the West that its interests would be best served by the survival of a weakened Qing Dynasty. Indeed, the Treaty of Tianjin granted Western nations the right to establish diplomatic residences in Peking and access to China's interior via waterways. At long last, the West seemed to be getting from China what it wanted. Ward benefited from this new backing of the Qing because, by fighting the insurgents, he no longer defied Western interests.[73]

Third, Ward had a startling insight. Combat against Taiping armies had led Ward to revise his assumptions regarding the fitness of the Chinese soldier. The latter could perform as capably as any soldier in the world, Ward believed, provided he received proper training, equipment, and pay. After persuading Wu and Yang to give him one more chance, Ward moved swiftly to realize his vision. He recruited men from Kiangsu Province and established his camp outside the walls of Sung-chiang. As intensive training began, the novelty of the sight attracted Chinese and Western observers. Villagers, as they watched Chinese men march to orders bellowed by an American drillmaster, at first laughed at the soldiers they derisively called "imitation foreign devils." One Western observer expressed wonder at the new kind of man evolving before his eyes: a Chinese who was "clothed, equipped and drilled in perfect unison with the modes of the European soldier." "The progress attained in so short a time" he remarked, "was the greatest of wonders." A proud Wu Hsü praised the orderliness of the soldiers, who marched "systematically like fish scales or comb teeth."[74]

Though Ward drilled his men according to modern military methods, he employed a personal command style that bordered on the mystical. Wearing a simple blue coat and white shirt, Ward led his men into combat carrying, not a sword or a sidearm, but a short rattan cane. In the minds of his men, this cane acquired powerful symbolism, signifying the invincibility of their leader. This interpretation, though based on superstition, had a favorable effect on the men's psychologies during combat: seeing a virtually unarmed Ward charge into the thick of battle bonded the men to their commander and inspired acts of daring. They believed that no opposing army could stop them.[75]

The Ever Victorious Army

By the close of 1861 the massing of rebel troops in cities outside Shanghai left no doubt as to Taiping intentions. Though Ward sought more time to prepare his men, he realized that the circumstances demanded action. A string of battles ensued, all of which took place within a thirty-mile radius of Shanghai. In January 1862 Ward launched a surprise attack on Kwan-fu-ling, a heavily fortified city that the rebels saw as vital to their planned invasion of Shanghai. For the assault, Ward employed tactics that he would repeat in each city he targeted. First, to rapidly deploy his forces, Ward took advantage of Kiangsu's latticework of rivers and canals by moving on steamers armed with artillery. Upon reaching the targeted city, Ward and his men would storm the walls while the heavy artillery, positioned on rotating platforms on the steamers' decks, blasted Taiping fortifications from the water.[76]

When conditions allowed, Ward would seal off gateways and points of egress, forcing his enemy to retreat in panicked disarray through a preselected channel. There, Ward's waiting troops would wreak death on them. In the coastal town of Kaochiao, which Ward attacked in February, the frantic Taiping retreat flowed over a long bridge that, according to Forester, "was turned into a slaughter-pen." "The enemy were packed in so closely, and we were at such short range, that our fire did terrible execution." Other rebel soldiers attempted to flee through a south gate, in the vain hope that they could reach the coast and escape by boat. "But once outside only the shores of the Yellow sea awaited them," Forester continued, "and upon its sands Death waited with open arms." Unable to reach their boats, desperate Taipings "leaped into the water, to be drowned."[77] In early March, Ward took the city of Hsiaotang in similar fashion. This successful siege concluded a remarkable five-week period during which Ward's army had won stirring victories at three Taiping strongholds in the Yangtze Delta region.[78] After the impressive run, the imperial viceroy of Kiangsu, Hsüeh Huan, suggested to the emperor a renaming. "Because of the extreme effectiveness of the 'Foreign Army Corps,'" he wrote, "I have selected the name of the 'Ever Victorious Army.'" Peking concurred.[79]

Encouraged by his victories, Ward looked to expand the Ever Victorious Army. In the spring of 1862 Hsüeh Huan authorized an increase to three thousand troops. He did so, however, with misgiving because he understood the risk involved. Here was an ambitious foreigner, whose long-term intentions remained mysterious, in command of fiercely loyal Chinese soldiers capable of defeating larger Qing armies. What would Ward do, Hsüeh Huan and others wondered, after the rebellion was crushed? The American needed to be not stopped but controlled. To benefit from Ward while mitigating the danger he posed, the Qing moved to integrate him into its own military; this way, Ward's irrepressible ambition could be safely channeled through the Qing system of promotions. Following this strategy, the Qing presented Ward with the blue button of a fourth-class mandarin and conferred on him the title of brigadier general. Ward was expected to reciprocate by accepting Chinese citizenship.[80]

Ward cooperated because doing so advanced his interests. He eyed the glory that promised to go to the generals who participated in the coming siege of Nanjing. Since China's top general, Zeng Guofan, would coordinate this massive operation, Ward could not achieve his goal by remaining outside the Chinese system. Acting pragmatically, Ward accepted his title and rank, assented to citizenship, and even took a Chinese wife, marrying Yang Fang's daughter, Chang Mei, considered bad luck after her first fiancé's untimely death. Despite Ward's ostensible Sinification, an inviolable core of individualism continued to govern his behavior. Though he donned a mandarin cap and gown for his wedding, he refused to wear the costume on any other day. He also did not shave his forehead and wear his hair in a queue. In a message to Zeng Guofan, Li Hongzhang expressed doubt as to the sincerity of Ward's conversion: "Although . . . he has not yet shaved his hair or called at my humble residence, I have no time to quarrel with foreigners over such a little ceremonial matter."[81]

Li was right to harbor skepticism. While Ward accepted the superficial trappings of a Chinese officer, becoming truly Chinese required one's complete submission to the Confucian system. In his heart, Ward remained an individualistic American, as the following example illustrates. After Ward and his men had defeated a Taiping contingent, a local mandarin followed by a swarm of villagers converged on the defeated Taipings. Though Ward had placed an injunction on looting, the mandarin, unwilling to check his appetite for plunder, chose to ignore the ban. Not taking this act of defiance lightly, Ward ordered one of his Chinese soldiers to shoot the mandarin. Realizing the ramifications of the order, the horrified soldier hesitated before ultimately refusing. Colonel Forester promptly gunned down the mandarin. The incident revealed the essential incompatibility of Ward and the hierarchical Confucian culture into which he was supposed to be assimilating.[82]

By the spring of 1862 Hsüeh Huan's opinion of Ward had darkened. The viceroy shared with the emperor his fear that Ward posed a danger to the state:

I have noticed that Ward is becoming more and more arrogant, treating the Ever Victorious Army as if it were his own. . . . [W]henever a battle is fought, he takes action before official orders reach him. His disobedience has become obvious. And after every battle he asks for a heavy reward, and it is not easy to satisfy his appetite. It is understood that foreigners love money and fame, but Ward's character is still too extreme and his heart is hard to fathom.[83]

Hsüeh Huan closed with a chilling warning: "If his army becomes too large, it will be a tail too big to wag." What was Ward's ultimate goal in China? Few were so naive as to believe that Ward would disband his army after the war. Some thought he intended to rise obediently within the Qing system. Others suspected his ambition was to carve out a piece of the empire and become a warlord. Still others speculated that he sought the overthrow of the Qing Dynasty. However, since Ward's heart was "hard to fathom," Chinese and foreigners could only guess as to his intentions. A well-aimed musket ball ensured that they would never find out.[84]

Conclusion

As one victory followed another, Ward drew up plans to increase the size of his army to twenty-five thousand men. He also showed a disturbing propensity to place himself in harm's way. Quite possibly, as his biographer Caleb Carr suspects, Ward had begun to believe the Chinese superstitions attributing invincibility to him. In September 1862 Ward paid a visit to his friend A. A. Hayes, a partner in Olyphant's Shanghai office. "You are taking fearful risks," Hayes warned Ward, in reference to his reckless style. "You may be killed at any moment." Hayes's admonitory words proved prescient. A few days later at the city of Tz'u-ch'i, Ward placed himself in enemy fire while preparing his men to scale the walls. Abruptly, he moved his hand to his side and exclaimed, "I have been hit." Hastily taken to his steamship, Ward expired twenty-four hours later. Before his death, he whispered instructions concerning his possessions to a lieutenant. After dividing his fortune among his wife, brother, and sister, he asked that Anson Burlingame serve as his executor.[85]

Appointed American minister to China by Abraham Lincoln in 1861, Anson Burlingame faced challenges in China. These, however, had little to do with the Taipings. Not long after Ward's death, the movement began to unravel, subjected as it was to internal decay and external pressure. In 1864 Zeng Guofan launched a siege of Nanjing that succeeded in taking the capital. Though Hong Xiuquan had earlier succumbed to sickness, imperial forces captured the Chung Wang. In an act of leniency, Zeng allowed his prisoner to write his autobiography from inside a wooden cage. In the final paragraph, written just before his execution, the Chung Wang groped for the meaning that, he thought, must lie behind the mass death and destruction. "The people were predestined to suffer in distress," he declared unconvincingly, before asking in vain, "In this suffering, why was the T'ien Wang [Hong Xiuquan] born to disturb the whole country?" and "Why did I . . . support and assist him?" He next reasserted his faith in providence— "It must have been the will of Heaven to make this happen"—before reverting to doubt in his final words: "Truly I do not understand this."[86]

For Anson Burlingame, understanding the blindly destructive forces unleashed by the Taiping Rebellion was less important than formulating a strategy for the altered geopolitical landscape they created. Burlingame recognized that China, in the rebellion's wake, was entering a new era in its relations with the outside world. If the earlier period had been, at least from the West's perspective, dominated by the problem of too much Chinese control, then this post-Taiping era would be shaped by its opposite— insufficient Chinese power. That the Western powers sensed China's weakness, Burlingame realized, posed a threat to China's sovereignty. Burlingame would need to decide exactly what U.S. policy should be. Yet while doing so, he also had to ask himself the humbling question: given the weakness of his country's official presence, did American policy even matter?

9

Cooperation

Burlingame and the Reinvention of Sino-Western Relations

I f Anson Burlingame wanted to grumble about his lot as U.S. minister to China, he had ample justification for doing so. Even a cursory look at the length of his predecessors' terms was sufficient to reveal a disturbing trend. Few lasted more than two years. None made it to three. Worse still, those were the official lengths of the terms; any minister's actual time spent in China was much shorter because one had to factor in months spent at sea. In the interim periods, Washington resorted to installing Parker or Williams as gap fillers. They provided continuity to an office that otherwise appeared as little more than a staccato sequence of broken segments. If the brevity of terms offered any indication, none of these men viewed the appointment as desirable. They all wanted out.

In reading the papers filed by his predecessors, Burlingame could easily isolate the source of discontent. In his final report, Humphrey Marshall (1852–1854) explained the cause of his frustration. "In surrendering the trust to my successor," he wrote, "I . . . add my sincere hope that he may be sustained by his government." Without "support" or the "disposal of force to sustain his efforts," he cannot possibly "win the success" to "compensate him for an exile from his native land."[1] The U.S. minister was empowered to speak on the behalf of his government, but since Washington, unlike London and Paris, failed to provide actual support, his words carried little weight. Williams, who dutifully served nine stints, stated the problem succinctly: "The United States authorities in China are invested with more authority than power."[2]

Recognizing this impotence, Qing officials could ignore the American minister without fear of repercussions. Parker learned this lesson in 1856, when he pressed China to renegotiate its U.S. treaty in the vain hope that he might secure the right to establish a legation in Peking. After the Chinese disregarded his request, Parker contrived a bizarre scheme whereby

Americans would seize Formosa (Taiwan) as a way to force China to the negotiating table. Though the Formosa scheme reeked of empire building, it was actually only one man's desperate attempt to gain leverage. When Washington received the proposal, policy makers scratched their heads in befuddlement before dismissing it outright.[3]

American expatriates could also ignore the U.S. minister without consequence. John Ward (1858–1860) wrote of his futile efforts to punish wrongdoers when his government failed to provide him with even a jail cell. If the British did not offer space in their facility, Ward had no choice but to let criminals go free.[4] In this environment, opium traffickers operated with impunity. William Reed (1857–1858) watched powerlessly as ships flying the American flag dealt "freely" in opium at "every port."[5] As for Burlingame, he harbored fatherly affection for Ward but could not deny that the latter's paramilitary force defied U.S. neutrality. "The United States authority was laughed at," Burlingame later wrote, "and our flag made the cover for the villains in China."[6]

Adding to any minister's humiliation, lack of military resources forced him to accept help from the British. Few things rankled Burlingame more than smug Englishmen who reminded him that the British navy, not U.S. forces, protected American citizens, ships, and assets from pirates or rebels. "You are indebted to the British," they condescended, "for what protection you have on the coast of China."[7] What could Burlingame do except swallow his pride? If these problems were not dispiriting enough, Burlingame had accepted the post mere months after the Confederate attack on Fort Sumter. If Washington had neglected China before, the onset of war almost guaranteed the continuation of federal apathy. Burlingame's term as minister appeared doomed from the start.

Or was it? Burlingame enjoyed several advantages over his predecessors. He was the first to reside in Peking, that right having been won not by Parker's shenanigans but by British and French forces in the Second Opium War. In the capital, Burlingame used his charisma to cultivate friendships with not only Western colleagues but also Qing officials running China's new foreign relations office. The office had a special fondness for Burlingame because he brought something rare to his office: sympathy for China. With political sensibilities forged during America's debate over slavery, Burlingame was driven by a moral obligation to protect the weak from the strong. Applying this principle in China, he opposed Western powers that used force to win concessions.

China's many wars also presented Burlingame with an opportunity. He could argue to Chinese and Western officials, both grown weary of fighting, that each stood to benefit from a new kind of relationship, one based on cooperation rather than conflict. In a remarkable achievement, Burlingame effected a temporary paradigm change in Sino-Western relations. Recognizing his talent and sympathies, the Chinese surprised him in 1868 by asking him to serve as China's envoy to the West. Burlingame accepted. If he could encase his cooperative principles within legally binding treaties, he could secure a favorable place for China in the world—and consummate his personal dream in the process.

Self-Strengthening

In the early 1860s the Qing Dynasty teetered on the brink of collapse. Western and Chinese observers alike had witnessed the rapid advance of Taiping armies in the 1850s, the ease with which small European forces cut through lines of Qing troops, the inability of China's coastal forts to stop foreign gunboats, and the burning of the Summer Palace at the hands of Anglo-French soldiers in 1860. Few observers thought the Qing government could develop solutions to problems of this magnitude. "The old foundations of government are thoroughly rotten," observed the *North China Herald* in 1860, "its ranks and orders are broken; and its gorgeous decorations are in tatters." According to the historian Mary Wright, only a miracle could save the dynasty and forestall China's slide into anarchy.[8]

In the early 1860s a group of progressive Qing officials rose to the challenge. The leader, Prince Gong, was the half brother of the Xianfeng emperor, who died in 1861 after fleeing the capital to escape invading Anglo-French forces. Since Xianfeng's son, Tongzhi, was still a child upon assuming the throne, Prince Gong and the Empress Dowager Cixi (Tongzhi's mother) became regents after ousting the former regent in a coup. In plotting a new course for China, Prince Gong recruited a small cadre of capable men: Wenxiang, Zeng Guofan, Zuo Zongtang, and Li Hongzhang, among others.

To stave off destruction, Prince Gong and his cohort initiated a sweeping, "self-strengthening" reform program. They identified key areas under Qing governance where they could, by applying Western models, either modernize old institutions or form new ones. Though self-strengthening entailed learning from the West, the movement did not require the apostasy of its advocates. Self-strengtheners could maintain their faith in the Confucian traditions that had structured Chinese society and statecraft for centuries. Their goal, in other words, was preservationist not revolutionary: they sought to shield the cherished Confucian essence from threats by encasing it within a protective shell composed of Western science and technology.[9]

Since wars constituted the greatest threat to Qing sovereignty, reformers made the acquisition of Western military technology their highest priority. "If we wish to find a method of self-strengthening," Zeng Guofan wrote in 1862, "we should . . . regard learning to make explosive shells and steamships and other instruments as the work of first importance." Once in possession of these "superior techniques," China could reward Western nations "when they are obedient" and "avenge our grievances when they are disloyal."[10] To revamp the army, reformers reduced the overall number of troops while improving each one's fighting ability by hiring foreign drillmasters. They organized the Yangtze Navy according to the Western model, and to furnish it with a modern fleet, they established the Fuzhou Shipyard, which they placed under the supervision of French engineers. Similarly, at the Kiangnan Arsenal, foreign arms manufacturers supervised the assembly of modern artillery.[11]

Self-strengtheners also pursued nonmilitary reforms. For example, Prince Gong's ruling faction defined Western learning, broadly construed, as a pressing need. Though isolated scholar officials had reached this conclusion earlier, Peking had not welcomed their unorthodox views. After publishing his pioneering study on the West (see Chapter 7), Xu Jiyu received a demotion. In 1851 he was removed from office altogether. In 1862 the Qing—in a complete reversal—established a foreign language school, the Tongwen Guan, to translate Western books. In 1869 progressive officials appointed the American W.A.P. Martin, previously the school's chair of International Law and Political Economy, as its head. While stressing foreign languages, Martin designed a Western-style curriculum that also emphasized mathematics and natural sciences.[12]

As its greatest innovation, the Qing established in 1861 a government office, the Zongli Yamen, to handle diplomacy with the Western powers. Previously, China had lacked a bureau charged specifically with this responsibility; regional viceroys and local officials had always handled foreign relations. In the Zongli Yamen, however, a group of skilled statesmen could subject Western diplomacy to close study. As a sign of the times, Prince Gong resuscitated the career of the once-disgraced Xu Jiyu, granting him a position in the new foreign affairs office. When William Seward, Lincoln's secretary of state, learned of Xu's admiration for George Washington, he sent Xu a portrait of the first president. The man handing Xu this gift was Anson Burlingame, the first U.S. minister to reside in Peking.[13]

Anson Burlingame

In July 1862 Samuel Wells Williams wrote to his wife from a location that, just a few years earlier, would have been unimaginable. "You think I ought to tell you something about Peking," he wrote, "but descriptions fail woefully when there is so little in common with what you've seen." Deciding to take a stab at it, Williams described his effort to climb the city walls, "about seventy [feet] high," to obtain an extraordinary view of the city: "One sees a vast array of houses stretching away out of sight." Williams selected one of these structures, a modest dwelling in need of repairs, to serve as Anson Burlingame's residence.[14]

Williams and Burlingame enjoyed an excellent working relationship, perhaps because of their similar backgrounds. Like the missionary, the politician was born in upstate New York to devoutly Protestant parents. His father, who became a preacher, frequently took the family to Methodist camp meetings. In 1823, when Burlingame was three, the family moved to

Ohio, settling later in the Michigan territory, where Burlingame attended college. Though gravitating toward law and politics, Burlingame maintained the habits formed during a youth steeped in evangelical Christianity: he was zealous in his advocacy of his ideals, such as the equality of all men, and he had a gift for oratory rivaling that of any charismatic minister. After graduating from Harvard Law School in 1846, he practiced law in Boston before entering politics, serving three terms in the House of Representatives (1855–1861).[15]

In Congress, Burlingame developed a reputation not just for eloquent words but for determined action. In 1856 he emerged as a hero in the North after risking his life to defend his friend Senator Charles Sumner and the antislavery principle. When Sumner spoke out against slavery in Kansas, his words infuriated Congressman Preston Brooks, who charged that Sumner had insulted the honor of his cousin, Andrew Butler, a South Carolina senator. An enraged Brooks savagely beat Sumner with his cane in the Senate chamber. Burlingame denounced the act as cowardly, prompting Brooks to challenge him to a duel. Burlingame accepted and shrewdly chose the Canadian side of Niagara Falls as the site. Claiming the site was too far to the north, and therefore on ground hostile to a proslavery Southerner, Brooks backed out. From Burlingame's perspective, events could not have unfolded any better. He had won the respect of colleagues in Congress and members of the press, who lauded him for acting courageously on his principles. He had done so without firing a gun.[16]

The confrontation with Brooks provides us with a glimpse into Burlingame's character. Though he had acted in accordance to principle, he had also picked the ideal controversy in which to showcase his personal charisma, rhetorical flourish, and natural theatricality. Indeed, he understood that, if one hoped to influence people, it was not enough to be righteous— one had to *perform righteousness* convincingly before one's audience. According to James Blaine, a congressman from Maine, Burlingame possessed a personal magnetism, a quality that Blaine struggled to pin down. "What we mean precisely by magnetism it might be difficult to define," he wrote, "but it is undoubtedly true that Mr. Burlingame possessed an immense reserve of that subtle, forceful, overwhelming power." If he believed something, he did so "with such intensity" and "fervour" that the "impulse" of his audience was "to believe and assent to be convinced." Magnetism clearly contributed to Burlingame's success in American politics. Would the ineffable power transfer to China?[17]

The Cooperative Policy

In 1860 Burlingame campaigned so energetically for Lincoln that he neglected to win his own congressional seat. Lincoln offered the defeated Burlingame the appointment in China. Upon reading his instructions from Secretary of State Seward, Burlingame learned that, if he was to make his mark in China, he would have to do so without much help from his government. French and British "agents are supported by land and naval forces," a candid Seward wrote, "while, unfortunately, you are not." "You are, therefore, instructed to consult and co-operate with them." He would not be a unique American voice in China, Burlingame learned, because Washington demanded that he fall in line with Britain and France.[18]

Burlingame regarded these orders as incompatible with his personal beliefs, which he had forged during the great debate over slavery that roiled American politics before the Civil War. In China, Burlingame viewed Britain's conduct through the moral lens of the antislavery cause. Making the linkage to slavery explicit, he believed that his mission was "to end a system of overseerism" perpetrated by "British officers who look upon China as a kind of English preserve." He could not, in good conscience, support the policies of Britain or France, who used their superior militaries to bully China. Unfortunately, since his orders from the State Department were explicitly clear on the matter, he faced a conundrum.[19]

Though the deck was stacked against him, Burlingame saw one cause for hope. In Peking he would be working not with nations but with individuals representing nations. In the past, he had always been able to win people over with the sheer force of his "magnetism." If he could persuade British and French officials to settle disputes with China without resorting to force, he could act in accordance with his own principles while still complying with Seward's instructions. Of course, before the Europeans would adopt such a pacific policy, they would need to know that the Chinese planned to act in good faith—that is, to honor their treaties. Burlingame believed the Chinese could be convinced to abide by their treaties if they thought that, by doing so, they could avoid disastrous wars. For their part, the Chinese would need assurances that the European powers would not, at the slightest disagreement, send gunboats to blast China into submission. Burlingame's insight, in other words, was to reduce the seemingly intractable Sino-European conflict into something simple and soluble: a mutual lack of trust.

Burlingame next moved to persuade each side of the other's sincere desire to cooperate. "He is one of the most enthusiastic of men," Williams observed. "His influence here upon the Chinese has been considerable, and still greater upon the other ministers."[20] Working with both sides, Burlingame outlined a cooperative policy composed of four basic principles that all parties would agree to follow: first, that all foreign powers must respect the interests, autonomy, and territorial integrity of China; second, that foreign envoys must act not unilaterally but in concert with each other, recognizing that all foreign powers automatically received any privileges granted to a single nation (thanks to most-favored-nation clauses in each nation's treaty); third, that foreign envoys, when addressing a grievance, must cooperate with their Chinese counterparts who, conversely, must work with them to achieve a fair solution; and fourth, that both sides respect the authority of the treaties when any question arose. "We are making an effort," Burlingame wrote, "to substitute fair diplomatic action in China for force."[21]

Though incurably optimistic, Burlingame had legitimate reason to believe in the cooperative policy's viability. In his reading of the current geopolitical dynamic, events favored a policy that would have been unthinkable just a few years earlier. "The circumstances conspire," he wrote Seward, "to make this a fortunate moment in which to inaugurate the co-operative policy."[22] What were these circumstances? First, the foreign envoys were all "men of modern ideas," Burlingame noted, referring to Frederick Bruce (Britain), Jules Berthemy (France), and L. D. Balluzek (Russia). Of the "four B's," Bruce impressed Burlingame the most.[23] In Peking the two envoys spent most evenings in Burlingame's home playing cards, smoking cigars, and discussing diplomacy. There are "two schools of Englishman," Burlingame observed, one who would "take the Chinese by the throat" and seize territory "*a la* India" and the other who would "deal fairly by them" and seek to "maintain the integrity of the Chinese Empire." Bruce belonged to "the latter school."[24] Given the closeness of this partnership, some historians credit Bruce with coauthorship of the cooperative policy.[25]

Second, a shift in British public opinion buoyed Burlingame's hopes. Though Bruce accepted the cooperative policy on its merits, he also possessed a strong political incentive to embrace any alternative to force. The English public had grown weary of costly conflicts in China and now demanded that its government exhaust all options before declaring war. "He who next plunges the country into a Chinese war without first making every admissible effort to avert it," the *North China Herald* warned in 1860, will face "an indignant British public." To Burlingame, the cooperative policy shimmered as a noble humanitarian ideal, comparable to antislavery. The British, in contrast, saw it as a practical policy that spared the country from expensive wars.[26]

Third, foreign envoys in Peking became suffused with what Mary Wright has termed "Sinophilism." For decades, the Qing had tried to keep Western officials out of Peking (as Caleb Cushing discovered). Though Qing officials grudgingly made this concession, they discovered it presented unexpected advantages. Living far from the treaty ports, the envoys could ignore their countrymen's constant demands to take aggressive action against China. "Removed from any contact with foreign merchants," groused England's Chamber of Commerce from Shanghai, "the Foreign Ministers become . . . advocates of Chinese exclusiveness, rather than of the extension of foreign trade." Another disgruntled observer noted that Peking "bewitched" the envoys with its "scholastic and historical traditions." Living near China's ancient halls of power, the envoys became almost like protégés to the Chinese statesmen of the Zongli Yamen.[27]

The attraction was mutual. As a fourth circumstance favoring a cooperative policy, the Sinification of foreign envoys found its mirror image in the Westernization of the Zongli Yamen. In the eighteenth century, the Qing had tried without success to integrate Europeans into the Confucian tributary system. Because the previous twenty years had proved the futility of this model, the members of the Zongli Yamen, in a radical shift in thinking, abandoned it in their dealings with the West. While the Sino-centric model would continue to define China's relationship to its satellite countries in Asia, the Zongli Yamen developed a parallel system exclusively for the West—a system based on treaties rather than tribute bearing. For these reasons, conditions seemed to favor cooperation. If Burlingame had his way, he would personally bring about a paradigm shift in Sino-Western relations.[28]

International Law

The success of the cooperative policy hinged on China's acceptance of the treaties as legally binding documents. At first, the Zongli Yamen looked leery-eyed at any treaty, regarding it as a bitter pill to swallow. These nimble operators realized, however, that the treaty when properly understood presented an unanticipated advantage. Since Western nations respected treaties, these documents could be used to limit the advances of the grasping West. If a Western nation made a demand explicitly included in its treaty, the Zongli Yamen would grant the request, promptly and without argument. Conversely, if no treaty article provided for the demand in question, the Zongli Yamen felt empowered to deny the request. The treaty allowed China to draw a line in the dirt that foreigners could not cross.[29]

Issues sometimes arose, however, that existed outside a treaty's clearly demarcated legal coverage. In such cases, the Zongli Yamen learned that Westerners consulted a different authority, something called international law. In 1836 Henry Wheaton, a Harvard professor who had represented the United States in Europe, composed the first English-language text on the subject. In little time *Wheaton's Elements of International Law* became the authority, replacing Vattel's earlier work, some of which Peter Parker had translated for Lin Zexu. Fond of the text, Burlingame urged the Zongli Yamen to consult it during disputes. Of course, since these officials could not read English, they would require a translation. As luck would have it, a translation project was already under way.

Born in Indiana, W.A.P. Martin sailed to China in 1850 to join the Presbyterian mission in Ningbo. Looking for a suitable evangelical model, Martin turned to neither Gützlaff nor Bridgman but a Jesuit from an earlier era. After studying the career of Mateo Ricci (1552–1610), Martin decided to fashion himself as the modern equivalent. Content to live in Ningbo for the short term, Martin set his ultimate sights on Peking because Ricci had famously won access to the Forbidden City. How had Ricci gotten in? By tethering Christianity to astronomy and mathematics. "Careful to avoid giving offense," Martin wrote of Ricci, "his science proved to be the master-key." Imitating his hero, Martin resolved to hitch Christianity to Western learning.[30]

In 1858 U.S. minister William Reed hired Martin as his translator. By this time, Martin had taken up the translation of Wheaton's text on the assumption that international law, like Ricci's astronomy, could serve as his "master-key." "I was led to undertake it," Martin wrote of this project, "without the suggestion of anyone, but providentially I doubt not." Had it not been for Burlingame, Martin's work might have languished in obscurity. When Wenxiang, then in a thorny diplomatic dispute with France, asked Burlingame to suggest a book on international law, he recommended Wheaton, unaware of Martin's ongoing project. Shortly thereafter, Burlingame learned of Martin's work and hastily brought the missionary to the Zongli Yamen.[31]

Prince Gong eagerly sought out Martin's translation.[32] After reading it, the skeptical prince questioned both the text's utility and the author's motives, speculating that the author intended "to imitate men like Matteo Ricci."[33] Though Gong had Martin pegged, he nevertheless saw just enough promise in the translation to assign four Chinese scholars to the job of smoothing Martin's imperfect Chinese.[34] In 1864 a diplomatic crisis presented Prince Gong with an opportunity to test Wheaton's ideas.

As the new Prussian minister, M. von Rehfues, approached China in a man-of-war, he encountered three Danish vessels off the coast. Since Prussia was then at war with Denmark, von Rehfues happily captured the vessels, considering them spoils of war. Alarmed, Prince Gong immediately protested the seizure; inaction on China's part, he knew, would set a dangerous precedent, allowing Western conflicts to extend into China's territorial waters. In talks with von Rehfues, Prince Gong stealthily inserted Wheaton's principles, without labeling them as such, on questions of jurisdiction within a nation's coastal waters. To his astonishment, von Rehfues backed off and released the Danish ships. Though "this book of foreign laws does not entirely agree with our own laws," Prince Gong advised the emperor, it contained "occasional passages which are useful." He went on to explain that, in talks with the Prussian minister, "we used some sentences from the book, without expressly saying so." That the minister then "acknowledged his mistake without saying a word . . . seems a good proof."[35] The Chinese "have shown in these negotiations," observed a British diplomat, "that they have read their translation of Wheaton with profit."[36]

As further proof of the translation's usefulness, it attracted the ire of a French official who angrily accosted Burlingame after the incident. "Who is this man who is going to give the Chinese an insight into our European international law?" M. Klecskowsky demanded. "Kill him—choke him off; he will make us endless trouble." Upon learning of the threat, Martin was positively gleeful. After all, if his translation infuriated European bullies, then it was having the desired impact. Intoxicated with pride, Martin succumbed to hyperbole when forecasting the book's future. "I am not sure it will not stand second in influence to the translation of the Bible!" Williams also approved of the Martin-Burlingame effort, which he contrasted with extraterritoriality, a doctrine he despised. If the latter aimed for the "subversion of the native," the former aspired "to elevate these eastern peoples" to the "level" of Westerners. Prince Gong arranged for an official photograph in which he would pose holding a copy of Wheaton.[37]

Martin dedicated the work to Burlingame, its advocate and patron.[38] The latter, thrilled by the book's impact, sent a copy to Seward, who responded by inviting China to send an envoy to Washington. The "harmonious" nature of Sino-American relations, Seward insisted, warranted the taking of this "unprecedented" step. Though China was not ready to send an envoy, Qing trust in the United States had never been greater, thanks almost entirely to the efforts of Burlingame. Two years earlier, he had earned the gratitude of Qing officials by intervening on their behalf to resolve a potentially explosive conflict with the British.[39]

The Lay-Osborne Flotilla

In 1862 the war against the Taipings took a turn for the worse. Desperate for more military power, the Zongli Yamen dispatched Horatio Nelson Lay to England to purchase a flotilla of gunboats. A former British diplomat, Lay had worked for the Qing since 1854 as chief inspector of China's Imperial Maritime Customs. The flotilla promised to be extremely costly, and thus Wenxiang and Prince Gong were staking their reputations on its effectiveness. Even more importantly, self-strengthening itself hung in the balance. If the fleet proved to be an expensive mistake, the failure would weaken the support enjoyed by the progressive self-strengtheners and embolden conservative elements within the Qing government.

Tragically, China had entrusted precisely the wrong man with this assignment. Horatio Lay harbored a secret design that threatened to undermine China's entire purpose in securing a fleet. While the Chinese expected to deploy the fleet against the rebels, Lay planned to use it to patrol the Yangtze, crush the piracy that interfered with British shipping, and save Britain the expense of maintaining a fleet in Chinese waters (Imperial Maritime Customs, which Lay controlled, would fund the flotilla). Lay's scheme would not have mattered had the Sino-British agreement been more clearly written. Problematically, however, the document contained ambiguous language on the crucial issue of command of the flotilla, ambiguity that Lay planned to seize on to assert control over the fleet.

After reaching England, Lay drafted a formal set of instructions for the flotilla's appointed commander, Captain Sherard Osborne. He directed Osborne to ignore all orders except those issued by the emperor and communicated through Lay. Additionally, Lay reserved the right "to refuse to be the medium of any orders of the reasonableness of which he is not satisfied." The hubris of Lay's scheme was stunning. Theoretically, Osborne could reject any order not originating from the throne (or from the regent). Moreover, should the emperor issue a command that met with Lay's disapproval, Lay could override the monarch's will with his veto. If Lay had his way, he would wield total control over the most formidable force in Asia.[40]

When Lay arrived in China in 1863 in advance of the flotilla, Prince Gong quickly recognized Lay's naked grasp for power. Yet this realization did not, by itself, suggest a clear course of action. Because the Qing Dynasty was fighting for its very survival against Taiping rebels, the prince could not afford to offend Britain by rejecting the flotilla and reprimanding Lay. That said, Gong also understood that, were he to accept the flotilla on Lay's terms, he would in effect be conceding control of the coast and the Yangtze to the vainglorious Lay.

Presented with no good choices, Prince Gong turned to Burlingame, who immediately grasped the gravity of the situation. Lay had demanded not only "that the flotilla . . . be placed in his hands," Burlingame later wrote, but also that he enjoy total control over customs revenue. Burlingame sent the prince a clear set of instructions: first, China must neither accept the flotilla nor concede control to Lay; second, China should explain its position to Frederick Bruce, who could help China work with the British government; and third, China should, after receiving Britain's support, politely but firmly ask Osborne to return the flotilla to England. In insisting on the flotilla's return to England, Burlingame was thinking partly of American interests. If Lay, in an attempt to unload the flotilla, were to sell it to the highest bidder, the Confederate navy might take possession.

Since China's response depended on British cooperation, Burlingame began to work back channels. He approached Bruce, who at first indicated his intention to back Lay. However, after spending several evenings pacing the floor in Burlingame's home, Bruce accepted his friend's assessment of Lay's dark motives. However, if Bruce was going to take China's side in a dispute involving a countryman, he would require American support—support that Burlingame agreed to provide. Burlingame contacted Seward in Washington, advising him to commend Bruce's conduct to the British government. In the end, China rejected the flotilla when it arrived, Bruce arranged for it to return to England, and China relieved Lay as customs inspector. To replace Lay, Burlingame and Bruce recommended Robert Hart, who would occupy the office until 1908.[41]

First Departure

In 1864 Burlingame applied for temporary leave, citing fatigue in his communication to Seward. After three years abroad, he and his wife, Jane, also wanted to see their children.[42] "I hope that the government will not refuse Anson leave to go," Jane wrote her father. "We have the satisfaction of feeling that we shall be regretted in Peking," but Anson "is not to be persuaded" to stay.[43] Saddened by the news, the Zongli Yamen met with Burlingame several times in the American legation. According to one Chinese official, this was an unprecedented honor. The "Chinese Government," he said, "had never given such a demonstration . . . in which the Prince Gong & the highest Officials had visited day after day at the American Legation." During one meeting, Burlingame shared "two methods" he thought could help China during disputes with foreigners. First, the Chinese should, after confirming the correctness of their position, send a clear statement to the foreign envoy, with instructions to publish it in their respective nations. "The fear of public opinion," Burlingame explained, "would prove a wholesome safeguard against violent . . . proceedings." Second, China must *"send a diplomatic mission to the West."*[44]

Later, Prince Gong sat down with Burlingame to solidify their friendship and test the waters for a future partnership. "It is not without sincere regret that we part with one whom we have found to be our true friend," the prince began, citing Burlingame's help with the flotilla. "I cannot refrain from asking, is it necessary that you should leave us?" After Burlingame dodged the question by referring vaguely to his "temporary leave," Gong asserted, "Your president has a second term and you ought to have another." When Burlingame conspicuously avoided confirming his return to China, Gong adamantly declared, "We will take no denial," and he demanded that Burlingame "pledge yourself to return to us." "If you are willing to resume your mission," Gong continued, raising a glass, "you will join me in draining a glass in token of consent." Burlingame paused momentarily before emptying his glass. "The covenant is ratified," the prince announced, because "friends are not allowed to forget a promise sealed in a glass of wine."[45]

Why did the usually verbose Burlingame become reticent on the subject of his leave? By this time, he had likely received a communication from the State Department informing him that his request had been declined. If so, he understandably avoided sharing details for a departure that violated official orders. The planned departure, however, raises another question: Why was Burlingame so anxious to leave China as to defy his government? According to historian Martin Ring, a likely possibility is that the unresolved nature of the Lay-Osborne flotilla had left Wenxiang, the plan's most enthusiastic backer, in a precarious position. Even though the flotilla had been turned away, Britain had yet to reimburse China. As long as the outstanding balance remained, the matter was not officially closed and Wenxiang remained the target of conservatives. These critics could claim that he first entered into an ill-advised deal with a crooked man, then bungled the transfer of the fleet to China, and finally failed to recoup the lost money. It was exactly the sort of fiasco that could destroy a career. By hastening to London, Burlingame hoped to help his friend by expediting the payment process. He could also protect his fragile cooperative policy, the fate of which depended on his Chinese colleagues. Should they fall out of power, China would revert to its stubborn ways, the Western powers would return to gunboat diplomacy, and the policy would collapse.[46]

In April 1865 the Burlingames departed Shanghai. Upon reaching Singapore, they heard the news, at once exhilarating and horrifying, that General Lee had surrendered at Appomattox but that Lincoln had been assassinated. As he looked forward to his arrival in the United States, Burlingame could predict neither how the political landscape would change in light of these events nor how his personal fortunes would be affected. When he looked back on China, however, he recognized that something significant had taken place during his meetings with the Zongli Yamen. He had become bonded to China in a profound way.[47]

A Surprising Offer

Burlingame did return to China. Though his loyalty to Prince Gong factored into his decision, he came back mostly out of fear that the cooperative policy would collapse in his absence. He had ample cause for this concern. Though his faith in the intrinsic righteousness of cooperation never wavered, he worried about its durability. It was, after all, a multiple-party accord in which members were not obliged by any treaty to abide by its principles. A voluntary pact, the cooperative policy would endure only if all parties involved, without exception, agreed on its basic principles and trusted in the good intentions of the others. This is what Burlingame had meant in 1863 in observing to Seward that "our only hope is in . . . perfect union among ourselves."[48]

While Seward approved of the policy, he also recognized its fragility. A state of "perfect union" among Chinese and foreign officials, after all, was difficult to sustain. Should even one of these men, Seward ominously noted, be replaced by a "less intelligent and able statesman," the accord would fall into "disuse."[49] While Burlingame was away, cracks began to appear on the delicate China vase of the policy. Most crucially, after Bruce and Berthemy stepped down, men unsupportive of the policy replaced them. When Burlingame returned to Peking in 1866, he discovered that strife, not harmony, had become the norm.[50] "The apple of discord has found its way into the peaceful community," Jane wrote her father in 1867, "and everybody runs to Anson to settle disputes. He is called 'peacemaker,' and is talking from morning until night, with one party or another."[51] During these trying times, Burlingame probably wondered whether the cooperative policy could be installed in the permanent legal framework of diplomacy. Only then could it endure in his absence.

In 1867 Burlingame prepared to leave China for good. Before departing, he composed a report for Seward summarizing the changes that had taken place during his terms. "When I came to China, in 1861," he began, "the force policy was the rule" because the consensus among Westerners was that "the Chinese are conceited barbarians, and . . . you must take them by the throat." In a few short years, he and his colleagues had developed a new diplomatic model. Under the cooperative policy, they had substituted "fair diplomatic action" for gunboat diplomacy and, by doing so, had earned "the confidence of this people." Burlingame proudly listed the gains that flowed out of his approach: Christian "missions have [been] extended," "trade has increased three-fold," "scientific men have been employed," Wheaton has been translated, "military instruction accepted," "steam-boats multiplied," and the "way slowly opened for . . . telegraphs and railroads." The future looked bright, as long as cooperation held.[52]

Before Burlingame embarked, the Chinese dropped a bombshell. "Events of such importance have transpired within a few days," Jane wrote her son in November 1867, "that I take advantage of the Russian mail . . . to write you something about them." Burlingame had been appointed "Ambassador from China to all the Treaty Powers!" According to Jane, Wenxiang first floated the idea past Burlingame at a formal breakfast. "You must be our friend in foreign lands," Wenxiang urged him, "where we are so misunderstood." After Burlingame responded that he could best serve China from America, "the idea seems to have flashed upon them . . . that if they appointed your father their Ambassador, it would do wonders for China." Days later, Prince Gong formally tendered the offer, which Burlingame accepted. The world's "oldest nation," Jane exclaimed to her father, had elected to use "the youngest to represent her throughout the world!" In the remarkable appointment, Williams discerned the "hand of Providence."[53]

This sequence of events notwithstanding, the Burlingame mission was born less out of spontaneity (or act of God) and more out of need. Previously, Robert Hart had urged this course of action, on the grounds that China's isolation from the West left it at a disadvantage. In disputes, overbearing foreign envoys and aggressive merchants enjoyed the upper hand as long as China lacked a direct channel to Western governments. "When the envoys . . . are perverse, headstrong and unreasonable," the Zongli Yamen discovered, "we can only restrain them with dignified words; we cannot question their respective governments about it." With the ten-year revision of the Treaty of Tianjin (1858) looming, the Zongli Yamen hoped that the Burlingame mission could strengthen its hand before negotiations commenced.[54]

After resigning as U.S. minister, Burlingame asked the dependable Williams to fill the void. "He is the best man the Chinese could have found," Williams wrote of Burlingame, "and if any one could give . . . those countries a favorable view of this empire, he is likely to do so."[55] During a sleepless period of whirlwind preparations, Burlingame worked with the Zongli Yamen to handpick the other members of the mission. So as to have Britain and France represented, they chose John McLeavey Brown, Chinese secretary of the British legation, and Emile de Champs, a French commissioner of Maritime Customs. From the Zongli Yamen, they selected Chih Kang,

Sun Chia-ku, and a handful of minor officials. On November 25, 1867, the Burlingame mission departed the capital on horseback. After a harrowing five-day trip, during which they endured a dust storm and eluded bandits, the party reached the port of Tianjin.[56]

The Burlingame Mission

On the steamship Burlingame noted the eight hundred Cantonese passengers bound for San Francisco. He understood their relevance to his mission. Because of Chinese immigration, the Sino-American relationship possessed a dimension that Sino-European relations lacked, the latter being centered on trade and little else. Recognizing that any treaty must address Chinese migrants, Burlingame urged Chih Kang and Sun Chia-ku to reach out to Chinese communities in San Francisco to learn about their experience. However, as that city drew near, extreme dread crept into Burlingame's thoughts. In Shanghai a newspaper had branded him a traitor to his country. If his countrymen shared this view, how would he be greeted?[57]

As the ship approached the wharf in April 1868, Burlingame observed a large crowd, which he feared had gathered to "jeer and insult him." Accosting the first man he met, Burlingame learned that "the whole city is here to welcome the new Chinese minister." "Thank God!" the relieved ambassador exclaimed.[58] Besieged by visitors, Burlingame talked incessantly at parties and dinners, becoming so hoarse, according to Jane, that he had "to lock his door" to "save his voice."[59] According to the historian John Schrecker, press coverage of the Burlingame mission indicates that Americans understood it by placing it in the context of Reconstruction. Predictably, responses to Burlingame followed party lines. Republican newspapers, which favored the extension of rights to freed slaves, supported Burlingame's efforts on behalf of the Chinese. Conversely, Democratic newspapers, which opposed initiatives to uplift former slaves, despised the man who would strengthen China's position in the world.[60]

After departing San Francisco, the mission steamed to Panama, crossed the isthmus by train, and then took a ship to New York, arriving in late May. In New York Burlingame enjoyed the support of Horace Greeley, editor of the *Tribune*, who promoted the mission in his paper. The Democratic *World*, however, preserved political symmetry by assailing Burlingame. Leaving New York, the delegation traveled by train to Washington, where Seward hosted them several times and the House and Senate, both dominated by Republicans, honored them with receptions. The delegation also visited the White House to meet with Andrew Johnson, who had recently survived impeachment proceedings. During the Washington sojourn, Burlingame met privately with Seward to hammer out the terms of "the Burlingame Treaty" (Figure 9.1).[61]

Figure 9.1. Anson Burlingame, standing beside the seated Chih Kang and Sun Chia-ku. *(Library of Congress Prints and Photographs Division, Washington, D.C.)*

In its eight brief articles, the Burlingame Treaty codified the basic principles of the cooperative policy. Three of the articles (1, 2, and 8) addressed the issue of Chinese sovereignty by guaranteeing China dominion over its territories, by conceding control of inland navigation to China, and by acknowledging the emperor's right to introduce internal improvements at his own pace and without external interference. In response to the unequal nature of China's earlier treaties, five articles (3–7) increased the symmetry of the Sino-American relationship by defining most rights as reciprocal. For example, Americans in China and, reciprocally, Chinese in America, would enjoy access to any schools under government control. The United States assigned consuls to Chinese ports, and the treaty rectified the earlier incongruity by granting China the same privilege in America. It also allowed both Americans and Chinese to enjoy unrestricted travel to, and residence in, each other's countries. Though the treaty forbade the naturalization of Chinese living in the United States, it preserved symmetry by denying Chinese citizenship to Americans. Similarly, an article protecting expatriates from religious persecution, though ostensibly favoring missionaries in China, also served China's interests.[62] As Chih Kang explained to the Zongli Yamen, Chinese migrants complained to him that Americans mistreated them because they were "of another religion which does not believe in Jesus."[63] This article forbade religious discrimination in both countries.

The Burlingame Treaty became China's first equal treaty with a Western nation. It was signed in Washington on July 28, 1868, the same date that saw the ratification of the Fourteenth Amendment to the Constitution. For Burlingame, the synchronicity held symbolic significance because both the treaty and the amendment advanced the principle of equality, whether among nations or between races. When Burlingame traveled in August to Massachusetts, a former stronghold of abolitionism, he received a stirring reception. "Here, I learned to denounce that pride of race which denies the brotherhood of man," he declared during a speech in Cambridge, "here I learned to plead for four millions of human beings," referring to slaves, "as I now speak for four hundred millions of human beings," meaning the Chinese.[64] While touring the Boston area, the delegation paraded down streets lined with people, many of whom climbed trees to obtain a better view. According to Zhang Deyi, a minor official, people greeted them by "doffing hats, waving handkerchiefs, applauding, throwing flowers and shouting 'hooray!'" Others waved Chinese goods out their windows—porcelain dishes, silks, and umbrellas.[65]

Speaking in Boston to an audience that included Ralph Waldo Emerson, Charles Sumner, and Caleb Cushing, Burlingame framed the treaty as a major step forward in human rights. "This treaty recognizes China as an equal among nations," he proclaimed, "in opposition to the old doctrine that because she was not a Christian nation, she could not be placed in the roll of nations." Without referring explicitly to Cushing, Burlingame implied that his mission constituted a moral correction to Cushing's, which had extracted concessions from China. "The United States have asked nothing for themselves," he continued, and "I am proud that this country has made a treaty which is, every line of it, in the present interests of China." Aware that the treaty "will be . . . resisted by the spirit of the old opium smuggler," he manifested no fear because "it is founded in right, it is founded in justice."[66]

Burlingame delivered his most famous speech in New York. His performance showcased at once his great talent for oratory and a tragic flaw that left him vulnerable to critics. In June, before the treaty had been signed, the delegation attended a banquet in its honor. Rising to speak, Burlingame described China as a proud nation of scholars and traditions that responded to modern challenges as best it could. If Americans would resist the temptation to lecture and instead lend China a hand, that nation would modernize, slowly but surely. As Burlingame described China's grand gesture in sending this mission, audible silk passed through his lips:

> She . . . comes out to you and extends her hand. She tells you she is ready to take upon her ancient civilization the graft of your civilization. . . . She tells you that she is willing to trade with you, to buy of you, to sell to you. . . . She invites your merchants, she invites your missionaries. She tells the latter to plant the shining cross on every hill.[67]

Was China really this open to free trade, evangelism, and American civilization? At the banquet, the truth hardly mattered as Burlingame sat down to thunderous applause. However, concerned that the public might misunderstand his mission, Burlingame secretly met with Mark Twain to collaborate on an article for the *Tribune*: "The Treaty with China—Its Provisions Explained." Though Burlingame had a hand in writing this piece, the *Tribune* listed Mark Twain as the sole author.[68]

Burlingame's concerns were well-founded: critics attacked him, his grandiloquent speeches, and his far-reaching treaty. In California, Democrats fixated on the article guaranteeing free and unregulated Chinese migration. "This country cannot be given up to hordes of Asiatics," blasted one paper, "in order to please a few Eastern humanitarians and usurping politicians."[69] Another paper, one that also feared "Asiaticization," lashed out against treaty provisions empowering the Chinese to practice "Heathenism and Idolatry" in the United States, to establish consuls, and to send their children to American schools. "All the advantages . . . are gained by the Chinese," the paper complained, while the United States would "surrender everything—even decency and manliness," all "thanks to a renegade American, who prefers to wear the livery of a Pagan Emperor rather than the costume of an American citizen."[70]

Outside the United States, the New York speech fared poorly. Utterly bewildered, Europeans thought Burlingame's fantastic depiction of an open and progressive China showed either hopeless naivete or a penchant for exaggeration.[71] In Shanghai the foreign community accused Burlingame of grossly misrepresenting the Chinese. "The conduct of Mr. Burlingame . . . has destroyed our pleasing anticipations," wrote the *North China Herald*. "His absurd description of China in a public speech in New York has covered him with ridicule from all who know how different is the original from the picture."[72] Even Williams admitted his friend had succumbed to hyperbole. Burlingame "exaggerates in many ways," he wrote, and placed so much trust in the Qing that he mistakenly "[did] not . . . urge them on as they should have been." Certainly, China had made some progress, Williams admitted, "but what is their starting point? A baby makes great progress in ten years too."[73]

Across the Atlantic

"I have done something," Burlingame reflected on the eve of his departure for London, "the past is secure, but how about the future?" Cooperation would not become the new paradigm unless Burlingame could win over the other Western powers. "Nothing is finished and England . . . is rising up against me." Indeed, upon reaching London in September 1868, Burlingame found that the press, having received messages from expatriates in Shanghai, either dismissed his mission as "humbug" or saw it as a Chinese ploy to stall reform initiatives. For two months, British officials kept the delegation waiting while they figured out how to handle it. Finally, Burlingame received an invitation to an audience with Queen Victoria in Windsor Castle.

After that mostly ceremonial occasion, Burlingame began having discussions with policy makers and members of Parliament. During these face-to-face meetings, his personal charisma worked to his advantage. Most importantly, the Earl of Clarendon, secretary of state for foreign affairs in the Gladstone administration, expressed his general approval of the mission's objectives. Working closely with Chih Kang, Burlingame drafted a "Clarendon-Burlingame understanding" in which Britain and China agreed to redefine their relationship according to cooperation policy principles. After this breakthrough, the once-antagonistic press started to turn in Burlingame's favor. "I have won the field here," he wrote triumphantly to Williams, "Press, Gov't and all for the views of the treaty." When Burlingame departed for France in January 1869, he felt confident that his "understanding" with Clarendon would hold.[74]

In Paris the French feted the delegates with balls and banquets. However, discussions with the ministers of Napoleon III produced nothing substantive. After a nine-month residence, Burlingame accepted failure and led the mission to Sweden, Denmark, and Holland. Though these countries treated the delegation well, the talks yielded nothing encouraging. In Berlin Burlingame's spirits were buoyed by the news that China had ratified its U.S. treaty and by the favorable reception of Chancellor Otto Bismarck to cooperation policy ideals. As the mission commenced its long trek to St. Petersburg, Burlingame confidently reported to Williams that "America, England, and Prussia, the three great trading nations in China, are united."[75]

Reaching St. Petersburg in the dead of winter, Burlingame contended for the first time with Sino-Russian relations, which revolved around the nations' shared border. A novice in this arena, Burlingame worried that an error on his part might cause China to lose face and damage his chances for a treaty. The delegation's initial meeting with Czar Alexander II, however, alleviated many of his concerns. The czar expressed interest in Burlingame's initiatives and invited the group to tour the hermitage. Though Burlingame caught what appeared to be a cold, his mind was energized by his diplomatic prospects and he thought little of it.[76]

"Father is ill. Lungs and fever," read the urgent telegram from Edward Burlingame in St. Petersburg to his brother Walter in Berlin. "Do not be alarmed, no immediate danger but we thought you would feel better to come." Walter left Berlin immediately, traveling as fast as he could to the Russian capital. He did not arrive in time to see his father alive. After catching what was probably pneumonia, Burlingame deteriorated rapidly, responding to none of the treatments prescribed by his Russian doctor. From his bed, he asked repeatedly for news from London: had John McLeavey Brown sent any updates? Sensing the end was near, he expressed to Edward the agony of knowing he would die before the mission's goals could be consummated. If nations were not legally bound to uphold cooperation policy principles, this most enlightened policy would vanish from the earth. Burlingame died February 23, 1870. His body, after being shipped to Boston, was interred in Mount Auburn Cemetery in a coffin draped in Chinese and American colors.[77]

Things Fall Apart

Following the death of its champion, cooperative policy lived on, but not for long. Indeed, events unfolded according to a sequence so disastrous that Burlingame, had he lived to witness the fate of his dream, would have judged it a nightmare. Under new leadership, the delegation limped back to Europe in 1870, eventually reaching Paris, where members held out faint hopes that a second round of negotiations might yield a written understanding. Their timing could not have been worse. Shortly after the resumption of talks in July, Parisian newspapers reported disturbing news from China. In Tianjin, a Chinese mob had broken into a French mission and orphanage, murdering the nuns, priests, staff, and Chinese converts inside. In the streets of the French capital, Parisians glared at Chih Kang, as if to hold him responsible for the atrocity. Fearing for its members' safety, the delegation left France without securing an agreement. Visiting other

European capitals, the delegation discovered that the Tianjin Massacre had soured all of Europe on China. After the demoralized delegation returned to Peking, Chih Kang learned that he had been assigned to a remote post in Mongolia, his own government suspecting that his experience in the West had polluted his mind.[78]

In all places where Burlingame had pushed for cooperation, his work began to unravel. In England Lord Clarendon died in June 1870. His successor dismissed the Sino-British understanding as the nonbinding opinion of a deceased statesman—a piece of paper one could file away. In China Burlingame's appointed replacement as U.S. minister, J. Ross Browne, rejected cooperation on the grounds that it was founded on his predecessor's naive faith in Chinese officials. "Too sanguine a representation of the intelligence of the Chinese and their ability, statesmanship and desire to advance," Browne wrote to Seward, "has a tendency to create exciting illusions and can only result in disappointment." Burlingame had viewed the Chinese through a rose-tinted lens, Browne claimed, and the impractical cooperative policy had resulted from this error. Reverting to older ways, Browne distrusted Chinese officials and supported Britain's use of force when necessary.[79]

In California rising anti-Chinese sentiment threatened the viability of the Burlingame Treaty. During the 1860s Western industries had actively recruited Chinese labor from Guangdong Province. Burlingame's treaty, in other words, had provided the legal framework for an already-existing migratory pipeline. California's white working-class population had tolerated, if not embraced, the growing Chinese population. With the Civil War interrupting the flow of eastern goods to the west, Californian industries had hired laborers of all colors to meet demand. This high employment had worked to mitigate racial tensions.

In the early 1870s, however, a radically altered economic landscape rendered the Chinese politically radioactive. With the end of the Civil War (1865) and the completion of the transcontinental railroad (1869), cheap manufactured goods from the east flooded California's markets, forcing many industries into bankruptcy. Those companies that survived often preferred Chinese laborers, who accepted lower wages than their white counterparts. As unemployment among white men surged, the demagogue Dennis Kearney stirred up racial hatred by pointing an accusatory finger at the Chinese, a most convenient scapegoat. Mobs of angry Californians harassed the Chinese in the streets, destroyed Chinese-owned property, and even murdered Chinese, all in direct defiance to the protections supposedly guaranteed by the Burlingame Treaty.[80]

During the turbulent 1870s, the reputation of the Burlingame Treaty suffered. In 1876 a poignant article in the *New York Telegram* used anecdotes to explain the treaty's fall from grace. It cited William Piper, a Democratic congressman from California, who insinuated that Burlingame had not died of illness, as had been reported: the Chinese in the delegation had conspired to murder him. The article's author, after checking accounts of Burlingame's death, dismissed Piper's malicious innuendo as baseless. To create a meaningful juxtaposition, he next described a solemn scene he witnessed in Mount Auburn Cemetery. "We were wandering at sunset," he wrote, "when the unusual sight of two young Chinamen" bearing flower wreaths "caught our eyes." Approaching Burlingame's grave "as if they were familiar with the place," they set the flowers "tenderly upon the white block" and exchanged a few hushed words. Their ritual complete, they "climbed the green hill . . . and disappeared."[81] In a short span of years, politics had changed so rapidly as to consign Burlingame and his treaty to irrelevance. Only the Chinese cherished his memory, and few of them voted.

What about Burlingame's own Republican Party? The same article observed that Republicans and Democrats "rival one another in painting the whole Chinese nation . . . as black as the devil."[82] Though the author referred only to Californian politicians, Republicans everywhere had begun to abandon Burlingame and the Chinese by the late 1870s. Why the about-face? Republican office seekers realized they had little to gain from a pro-Chinese platform and plenty to lose—a political reality that the conversion of James Blaine illustrates. In 1868 Blaine applauded the Burlingame mission, calling it "the most important mission which China ever sent to Christian nations." More than a decade later, Blaine, now a presidential hopeful, made the calculated decision to reverse his position to secure his party's nomination for the 1880 election. Since several Western states split their support evenly between the two parties, Blaine believed that, by calling for an exclusionary immigration policy, he could tip the balance in his favor in these states.[83] "The question lies in my mind," he declared before the Senate, "either the Anglo-Saxon race will possess the Pacific coast or the Mongolians will."[84] It was political pragmatism at its worst.

Those who joined Blaine in calling for Chinese exclusion faced one major obstacle. The Burlingame Treaty, despite its unpopularity, had been ratified in the United States and China. Before Washington could block Chinese immigration, Peking would have to consent to revise the existing treaty. To this end, the United States sent a commission to China in 1880. The group was headed by James Angell, the president of the University of Michigan, who, though not supportive of outright exclusion, believed the United States needed more authority to regulate immigration than the Burlingame Treaty provided. In Peking, Angell negotiated with two Chinese ministers, Pao Chun and Li Hungtsao, who expressed initial skepticism. Since it was only the "rabble" in California who clamored for exclusion, they argued, the U.S. government must resist bending to the will of "violent men." Though Pao and Li were inclined to oppose any change to the treaty, more pressing issues prevented them from objecting too strenuously. Faced with the twin threats of a Russian attack and a war with Japan, China could not allow a squabble to jeopardize its friendship with the United States. With misgiving, they agreed to a new treaty that gave the United

States the power to "regulate, limit, or suspend" the "coming of Chinese laborers to the United States."[85]

The roadway now cleared of its largest obstacle, a Chinese exclusion bill rolled inexorably toward passage in Congress.[86] In Boston an indignant John Murray Forbes decried "the madness which prevails." "Much talk is made of the bad morals of the China coolie," Forbes wrote. "The real trouble is he is such a good, thorough, and steady worker that the shiftless Irish or Yankee or Californian," who "look on him as a dangerous competitor," tries to "scare" the "the innocents with predictions of being swamped by the millions from China."[87] Watching from New Haven, the elderly Williams, now a professor of Chinese at Yale, labored away on a second edition of *The Middle Kingdom* in the vain hope that more education might cure his country of its irrational paranoia. He also urged the president and lawmakers to stop the insanity, but to no avail. The Exclusion Act was signed into law in 1882, effectively nullifying the Burlingame Treaty.[88]

Conclusion

Most U.S. ministers in China decried the lack of federal support they received. Burlingame spied an opportunity. In Peking his overflowing personality expanded to fill the void created by the virtually nonexistent American government presence. He formed a dream that, in size and scope, matched even that of the Millennialists. This reference to the missionaries is not accidental. While maintaining the zeal of his Protestant roots, Burlingame replaced the Gospel with a humanitarian principle forged in the crucible of America's great debate over slavery: he believed in the essential equality of men and nations. Using the Burlingame mission as his pulpit, he tried to persuade Europe and the United States to revise their relationships with China, abandoning belligerence in favor of cooperation. More than just Sino-Western relations were at stake here, as Burlingame was surely aware. Had the cooperative policy gained acceptance in the West, it could conceivably have become the standard model guiding all ensuing treaty negotiations between Western and non-Western nations. Burlingame would have changed the world. Unfortunately, racial, economic, and political forces far more powerful than Burlingame himself overwhelmed and destroyed his dream. Still, his model of diplomacy—born as it was out of religious revivals, slavery debates, and his own irrepressible individualism—was distinctly American.

Conclusion

At Anson Burlingame's funeral, the Reverend George W. Briggs observed that the life of the deceased envoy "seems like a tale of romance." Burlingame, he implied, had been a lone knight on a moral quest to obtain a holy grail of his own making.[1] Though Briggs referred to only Burlingame, his eulogy could just as easily have applied to many of the Americans who journeyed to China before him. For this reason, Burlingame's funeral marked the end of not just one man's crusade but the first era of America's involvement in China. Since the official U.S. presence remained minimal throughout the period, the country expressed itself through the actions of individual citizens, many of whom, like Burlingame, projected personal dreams onto China's vast canvas: to rise in class status, corner entire markets, bring about the Millennium, introduce modern technology to China, explain China to Americans, win military glory, or establish a new diplomatic paradigm. These dreams inspired Americans between the sailing of the *Empress of China* in 1784 and the death of Burlingame in 1870.

The American presence in China would expand dramatically in the era to follow (1871–1949), eventually eclipsing the British in terms of total influence. However, the nature of that presence would undergo a fundamental shift. The activities of energetic individuals shaped the first era; in the second era the United States would assert itself primarily through institutions: corporations, governmental agencies, military units, news organs, educational institutions, and philanthropic organizations. Thanks to this institution building, Americans and Chinese formed what Michael Hunt calls a "special relationship" in the twentieth century.[2] To both sides, this relationship appeared to be on the verge of consummation during the Second World War before utterly collapsing with the Communist takeover of 1949. Indeed, it was really in the second era that the United States achieved widespread influence in China. In the final analysis, what was the legacy of the first era? In three ways, Sino-American interaction during the first era laid the intellectual and imaginative groundwork for the special relationship of the second.

First, *Americans of the first era built the infrastructure that made possible the cultural and intellectual exchanges of the second era.* In 1841 Samuel Brown, who ran a school for Chinese children in Macau, explained to his sponsor, the Morrison Educational Society, why he dedicated himself to the study of Chinese language and culture. A good teacher, he said, must know the minds of his students. Without this knowledge, how could meaningful communication take place? However, because of Qing injunctions, the West had remained in a state of "ignorance respecting the peculiar feelings, prejudices, habits, and history of the Chinese." In hauntingly vivid language, Brown described the current state of Sino-Western interaction:

> Our intercourse is much like that of two untaught mutes, that meet with ideas circumscribed by the limits of what their eyes have seen, and picture to each other in pantomime, the mere outlines of the few thoughts they have in common, and then part again in utter ignorance of each other's spiritual being.[3]

Chinese and Americans could not talk to each other, and without communication they could not understand one another's inner thoughts. In slow and laborious fashion, Bridgman, Williams, and others rectified this problem by constructing the cultural and linguistic infrastructure that allowed exchange to take place. In the second era, Americans enjoyed dialogues and partnerships with Chinese that were impossible back when Brown made this statement. They also founded colleges and universities, encasing Bridgman's vision in stone, brick, and mortar.

Second, *Americans of the first era painted a portrait of China that those of the second era found imaginatively useful.* Thanks to the lore of China traders, China glowed in the American imagination as a place where vast fortunes were made, this despite two severe limitations: China had been closed and American industry had yet to mature. Imagine the possibilities, businessmen of the Gilded Age could say, now that China is open and the American industrial sector outperforms all rivals! If the China trade of the first era had seduced ambitious merchants, the China market of the second would beckon corporations with its seemingly limitless potential—"400 million customers," in the famous words of one writer.[4] First-era missionaries also contributed to China's attractive power. Though they failed to win many converts, they accomplished more realistic goals, such as the establishment of missionary stations in treaty ports. And because they or their descendents published accounts of their labors, first-era missionaries inspired later generations of Christians with their heroic examples. For these reasons, the China they left was more exciting, in terms of its evangelical promise, than the China they had found. By century's end, Americans would think of the missionary movement not as single individuals but as waves of volunteers.

Though Millennial fervor dissipated after the Civil War, the rise of the United States as a world power in the late nineteenth and early twentieth centuries fed the growth of its secular replacement: American Exceptionalism. According to this national mythology, American civilization alone possessed the right mix of free market capitalism, rugged individualism, Christian morality, technological genius, and democratic principles—or so many Americans thought. Interestingly, the triumph of Exceptionalism necessitated its undoing. If there truly was a distinct American civilization that was better than all others, Americans would have to prove its superiority by successfully exporting it throughout the world—rendering their way of life *un*exceptional in the process. China provided the perfect test. Not only was China vast and culturally different, its people harbored a strong sense of Chinese Exceptionalism. More than any other country, therefore, China could validate Americans by embracing their values, beliefs, and institutions. In the twentieth century, John Hersey (1914–1993), born in China to a missionary family, captured this need to be needed in his novels set in China.[5] In the second era, Americans pursued this secular goal with an ardor reminiscent of the first era's Millennialism.

Third, *Americans in the first era established the United States as a different kind of player in China*, one that intrigued the Chinese as it perplexed them. Here, after all, was a country that at times imitated the overbearing British yet at other times surprised and delighted the Chinese by deviating from the European model. Though showing they could go off script (or perhaps that they lacked a script altogether), Americans proved unable to sustain any movement long enough to establish a permanent model of their own, as Burlingame's example illustrates. From the Chinese perspective, this erratic behavior, vexing though it was, at the very least demonstrated that the American presence, unlike the British presence, was not monolithic. That being said, American behavior was too inconsistent and unpredictable to inspire China's outright trust. Though we do not, for this reason, see the emergence of a genuine and lasting Sino-American friendship in the first era, we can say that the Chinese recognized a tantalizing potential in the Americans—one that was unique among the Western powers. Thus, when the wave of institution building began in the second era, Americans encountered a China that was, if not exactly enthusiastic, at least receptive to their overtures.

Notes

INTRODUCTION

1. Samuel Shaw, *The Journals of Major Samuel Shaw, the First American Consul at Canton, with a Life of the Author by Josiah Quincy*, ed. Josiah Quincy (Boston: Wm. Crosby and H. P. Nichols, 1847), 199–200.

2. Letters from Jane Burlingame to her son and father, November 23, 1867, Jane Burlingame Outgoing Correspondence, 1867–1870 folder, Container 3, Anson Burlingame and Edward L. Burlingame Family Papers, Manuscript Division, Library of Congress.

3. See, for example, Philip Chadwick Foster Smith, *The Empress of China* (Philadelphia: Philadelphia Maritime Museum, 1984); Charles Stelle, *Americans and the China Opium Trade in the Nineteenth Century* (New York: Arno Press, 1981); Jacques Downs, *The Golden Ghetto: The American Commercial Community at Canton and the Shaping of American China Policy, 1784–1844* (Bethlehem, PA: Lehigh University Press, 1997); and Murray Rubinstein, *The Origins of the Anglo-American Missionary Enterprise in China, 1807–1840* (Lanham, MD: Scarecrow Press, 1996).

CHAPTER 1

1. Philip Chadwick Foster Smith, *The Empress of China* (Philadelphia: Philadelphia Maritime Museum, 1984), 70–71.

2. Kendall Johnson, "A Question of Character: The Romance of Early Sino-American Commerce in *The Journals of Major Samuel Shaw, the First American Consul at Canton* (1847)," in *Narratives of Free Trade: The Commercial Cultures of Early U.S.-China Relations*, ed. Kendall Johnson (Hong Kong: Hong Kong University Press, 2012), 37.

3. John Ledyard, *The Last Voyage of Captain Cook: The Collected Writings of John Ledyard*, ed. James Zug (Washington, DC: National Geographic Adventure Classics, 2005), 46.

4. Ibid.

5. Ibid., xvi.

6. James Zug, *American Traveler: The Life and Death of John Ledyard, the Man Who Dreamed of Walking the World* (New York: Basic Books, 2005), 132.

7. Zug, *American Traveler*, 133–135; Smith, *Empress of China*, 14–30; Jean Gordon Lee, *Philadelphians and the China Trade, 1784–1844* (Philadelphia: University of Pennsylvania Press, 1984), 25.

8. Zug, *American Traveler*, 133–135.

9. Ibid., 135–137; Lee, *Philadelphians and the China Trade*, 25.

10. Zug, *American Traveler*, 159–163; Ledyard, *Last Voyage*, xvii.

11. Smith, *Empress of China*, 31–42; Davis Taylor, *Ginseng: The Divine Root* (Chapel Hill, NC: Algonquin Books, 2006), 118–134.

12. Paul A. Van Dyke, "Macao, Hawaii, and Sino-American Trade: Some Historical Observations, Interactions, and Consequences," in *Macao and Sino-U.S. Relations*, ed. Yufan Hao and Jianwei Wang (Lanham, MD: Lexington Books, 2011), 85.

13. John Adams, *The Works of John Adams, Second President of the United States*, vol. 10, ed. Charles Francis Adams (Boston: Little, Brown, 1856), 283.

14. Joyce Appleby, *Inheriting the Revolution: The First Generation of Americans* (Cambridge, MA: Harvard University Press, 2000), 240.

15. Caroline Frank, *Objectifying China, Imagining America: Chinese Commodities in Early America* (Chicago: University of Chicago Press, 2011), 24–28.

16. Smith, *Empress of China*, 7–8.

17. Van Dyke, "Macao," 78.

18. Zug, *American Traveler*, 135–136.

19. Samuel Shaw, *The Journals of Major Samuel Shaw, the First American Consul at Canton, with a Life of the Author by Josiah Quincy*, ed. Josiah Quincy (Boston: Wm. Crosby and H. P. Nichols, 1847), 133.

20. Zug, *American Traveler*, 135–136.

21. Smith, *Empress of China*, 64.

22. Shaw, *Journals of Major Samuel Shaw*, 134–136, 139, 140–141.

23. Ibid., 152–155; Yen-P'ing Hao, "Chinese Teas to America—a Synopsis," in *America's China Trade in Historical Perspective: The Chinese and American Performance*, ed. Ernest May and John K. Fairbank (Cambridge, MA: Harvard University Press, 1986), 12.

24. Paul Van Dyke, *The Canton Trade: Life and Enterprise on the China Coast, 1700–1845* (Hong Kong: Hong Kong University Press, 2005), 6–8, 165.

25. Ibid., 9–17, 36.

26. Smith, *Empress of China*, 148; Lee, *Philadelphians and the China Trade*, 34.

27. Kuo-Tung Anthony Ch'en, *The Insolvency of the Chinese Hong Merchants, 1760–1843* (Taipei: Institute of Economics, Academia Sinica, 1990), 97; C. Toogood Downing, *The Fan-qui in China*, vol. 1 (London: Henry Colburn, 1838), 117–118; Van Dyke, *Canton Trade*, 10, 24–25.

28. Shaw, *Journals of Major Samuel Shaw*, 176–177.

29. Van Dyke, *Canton Trade*, 25; Jacques Downs, *The Golden Ghetto: The American Commercial Community at Canton and the Shaping of American China Policy, 1784–1844* (Bethlehem, PA: Lehigh University Press, 1997), 22.

30. Shaw, *Journals of Major Samuel Shaw*, 174.

31. Yen-P'ing Hao, *The Comprador in Nineteenth Century China: Bridge between the East and West* (Cambridge, MA: Harvard University Press, 1970), 2;

Shaw, *Journals of Major Samuel Shaw*, 176; Downs, *Golden Ghetto*, 19, 22, 36–37, 78; Van Dyke, *Canton Trade*, 11.

32. Shaw, *Journals of Major Samuel Shaw*, 178–179.

33. Tyler Dennett, *Americans in Eastern Asia* (New York: Macmillan, 1922), 49; Foster Rhea Dulles, *The Old China Trade* (Boston: Houghton Mifflin, 1930), 18–19.

34. Shaw, *Journals of Major Samuel Shaw*, 178–179.

35. Downs, *Golden Ghetto*, 37.

36. Smith, *Empress of China*, 189–192.

37. Jean Sutton, *The East India Company's Maritime Service, 1746–1834: Masters of the Eastern Seas* (Woodbridge, Suffolk, UK: Boydell Press, 2010), 148; Samuel Woodhouse, "The Voyage of the Empress of China," *Pennsylvania Magazine of History and Biography* 63 (1939): 29–30.

38. Woodhouse, "The Voyage of the Empress of China," 29–30.

39. Shaw, *Journals of Major Samuel Shaw*, 179–180.

40. Robert Hall Jr., "Chinese Pidgin English Grammar and Texts," *Journal of the American Oriental Society* 64 (1944): 95; William C. Hunter, *The "Fan Kwae" at Canton before Treaty Days, 1825–1844* (1882; repr., Shanghai: Oriental Affairs, 1938), 36–37.

41. Weng Eang Cheong, *The Hong Merchants of Canton: Chinese Merchants in Sino-Western Trade* (Surrey, UK: Curzon Press, 1997), 161; Shaw, *Journals of Major Samuel Shaw*, 183.

42. Ch'en, *Insolvency of the Chinese Hong Merchants*, 53–54, 143–145, 167–168, 252–254; Paul Van Dyke, *Merchants of Canton and Macao: Politics and Strategies in Eighteenth-Century Chinese Trade* (Hong Kong: Hong Kong University Press, 2011), 9, 20–22.

43. Van Dyke, *Merchants*, 53–55; Sutton, *East India Company's Maritime Service*, 2, 8–11.

44. Anne White, "The Hong Merchants of Canton" (Ph.D. diss., University of Pennsylvania, 1967), 76.

45. Van Dyke, *Merchants*, 62–66.

46. Ch'en, *Insolvency of the Chinese Hong Merchants*, 274.

47. White, "Hong Merchants," 70–72; Ch'en, *Insolvency of the Chinese Hong Merchants*, 196–205; Cheong, *Hong Merchants of Canton*, 153, 167, 186.

48. Ch'en, *Insolvency of the Chinese Hong Merchants*, 88–92.

49. Smith, *Empress of China*, 172.

50. Shaw, *Journals of Major Samuel Shaw*, 179–180.

51. Hosea Ballou Morse, *The Chronicles of the East India Company Trading to China, 1635–1834* (Taipei: Ch'eng-Wen, 1966), 94–109; Shaw, *Journals of Major Samuel Shaw*, 186–195.

52. "From Samuel Shaw to John Jay," in *The Diplomatic Correspondence of the United States*, vol. 7 (Washington, DC: Francis Preston Blair, 1834), 432–435.

53. Shaw, *Journals of Major Samuel Shaw*, 189–190.

54. Ibid., 188–189.

55. Ibid., 189–195, 337–341.

56. Ibid., 193.

57. Smith, *Empress of China*, 196–202. Despite British indignation, Li Chen shows that the defendant would have likely been charged with manslaughter, if not murder, in an English court. See "Law, Empire, and Historiography of Modern Sino-Western Relations: A Case Study of the *Lady Hughes* Controversy in 1784," *Law and History Review* 27 (2009): 1–53.

58. Smith, *Empress of China*, 206; Shaw, *Journals of Major Samuel Shaw*, 218; Appleby, *Inheriting the Revolution*, 74.

59. Philip Freneau, *Poems Written and Published during the American Revolutionary War*, vol. 2 (Philadelphia: Lydia R. Bailey, 1809), 181–182.

60. Shaw, *Journals of Major Samuel Shaw*, 337–341.

61. Paul E. Fontenoy, "Ginseng, Otter Skins, and Sandalwood: The Conundrum of the China Trade," *Northern Mariner* 7 (1997): 5.

62. Shaw, *Journals of Major Samuel Shaw*, 231–232.

63. Woodhouse, "Voyage of the Empress of China," 29.

64. Fontenoy, "Ginseng, Otter Skins, and Sandalwood," 5–6.

65. Minor Myers, *Liberty without Anarchy: A History of the Society of the Cincinnati* (Charlottesville: University of Virginia Press, 1983), 76; Smith, *Empress of China*, 6, 45–46; Shaw, *Journals of Major Samuel Shaw*, 199.

66. Alan Taylor, *William Cooper's Town: Power and Persuasion on the Frontier of the Early American Republic* (New York: Vintage Books, 1996), 13–14; Myers, *Liberty without Anarchy*, xiv.

67. Frank, *Objectifying China, Imagining America*, 205; James Fichter, *So Great a Proffit: How the East Transformed Anglo-American Capitalism* (Cambridge, MA: Harvard University Press, 2010), 39–41.

68. Fichter, *So Great a Proffit*, 26, 43.

69. "Perkins and Company, 1803–1827," *Bulletin of the Business Historical Society* 6 (1932): 1; Shaw, *Journals of Major Samuel Shaw*, 111–112, 117; Fichter, *So Great a Proffit*, 43–44.

70. Winthrop Marvin, *The American Merchant Marine* (New York: Scribner, 1916), 77; Fichter, *So Great a Proffit*, 42–44.

71. Amasa Delano, *Narrative of Voyages and Travels in Northern and Southern Hemispheres* (Boston: E. G. House, 1817), 21.

72. Smith, *Empress of China*, 249–250.

73. Ibid., 240–249.

CHAPTER 2

1. James Fichter, *So Great a Proffit: How the East Transformed Anglo-American Capitalism* (Cambridge, MA: Harvard University Press, 2010), 43–44; Amasa Delano, *Narrative of Voyages and Travels in Northern and Southern Hemispheres* (Boston: E. G. House, 1817), 21–40. Quotation from Delano, *Narrative of Voyages and Travels*, 23.

2. Caroline Frank, *Objectifying China, Imagining America: Chinese Commodities in Early America* (Chicago: University of Chicago Press, 2011), 205.

3. Delano, *Narrative of Voyages and Travels*, 21.

4. Freeman Hunt, *Lives of American Merchants*, vol. 2 (New York: Derby and Jackson, 1858), 56; Thomas G. Carey, *Memoir of Thomas Handasyd Perkins* (Boston: Little, Brown, 1856), 8; Henry Lee, "The Magee Family and the Origins of the China Trade," *Proceedings of the Massachusetts Historical Society* 81 (1969): 105–106.

5. Carl Seaburg and Stanley Paterson, *Merchant Prince of Boston: Colonel T.H. Perkins, 1764–1854* (Cambridge, MA: Harvard University Press, 1971), 42–44.

6. Hunt, *Lives of American Merchants*, 61.

7. Seaburg and Paterson, *Merchant Prince of Boston*, 46–47.

8. Lee, "Magee," 108–109; Hunt, *Lives of American Merchants*, 57–66; Seaburg and Paterson, *Merchant Prince of Boston*, 53–54.

9. Carey, *Memoir of Thomas Handasyd Perkins*, 42–43.

10. Seaburg and Paterson, *Merchant Prince of Boston*, 156.

11. Ibid., 301, 313–314.

12. Ibid., 181, 285.

13. Nancy Ellen Davis, "The American China Trade, 1784–1844: Products for the Middle Class" (Ph.D. diss., George Washington University, 1987), 42–44.

14. Lee, "Magee," 109; Seaburg and Paterson, *Merchant Prince of Boston*, 55.

15. Seaburg and Paterson, *Merchant Prince of Boston*, 93, 143–146, 183.

16. Ibid., 156.

17. James Gibson, *Otter Skins, Boston Ships, and China Goods: The Maritime Fur Trade of the Northwest Coast, 1785–1841* (Seattle: University of Washington Press, 1992), 59, 299–310.

18. Ibid., 135, 165–166, 183; Seaburg and Paterson, *Merchant Prince of Boston*, 160–161, 181; Lee, "Magee," 114–115.

19. Seaburg and Paterson, *Merchant Prince of Boston*, 160–161.

20. Ibid., 158–161.

21. Ibid., 163–164.

22. Ibid.

23. "Perkins and Company," 2.

24. Seaburg and Paterson, *Merchant Prince of Boston*, 161–166.

25. Fichter, *So Great a Proffit*, 1; Seaburg and Paterson, *Merchant Prince of Boston*, 93, 143–146, 183.

26. Phyllis Forbes Kerr, *Letters from China: The Canton-Boston Correspondence of Robert Bennet Forbes* (Mystic, CT: Mystic Seaport Museum, 1996), 123.

27. Joan Kerr Facey Thill, "A Delawarean in the Celestial Empire: John Richardson Latimer and the China Trade" (master's thesis, University of Delaware, 1973), 34–35.

28. James Fenimore Cooper, *Afloat and Ashore: A Sea Tale*, vol. 2 (1844; repr., New York: Stringer and Townsend, 1852), 58, 78.

29. Johnathan Farris, "Thirteen Factories of Canton: An Architecture of Sino-Western Collaboration and Confrontation," *Buildings and Landscapes* 14 (Fall 2007): 70–71; William C. Hunter, *The "Fan Kwae" at Canton before Treaty Days, 1825–1844* (1882; repr., Shanghai: Oriental Affairs, 1938), 14–15.

30. Farris, "Thirteen Factories of Canton." 73–74; Jacques Downs, *The Golden Ghetto: The American Commercial Community at Canton and the Shaping of American China Policy, 1784–1844* (Bethlehem, PA: Lehigh University Press, 1997), 94.

31. Osmond Tiffany, *The Canton Chinese* (Boston: James Monroe, 1849), 223.

32. Nan Hodges and Arthur Hummel, eds., *Lights and Shadows of a Macao Life: The Journal of Harriet Low, Travelling Spinster* (Woodinville, WA: History Bank, 2002), 400 (emphasis in original).

33. C. Toogood Downing, *The Fan-qui in China*, vol. 1 (London: Henry Colburn, 1838), 298–299.

34. Ibid., 298–299.

35. Kerr, *Letters from China*, 130.

36. William C. Hunter, *Bits of Old China* (1855; repr., Taipei: Ch'eng-Wen, 1966), 15–17.

37. Downing, *Fan-qui*, 1:163.

38. Downs, *Golden Ghetto*, 236. See also John Frederick Martin, *Profits in the Wilderness: Entrepreneurship and the Founding of New England Towns in the Seventeenth Century* (Chapel Hill: University of North Carolina Press, 1991); and Richard Bushman, *From Puritan to Yankee: Character and the Social Order in Connecticut, 1690–1765* (Cambridge, MA: Harvard University Press, 1980).

39. Robert B. Forbes, *Personal Reminiscences*, 2nd ed. (Boston: Little, Brown, 1882), 338.

40. Carey, *Memoir of Thomas Handasyd*, 42–43; Lee, "Magee," 108.

41. Kuo-Tung Anthony Ch'en, *The Insolvency of the Chinese Hong Merchants, 1760–1843* (Taipei: Institute of Economics Academia Sinica, 1990), 14, 22–23, 280; James Thomson, Peter Stanley, and John Curtis Perry, *Sentimental Imperialists: The American Experience in East Asia* (New York: Harper and Row, 1981), 21–22.

42. Anne White, "The Hong Merchants of Canton" (Ph.D. diss., University of Pennsylvania, 1967), 98; Ch'en, *Insolvency of the Chinese Hong Merchants*, 168–170, 223, 244–245.

43. Downs, *Golden Ghetto*, 154.

44. Fichter, *So Great a Proffit*, 280.

45. Richard Hildreth, *Our First Men: A Calendar of Wealth, Fashion and Gentility* (Boston, 1846), 5.

46. Weng Eang Cheong, *The Hong Merchants of Canton: Chinese Merchants in the Sino-Western Trade* (Surrey, UK: Curzon Press, 1997), 267–268; Yen-P'ing Hao, *The Comprador in Nineteenth Century China: Bridge between the East and West* (Cambridge, MA: Harvard University Press, 1970), 6; Valery Garrett, *Chinese Dress from the Qing Dynasty to the Present* (North Clarendon, VT: Tuttle, 2007), 70.

47. Downing, *Fan-qui*, 1:116 (emphasis in original).

48. Paul Van Dyke, *Merchants of Canton and Macao: Politics and Strategies in Eighteenth-Century Chinese Trade* (Hong Kong: Hong Kong University Press, 2011), 14; Betty Peh-T'i Wei, *Ruan Yuan, 1764–1849: The Life and Work of a Major Scholar Official in Nineteenth Century China before the Opium War* (Hong Kong: Hong Kong University Press, 2006), 146.

49. Frederic Grant, "Merchant Litigation in the American Courts," *Proceedings of the Massachusetts Historical Society* 99 (1987): 48, 54; Downs, *Golden Ghetto*, 152; White, "Hong Merchants," 96–97.

50. Gibson, *Otter Skins*, 191.

51. Downs, *Golden Ghetto*, 152–156; Sibing He, "Russell and Company, 1818–1891: America's Trade and Diplomacy in Nineteenth-Century China" (Ph.D. diss., Miami University, Department of History, 1997), 82. Also see Hildreth, *Our First Men*.

52. Charles Tyng, *Before the Wind: The Memoir of an American Sea Captain, 1808–1833* (New York: Viking, 1999), 64–67.

53. Ibid., 67.

54. Sarah Forbes Hughes, ed., *Letters and Recollections of John Murray Forbes* (Boston: Houghton, Mifflin, 1900), 57.

55. Charles C. Stelle, "American Trade in Opium to China, Prior to 1820," *Pacific Historical Review* 9 (1940): 432.

56. Ibid., 435.

57. Seaburg and Paterson, *Merchant Prince of Boston*, 263–266.

58. Stelle, "Prior to 1820," 439.

59. Seaburg and Paterson, *Merchant Prince of Boston*, 285.

60. "Perkins and Company," 3–4.

61. Tyng, *Before the Wind*, 100.

62. Paul Van Dyke, *The Canton Trade: Life and Enterprise on the China Coast, 1700–1845* (Hong Kong: Hong Kong University Press, 2005), 135–137.

63. Seaburg and Paterson, *Merchant Prince of Boston*, 313–314.

64. Jacques Downs, "American Merchants and the China Opium Trade, 1800–1840," *Business History Review* 42 (1968): 430–432 (emphasis added).

65. Charles C. Stelle, "American Trade in Opium to China, 1821–1839," *Pacific Historical Review* 10 (1941): 64–66.

66. Downs, "American Merchants," 431.

67. Stelle, "1821–1839," 64–66.

68. John Perkins Cushing, "Memo. for Mr. Forbes Respecting Canton Affairs," *Business History Review* 40 (1966): 105–107 (emphasis added).

69. Downing, *Fan-qui*, 1:257.

70. Seaburg and Paterson, *Merchant Prince of Boston*, 337.

71. Hodges and Hummel, *Lights and Shadows*, 401–402; Downs, *Golden Ghetto*, 242.

72. Seaburg and Paterson, *Merchant Prince of Boston*, 359–360, 372–373.

73. Forbes, *Personal Reminiscences*, 128–130; Kerr, *Letters from China*, 12; Seaburg and Paterson, *Merchant Prince of Boston*, 296, 368–373.

74. Cushing, "Memo.," 105.

75. He, "Russell," 46–47, 54, 57–58.

76. Hodges and Hummel, *Lights and Shadows*, 401–402.

77. Alan Emmet, *So Fine a Prospect: Historic New England Gardens* (Hanover, NH: University Press of New England, 1996), 60; Judith Major, *To Live in the New World: A.J. Downing and American Landscape Gardening* (Cambridge, MA: MIT Press, 1997), 46, 76–78; Seaburg and Paterson, *Merchant Prince of Boston*, 374; Downs, *Golden Ghetto*, 244–246.

78. Downs, *Golden Ghetto*, 151–154; White, "Hong Merchants," 146–147; He, "Russell," 85; Seaburg and Paterson, *Merchant Prince of Boston*, 371.

CHAPTER 3

1. William Rowe, *China's Last Empire: The Great Qing* (Cambridge, MA: Harvard University Press, 2009), 146–147.

2. William Bentley, *The Diary of William Bentley, D.D. Pastor of the East Church, Salem Massachusetts*, vol. 3 (Salem, MA: Essex Institute, 1911), 68; James M. Lindgren, "'That Every Mariner May Possess the History of the World': A Cabinet for the East India Marine Society of Salem," *New England Quarterly* 68 (1995): 184. (All quotations from Lindgren.)

3. Caroline Howard King, *When I Lived in Salem, 1822–1866* (Brattleboro, VT: Stephen Daye Press, 1937), 28–30; Walter Muir Whitehill, *The East India Marine Society and the Peabody Museum of Salem, a Sesquicentennial History* (Salem, MA: Peabody Museum, 1949), 37–38, 45–46; Lindgren, "'That Every Mariner May Possess the History of the World,'" 185–187.

4. Ping Chia Kuo, "Canton and Salem: The Impact of Chinese Culture upon New England Life during the Post-Revolutionary Era," *New England Quarterly* 3 (1930): 421–423.

5. Jean Mudge, *Chinese Export Porcelain for the American Trade, 1785–1835* (Newark: University of Delaware Press, 1981), 145–146.

6. Gideon Nye, *Tea: And the Tea Trade* (New York: Geo. W. Wood, 1850), 23–24.

7. Mudge, *Chinese Export Porcelain for the American Trade*, 145–146.

8. Ibid., 67–71.

9. "Description of a Tea Plant," *Chinese Repository* 8 (1839): 132–164.

10. Paul Van Dyke, *Merchants of Canton and Macao: Politics and Strategies in Eighteenth-Century Chinese Trade* (Hong Kong: Hong Kong University Press, 2011), 14–16.

11. Osmond Tiffany, *The Canton Chinese* (Boston: James Monroe, 1849), 112, 115.

12. Charles Tyng, *Before the Wind: The Memoir of an American Sea Captain, 1808–1833* (New York: Viking, 1999), 36.

13. Lillian Li, "The Silk Export Trade and Economic Modernization in China and Japan," in *America's China Trade in Historical Perspective: The Chinese and American Performance*, ed. Ernest May and John K. Fairbank (Cambridge, MA: Harvard University Press, 1986), 83; Jacques Downs, *The Golden Ghetto: The American Commercial Community at Canton and the Shaping of American China Policy, 1784–1844* (Bethlehem, PA: Lehigh University Press, 1997), 73–74; Ping Chia Kuo, "Canton and Salem," 426–427, 434; Jonathan Goldstein, *Philadelphia and the China Trade, 1682–1846* (University Park: Penn State University Press, 1978), 3.

14. John K. Fairbank, "Introduction," in *America's China Trade in Historical Perspective: The Chinese and American Performance*, ed. Ernest May and John K. Fairbank (Cambridge, MA: Harvard University Press, 1986), 3. See also William Rowe, *Hankow: Commerce and Society in a Chinese City, 1796–1889* (Stanford, CA: Stanford University Press, 1984).

15. James Gibson, *Otter Skins, Boston Ships, and China Goods: The Maritime Fur Trade of the Northwest Coast, 1785–1841* (Seattle: University of Washington Press, 1992), 106.

16. John Denis Haeger, *John Jacob Astor: Business and Finance in the Early Republic* (Detroit, MI: Wayne State University Press, 1991), 83.

17. Downs, *Golden Ghetto*, 107–108; James Fichter, *So Great a Proffit: How the East Transformed Anglo-American Capitalism* (Cambridge, MA: Harvard University Press, 2010), 32.

18. "The Edible Birds'-Nests of China," *Harper's New Monthly Magazine* 2 (1850): 397. See also Samuel Goodrich, *The Voyages, Travels and Adventures of Gilbert Go-Ahead in Foreign Parts* (New York: J. C. Derby, 1855), 75–76.

19. Edmund Fanning, *Voyages round the World: With Selected Sketches of Voyages to the South Seas, North and South Pacific Oceans, China, Etc.* (New York: Collins and Hannay, 1833), 454–467.

20. Dorothy Shineburg, *They Came for Sandalwood: A Study of the Sandalwood Trade in the South-west Pacific, 1830–1865* (Melbourne, Australia: Melbourne University Press, 1967), 1–2, 8–9.

21. Gibson, *Otter Skins*, 257.

22. Paul E. Fontenoy, "Ginseng, Otter Skins, and Sandalwood: The Conundrum of the China Trade," *Northern Mariner* 7 (1997): 11–12.

23. Gibson, *Otter Skins*, 253.

24. Cooper, *The Sea Lions*, vol. 1 (New York: Stringer and Townsend, 1849), 46.

25. Fanning, *Voyages round the World*, 116–117.

26. Dick Wilson, "King George's Men: British Ships and Sailors in the Pacific Northwest–China Trade, 1785–1821" (Ph.D. diss., University of Idaho, 2004), 124.

27. Gibson, *Otter Skins*, 58.

28. Carl Seaburg and Stanley Paterson, *Merchant Prince of Boston: Colonel T.H. Perkins, 1764–1854* (Cambridge, MA: Harvard University Press, 1971), 55; Gibson, *Otter Skins*, 299; Fichter, *So Great a Proffit*, 47–52.

29. Frederic Howay, ed., *Voyages of the "Columbia" to the Northwest Coast, 1787–1790 and 1790–1793* (New York: Da Capo Press, 1941), 48–49.

30. Gibson, *Otter Skins*, 131.

31. Henry Lee, "The Magee Family and the Origins of the China Trade," *Proceedings of the Massachusetts Historical Society* 81 (1969): 109–110.

32. Gibson, *Otter Skins*, 120–123, 129, 215–216, 225.

33. Ibid., 35, 54–57, 135.

34. Richard Henry Dana, *Two Years before the Mast* (Cambridge, MA: Riverside Press, 1868), 413.

35. Seaburg and Paterson, *Merchant Prince of Boston*, 182.

36. Gibson, *Otter Skins*, 182.

37. Jacques Downs, "American Merchants and the China Opium Trade, 1800–1840," *Business History Review* 42 (1968): 422.

38. Joseph Ellis, *American Sphinx: The Character of Thomas Jefferson* (New York: Alfred A. Knopf, 1997), 237.

39. Arthur Bonner, *Alas! What Brought Thee Hither? The Chinese in New York, 1800–1950* (Madison, NJ: Farleigh Dickinson University Press, 1997), 1; Francis Ruley Karttunen, *The Other Islanders: People Who Pulled Nantucket's Oars* (New Bedford, MA: Spinner, 2005), 146; Seaburg and Paterson, *Merchant Prince of Boston*, 193–198.

40. Haeger, *John Jacob Astor*, 83–91.

41. Ibid., 98–99.

42. James P. Ronda, *Astoria and Empire* (Lincoln: University of Nebraska Press, 1990), 2.

43. Haeger, *John Jacob Astor*, 94–119.

44. Ronda, *Astoria and Empire*, 236–237.

45. Haeger, *John Jacob Astor*, 182, 119–124, 158–159, 165–166.

46. Ibid., 173–175, 182–183, 94–95, 204.

47. Fichter, *So Great a Proffit*, 216–217; Seaburg and Paterson, *Merchant Prince of Boston*, 267–268; Gibson, *Otter Skins*, 26.

48. Downs, *Golden Ghetto*, 195.

49. Fichter, *So Great a Proffit*, 209–210.

50. Tyng, *Before the Wind*, 32.

51. Fichter, *So Great a Proffit*, 209–210.

52. Yen-P'ing Hao, "Chinese Teas to America—a Synopsis," in May and Fairbank, *America's China Trade in Historical Perspective*, 23.

53. Gibson, *Otter Skins*, 177.

54. Tyler Dennett, *Americans in Eastern Asia* (New York: Macmillan, 1922), 20 (emphasis in original).

55. Hsin-pao Chang, *Commissioner Lin and the Opium War* (Cambridge, MA: Harvard University Press, 1964), 219, appendix A; Charles C. Stelle, "American Trade in Opium to China, Prior to 1820," *Pacific Historical Review* 9 (1940): 427–430; Downs, "American Merchants," 423; Seaburg and Paterson, *Merchant Prince of Boston*, 265.

56. Stelle, "Prior to 1820," 429–430.

57. Goldstein, *Philadelphia*, 53–54.

58. Stelle, "Prior to 1820," 434.

59. Goldstein, *Philadelphia*, 53–54; Downs, "American Merchants," 425.

60. Stelle, "Prior to 1820," 440.

61. Downs, "American Merchants," 424.

62. Van Dyke, *Canton Trade*, 10, 122–123, 132–133, 165.

63. Van Dyke, "Macao," 78.

64. Betty Peh-T'i Wei, *Ruan Yuan, 1764–1849: The Life and Work of a Major Scholar Official in Nineteenth Century China before the Opium War* (Hong Kong: Hong Kong University Press, 2006), 154–155; Charles C. Stelle, "American Trade in Opium to China, 1821–1839," *Pacific Historical Review* 10 (1941): 57–59; Downs, "American Merchants," 427–428.

65. Wei, *Ruan Yuan*, 156.

66. Stelle, "Prior to 1820," 437.

67. Wei, *Ruan Yuan*, 156.

68. Stelle, "1821–1839," 59.

69. Anne White, "The Hong Merchants of Canton" (Ph.D. diss., University of Pennsylvania, 1967), 129; Downs, "American Merchants," 427–428, 430–431.

70. Jonathan Spence, "Opium Smoking in Ch'ing China," in *Conflict and Control in Late Imperial China*, ed. Frederic Wakeman Jr. and Carolyn Grant (Berkeley: University of California Press, 1975), 162–163.

71. Phyllis Forbes Kerr, *Letters from China: The Canton-Boston Correspondence of Robert Bennet Forbes* (Mystic, CT: Mystic Seaport Museum, 1996), 101–105; Downs, *Golden Ghetto*, 109.

72. Hao, "Chinese Teas," 23.

73. Downs, *Golden Ghetto*, 155; Sibing He, "Russell and Company, 1818–1891: America's Trade and Diplomacy in Nineteenth-Century China" (Ph.D. diss., Miami University, Department of History, 1997), 59–61; Seaburg and Paterson, *Merchant Prince of Boston*, 333.

74. Philip Ziegler, *The Sixth Great Power: Barings, 1762–1929* (London: William Collins Sons, 1988), 123–129, 143.

75. Robert Bennet Forbes, *Remarks on China and the China Trade* (Boston: Samuel N. Dickinson, 1844), 24–25, 55–56; Samuel Wells Williams, "The Present Position of the Chinese Empire," *Transactions of the American Ethnological Society* (New York: Bartlett and Welford, 1848), 279.

76. Fichter, *So Great a Proffit*, 28.

77. Ibid., 4; Downs, "American Merchants," 419.

CHAPTER 4

1. W. J. Townsend, *Robert Morrison: Pioneer of Missions to China* (Pickering and Inglis, 1928), 40; Murray Rubinstein, *The Origins of the Anglo-American Missionary Enterprise in China, 1807–1840* (Lanham, MD: Scarecrow Press, 1996),

63–68, 76; Edwin Stevens, "Obituary Notice of the Reverend Robert Morrison," *Chinese Repository* 3 (1834): 180.

2. Rubinstein, *Origins of the Anglo-American Missionary Enterprise*, 77–81, 150; Townsend, *Robert Morrison*, 55–57.

3. Rubinstein, *Origins of the Anglo-American Missionary Enterprise*, 175.

4. Ibid., 99–101.

5. Ibid., 151, 196, 205, 217–223.

6. Samuel Hopkins, *The Works of Samuel Hopkins*, vol. 2 (Boston: Doctrinal Tract and Book Society, 1852), 232.

7. William Hutchison, *Errand to the World: American Protestant Thought and Foreign Missions* (Chicago: University of Chicago Press, 1993), 61; James West Davidson, *The Logic of Millennial Thought: Eighteenth-Century New England* (New Haven, CT: Yale University Press, 1977), ix–xi.

8. John A. Andrew, *Rebuilding the Christian Commonwealth: New England Congregationalists and Foreign Missions, 1800–1830* (Lexington: University of Kentucky Press, 1976), 2.

9. Eliza Bridgman, *The Pioneer of American Missions in China: The Life and Labors of Elijah Coleman Bridgman* (New York: Anson D. F. Randolph, 1864), 3.

10. Fred Drake, "Bridgman in China in the Early Nineteenth Century," *American Neptune* 46 (1986): 35.

11. Michael Lazich, *E. C. Bridgman (1801–1861), America's First Missionary to China*, (Lewiston, NY: Edwin Mellen Press, 2000), 30–31 (emphasis in original).

12. Ibid., 13–15, 39–40 (emphasis in original).

13. Ibid., 36–38, 44.

14. Rubinstein, *Origins of the Anglo-American Missionary Enterprise*, 110.

15. Ibid., 218.

16. Ibid., 217–224; Lazich, *Bridgman*, 44–49; Conrad Edick Wright, "Merchants and Mandarins: New York and the Early China Trade," in *New York and the China Trade*, ed. David Sanctuary Howard (New York: New-York Historical Society, 1984), 30.

17. David Abeel, *Journal of a Residence in China and the Neighboring Countries* (New York: J. Abeel Williamson, 1836), 31–33.

18. Lazich, *Bridgman*, 55.

19. Drake, "Bridgman," 34.

20. Eliza Bridgman, *Pioneer of American Missions*, 21–23.

21. Ibid., 21–25.

22. Ibid., 30–33 (emphasis in original).

23. Phyllis Forbes Kerr, *Letters from China: The Canton-Boston Correspondence of Robert Bennet Forbes* (Mystic, CT: Mystic Seaport Museum, 1996), 113.

24. Lazich, *Bridgman*, 64–66.

25. Abeel, *Journal*, 77–85.

26. Ibid., 94–95.

27. Charles Tyng, *Before the Wind: The Memoir of an American Sea Captain, 1808–1833* (New York: Viking, 1999), 30.

28. Abeel, *Journal*, 94–95.

29. Eliza Bridgman, *Pioneer of American Missions*, 42–43.

30. Lazich, *Bridgman*, 66–67.

31. Ibid., 66, 70.

32. Lazich, *Bridgman*, 69.

33. Ibid., 75–79.

34. Elijah Bridgman, *Letters to Children* (Boston: Massachusetts Sabbath School Society, 1834), 7–10, 17, 29–30, 84–85, 115–117, 124 (emphasis in original).

35. Lazich, *Bridgman*, 94, 122.

36. Ibid., 99–100.

37. William Elliot Griffis, *A Maker of the New Orient: Samuel Robbins Brown* (New York: Fleming H. Revell, 1902), 31, 58–71.

38. Lazich, *Bridgman*, 114.

39. Ibid., 134–142.

40. Drake, "Bridgman," 41; Suzanne Wilson Barnett, "Protestant Expansion and Chinese Views of the West," *Modern Asian Studies* 6 (1972): 138, 145–148; Lazich, *Bridgman*, 143, 152–155.

41. Lazich, *Bridgman*, 156–158.

42. Drake, "Bridgman," 38–39.

43. Elizabeth L. Malcolm, "The Chinese Repository and Western Literature on China 1800 to 1850," *Modern Asian Studies* 7 (1973): 166.

44. Jessie Lutz, *Opening China: Karl F. A. Gützlaff and Sino-Western Relations, 1827–1852* (Grand Rapids, MI: William B. Eerdman, 2008), 20–23.

45. Ibid., 38–40.

46. Ibid., 38–41, 48–50.

47. Ibid., 51–54.

48. Jessie Lutz, "The Grand Illusion: Karl Gützlaff and Popularization of China Missions in the United States during the 1830s," in *United States Attitudes and Policies toward China: The Impact of American Missionaries*, ed. Patricia Neils (Armonk, NY: M. E. Sharpe, 1990), 46–47.

49. Lutz, *Opening*, 69–80.

50. Hsin-pao Chang, *Commissioner Lin and the Opium War* (Cambridge, MA: Harvard University Press, 1964), 23–24.

51. Lutz, *Opening*, 80 (emphasis added).

52. Charles Gützlaff, "Journal of a Residence in Siam, and of a Voyage along the Coast of China to Mantchou Tartary," *Chinese Repository* 1 (1832): 139–140 (emphasis in original).

53. Ibid.

54. Lutz, "Grand Illusion," 46, 53.

55. Ibid., 48–52.

56. Margaret Coughlin, "Strangers in the House: J. Lewis Shuck and Issachar Roberts, First American Baptist Missionaries to China" (Ph.D. diss., University of Virginia, 1972), 26, 37.

57. Rubinstein, *Origins of the Anglo-American Missionary Enterprise*, 294–295.

58. Edwin Stevens, "Expedition to the Bohea (Wooe) Hills," *Chinese Repository* 4 (1835): 82, 89–90, 93–94.

59. Eliza Bridgman, *Pioneer of American Missions*, 69.

60. Rubinstein, *Origins of the Anglo-American Missionary Enterprise*, 297.

61. Patrick Hanan, *Chinese Fiction of the Nineteenth and Early Twentieth Centuries* (New York: Columbia University Press, 2004), 62–63.

62. Lutz, "Grand Illusion," 62–65.

63. Lazich, *Bridgman*, 91–92.

64. Frederick Wells Williams, *The Life and Letters of Samuel Wells Williams, LL.D.* (New York: Putnam, 1889), 63–66; Samuel Wells Williams, "Autobiographical Sketch," April 1878, Box 13, Series 2, Samuel Wells Williams Family Papers, Manuscript Collections, Yale University Library.

65. Samuel Wells Williams, "Review of *China Opened,*" *Chinese Repository* 8 (1839): 84–98.

66. Lazich, *Bridgman,* 105.

67. Clifton Jackson Phillips, *Protestant America and the Pagan World: The First Half Century of the American Board of Commissioners for Foreign Missions, 1810–1860* (Cambridge, MA: East Asian Research Center, Harvard University, 1969), 29–31.

68. Edward Gulick, *Peter Parker and the Opening of China* (Cambridge, MA: Harvard University Press, 1973), 4–5, 30.

69. George Stevens, *The Life, Letters, and Journals of the Rev. and Hon. Peter Parker, M.D.* (Wilmington, DE: Scholarly Resources, 1972), 56–57.

70. Ibid., 24–25, 32.

71. Gulick, *Peter Parker,* 12–16.

72. Ibid., 7–9.

73. Stevens, *Parker,* 37.

74. Gulick, *Peter Parker,* 18–19.

75. Ira Rutkow, *American Surgery: An Illustrated History* (Philadelphia: Lippincott, 1998), 62, 65, 70, 83–88.

76. Stevens, *Parker,* 82–83.

77. Ibid.

78. Ibid., 96–98, 100–101.

79. Gulick, *Peter Parker,* 37–40.

80. Stevens, *Parker,* 111–112.

81. Gulick, *Peter Parker,* 43–44, 150–153.

82. Rutkow, *American Surgery,* 70.

83. Stevens, *Parker,* 123–125.

84. Ibid., 119.

85. Ibid.

86. Kerr, *Letters from China,* 70–71.

87. Peter Parker, "Ophthalmic Hospital at Canton: Third Quarterly Report," *Chinese Repository* 5 (1836): 189–192.

88. Kerr, *Letters from China,* 70–71.

89. Stevens, *Parker,* 132–133.

90. Robin Hutcheon, *Chinnery* (Hong Kong: FormAsia, 1989), 63–65; Kerr, *Letters from China,* 79; Rutkow, *American Surgery,* 75–77.

91. Stephen Rachman, "Memento Morbi: Lam Qua's Paintings, Peter Parker's Patients," *Literature and Medicine* 23 (2004): 134–136, 148–153.

92. Peter Parker, "Ophthalmic Hospital at Canton: Ninth Quarterly Report," *Chinese Repository* 7 (1839): 576–579.

93. Rachman, "Memento Morbi," 151.

94. Gulick, *Peter Parker,* 153.

95. Ibid., 58–60, 150–153; Stevens, *Parker,* 123–125.

96. Drake, "Bridgman," 35.

97. Gulick, *Peter Parker,* 205; Peter Fay, "The Protestant Mission and the Opium War," *Pacific Historical Review* 40 (1971): 148–155.

CHAPTER 5

1. Peter Parker, "Ophthalmic Hospital at Canton: Ninth Quarterly Report," *Chinese Repository* 7 (1839): 578; "Suspension of Trade," *Chinese Repository* 7 (1838): 437–456; Stephen Rachman, "Memento Morbi: Lam Qua's Paintings, Peter Parker's Patients," *Literature and Medicine* 23 (2004): 152.

2. Robert B. Forbes, *Personal Reminiscences*, 2nd ed. (Boston: Little, Brown, 1882), 31, 41, 49–50, 58; Phyllis Forbes Kerr, *Letters from China: The Canton-Boston Correspondence of Robert Bennet Forbes* (Mystic, CT: Mystic Seaport Museum, 1996), 12.

3. Forbes, *Personal Reminiscences*, 88, 11, 124.

4. Ibid., 57, 132, 133.

5. Ibid.

6. Margaret C. S. Christman, *Adventurous Pursuits: Americans and the China Trade* (Washington, DC: Smithsonian Institute Press, 1984), 114.

7. Forbes, *Personal Reminiscences*, 91, 144–145.

8. Ibid.

9. Geoffrey Ward, "A Fair, Honorable, and Legitimate Trade," *American Heritage* 37 (1986): 49–64.

10. William C. Hunter, *The "Fan Kwae" at Canton before Treaty Days, 1825–1844* (1882; repr., Shanghai: Oriental Affairs, 1938), 80.

11. R. K. Newman, "Opium Smoking in Late Imperial China: A Reconsideration," *Modern Asian Studies* 29 (1995): 766–767.

12. Jonathan Spence, "Opium Smoking in Ch'ing China," in *Conflict and Control in Late Imperial China*, ed. Frederic Wakeman Jr. and Carolyn Grant (Berkeley: University of California Press, 1975), 144–146.

13. Geoffrey Ward, *Before the Trumpet: Young Franklin Roosevelt 1882–1905* (New York: Harper and Row, 1985), 77–78.

14. Kerr, *Letters from China*, 101.

15. Ibid., 63, 210.

16. Ward, "Fair, Honorable," 49–64.

17. Hunter, *"Fan Kwae,"* 72–73 (emphasis in original).

18. Nan Hodges and Arthur Hummel, eds., *Lights and Shadows of a Macao Life: The Journal of Harriet Low, Travelling Spinster* (Woodinville, WA: History Bank, 2002), 4–5.

19. Hunter, *"Fan Kwae,"* 67.

20. Paul Pickowicz, "William Wood in Canton: A Critique of the China Trade before the Opium War," *Essex Institute Historical Collections* 107 (1971): 3–4.

21. Hunter, *"Fan Kwae,"* 67.

22. Alain Le Pichon, *China Trade and Empire: Jardine, Matheson and Co. and the Origins of British Rule in Hong Kong, 1827–1843* (New York: Oxford University Press, 2006), 67; Pickowicz, "William Wood in Canton," 12–14, 18–23; Hodges and Hummel, *Lights and Shadows*, 190–194.

23. Hodges and Hummel, *Lights and Shadows*, 7–9.

24. Christman, *Adventurous Pursuits*, 113.

25. Hodges and Hummel, *Lights and Shadows*, 4–13.

26. Jacques Downs, *The Golden Ghetto: The American Commercial Community at Canton and the Shaping of American China Policy, 1784–1844* (Bethlehem, PA: Lehigh University Press, 1997), 56, 201–207.

27. C. W. King, *The Opium Crisis: A Letter Addressed to Charles Elliot, Esq., Chief Superintendent of the British Trade with China by an American Merchant* (London: Edward Suter, 1839), 1–3.

28. "The Opium Trade," *Asiatic Journal and Monthly Register* 30 (1839): 234–235.

29. Michael Lazich, "American Missionaries and the Opium Trade in Nineteenth-Century China," *Journal of World History* 17 (2006): 202.

30. Kerr, *Letters from China*, 113, 164, 213.

31. John Haddad, *Romance of China: Excursions to China in U.S. Culture, 1776–1876* (New York: Columbia University Press, 2008), 86–88.

32. Ibid., 89.

33. Ibid., 90–91.

34. Ibid., 112.

35. Ibid., 93–100.

36. Ibid., 102–105.

37. E. C. Wines, *A Peep at China in Mr. Dunn's Chinese Collection* (Philadelphia: Ashmead, 1839), 10–11.

38. James Polachek, *The Inner Opium War* (Cambridge, MA: Harvard University Press, 1992), 106–108, 112–120; Paul Van Dyke, *The Canton Trade: Life and Enterprise on the China Coast, 1700–1845* (Hong Kong: Hong Kong University Press, 2005), 138; David Bello, *Opium and the Limits of Empire: Drug Prohibition in the Chinese Interior, 1729–1850* (Cambridge, MA: Harvard University Press, 2005), 131.

39. Polachek, *Inner Opium War*, 121–125, 322.

40. "Suspension of Trade," *Chinese Repository* 7 (1838): 439, 443–444.

41. Ibid., 440–441.

42. Ibid., 445.

43. Hunter, *"Fan Kwae,"* 45–47.

44. "The Opium Trade," 234–235.

45. "Suspension of Trade," 449.

46. Ibid., 452.

47. Michael Lazich, *E.C. Bridgman (1801–1861), America's First Missionary to China* (Lewiston, NY: Edwin Mellen Press, 2000), 195–196.

48. Polachek, *Inner Opium War*, 128–129; Maurice Collis, *Foreign Mud* (London: Faber and Faber, 1946), 203–204.

49. Lazich, *Bridgman*, 185–188.

50. George Stevens, *The Life, Letters, and Journals of the Rev. and Hon. Peter Parker, M.D.* (Wilmington, DE: Scholarly Resources, 1972), 171.

51. Edward Gulick, *Peter Parker and the Opening of China* (Cambridge, MA: Harvard University Press, 1973), 89.

52. Lazich, *Bridgman*, 189–190.

53. Haddad, *Romance*, 119.

54. Letter from Samuel Wells Williams to Sarah Walworth, August 30, 1847, Box 1, Series 1, Samuel Wells Williams Family Papers, Manuscript Collections, Yale University Library (hereafter SWWFP).

55. Lazich, "American Missionaries," 203–204.

56. Kerr, *Letters from China*, 109–110.

57. Forbes, *Personal Reminiscences*, 148.

58. Kerr, *Letters from China*, 112–114.

59. Lazich, "American Missionaries," 203–204.

60. Forbes, *Personal Reminiscences*, 149.

61. "Memorial of R.B. Forbes and Others," Doc. No. 40, House of Representatives, 26th Congress, First Session. The letter was reprinted in other periodicals, including *Hazard's United States Commercial and Statistical Register* 2 (1940): 162–163.

62. Kerr, *Letters from China*, 128–129, 131.

63. Arthur Waley, *The Opium War through Chinese Eyes* (Stanford, CA: Stanford University Press, 1958), 50–51.

64. Hsin-pao Chang, *Commissioner Lin and the Opium War* (Cambridge, MA: Harvard University Press, 1964), 174–175.

65. "Annihilation of the Opium Trade," *Asiatic Journal and Monthly Register* 30 (1839): 310.

66. Ward, "Fair, Honorable," 49–64.

67. "Destruction of the Opium at Chunhow (Chinkow)," *Chinese Repository* 8 (1839): 76.

68. Ibid., 70–77; "Annihilation of the Opium Trade," 310.

69. "Destruction of the Opium at Chunhow," 77.

70. Ibid., 70–77.

71. C. R., "Progress of the Difficulties between the English and Chinese," *Chinese Repository* 8 (1840): 453.

72. Ibid., 453–454.

73. Ibid., 455–456.

74. Kerr, *Letters from China*, 213.

75. "Reply to Article Second," *Chinese Repository* 8 (1840): 533.

76. Ibid., 535 (emphasis in original).

77. Ibid., 536 (emphasis in original).

78. Ibid., 540 (emphasis in original).

79. Lazich, *Bridgman*, 189.

80. "The New Year," *Chinese Repository* 8 (1840): 442–446.

81. Eliza Bridgman, *The Pioneer of American Missions in China: The Life and Labors of Elijah Coleman Bridgman* (New York: Anson D. F. Randolph, 1864), 113–114.

82. Letter from Samuel Wells Williams to Frederick Williams, November 30, 1840, Box 1, Series 1, SWWFP.

83. Kerr, *Letters from China*, 222–225, 239.

CHAPTER 6

1. Phyllis Forbes Kerr, *Letters from China: The Canton-Boston Correspondence of Robert Bennet Forbes* (Mystic, CT: Mystic Seaport Museum, 1996), 253–254.

2. Immanuel Hsü, *China's Entrance into the Family of Nations* (Cambridge, MA: Harvard University Press, 1960), 123–125.

3. Edward Gulick, *Peter Parker and the Opening of China* (Cambridge, MA: Harvard University Press, 1973), 89.

4. George Stevens, *The Life, Letters, and Journals of the Rev. and Hon. Peter Parker, M.D.* (Wilmington, DE: Scholarly Resources, 1972), 128.

5. Ibid., 184.

6. Gulick, *Peter Parker*, 98–99.

7. Stevens, *Parker*, 184–187 (emphasis in original).

8. Kenneth E. Shewmaker, "Forging the 'Great Chain': Daniel Webster and the Origins of American Foreign Policy toward East Asia and the Pacific, 1841–1852," *Proceedings of the American Philosophical Society* 129 (1985): 225.

9. Ibid., 226; John K. Rogers, "Daniel Webster and Col. T.H. Perkins. A Summer-Day Outing in 1817," *New England Magazine* 4 (1886): 13–26.

10. Shewmaker, "Forging the 'Great Chain,'" 229–230.

11. Macabe Keliher, "Anglo-American Rivalry and the Origins of U.S. China Policy," *Diplomatic History* 31 (2007): 247–249.

12. Stevens, *Parker*, 188; William J. Donahue, "The Caleb Cushing Mission," *Modern Asian Studies* 16 (1982): 196.

13. John Belohlavek, *Broken Glass: Caleb Cushing and the Shattering of the Union* (Kent, OH: Kent State University Press, 2005), 58, 153; Keliher, "Anglo-American Rivalry," 252.

14. Belohlavek, *Broken Glass*, 58, 93, 152–154.

15. Ibid., 22, 92–93.

16. *Congressional Globe*, 26th Congress, First Session, March 16, 1840, 275.

17. Carl Seaburg and Stanley Paterson, *Merchant Prince of Boston: Colonel T.H. Perkins, 1764–1854* (Cambridge, MA: Harvard University Press, 1971), 334–335, 408–409.

18. Claude Fuess, *The Life of Caleb Cushing*, vol. 1 (New York: Harcourt, Brace, 1923), 414–415.

19. Frederick Wells Williams, *The Life and Letters of Samuel Wells Williams, LL.D.* (New York: Putnam, 1889), 123.

20. July 24–31, 1843, folder, Box 40, Caleb Cushing Papers (hereafter CCP), Manuscript Division, Library of Congress.

21. April 23–30, 1843, folder, Box 39, CCP.

22. May 27–31, 1843, folder, Box 39, CCP.

23. Brooke Hindle, "The Transfer of Technology and American Industrial Fairs to 1853," in *XIVth International Congress of the History of Science, Proceedings No. 3* (Tokyo: Science Council of Japan, 1974), 146–148.

24. Tyler Dennett, *Americans in Eastern Asia* (New York: Macmillan, 1922), 137.

25. John Haddad, *Romance of China: Excursions to China in U.S. Culture, 1776–1876* (New York: Columbia University Press, 2008), 194–197.

26. July 1–10, 1843, folder, Box 40, CCP.

27. Donahue, "Caleb Cushing Mission," 198.

28. Ibid., 200.

29. Belohlavek, *Broken Glass*, 150, 159.

30. Robert Remini, *Daniel Webster: The Man and His Time* (New York: W. W. Norton, 1997), 578.

31. *Dictionary of American Naval Fighting Ships*, ed. James Mooney (Washington, DC: Naval Department, 1969), s.v. "Missouri"; Belohlavek, *Broken Glass*, 160.

32. Daniel Webster, "Mr. Webster to Mr. Cushing," in *The Diplomatic and Official Papers of Daniel Webster, while Secretary of State* (New York: Harper and Brothers, 1848), 361–362.

33. Belohlavek, *Broken Glass*, 160–162.

34. Dennett, *Americans in Eastern Asia*, 143.

35. Donahue, "Caleb Cushing Mission," 203.

36. See Manchu notebooks, Boxes 166–167, CCP; for Webster's teacher, see April 1–10, 1844, folder, Box 43, CCP.

37. Ping Chia Kuo, "Caleb Cushing and the Treaty of Wanghia," *Journal of Modern History* 5 (1933): 35–36.

38. Ibid.

39. Ibid., 38.

40. Donahue, "Caleb Cushing Mission," 205.

41. Kuo, "Cushing," 39–40.

42. Keliher, "Anglo-American Rivalry," 250.

43. Belohlavek, *Broken Glass*, 165.

44. Kuo, "Cushing," 43.

45. Donahue, "Caleb Cushing Mission," 206; Belohlavek, *Broken Glass*, 166.

46. Belohlavek, *Broken Glass*, 167.

47. Kuo, "Cushing," 43.

48. Earl Swisher, *China's Management of the American Barbarians: A Study of Sino-American Relations, 1841–1861, with Documents* (New Haven, CT: Far Eastern, 1953), 153–154, 158.

49. Belohlavek, *Broken Glass*, 168–171.

50. June 17–21, 1844, folder, Box 44, CCP.

51. Belohlavek, *Broken Glass*, 170–171.

52. Fuess, *Life of Caleb Cushing*, 1:436.

53. Paul H. Clyde, *United States Policy toward China: Diplomatic and Public Documents, 1839–1939* (New York: Russell and Russell, 1964), 17.

54. Kuo, "Cushing," 48–49.

55. Swisher, *China's Management of the American Barbarians*, 163.

56. Clyde, *United States Policy toward China*, 18, 20–21.

57. Swisher, *China's Management of the American Barbarians*, 163, 167–168.

58. Hsü, *China's Entrance*, 139.

59. April 1–10, 1844, folder, Box 43, CCP; "Destruction of the Opium at Chunhow (Chinkow)," *Chinese Repository* 8 (1839): 70–77; Jacques Downs, *The Golden Ghetto: The American Commercial Community at Canton and the Shaping of American China Policy, 1784–1844* (Bethlehem, PA: Lehigh University Press, 1997), 61; Jonathan Spence, *The Search for Modern China* (New York: W. W. Norton, 2001), 126–127.

60. "Memorial of R.B. Forbes and Others," Doc. No. 40, House of Representatives, 26th Congress, First Session.

61. "The American Flag-staff," *Chinese Repository* 13 (1844): 276–277.

62. Donahue, "Caleb Cushing Mission," 206–208.

63. For an account of the incident, see Cushing's correspondence for June and July 1844, Box 44, CCP.

64. Donahue, "Caleb Cushing Mission," 208.

65. Ibid., 212.

66. Belohlavek, *Broken Glass*, 174–177.

67. July 15–24, 1844, folder, Box 45, CCP.

68. Samuel Wells Williams, "A Journal of the Perry Expedition to Japan," *Transactions of the Asiatic Society of Japan* (1910): 145–148; Peter Booth Wiley, *Yankees in the Land of the Gods: Commodore Perry and the Opening of Japan* (New York: Viking, 1990), 364, 416.

69. Swisher, *China's Management of the American Barbarians*, 82–83, 98–99.

70. James Polachek, *The Inner Opium War* (Cambridge, MA: Harvard University Press, 1992), 137–141, 163–169.

71. Belohlavek, *Broken Glass*, 171.

72. Swisher, *China's Management of the American Barbarians*, 173.

73. Ibid., 177.

74. Mary Wright, *The Last Stand of Chinese Conservatism: The T'ung-Chih Restoration, 1862–1874* (New York: Atheneum, 1966), 222; John King Fairbank, "Introduction: The Old Order," in *The Cambridge History of China*, vol. 10, ed. John King Fairbank and K. C. Liu (Cambridge: Cambridge University Press, 1978), 33; Hsü, *China's Entrance*, 5–7.

75. Haddad, *Romance*, 200–205.

76. Belohlavek, *Broken Glass*, 178.

77. Fuess, *Life of Caleb Cushing*, 1:440.

78. Teemu Ruskola, "Canton Is Not Boston: The Invention of American Imperial Sovereignty," *American Quarterly* 57 (2005): 876.

79. Ibid., 861–863, 875–876.

80. Belohlavek, *Broken Glass*, 182–183, 189–190.

81. *Niles National Register*, November 1, 1845.

82. William C. Hunter, *The "Fan Kwae" at Canton before Treaty Days, 1825–1844* (1882; repr., Shanghai: Oriental Affairs, 1938), 155; Kerr, *Letters from China*, 185.

CHAPTER 7

1. G. R. Williamson, *Memoir of the Rev. David Abeel, D.D., Late Missionary to China* (Wilmington, DE: Scholarly Resources, 1972), 211.

2. Ibid., 218.

3. William J. Boone, *Address in Behalf of the China Mission* (New York: W. Osborne, 1837).

4. Williamson, *Abeel*, 225.

5. Fred Drake, "Mid-Nineteenth-Century Discovery of the Non-Chinese World," *Modern Asian Studies* 6 (1972): 207–210.

6. Fred Drake, *China Charts the World: Hsu Chi-yü and His Geography of 1848* (Cambridge, MA: Harvard University Press, 1975), 35–36.

7. "Journal of the Rev. David Abeel at Amoy," *Chinese Repository* 13 (1844): 236, 238.

8. Samuel Wells Williams, *The Middle Kingdom*, 2 vols. (New York: Wiley and Putnam, 1848).

9. Drake, *China Charts*, 150.

10. Ibid., 164–165 (emphasis in original).

11. John Haddad, *Romance of China: Excursions to China in U.S. Culture, 1776–1876* (New York: Columbia University Press, 2008).

12. Ralph Covell, *W.A.P. Martin: Pioneer of Progress in China* (Washington, DC: Christian University Press, 1978), 47.

13. Michael Lazich, *E.C. Bridgman (1801–1861), America's First Missionary to China* (Lewiston, NY: Edwin Mellen Press, 2000), 293.

14. Ibid., 298.

15. Ibid., 257–258.

16. Ibid., 258–262.

17. Frederick Wells Williams, *The Life and Letters of Samuel Wells Williams, LL.D.* (New York: Putnam, 1889), 166–167.

18. Lazich, *Bridgman*, 266, 275 (emphasis in original).

19. Ibid., 280–282.

20. Ibid., 290–291.

21. Frederick Wells Williams, *Life and Letters*, 173.

22. Ibid., 106, 203.

23. Ibid., 99–100, 168, 173, 178.

24. Edward Gulick, *Peter Parker and the Opening of China* (Cambridge, MA: Harvard University Press, 1973), 134–141, 166–167.

25. Frederick Wells Williams, *Life and Letters*, 234–238.

26. Gulick, *Peter Parker*, 193–197.

27. Frederick Wells Williams, *Life and Letters*, 246–247.

28. Ibid., 331.

29. Lazich, *Bridgman*, 381–385.

30. Frederick Wells Williams, *Life and Letters*, 332.

31. *Correspondence Relative to the Earl of Elgin's Special Missions to China and Japan, 1857–1859* (San Francisco: Chinese Materials Center, 1975), 393.

32. Tyler Dennett, *Americans in Eastern Asia* (New York: Macmillan, 1922), 306.

33. *Elgin's Special Missions*, 393–395.

34. J. Y. Wong, *Deadly Dreams: Opium, Imperialism, and the Arrow War* (Cambridge: Cambridge University Press, 1998), 414–415.

35. *Elgin's Special Missions*, 393–398.

36. Wong, *Deadly Dreams*, 415.

37. Dennett, *Americans in Eastern Asia*, 325.

38. Frederick Wells Williams, *Life and Letters*, 291–292, 375.

39. Ellsworth C. Carlson, *The Foochow Missionaries, 1847–1880* (Cambridge, MA: Harvard University Press, 1974), 70.

40. Carl Cutler, *Greyhounds of the Sea: The Story of the American Clipper Ship* (New York: Halcyon House, 1930), 118–123; Kwang-Ching Liu, *Anglo-American Steamship Rivalry in China, 1862–1874* (Cambridge, MA: Harvard University Press, 1962), 2.

41. Cutler, *Greyhounds of the Sea*, 111, 412–447.

42. Stephen Chapman Lockwood, *Augustine Heard and Company, 1858–1862* (Cambridge, MA: Harvard University Press, 1971), 6–7, 27–29.

43. Yen-P'ing Hao, *The Comprador in Nineteenth Century China: Bridge between the East and West* (Cambridge, MA: Harvard University Press, 1970), 4–5, 32–33.

44. Lockwood, *Augustine Heard*, 5–6, 37, 40, 45.

45. Ibid., 91–94.

46. Liu, *Steamship Rivalry*, 13, 16.

47. Ibid., 14–15.

48. Ibid., 20–22, 31 (emphasis in original).

49. Ibid., 24–29.

50. Ibid., 58–60, 73.

51. Sarah Forbes Hughes, ed., *Letters and Recollections of John Murray Forbes* (Boston: Houghton, Mifflin, 1900), 39–41; John Larson, *Bonds of Enterprise: John*

Murray Forbes and Western Development (Cambridge, MA: Harvard University Press, 1984), 10–11.

52. Larson, *Bonds of Enterprise*, 17–18.

53. Phyllis Forbes Kerr, *Letters from China: The Canton-Boston Correspondence of Robert Bennet Forbes* (Mystic, CT: Mystic Seaport Museum, 1996), 13; Hughes, *John Murray Forbes*, 62.

54. Hughes, *John Murray Forbes*, 6, 87–88.

55. Robert B. Forbes, *Personal Reminiscences*, 2nd ed. (Boston: Little, Brown, 1882), 138–139.

56. Larson, *Bonds of Enterprise*, 23.

57. Kerr, *Letters from China*, 13, 129.

58. Hughes, *John Murray Forbes*, 98–99.

59. Arthur Johnson and Barry Supple, *Boston Capitalists and Western Railroads: A Study in the Nineteenth-Century Railroad Investment Process* (Cambridge, MA: Harvard University Press, 1967), 93.

60. Hughes, *John Murray Forbes*, 90.

61. Larson, *Bonds of Enterprise*, 11.

62. Johnson and Supple, *Boston Capitalists and Western Railroads*, 30; Thomas Cochran, *Railroad Leaders, 1845–1890: The Business Mind in Action* (New York: Russell and Russell, 1966), 35.

63. Larson, *Bonds of Enterprise*, 22.

64. Ibid., 31–32.

65. Cochran, *Railroad Leaders*, 36, 326.

66. Johnson and Supple, *Boston Capitalists and Western Railroads*, 96–99.

67. Ibid., 30, 47, 110–111, 120.

68. Larson, *Bonds of Enterprise*, 52.

69. Cochran, *Railroad Leaders*, 331.

70. Ibid., 328.

71. R. C. Overton, "Charles Elliott Perkins," *Business History Review* 31 (1957): 304.

72. Johnson and Supple, *Boston Capitalists and Western Railroads*, 175.

73. Hughes, *John Murray Forbes*, 161.

74. Larson, *Bonds of Enterprise*, 85–89.

75. Hughes, *John Murray Forbes*, 148–151.

76. Haddad, *Romance*, 55–62, 129–155.

77. Peter Kwong and Dušanka Miščević, *Chinese America: The Untold Story of America's Oldest New Community* (New York: New Press, 2005), 35.

78. Ronald Takaki, *Strangers from a Different Shore* (Boston: Little, Brown, 1989), 33. See also "The Celestials at Home and Abroad," *Littell's Living Age* 430 (1852): 294.

79. *Biographical Dictionary of Chinese Women: The Qing Period, 1644–1911*, ed. Lily Xiao Hong Lee (New York: M. E. Sharpe, 1998), s.v. "Maria Seise."

80. Kwong and Miščević, *Chinese America*, 6.

81. Frederick Wells Williams, *Life and Letters*, 169–170.

82. Kwong and Miščević, *Chinese America*, 7–8.

83. Ibid., 11–15; Takaki, *Strangers from a Different Shore*, 84.

84. Takaki, *Strangers from a Different Shore*, 35.

85. Kwong and Miščević, *Chinese America*, 7.

86. Ibid.

87. Takaki, *Strangers from a Different Shore*, 31.

88. Hamilton Holt, *The Life Stories of Undistinguished Americans* (New York: Routledge, 1990), 178.

89. Takaki, *Strangers from a Different Shore*, 36.

90. Shih-shan H. Tsai, "American Involvement in the Coolie Trade," *American Studies* 6 (1976): 53; Kwong and Miščević, *Chinese America*, 35–37.

91. Tsai, "American Involvement in the Coolie Trade," 53–58.

92. Gulick, *Peter Parker*, 173.

93. Ibid., 174.

94. George Stevens, *The Life, Letters, and Journals of the Rev. and Hon. Peter Parker, M.D.* (Wilmington, DE: Scholarly Resources, 1972), 306.

95. Tsai, "American Involvement in the Coolie Trade," 65.

96. Mary Louis Pratt, *Imperial Eyes: Travel Writing and Transculturation* (London: Routledge, 1992), 6.

CHAPTER 8

1. "Obituary of the Rev. Edwin Stevens," *Sailor's Magazine and Naval Journal* 10 (1837): 115.

2. Jonathan Spence, *God's Chinese Son: The Taiping Heavenly Kingdom of Hong Xiuquan* (New York: W. W. Norton, 1996), 16.

3. Ibid., 18.

4. Michael Lazich, *E.C. Bridgman (1801–1861), America's First Missionary to China* (Lewiston, NY: Edwin Mellen Press, 2000), 97.

5. Spence, *God's Chinese Son*, 30–32.

6. P. Richard Bohr, "Liang Fa's Quest for Moral Power," in *Christianity in China: Early Protestant Missionary Writings*, ed. Suzanne Wilson Barnett (Cambridge, MA: Harvard University Press, 1985), 36–40.

7. Ibid., 41.

8. Ibid., 42–44.

9. Philip Kuhn, "Origins of the Taiping Vision: Cross-Cultural Dimensions of a Chinese Rebellion," *Comparative Studies in Society and History* 19 (1977): 354.

10. Spence, *God's Chinese Son*, 24–33.

11. Ibid., 47.

12. Ibid., 47–50.

13. Ibid., 64–67.

14. Yuan Chung Teng, *Americans and the Taiping Rebellion: A Study of American-Chinese Relationship, 1847–1864* (Taipei: China Academy, 1982), 8.

15. Margaret Coughlin, "Strangers in the House: J. Lewis Shuck and Issachar Roberts, First American Baptist Missionaries to China" (Ph.D. diss., University of Virginia, 1972), 37–40.

16. Ibid., 41–42 (emphasis in original).

17. Ibid., 43, 47, 50–52.

18. Ibid., 131.

19. Ibid., 75–76 (emphasis in original).

20. Ibid.

21. Ibid., 76.

22. Arthur Waley, *The Opium War through Chinese Eyes* (Stanford, CA: Stanford University Press, 1958), 229–233.

23. Coughlin, "Strangers in the House," 81.

24. Frederic Wakeman Jr., *Strangers at the Gate: Social Disorder in South China, 1839–1861* (Berkeley: University of California Press, 1966), 14–21.

25. Coughlin, "Strangers in the House," 188–189.

26. Ibid., 227–228.

27. Ibid., 254.

28. George Blackburn Pruden, "Issachar Jacox Roberts and American Diplomacy in China during the Taiping Rebellion" (Ph.D. diss., American University, 1977), 158–159.

29. Coughlin, "Strangers in the House," 255–256.

30. Ibid., 254–257.

31. Issachar Jacox Roberts, "Tae Ping Wang," *Putnam's Magazine* 8 (1856): 380–384.

32. Ibid., 383–384.

33. Coughlin, "Strangers in the House," 229–231.

34. Ibid., 95–101 (emphasis in original).

35. Pruden, "Issachar Jacox Roberts," 161–162.

36. Ibid., 161–163.

37. Coughlin, "Strangers in the House," 105–106.

38. Pruden, "Issachar Jacox Roberts," 163–165.

39. Lazich, *Bridgman*, 300, 304–306.

40. Coughlin, "Strangers in the House," 109–110.

41. Ibid., 118.

42. Ibid., 112–119.

43. Teng, *Americans*, 14–15; Spence, *God's Chinese Son*, 98, 107, 115, 126, 132.

44. Yuan Chung Teng, "Reverend Issachar Jacox Roberts and the Taiping Rebellion," *Journal of Asian Studies* 23 (1963): 59.

45. Coughlin, "Strangers in the House," 265.

46. Pruden, "Issachar Jacox Roberts," 207.

47. Teng, "Roberts," 60.

48. Teng, *Americans*, 164.

49. Spence, *God's Chinese Son*, 286.

50. Coughlin, "Strangers in the House," 269–270.

51. Spence, *God's Chinese Son*, 287.

52. Teng, "Roberts," 63–64.

53. Wing Yung, *My Life in China and America* (Hong Kong: China Economic Review, 2007), 64.

54. Spence, *God's Chinese Son*, 288–290.

55. Coughlin, "Strangers in the House," 131.

56. Ibid., 275–277.

57. John A. Rapp, "Clashing Dilemmas: Hong Rengan, Issachar Roberts, and a Taiping 'Murder' Mystery," *Journal of Historical Biography* 4 (2008): 34–35.

58. Coughlin, "Strangers in the House," 277.

59. Rapp, "Clashing Dilemmas," 27–28, 34–35.

60. Ibid., 27–29, 35–36.

61. Prescott Clarke and J. S. Gregory, *Western Reports on the Taiping: A Selection of Documents* (Canberra: Australian National University Press, 1982), 314–316.

62. Ibid.

63. Caleb Carr, *The Devil Soldier: The Story of Frederick Townsend Ward* (New York: Random House, 1992), 10.

64. Spence, *God's Chinese Son*, 311–312.

65. Jonathan Spence, *To Change China: Western Advisers in China 1620–1960* (New York: Penguin Books, 1986), 60; Carr, *Devil Soldier*, 13, 76–78; Edward Rhoads, *Manchu and Han: Ethnic Relations and Political Power in Late Qing and Early Republican China, 1861–1928* (Seattle: University of Washington, 2000), 6–10.

66. Carr, *Devil Soldier*, 26–32.

67. Ibid., 34–38, 59, 58–61, 65, 67.

68. Ibid., 39, 81, 82, 88; Spence, *To Change China*, 61–62.

69. Carr, *Devil Soldier*, 89–90.

70. Ibid., 91, 106–109.

71. Ibid., 118–119.

72. Ibid., 27–83.

73. Franz Michael, *The Taiping Rebellion History and Documents*, vol. 3 (Seattle: University of Washington Press, 1971), 729–1380; Kwan-wai So, Eugene P. Boardman, and Ch'iu P'ing, "Hung Jen-Kan, Taiping Prime Minister, 1859–1864," *Harvard Journal of Asiatic Studies* 20 (1957): 275–276; Spence, *To Change China*, 64.

74. Carr, *Devil Soldier*, 138–142, 161–164.

75. Ibid., 106–107.

76. Ibid., 165–166.

77. Ibid., 195.

78. Hallett Abend, *The God from the West: A Biography of Frederick Townsend Ward* (New York: Doubleday, 1947), 138–148.

79. Carr, *Devil Soldier*, 214.

80. Ibid., 230–231; Spence, *To Change China*, 70.

81. Carr, *Devil Soldier*, 87, 209–212, 220, 272, 280.

82. Ibid., 232.

83. Ibid., 238.

84. Ibid., 7, 236–238.

85. Ibid., 290–295.

86. Michael, *Taiping Rebellion*, 1496.

CHAPTER 9

1. Yuan Chung Teng, *Americans and the Taiping Rebellion: A Study of American-Chinese Relationship, 1847–1864* (Taipei: China Academy, 1982), 72–73.

2. Frederick Wells Williams, *The Life and Letters of Samuel Wells Williams, LL.D.* (New York: Putnam, 1889), 360.

3. Edward Gulick, *Peter Parker and the Opening of China* (Cambridge, MA: Harvard University Press, 1973), 189–193.

4. Caleb Carr, *The Devil Soldier: The Story of Frederick Townsend Ward* (New York: Random House, 1992), 29.

5. Jonathan Goldstein, *Philadelphia and the China Trade, 1682–1846* (University Park, PA: Penn State University Press, 1978), 68.

6. Eileen Scully, *Bargaining with the State from Afar: American Citizenship in Treaty Port China, 1844–1942* (New York: Columbia University Press, 2001), 69.

7. David Anderson, *Imperialism and Idealism: American Diplomats in China, 1861–1898* (Bloomington: Indiana University Press, 1985), 35.

8. Mary Wright, *The Last Stand of Chinese Conservatism: The T'ung-Chih Restoration, 1862–1874* (New York: Atheneum, 1966), 7–8, 11.

9. Ibid., 14.

10. Jonathan Spence, *To Change China: Western Advisers in China 1620–1960* (New York: Penguin Books, 1986), 146.

11. Wright, *Last Stand*, 210–212.

12. Ralph Covell, *W.A.P. Martin: Pioneer of Progress in China* (Washington, DC: Christian University Press, 1978), 172–174; Wright, *Last Stand*, 229.

13. Wright, *Last Stand*, 225; Joseph L. Morrow, "Anson Burlingame, His Life and Services," in *New Berlin Centennial* (New Berlin, NY: Unadilla Valley Historical Society, 1908), 79; Miscellany—Printed Material folder, Container 2, Anson Burlingame and Edward L. Burlingame Family Papers, Manuscript Division, Library of Congress (hereafter ABFP).

14. Frederick Wells Williams, *Life and Letters*, 338, 363.

15. Frederick Wells Williams, *Anson Burlingame and the First Chinese Mission to Foreign Powers* (New York: Scribner, 1912), 3–6.

16. Anderson, *Imperialism and Idealism*, 18–19.

17. Frederick Wells Williams, *Burlingame*, 7.

18. Anderson, *Imperialism and Idealism*, 24–25.

19. Ibid., 35.

20. Frederick Wells Williams, *Life and Letters*, 358.

21. Wright, *Last Stand*, 22.

22. Frederick Wells Williams, *Burlingame*, 33–35.

23. Anderson, *Imperialism and Idealism*, 25.

24. Ibid., 32.

25. S. S. Kim, "Burlingame and the Inauguration of the Co-Operative Policy," *Modern Asian Studies* 5 (1971): 353.

26. Wright, *Last Stand*, 26.

27. Ibid., 39–40, 226.

28. Ibid., 222–224.

29. Ibid., 231–232.

30. Spence, *To Change China*, 133–134.

31. Covell, *W.A.P. Martin*, 146–147.

32. Immanuel Hsü, *China's Entrance into the Family of Nations* (Cambridge, MA: Harvard University Press, 1960), 127–128.

33. Spence, *To Change China*, 134.

34. Richard Steven Horowitz, "Central Power and State Making: The Zongli Yamen and Self-Strengthening in China, 1860–1880," (Ph.D. diss., Harvard University, 1998), 275–276.

35. Covell, *W.A.P. Martin*, 147.

36. Horowitz, "Central Power and State Making," 279.

37. Hsü, *China's Entrance*, 136–138.

38. Ibid., 128.

39. Carl Yeager, "Anson Burlingame: His Mission to China and the First Chinese Mission to Western Nations" (master's thesis, Georgetown University, 1950), 42–43.

40. Spence, *To Change China*, 108–109.

41. Yeager, "Anson Burlingame," 32–36; David Anderson, "Anson Burlingame: American Architect of the Cooperative Policy in China, 1861–1871," *Diplomatic*

History 1 (1977): 247; Anderson, *Imperialism and Idealism*, 31; Spence, *To Change China*, 110–112.

42. Martin Ring, "Anson Burlingame, S. Wells Williams and China, 1861–1870: A Great Era in Chinese-American Relations" (Ph.D. diss., Tulane University, 1977), 167–168.

43. Letter from Jane Burlingame to Isaac Livermore, January 20, 1865, Jane Burlingame Outgoing Correspondence, 1864–1867 folder, Container 3, ABFP.

44. W.A.P. Martin, "Mr. Burlingame's Last Interview with Prince Kung and the Officers of the Foreign Board," State Department—Diplomatic Documents folder, Container 2, ABFP (emphasis in original).

45. Ibid.

46. Ring, "Anson Burlingame, S. Wells Williams," 170–177; Frederick Wells Williams, *Burlingame*, 113.

47. Martin, "Last Interview"; letter from Jane Burlingame to Isaac Livermore, July 1, 1865, Jane Burlingame Outgoing Correspondence, 1864–1867 folder, Container 3, ABFP.

48. Frederick Wells Williams, *Burlingame*, 33–35.

49. Anderson, *Imperialism and Idealism*, 27.

50. Ring, "Anson Burlingame, S. Wells Williams," 176–177.

51. Letter from Jane Burlingame to Isaac Livermore, 1867, Jane Burlingame Outgoing Correspondence, 1867–1870 folder, Container 3, ABFP.

52. Frederick Wells Williams, *Burlingame*, 65.

53. Letters from Jane Burlingame to her son and father, November 23, 1867, Jane Burlingame Outgoing Correspondence, 1867–1870, folder, Container 3, ABFP.

54. Hsü, *China's Entrance*, 163–164.

55. Frederick Wells Williams, *Life and Letters*, 376.

56. "The Chinese Embassy to All the Treaty Powers," Miscellany—Printed Material folder, Container 2, ABFP; Ring, "Anson Burlingame, S. Wells Williams," 220–224.

57. Ring, "Anson Burlingame, S. Wells Williams," 236–237.

58. Frederick Wells Williams, *Burlingame*, 117.

59. Letter from Jane Burlingame to Isaac Livermore, April 26, 1868, Jane Burlingame Outgoing Correspondence, 1867–1870, folder, Container 3, ABFB.

60. John Schrecker, "'For the Equality of Men—for the Equality of Nations': Anson Burlingame and China's First Embassy to the United States, 1868," *Journal of American–East Asian Relations* 17 (2010): 11.

61. Ibid., 15–16.

62. Frederick Wells Williams, *Burlingame*, 147–148; Ring, "Anson Burlingame, S. Wells Williams," 254–256.

63. Ring, "Anson Burlingame, S. Wells Williams," 254.

64. Schrecker, "'For the Equality of Men,'" 11, 20–21, 27.

65. Zhang Deyi, *Diary of a Chinese Diplomat* (Beijing: Chinese Literature Press, 1992), 134.

66. Frederick Wells Williams, *A Sketch of the Relations between the United States and China* (Boston: Thomas Crowell, 1910), 64–65.

67. *Banquet to His Excellency Anson Burlingame, and his Associates of the Chinese Embassy* (New York: Sun Book and Job Printing House, 1868), 16–17.

68. Schrecker, "'For the Equality of Men,'" 31.

69. Ibid., 34.

70. "The New Chinese Treaty—Infamous Diplomacy," Miscellany Clippings folder, Container 2, ABFP.

71. Frederick Wells Williams, *Burlingame*, 123.

72. Ring, "Anson Burlingame, S. Wells Williams," 252.

73. Ibid., 262–263.

74. Ibid., 260, 288–299.

75. Ibid., 299–300, 317–322.

76. Anson Burlingame Correspondence from St. Petersburg, February 23, 1870, Miscellany Clippings folder, Container 2, ABFP; Ring, "Anson Burlingame, S. Wells Williams," 323–325.

77. Telegraph from Edward to Walter Burlingame, Edward Burlingame (Son) Family Correspondence, 1858–1870, folder, Container 3, ABFP; Anson Burlingame Correspondence from St. Petersburg, February 23, 1870, Miscellany Clippings folder, Container 2, ABFP.

78. Ring, "Anson Burlingame, S. Wells Williams," 329–331; Hsü, *China's Entrance*, 171.

79. Ring, "Anson Burlingame, S. Wells Williams," 273, 332.

80. Iris Chang, *The Chinese in America: A Narrative History* (New York: Viking, 2003), 116–129.

81. "The Burlingame Treaty," *New York Telegram*, May 23, 1876, Miscellany Clippings folder, Container 2, ABFP.

82. Ibid.

83. Andrew Gyory, *Closing the Gate: Race, Politics, and the Chinese Exclusion Act* (Chapel Hill: University of North Carolina Press, 1998), 1, 27–28, 145–146.

84. Willis Fletcher Johnson, *Life of James G. Blaine, "the Plumed Knight"* (Philadelphia: Atlantic, 1893), 216.

85. Gyory, *Closing the Gate*, 212–216.

86. Ibid., 238.

87. Robert B. Forbes, *Personal Reminiscences*, 2nd ed. (Boston: Little, Brown, 1882), 411.

88. John Haddad, *Romance of China: Excursions to China in U.S. Culture, 1776–1876* (New York: Columbia University Press, 2008), 293–296.

CONCLUSION

1. Obituary for Anson Burlingame, State Department—Diplomatic Documents, 1861–1870 folder, Container 2, Anson Burlingame and Edward L. Burlingame Family Papers, Manuscript Division, Library of Congress.

2. Michael Hunt, *The Making of a Special Relationship: The United States and China to 1914* (New York: Columbia University Press, 1983).

3. "Morrison Educational Society," *Chinese Repository* 10 (October 1841): 572.

4. Carl Crow, *Four Hundred Million Customers* (New York: Harper, 1937).

5. See John Hersey, *A Single Pebble* (New York: Alfred A. Knopf, 1956), and John Hersey, *The Call* (New York: Alfred A. Knopf, 1985).

Bibliography

ARCHIVES, LIBRARIES, AND COLLECTIONS

ABFP—Anson Burlingame and Edward L. Burlingame Family Papers. Manuscript Division. Library of Congress.
CCP—Caleb Cushing Papers. Manuscript Division. Library of Congress.
SWWFP—Samuel Wells Williams Family Papers. Manuscript Collections. Yale University Library.

NEWSPAPERS AND MAGAZINES

Asiatic Journal and Monthly Register
Chinese Repository
Congressional Globe
Harper's New Monthly Magazine
Hazard's United States Commercial and Statistical Register
Littell's Living Age
Niles National Register
Putnam's Magazine
Sailor's Magazine and Naval Journal

BOOKS, JOURNALS, AND PAPERS

Abeel, David. *Journal of a Residence in China and the Neighboring Countries.* New York: J. Abeel Williamson, 1836.
Abend, Hallett. *The God from the West: A Biography of Frederick Townsend Ward.* New York: Doubleday, 1947.
Adams, John. *The Works of John Adams, Second President of the United States.* Edited by Charles Francis Adams. 10 vols. Boston: Little, Brown, 1856.
Anderson, David. "Anson Burlingame: American Architect of the Cooperative Policy in China, 1861–1871." *Diplomatic History* 1 (1977): 239–255.

————. *Imperialism and Idealism: American Diplomats in China, 1861–1898.* Bloomington: Indiana University Press, 1985.

Andrew, John A. *Rebuilding the Christian Commonwealth: New England Congregationalists and Foreign Missions, 1800–1830.* Lexington: University of Kentucky Press, 1976.

Appleby, Joyce. *Inheriting the Revolution: The First Generation of Americans.* Cambridge, MA: Harvard University Press, 2000.

Banquet to His Excellency Anson Burlingame, and his Associates of the Chinese Embassy by the Citizens of New York on Tuesday, June 23, 1868. New York: Sun Book and Job Printing House, 1868.

Barnett, Suzanne Wilson. "Protestant Expansion and Chinese Views of the West." *Modern Asian Studies* 6 (1972): 129–149.

Bello, David. *Opium and the Limits of Empire: Drug Prohibition in the Chinese Interior, 1729–1850.* Cambridge, MA: Harvard University Press, 2005.

Belohlavek, John. *Broken Glass: Caleb Cushing and the Shattering of the Union.* Kent, OH: Kent State University Press, 2005.

Bentley, William. *The Diary of William Bentley, D.D. Pastor of the East Church, Salem Massachusetts.* Vol. 3. Salem, MA: Essex Institute, 1911.

Bohr, Richard P. "Liang Fa's Quest for Moral Power." In *Christianity in China: Early Protestant Missionary Writings*, edited by Suzanne Wilson Barnett, 35–46. Cambridge, MA: Harvard University Press, 1985.

Bonner, Arthur. *Alas! What Brought Thee Hither?: The Chinese in New York, 1800–1950.* Madison, NJ: Farleigh Dickinson University Press, 1997.

Boone, William J. *Address in Behalf of the China Mission.* New York: W. Osborne, 1837.

Bridgman, Elijah C. *Letters to Children.* Boston: Massachusetts Sabbath School Society, 1834.

Bridgman, Eliza. *The Pioneer of American Missions in China: The Life and Labors of Elijah Coleman Bridgman.* New York: Anson D. F. Randolph, 1864.

Bushman, Richard. *From Puritan to Yankee: Character and the Social Order in Connecticut, 1690–1765.* Cambridge, MA: Harvard University Press, 1980.

Carey, Thomas G. *Memoir of Thomas Handasyd Perkins.* Boston: Little, Brown, 1856.

Carlson, Ellsworth C. *The Foochow Missionaries, 1847–1880.* Cambridge, MA: Harvard University Press, 1974.

Carr, Caleb. *The Devil Soldier: The Story of Frederick Townsend Ward.* New York: Random House, 1992.

Chang, Hsin-pao. *Commissioner Lin and the Opium War.* Cambridge, MA: Harvard University Press, 1964.

Chang, Iris. *The Chinese in America: A Narrative History.* New York: Viking, 2003.

Ch'en, Kuo-Tung Anthony. *The Insolvency of the Chinese Hong Merchants, 1760–1843.* Taipei: Institute of Economics, Academia Sinica, 1990.

Chen, Li. "Law, Empire, and Historiography of Modern Sino-Western Relations: A Case Study of the *Lady Hughes* Controversy in 1784." *Law and History Review* 27 (2009): 1–53.

Cheong, Weng Eang. *The Hong Merchants of Canton: Chinese Merchants in the Sino-Western Trade.* Surrey, UK: Curzon Press, 1997.

Christman, Margaret C. S. *Adventurous Pursuits: Americans and the China Trade.* Washington, DC: Smithsonian Institute Press, 1984.

Clarke, Prescott, and J. S. Gregory. *Western Reports on the Taiping: A Selection of Documents*. Canberra: Australian National University Press, 1982.

Clyde, Paul H. *United States Policy toward China: Diplomatic and Public Documents, 1839–1939*. New York: Russell and Russell, 1964.

Cochran, Thomas. *Railroad Leaders 1845–1890: The Business Mind in Action*. New York: Russell and Russell, 1966.

Collis, Maurice. *Foreign Mud*. London: Faber and Faber, 1946.

Cooper, James Fenimore. *Afloat and Ashore: A Sea Tale*. Vol. 2. 1844. Reprint, New York: Stringer and Townsend, 1852.

———. *The Sea Lions*. Vol. 1. New York: Stringer and Townsend, 1849.

Correspondence Relative to the Earl of Elgin's Special Missions to China and Japan, 1857–1859. San Francisco: Chinese Materials Center, 1975.

Coughlin, Margaret. "Strangers in the House: J. Lewis Shuck and Issachar Roberts, First American Baptist Missionaries to China." Ph.D. diss., University of Virginia, 1972.

Covell, Ralph. *W.A.P. Martin: Pioneer of Progress in China*. Washington, DC: Christian University Press, 1978.

Crow, Carl. *Four Hundred Million Customers*. New York: Harper, 1937.

Cushing, John Perkins. "Memo. for Mr. Forbes Respecting Canton Affairs." *Business History Review* 40 (1966): 98–107.

Cutler, Carl. *Greyhounds of the Sea: The Story of the American Clipper Ship*. New York: Halcyon House, 1930.

Dana, Richard Henry. *Two Years before the Mast*. Cambridge, MA: Riverside Press, 1868.

Davidson, James West. *The Logic of Millennial Thought: Eighteenth-Century New England*. New Haven, CT: Yale University Press, 1977.

Davis, Nancy Ellen. "The American China Trade, 1784–1844: Products for the Middle Class." Ph.D. diss., George Washington University, 1987.

Delano, Amasa. *Narrative of Voyages and Travels in Northern and Southern Hemispheres*. Boston: E. G. House, 1817.

Dennett, Tyler. *Americans in Eastern Asia*. New York: Macmillan, 1922.

Donahue, William J. "The Caleb Cushing Mission." *Modern Asian Studies* 16 (1982): 193–216.

Downing, C. Toogood. *The Fan-qui in China*. Vol. 1. London: Henry Colburn, 1838.

Downs, Jacques. "American Merchants and the China Opium Trade, 1800–1840." *Business History Review* 42 (1968): 418–442.

———. *The Golden Ghetto: The American Commercial Community at Canton and the Shaping of American China Policy, 1784–1844*. Bethlehem, PA: Lehigh University Press, 1997.

Drake, Fred. "Bridgman in China in the Early Nineteenth Century." *American Neptune* 46 (1986): 34–42.

———. *China Charts the World: Hsu Chi-yü and His Geography of 1848*. Cambridge, MA: Harvard University Press, 1975.

———. "Mid-Nineteenth-Century Discovery of the Non-Chinese World." *Modern Asian Studies* 6 (1972): 205–224.

Dulles, Foster Rhea. *The Old China Trade*. Boston: Houghton Mifflin, 1930.

Ellis, Joseph. *American Sphinx: The Character of Thomas Jefferson*. New York: Alfred A. Knopf, 1997.

Emmet, Alan. *So Fine a Prospect: Historic New England Gardens.* Hanover, NH: University Press of New England, 1996.

Fairbank, John K. "Introduction." In *America's China Trade in Historical Perspective: The Chinese and American Performance*, edited by Ernest May and John K. Fairbank, 1–10. Cambridge, MA: Harvard University Press, 1986.

———, ed. "Introduction: The Old Order." In *The Cambridge History of China*, vol. 10, edited by John King Fairbank and K. C. Liu. Cambridge: Cambridge University Press, 1978.

Fanning, Edmund. *Voyages round the World: With Selected Sketches of Voyages to the South Seas, North and South Pacific Oceans, China, Etc.* New York: Collins and Hannay, 1833.

Farris, Johnathan. "Thirteen Factories of Canton: An Architecture of Sino-Western Collaboration and Confrontation." *Buildings and Landscapes* 14 (Fall 2007): 66–83.

Fay, Peter. "The Protestant Mission and the Opium War." *Pacific Historical Review* 40 (1971): 145–161.

Fichter, James. *So Great a Proffit: How the East Transformed Anglo-American Capitalism.* Cambridge, MA: Harvard University Press, 2010.

Fontenoy, Paul E. "Ginseng, Otter Skins, and Sandalwood: The Conundrum of the China Trade." *Northern Mariner* 7 (1997): 1–16.

Forbes, Robert B. *Personal Reminiscences.* 2nd ed. Boston: Little, Brown, 1882.

———. *Remarks on China and the China Trade.* Boston: Samuel N. Dickinson, 1844.

Frank, Caroline. *Objectifying China, Imagining America: Chinese Commodities in Early America.* Chicago: University of Chicago Press, 2011.

Freneau, Philip. *Poems Written and Published during the American Revolutionary War.* Philadelphia: Lydia R. Bailey, 1809.

Fuess, Claude. *The Life of Caleb Cushing.* Vol. 1. New York: Harcourt, Brace, 1923.

Garrett, Valery. *Chinese Dress from the Qing Dynasty to the Present.* North Clarendon, VT: Tuttle, 2007.

Gibson, James. *Otter Skins, Boston Ships, and China Goods: The Maritime Fur Trade of the Northwest Coast, 1785–1841.* Seattle: University of Washington Press, 1992.

Goldstein, Jonathan. *Philadelphia and the China Trade, 1682–1846.* University Park: Penn State University Press, 1978.

Grant, Frederic. "Merchant Litigation in the American Courts." *Proceedings of the Massachusetts Historical Society* 99 (1987): 44–62.

Griffis, William Elliot. *A Maker of the New Orient: Samuel Robbins Brown.* New York: Fleming H. Revell, 1902.

Gulick, Edward. *Peter Parker and the Opening of China.* Cambridge, MA: Harvard University Press, 1973.

Gyory, Andrew. *Closing the Gate: Race, Politics, and the Chinese Exclusion Act.* Chapel Hill: University of North Carolina Press, 1998.

Haddad, John. *Romance of China: Excursions to China in U.S. Culture, 1776–1876.* New York: Columbia University Press, 2008.

Haeger, John Denis. *John Jacob Astor: Business and Finance in the Early Republic.* Detroit, MI: Wayne State University Press, 1991.

Hall, Robert, Jr. "Chinese Pidgin English Grammar and Texts." *Journal of the American Oriental Society* 64 (1944): 95–113.

Hanan, Patrick. *Chinese Fiction of the Nineteenth and Early Twentieth Centuries.* New York: Columbia University Press, 2004.

Hao, Yen-P'ing. "Chinese Teas to America—a Synopsis." In *America's China Trade in Historical Perspective: The Chinese and American Performance*, edited by Ernest May and John K. Fairbank, 11–31. Cambridge, MA: Harvard University Press, 1986.

———. *The Comprador in Nineteenth Century China: Bridge between the East and West*. Cambridge, MA: Harvard University Press, 1970.

He, Sibing. "Russell and Company, 1818–1891: America's Trade and Diplomacy in Nineteenth-Century China." Ph.D. diss., Miami University, 1997.

Hersey, John. *The Call*. New York: Alfred A. Knopf, 1985.

———. *A Single Pebble*. New York: Alfred A. Knopf, 1956.

Hildreth, Richard. *Our First Men: A Calendar of Wealth, Fashion and Gentility*. Boston: 1846.

Hindle, Brooke. "The Transfer of Technology and American Industrial Fairs to 1853." In *XIVth International Congress of the History of Science, Proceedings No. 3*. Tokyo: Science Council of Japan, 1974.

Hodges, Nan, and Arthur Hummel, eds. *Lights and Shadows of a Macao Life: The Journal of Harriet Low, Travelling Spinster*. Woodinville, WA: History Bank, 2002.

Holt, Hamilton. *The Life Stories of Undistinguished Americans*. New York: Routledge, 1990.

Hopkins, Samuel. *The Works of Samuel Hopkins*. Vol. 2. Boston: Doctrinal Tract and Book Society, 1852.

Horowitz, Richard Steven. "Central Power and State Making: The Zongli Yamen and Self-Strengthening in China, 1860–1880." Ph.D. diss, Harvard University, 1998.

Howay, Frederic, ed. *Voyages of the "Columbia" to the Northwest Coast, 1787–1790 and 1790–1793*. New York: Da Capo Press, 1941.

Hsü, Immanuel C. Y. *China's Entrance into the Family of Nations*. Cambridge, MA: Harvard University Press, 1960.

Hughes, Sarah Forbes, ed. *Letters and Recollections of John Murray Forbes*. Boston: Houghton, Mifflin, 1900.

Hunt, Freeman. *Lives of American Merchants*. Vol. 2. New York: Derby and Jackson, 1858.

Hunt, Michael. *The Making of a Special Relationship: The United States and China to 1914*. New York: Columbia University Press, 1983.

Hunter, William C. *Bits of Old China*. 1855. Reprint, Taipei: Ch'eng-Wen, 1966.

———. *The "Fan Kwae" at Canton before Treaty Days, 1825–1844*. 1882. Reprint, Shanghai: Oriental Affairs, 1938.

Hutcheon, Robin. *Chinnery*. Hong Kong: FormAsia, 1989.

Hutchison, William. *Errand to the World: American Protestant Thought and Foreign Missions*. Chicago: University of Chicago Press, 1993.

Johnson, Arthur, and Barry Supple. *Boston Capitalists and Western Railroads: A Study in the Nineteenth-Century Railroad Investment Process*. Cambridge, MA: Harvard University Press, 1967.

Johnson, Kendall. "A Question of Character: The Romance of Early Sino-American Commerce in *The Journals of Major Samuel Shaw, the First American Consul at Canton* (1847)." In *Narratives of Free Trade: The Commercial Cultures of Early U.S.-China Relations*, edited by Kendall Johnson, 33–56. Hong Kong: Hong Kong University Press, 2012.

Johnson, Willis Fletcher. *Life of James G. Blaine, "the Plumed Knight."* Philadelphia: Atlantic, 1893.

Karttunen, Francis Ruley. *The Other Islanders: People Who Pulled Nantucket's Oars.* New Bedford, MA: Spinner, 2005.

Keliher, Macabe. "Anglo-American Rivalry and the Origins of U.S. China Policy." *Diplomatic History* 31 (2007): 227–258.

Kerr, Phyllis Forbes. *Letters from China: The Canton-Boston Correspondence of Robert Bennet Forbes.* Mystic, CT: Mystic Seaport Museum, 1996.

Kim, S. S. "Burlingame and the Inauguration of the Co-operative Policy." *Modern Asian Studies* 5 (1971): 337–354.

King, C. W. *The Opium Crisis: A Letter Addressed to Charles Elliot, Esq., Chief Superintendent of the British Trade with China by an American Merchant.* London: Edward Suter, 1839.

King, Caroline Howard. *When I Lived in Salem, 1822–1866.* Brattleboro, VT: Stephen Daye Press, 1937.

Kuhn, Philip A. "Origins of the Taiping Vision: Cross-Cultural Dimensions of a Chinese Rebellion." *Comparative Studies in Society and History* 19 (1977): 350–366.

Kuo, Ping Chia. "Caleb Cushing and the Treaty of Wanghia." *Journal of Modern History* 5 (1933): 34–54.

———. "Canton and Salem: The Impact of Chinese Culture upon New England Life during the Post-Revolutionary Era." *New England Quarterly* 3 (1930): 420–442.

Kwong, Peter, and Dušanka Miščević *Chinese America: The Untold Story of America's Oldest New Community.* New York: New Press, 2005.

Larson, John. *Bonds of Enterprise: John Murray Forbes and Western Development.* Cambridge, MA: Harvard University Press, 1984.

Lazich, Michael. "American Missionaries and the Opium Trade in Nineteenth-Century China." *Journal of World History* 17 (2006): 197–223.

———. *E. C. Bridgman (1801–1861), America's First Missionary to China.* Lewiston, NY: Edwin Mellen Press, 2000.

Ledyard, John. *The Last Voyage of Captain Cook: The Collected Writings of John Ledyard.* Edited by James Zug. Washington, DC: National Geographic Adventure Classics, 2005.

Lee, Henry. "The Magee Family and the Origins of the China Trade." *Proceedings of the Massachusetts Historical Society* 81 (1969): 104–119.

Lee, Jean Gordon. *Philadelphians and the China Trade, 1784–1844.* Philadelphia: University of Pennsylvania Press, 1984.

Lee, Lily Xiao Hong, ed. *Biographical Dictionary of Chinese Women: The Qing Period, 1644–1911.* New York: M. E. Sharpe, 1998.

Le Pichon, Alain. *China Trade and Empire: Jardine, Matheson and Co. and the Origins of British Rule in Hong Kong, 1827–1843.* New York: Oxford University Press, 2006.

Li, Lillian. "The Silk Export Trade and Economic Modernization in China and Japan." In *America's China Trade in Historical Perspective: The Chinese and American Performance,* edited by Ernest May and John K. Fairbank, 77–99. Cambridge, MA: Harvard University Press, 1986.

Lindgren, James M. "'That Every Mariner May Possess the History of the World': A Cabinet for the East India Marine Society of Salem." *New England Quarterly* 68 (1995): 179–205.

Liu, Kwang-Ching. *Anglo-American Steamship Rivalry in China, 1862–1874.* Cambridge, MA: Harvard University Press, 1962.

Lockwood, Stephen Chapman. *Augustine Heard and Company, 1858–1862.* Cambridge, MA: Harvard University Press, 1971.

Lutz, Jessie Gregory. "The Grand Illusion: Karl Gützlaff and Popularization of China Missions in the United States during the 1830s." In *United States Attitudes and Policies toward China: The Impact of American Missionaries,* edited by Patricia Neils, 46–77. Armonk, NY: M. E. Sharpe, 1990.

———. *Opening China: Karl F. A. Gützlaff and Sino-Western Relations, 1827–1852.* Grand Rapids, MI: William B. Eerdman, 2008.

Major, Judith. *To Live in the New World: A.J. Downing and American Landscape Gardening.* Cambridge, MA: MIT Press, 1997.

Malcolm, Elizabeth L. "The Chinese Repository and Western Literature on China 1800 to 1850." *Modern Asian Studies* 7 (1973).

Malloy, Mary. *"Boston Men" on the Northwest Coast: The American Maritime Fur Trade, 1788–1844.* Kingston, Ontario, Canada: Limestone Press, 1998.

Martin, John Frederick. *Profits in the Wilderness: Entrepreneurship and the Founding of New England Towns in the Seventeenth Century.* Chapel Hill: University of North Carolina Press, 1991.

Marvin, Winthrop. *The American Merchant Marine.* New York: Scribner, 1916.

Michael, Franz. *The Taiping Rebellion: History and Documents.* Vol. 3. Seattle: University of Washington Press, 1971.

Mooney, James, ed. *Dictionary of American Naval Fighting Ships.* Vol. 4. Washington, DC: Naval Department, 1969.

Morrow, Joseph L. "Anson Burlingame, His Life and Services." *New Berlin Centennial.* New Berlin, NY: Unadilla Valley Historical Society, 1908.

Morse, Hosea Ballou. *The Chronicles of the East India Company Trading to China, 1635–1834.* Taipei: Ch'eng-Wen, 1966.

Mudge, Jean. *Chinese Export Porcelain for the American Trade, 1785–1835.* Newark: University of Delaware Press, 1981.

Myers, Minor. *Liberty without Anarchy: A History of the Society of the Cincinnati.* Charlottesville: University of Virginia Press, 1983.

Newman, R. K. "Opium Smoking in Late Imperial China: A Reconsideration." *Modern Asian Studies* 29 (1995): 765–794.

Nye, Gideon. *Tea: And the Tea Trade.* New York: Geo. W. Wood, 1850.

Overton, R. C. "Charles Elliott Perkins." *Business History Review* 31 (1957): 292–309.

"Perkins and Company, 1803–1827," *Bulletin of the Business Historical Society* 6 (1932): 1–5.

Phillips, Clifton Jackson. *Protestant America and the Pagan World: The First Half Century of the American Board of Commissioners for Foreign Missions, 1810–1860.* Cambridge, MA: East Asian Research Center, Harvard University, 1969.

Pickowicz, Paul. "William Wood in Canton: A Critique of the China Trade before the Opium War." *Essex Institute Historical Collections* 107 (1971): 3–34.

Polachek, James. *The Inner Opium War.* Cambridge, MA: Harvard University Press, 1992.

Pratt, Mary Louis. *Imperial Eyes: Travel Writing and Transculturation.* London: Routledge, 1992.

Pruden, George Blackburn. "Issachar Jacox Roberts and American Diplomacy in China during the Taiping Rebellion." Ph.D. diss., American University, 1977.

Rachman, Stephen. "Memento Morbi: Lam Qua's Paintings, Peter Parker's Patients." *Literature and Medicine* 23 (2004): 134–159.

Rapp, John A. "Clashing Dilemmas: Hong Rengan, Issachar Roberts, and a Taiping 'Murder' Mystery." *Journal of Historical Biography* 4 (2008): 27–58.

Remini, Robert. *Daniel Webster: The Man and His Time.* New York: W. W. Norton, 1997.

Rhoads, Edward. *Manchu and Han: Ethnic Relations and Political Power in Late Qing and Early Republican China, 1861–1928.* Seattle: University of Washington Press, 2000.

Ring, Martin. "Anson Burlingame, S. Wells Williams and China, 1861–1870: A Great Era in Chinese-American Relations." Ph.D. diss., Tulane University, 1977.

Rogers, John K. "Daniel Webster and Col. T.H. Perkins. A Summer-Day Outing in 1817." *New England Magazine* 4 (1886): 13–26.

Ronda, James P. *Astoria and Empire.* Lincoln: University of Nebraska Press, 1990.

Rowe, William. *China's Last Empire: The Great Qing.* Cambridge, MA: Harvard University Press, 2009.

———. *Hankow: Commerce and Society in a Chinese City, 1796–1889.* Stanford, CA: Stanford University Press, 1984.

Rubinstein, Murray. *The Origins of the Anglo-American Missionary Enterprise in China, 1807–1840.* Lanham, MD: Scarecrow Press, 1996.

Ruskola, Teemu. "Canton Is Not Boston: The Invention of American Imperial Sovereignty." *American Quarterly* 57 (2005): 859–884.

Rutkow, Ira. *American Surgery: An Illustrated History.* Philadelphia: Lippincott, 1998.

Schrecker, John. "'For the Equality of Men—For the Equality of Nations': Anson Burlingame and China's First Embassy to the United States, 1868." *Journal of American–East Asian Relations* 17 (2010): 9–34.

Scully, Eileen. *Bargaining with the State from Afar: American Citizenship in Treaty Port China, 1844–1942.* New York: Columbia University Press, 2001.

Seaburg, Carl, and Stanley Paterson. *Merchant Prince of Boston: Colonel T.H. Perkins, 1764–1854.* Cambridge, MA: Harvard University Press, 1971.

Shaw, Samuel. "From Samuel Shaw to John Jay." In *The Diplomatic Correspondence of the United States,* vol. 7. Washington, DC: Francis Preston Blair, 1834.

———. *The Journals of Major Samuel Shaw, the First American Consul at Canton, with a Life of the Author by Josiah Quincy.* Edited by Josiah Quincy. Boston: Wm. Crosby and H. P. Nichols, 1847.

Shewmaker, Kenneth E. "Forging the 'Great Chain': Daniel Webster and the Origins of American Foreign Policy toward East Asia and the Pacific, 1841–1852." *Proceedings of the American Philosophical Society* 129 (1985): 225–259.

Shineburg, Dorothy. *They Came for Sandalwood: A Study of the Sandalwood Trade in the South-west Pacific, 1830–1865.* Melbourne, Australia: Melbourne University Press, 1967.

Smith, Philip Chadwick Foster. *The Empress of China.* Philadelphia: Philadelphia Maritime Museum, 1984.

So, Kwan-wai, Eugene P. Boardman, and Ch'iu P'ing. "Hung Jen-Kan, Taiping Prime Minister, 1859–1864." *Harvard Journal of Asiatic Studies* 20 (1957): 262–294.

Spence, Jonathan. *God's Chinese Son: The Taiping Heavenly Kingdom of Hong Xiuquan.* New York: W. W. Norton, 1996.

———. "Opium Smoking in Ch'ing China." In *Conflict and Control in Late Imperial China,* edited by Frederic Wakeman Jr. and Carolyn Grant, 143–173. Berkeley: University of California Press, 1975.

————. *The Search for Modern China.* New York: W. W. Norton, 2001.

————. *To Change China: Western Advisers in China, 1620–1960.* New York: Penguin Books, 1986.

Stelle, Charles. *Americans and the China Opium Trade in the Nineteenth Century.* New York: Arno Press, 1981.

————. "American Trade in Opium to China, prior to 1820." *Pacific Historical Review* 9 (1940): 425–444.

————. "American Trade in Opium to China, 1821–1839." *Pacific Historical Review* 10 (1941): 57–74.

Stevens, George. *The Life, Letters, and Journals of the Rev. and Hon. Peter Parker, M.D.* Wilmington, DE: Scholarly Resources, 1972.

Sutton, Jean. *The East India Company's Maritime Service, 1746–1834: Masters of the Eastern Seas.* Woodbridge, Suffolk, UK: Boydell Press, 2010.

Swisher, Earl. *China's Management of the American Barbarians: A Study of Sino-American Relations, 1841–1861, with Documents.* New Haven, CT: Far Eastern, 1953.

Takaki, Ronald. *Strangers from a Different Shore.* Boston: Little, Brown, 1989.

Taylor, Alan. *William Cooper's Town: Power and Persuasion on the Frontier of the Early American Republic.* New York: Vintage Books, 1996.

Taylor, Davis. *Ginseng: The Divine Root.* Chapel Hill, NC: Algonquin Books, 2006.

Teng, Yuan Chung. *Americans and the Taiping Rebellion: A Study of American-Chinese Relationship, 1847–1864.* Taipei: China Academy, 1982.

————. "Reverend Issachar Jacox Roberts and the Taiping Rebellion." *Journal of Asian Studies* 23 (1963): 55–67.

Thill, Joan Kerr Facey. "A Delawarean in the Celestial Empire: John Richardson Latimer and the China Trade." Master's thesis, University of Delaware, 1973.

Thomson, James, Peter Stanley, and John Curtis Perry. *Sentimental Imperialists: The American Experience in East Asia.* New York: Harper and Row, 1981.

Tiffany, Osmond. *The Canton Chinese.* Boston: James Monroe, 1849.

Townsend, W. J. *Robert Morrison: Pioneer of Missions to China.* London: Pickering and Inglis, 1928.

Tsai, Shih-shan H. "American Involvement in the Coolie Trade." *American Studies* 6 (1976): 49–66.

Tyng, Charles. *Before the Wind: The Memoir of an American Sea Captain, 1808–1833.* New York: Viking, 1999.

Van Dyke, Paul. *The Canton Trade: Life and Enterprise on the China Coast, 1700–1845.* Hong Kong: Hong Kong University Press, 2005.

————. "Macao, Hawaii, and Sino-American Trade: Some Historical Observations, Interactions, and Consequences." In *Macao and Sino-U.S. Relations,* edited by Yufan Hao and Jianwei Wang, 71–96. Lanham, MD: Lexington Books, 2011.

————. *Merchants of Canton and Macao: Politics and Strategies in Eighteenth-Century Chinese Trade.* Hong Kong: Hong Kong University Press, 2011.

Wakeman, Frederic, Jr. *Strangers at the Gate: Social Disorder in South China, 1839–1861.* Berkeley: University of California Press, 1966.

Waley, Arthur. *The Opium War through Chinese Eyes.* Stanford, CA: Stanford University Press, 1958.

Ward, Geoffrey. *Before the Trumpet: Young Franklin Roosevelt, 1882–1905.* New York: Harper and Row, 1985.

————. "A Fair, Honorable, and Legitimate Trade." *American Heritage* 37 (1986): 49–64.

Weber, Charles. "Conflicting Cultural Traditions in China: Baptist Educational Work in the Nineteenth Century." In *United States Attitudes and Policies toward China: The Impact of American Missionaries*, edited by Patricia Neils, 25–45. Armonk, NY: M. E. Sharpe, 1990.

Webster, Daniel. "Mr. Webster to Mr. Cushing." In *The Diplomatic and Official Papers of Daniel Webster, while Secretary of State*, 360–365. New York: Harper, 1848.

Wei, Betty Peh-T'i. *Ruan Yuan, 1764–1849: The Life and Work of a Major Scholar Official in Nineteenth Century China before the Opium War*. Hong Kong: Hong Kong University Press, 2006.

White, Anne. "The Hong Merchants of Canton." Ph.D. diss., University of Pennsylvania, 1967.

Whitehill, Walter Muir. *The East India Marine Society and the Peabody Museum of Salem, a Sesquicentennial History*. Salem, MA: Peabody Museum, 1949.

Wiley, Peter Booth. *Yankees in the Land of the Gods: Commodore Perry and the Opening of Japan*. New York: Viking, 1990.

Williams, Frederick Wells. *Anson Burlingame and the First Chinese Mission to Foreign Powers*. New York: Scribner, 1912.

————. *The Life and Letters of Samuel Wells Williams, LL.D.* New York: Putnam, 1889.

————. *A Sketch of the Relations between the United States and China*. Boston: Thomas Crowell, 1910.

Williams, Samuel Wells. "A Journal of the Perry Expedition to Japan." *Transactions of the Asiatic Society of Japan* 37 (1910): 1–261.

————. *The Middle Kingdom*. 2 vols. New York: Wiley and Putnam, 1848.

————. "The Present Position of the Chinese Empire." *Transactions of the American Ethnological Society*. New York: Bartlett and Welford, 1848.

Williamson, G. R. *Memoir of the Rev. David Abeel, D.D., Late Missionary to China*. Wilmington, DE: Scholarly Resources, 1972.

Wilson, Dick. "King George's Men: British Ships and Sailors in the Pacific Northwest—China Trade, 1785–1821." Ph.D. diss., University of Idaho, 2004.

Wines, E. C. *A Peep at China in Mr. Dunn's Chinese Collection*. Philadelphia: Ashmead, 1839.

Wong, J. Y. *Deadly Dreams: Opium, Imperialism, and the Arrow War*. Cambridge: Cambridge University Press, 1998.

Wood, William. *Sketches of China*. Philadelphia: Carey and Lea, 1830.

Woodhouse, Samuel. "The Voyage of the Empress of China." *Pennsylvania Magazine of History and Biography* 63 (1939): 30–36.

Wright, Conrad Edick. "Merchants and Mandarins: New York and the Early China Trade." In *New York and the China Trade*, edited by David Sanctuary Howard, 17–54. New York: New-York Historical Society, 1984.

Wright, Mary. *The Last Stand of Chinese Conservatism: The T'ung-Chih Restoration, 1862–1874*. New York: Atheneum, 1966.

Yeager, Carl. "Anson Burlingame: His Mission to China and the First Chinese Mission to Western Nations." Master's thesis, Georgetown University, 1950.

Yung, Wing. *My Life in China and America*. Hong Kong: China Economic Review, 2007.

Zhang, Deyi. *Diary of a Chinese Diplomat.* Beijing: Chinese Literature Press, 1992.
Ziegler, Philip. *The Sixth Great Power: Barings, 1762–1929.* London: William Collins Sons, 1988.
Zug, James. *American Traveler: The Life and Death of John Ledyard, the Man Who Dreamed of Walking the World.* New York: Basic Books, 2005.

Index

Italic page numbers indicate material in figures.

John R. Haddad is an Associate Professor of American Studies and Popular Culture at Penn State Harrisburg. He was awarded the Gutenberg-e Prize in 2002 for his dissertation, which was published as *The Romance of China: Excursions to China in U.S. Culture, 1776–1876*. In 2010, he was awarded a Fulbright Scholar grant to teach and research at the University of Hong Kong.